IT'S NOT ABOUT A SALARY . . .

v

The Haymarket Series

Editors: Mike Davis and Michael Sprinkler

The Haymarket Series is a new publishing initiative by Verso offering original studies of politics, history and culture focused on North America. The series presents innovative but representative views from across the American left on a wide range of topics of current and continuing interest to socialists in North America and throughout the world. A century after the first May Day, the American left remains in the shadow of those martyrs whom this series honours and commemorates. The studies in the Haymarket Series testify to the living legacy of activism and political commitment for which they gave up their lives.

IT'S NOT ABOUT A SALARY . . .

Rap, Race and Resistance
in Los Angeles

Brian Cross

VERSO

London · New York

*This book is dedicated to Geronimo Gi Jagga Pratt, an
African-American leader, wrongfully
imprisoned for the last twenty years in this country
and to
my parents, Richard and Helen Cross, my sister Sinead
and all my friends and relatives in Ireland*

First published by Verso 1993
© Brian Cross 1993

Verso
UK: 6 Meard Street, London W1V 3HR
USA: 29 West 35th Street, New York, NY 10001–2291

Verso is the imprint of New Left Books

ISBN 0–86091–445–3
ISBN 0–86091–620–0 (pbk)

British Library Cataloguing in Publication Data
A catalogue record for this book is available from the British Library

Library of Congress Cataloging-in-Publication Data
A catalogue record for this book is available from the Library of Congress

Typeset by York House Typographic Ltd, London W13
Printed in the U.S.A. by Courier Companies Inc.

CONTENTS

ACKNOWLEDGEMENTS

Although one name appears on the cover of this book, all the great things that appear between its covers are the product of many. The hiphop community of Los Angeles has shown me great generosity, patience and loyalty, for which I am profoundly grateful.

Although the faults of this book are entirely the responsibility of its author, below is a list of those who have helped make the book possible: Mike Davis for coming up with the hare-brained idea of my doing a book; Colin Robinson for believing; Raegan Kelly for just being an incredible person, putting in endless hours of transcription and still being a friend after this; Raymond Roker for putting out the dopest magazine (*URB*); Danny Boy and Everlast for helping a homie out when he was low; T-Love for being an explosion of energy; AUG for stayin' up; Bree for transcribing and being there; Kiilu, Mike, Acey, Jup, Peace, Ganjah K and the Freestyle amalgamation for inspiration; the Watts Prophets, especially Amdee, for being special people and stayin' true. To Roy Porter, Kamau, Horace, JMD, Flash, Lonzo, Michael Mixxin' Moor, Lovin' C, Captain Rapp, Greg Mack, Toddy Tee, Big Boy, Boo Yaa Tribe, Afrika Islam, G Bone, Matt Robinson, Ice T, Kid Frost, Dre, Eazy, Cube, Jinx, Pooh, Mike N, OMD, SIN, YoYo, Criminal Mindead, Brown Town, Madkap and Broadway, King Tee, Taters, Matt McDaniel, Lench Mob, Cypress, House of Pain, Blood of Abraham, Bilal Bashir, Lett Loose, Epic, Quik, OFTB, Pharcyde, FunkDoobiest, Nef, Shadow (dope), BJ ya know it, Chino and Joyce thanks for sharing.

To Dick Hebdidge, George Lipsitz, James Spady, Charlotte Greig, and thanks for reading. Big ups to DJ Zen for stayin' up all night to edit when nobody else would have. To Sheena, Randolph, Akwanza, Gabe, Laurie, and Bilal for being great employers at RapPages. To Crozier, Natasha, Cathy Opie, Ken, Maureen, Shannon, Felix, Jonathan, Billy, Len and everybody at Pan for being cool. To all the publicists, Susan Mainzer, Jazzmyne, Charlene at Inner Circle, Lesley Pitts, Ron, Ray Tammara, Goner, EMz and of course Lilian Matulick, thank you. To the DJs: Daz, Orlando, Punish, Marques, Homicide, Pen, Mark Luv, Bigga B, Curve, Battlecat, Rob One, the Baka Boyz, Tomas, Adam, P, thanks for the hours of great music. To 213 2432020G-Money for bein', well, yourself. To Danny Holloway, Bird, Vooodu!, Mia (whoomp!), Bobo and the True Sound/Smokin Vinyl posse for havin' me on deck.

To the Kelly family for being incredible surrogate parents for nearly three years. To my Irish homies, Paul TarpX, Paul Mc, Derek, Francis, Beano, Danny Mc, Gerry Bruen and all the buddah crew – peace! In Ireland, the Cross clan, the Noonan family, the McCarthy family, the Verlings, the Harrows, the Cuneens, the Tynans, the Hogans, the Dublin Road crew, all at Tom Collins', stay up. To all at NCAD, Joan Fowler, Charlie Cullen, Noel Sheridan, Up Garryowen, Eddie in the library, Tony, Paul O', The Reading Group, Cecily, Ollie, Aileen, Mick the photographer and Mick the sculptor, Brian King, Anthony Hobbs, Patricia Langlois, Steve, Ronan. To the Bluefunkers, Val, Brian, Tom, Kevin and Jackie, Evelyn wudd up. To CalArts, Alan Sekula, John Bache, Andy, Ellen, Tom, Michael Asher, Billy Woodberry, Cathi Love, Tom Lawson, Ruben Ortiz, Miles and Amy, Miira, Al, Clay and Chris, thanks. To John Roberts, thank you.

To hiphop LA big it up, Volume 10, Snoop, Kam, Ganjah K, Domino, Ded II Tha World, Funkytown Pros, Alladin, Battle Cat, Bronze Age, the Alkoholiks, Justin Warfield, QDIII, MC Eiht, Above the Law, Bobcat, B Hall, R Kain Blaze, Earthquake Brothers, Underground Railroad, Proper Dose, Mixmaster Spade, Rudy Ray Moore, the Wascals, Tweedy Bird Loc, 2nd II None, if this happens again you will be included. To all at the Good Life, to all the bombers, writers, piecers, to all the promoters, writers, artists, photographers, producers, MCs, Gs, vatos, skaters, surfers and of course B-boys and girls PEACE! To all the clothing companies, especially Weedwear, Third Rail, GAT, El Diablo, Dino and Stan, good looking out. To all at *URB* especially Todd, Jason, Michele, Cheo, Josh, Spence, Willy thanks. To all the magazines, *SFTL*, *The Bomb*, *Flava*, *One Nut Network*, *No Sell Out*, *Freestyle*, *Rapsheet*, *Beatdown*, *RnR Confidential*, *Hiphop Connection*, *Soul CD*, *NME*, *Artform* and *Grand Street*, thanks.

Finally special thanks to Liné Spencer, the finest girl I know and all the other homies I forgot.

The interviews contained within these covers are the result of two and a half years of work. The methodology for selecting interviewees was far from scientific. Truthfully the most important factor in selecting subjects was availability. Many people came close to being interviewed but for logistical reasons the interviews never happened. To those people I am sorry, but hopefully there will be other books. On three occasions I had technical failure: YoYo, Mike N and Menace were unfortunate enough to suffer the consequences of a cheap and over-used tape recorder – again, apologies.

Thanks in advance to all the publishing companies. Permission for the lyrics reprinted here pending.

So that's it, read and enjoy. And remember there ain't no party like a West Coast party, 'cos a West Coast party don't stop.

PREFACE

Eager? I heard about him in Watts. I like the way he blows tenor. Where the hell's Watts? You never heard of Watts, California? Sorry Mingus, I'm an apple man . . .

Charles Mingus, Beneath the Underdog

Beyond what can be learnt from the conventions of book jacket biographies, basically I am a product of post-Lamass Ireland. This should connote both positively and negatively, for indeed we (in Ireland) did develop a reasonably advanced and affordable educational system. Sizeable numbers of us, however, are forced to leave to pursue the high goals we have acquired or simply (in most cases) to survive. Thirty-thousand people emigrate every year between the ages of eighteen and thirty.

My undergraduate education was informed not only by photography but by a keen interest in the peculiar nature of our status. Punk (or new wave depending on your sensibility or location) music, particularly the British and later Irish strains (especially The Clash and Stiff Little Fingers) strongly influenced my transition to adolescence and helped me begin to think of myself as a political being.

Coming from a family with strong republican sympathies I was exposed to my share of traditional Irish folk music – narrative ballads like 'Sean Sabht of Garryowen' and 'The Ballad of Kevin Barry'. I must say I never really liked it. These stories seemed too nostalgic, especially in the face of the bombing campaigns of the early seventies. Then, in my home town of Limerick we began to get new stories from the streets of London, Belfast and Derry, stories that contained some of the anger, excitement and alienation we felt.

I'm a communist. But I don't believe in the communism where everybody wears overalls and work boots. I believe in the communism where everybody drives a Cadillac.

Mick Jones of The Clash in the movie Rude Boy, 1979

By 1982, new wave had expanded into a diverse field of music culling influences from many contemporary and previous models of resistance. It was at this time I started to hear 'other' stories – just as gritty but this time with a regular beat – first from New York, then DC and then Philly. Keith le Blanc came out with 'No Sell Out' in 1983/4, using the speeches of Malcolm X (with the permission of Betty Shabazz), and I and a lot of my friends were hooked. I still have difficulty explaining why and how we could make the transition from listening to punk to hiphop, but we did. To be honest, as consumers we didn't give it that much thought.

In 1987 I went to see Schooly D perform in Ireland (opening for Big Audio Dynamite) to a largely bemused crowd. My friends and I were thoroughly impressed by his verbal skills and humour, even if we did not fully understand the complexity of his performance. For instance, we didn't know what cheeba was: we had experienced its charm but we called it something else. What impressed us more though were the abilities of his DJ, Code Money. I admit to being still very biased towards Schooly, having seen him in tight red leather trousers and red Kangol hat without his shirt, grab his crotch and then reach into the crowd to shake hands with the confused Dublin skinheads assembled to hear Mick Jones's new outfit.

In May 1988 approximately 150 of us were lucky enough to be present for an amazing show at McGonagles, a tiny sweatbox in Dublin. By some amazing chance a small-time local promoter had secured the largely unknown Public Enemy. Both Chuck and Flav offered insight on the similarities of our situations (read Irish and African American) and said things on the stage that night that no Irish group would have attempted. Chuck's heavy rhetoric was offset by Flav's jester behaviour: Flav gave a talk on Irish Spring soap and Lucky Charms, two products I personally wasn't aware of until much later.

In the summer of 1988 I came to the US for the first time. Once here it struck me that hiphop had prepared me for the racial realities I encountered. The idea of music preparing you for the reality of walking down Mission Boulevard in San Francisco was a profound shock. Information about lowriders and crack sales and Burger King was useful in negotiating the Mission District. I spent every spare penny on records, coming home with no loot, except my vinyl. I also spent this time finding out as much as I could about everything from White Castles to Huey Newton in an effort to deepen my understanding of what I was hearing, not as a possible future writer but as a good fan.

> As forms of art, photography and jazz are roughly the same age; but photography – perhaps because its origins cannot be traced to 'niggers' – has been able to breach the walls of the University, whereas jazz, aside from some very rare exceptions has not.
> Frank Kofsky, *Black Nationalism and the Revolution in Music*, 1970

In 1991, I accepted Mike Davis's challenge to document hiphop in LA: a naive gesture. In my surroundings (graduate school) I knew as much as my peers about the history of the music, but I hadn't encountered the real experts yet. Since then I confess to having had my perspective on the music change more than twice.

As a term that describes a colloquial way of speaking, rapping has been part of the social fabric of black America since English become a language of the slaves. This form, usually in rhyming couplets, is a powerful tool of resistance, a way of delineating community and of communicating history.

The culture we know as hiphop is one that has, since its inception, simultaneously acted as a continuum to earlier traditions and as a kind of DIY response to new technological possibilities opening up through the advance of microelectronics through the seventies and into the eighties and nineties. Sampling and sequencing opened the door for relatively (read not that labour-intensive) cheap production of the music, and the expanded and changed realm of musical reception (read the collapse of some public spheres and the expansion of private ones, such as the Walkman) has certainly contributed too.

It is interesting to note that this whole book can be contained on four floppy discs; however the average hiphop album in samples alone (before vocals are laid) demands upwards of fifty floppies. In many ways this should illustrate the complexity of the heritage of the music. It may be possible at a future date to imagine whole essays on single Tony Williams snare samples or Ron Carter bass stabs.

If the phenomenon of hiphop tells us anything, it is that people have stories. These stories are specific and relate to the social geography that produces them. They exist in the real. While U2 were talking about 'The Streets with No Name', Eazy and Cube were talking about Crenshaw, Slauson, Gauge and Figeroa. U2 may have meant well with their liberal rhetoric, but they missed the kind of naming that occurs from below, even when there are no street signs. How else do you find your way home? Hiphop in many ways is a map for precisely this purpose.

The form of these stories – the relation between their content and how they are told – is significant. Mainstream culture of late seems to be caught between retroism and parody. While both retro-chic and parody can tell us something about the present, they are underpinned by a profound disdain for it. Many of us don't have a past we can truly celebrate and unfortunately we can't exactly rely on the future; so the present is all we have. Hiphop is the music of the present tense.

Hiphop culture, as we move towards the mid-nineties, is under attack at every turn, whether in the expected blurtings of the myopic religious right or the horror of the (fast becoming obsolete) liberals in the pages of journals from the *Los Angeles Weekly* to the *New Republic* or the confused left unable to decipher the *realpolitik* from the posturing of the MTV generation. This is perhaps the most interesting part of the music: nobody seems able either to ignore or make sense of it. The people with the best understanding of hiphop are those who produce it. While these men and women may not be equipped with the contrived vocabulary of the last twenty years of theoretical debate, they live the lifestyle. It is certainly possible and useful to construct arguments from the perspective of those who receive the music, and many have, but we must look at the impulses of those who produce it.

These interviews and brief introductions are an abbreviation of very large and complex stories. These men and women deserve to have far lengthier texts devoted to their practices; if nothing else this volume will encourage the production of such texts. Finally I should say (if it isn't obvious) that interviews are as dependent on the specifics of that day, the order, mode of delivery and type of question asked, the preconceived notions of both interviewer and interviewee/s as they are on a consensual agreement concerning revelation. Enjoy.

L. A. HIPHOP

A Brief History

Black Los Angeles

On Thursday 28 March 1946 at 1 p.m. on Santa Monica Boulevard, in Hollywood, the Charlie Parker Septet went into the Radio Recorders Studio and recorded four sides. The septet (Parker on alto, Miles Davis on trumpet, Lucky Thompson on tenor sax, Dodo Marmarosa on piano, Arv Garrison on guitar, Vic McMillan on bass and Roy Porter on drums) knew the session had to be finished in four hours because anything more was overtime and the record company, Dial, wouldn't pay for it.

In those four hours Bird, with several sizzling solos, managed to overhaul music. Roy Porter tells of how Parker finished writing 'Moose the Mooche' on the way to the studio in his (Roy's) car: Los Angeles has never had such beautiful music written on its streets since, although there is plenty of competition. Bird leapt into the unknown with the legendary four-bar break in 'Night in Tunisia'. The break so confused the young session players that Miles Davis had to count them back in after Bird's solo.

Bird came here with Dizzy Gillespie to work at Billy Berg's on Vine in Hollywood. That same year at Berg's, Billie Holiday stabbed a heckler but ended up being acquitted due to the efforts of a young lawyer and fan, Walter Gordon. Berg's was the northernmost point on the map for most black musicians in LA at that time; the real hub was south of downtown, on 'the Avenue'.

Across town at the same time Slim Gaillard, a young guitar player and vocal wizard from Detroit, was recording 'Fried Chicken O Routee', with Bam Brown on bass and Leo Watson on drums and vocals. Outside its reference to feathered species, 'Fried Chicken' had little thematically to do with Bird. Gaillard was involved in expanding the tradition of scatting (which is supposed to have been a substitute for words when a singer forgot his/her lines!) into a new language that reflected the urban scene. He called this humorous language *Vout*.

Both men continued traditions that were already old when their ancestors were brought to the US from west Africa. And they were but individual lights in the constellation that was the music scene of black LA at the advent of bop. Charlie Parker, Billie Holiday and Slim Gaillard, to quote George Lipsitz, were 'nodes in a complex network' of African-American cultural workers. Lester Young had his own language, as did Louis Jordan, and it is said that Bird just wanted to be Art Tatum's right hand. An arc of sound and shared historical experience stretches back through time across this city forming a bridge between bop and hiphop, rap and scat. LA is still the home of some of the world's hardest beats and complex rhymes.

> 'You must know where [the word] bop comes from,' said Simple, astonished at my ignorance.
> 'I do not know,' I said. 'Where?'
> 'From the police . . . from the police beating on Negroes' heads,' said Simple.
> 'Every time a cop hits a Negro with his billy club, that old club says "BOP! BOP! . . . BE BOP . . . MOP . . . BOP!" . . . That's where Bebop came from, beaten right out of some Negro's head into them horns and saxophones and piano keys that plays it . . .'
> Langston Hughes, *The Best of Simple*, quoted in Frank Kofsky, p. 271

> What's happenin' C.C., they still call it the White House, but that's just a temporary condition too. Can you dig it C.C. To each his reach and if I don't cop it ain't mine to have, but I'll be reachin' for ya – 'cos I love ya C.C. There's a lot of Chocolate Cities around, we've got Newark, we've got Gary, somebody told me we've got LA . . .
> Parliament, *Chocolate City*, 1975

Los Angeles has since the late nineteenth century been an important site for black migration. The two periods of greatest peacetime migration were 1910–20 and the late fifties/early sixties, but most black migration into Los Angeles happened during the employment boom created by the military industrial expansion of World War Two. The prospect of employment and a chance of owning property and thus participating in the 'American dream' has traditionally been the main prize for immigrants to southern California. This also applies to African Americans, together with the chance, for some, of escaping the racism so prevalent in the South. Most black Angelinos have some family connection to the southern states of Louisiana, Texas, Arkansas, Oklahoma and Kansas; and black culture in LA finds its roots in these states.

Jelly Roll Morton and Kid Ory were among the first important musicians to move to Los Angeles in the twenties. The main focus for these early migrants was Central Avenue from 5th Street downtown to 103rd Street Watts.

> Any discussion of the 1920s should begin with 'The Avenue'. The story of Central Avenue with its elegant neighborhood, jazz clubs, business districts and trolley cars full of black faces has grown to mythical proportions. Some remember the 'Avenue' as a miniature Harlem, where

musicians and literati gauged the community's pulse by day and transformed that energy into rhyme and music by night; others recall with pride the offices of the black physicians and dentists; the store fronts of black businesses, and the fabled Dunbar Hotel; many, however, see only the overcrowded homes and apartments, the underside of the Avenue with its faded remnants of the dream.

J. G. Bunch, *Twentieth Century Los Angeles, Power, Promotion and Social Conflict,*
ed. Klein and Schiesl, 1990

On Central, Howard McGhee would later bring bebop (and be scorned for it by Kid Ory). In the late forties on Central, Eric Dolphy first blew in Roy Porter's Big Band. It was possible to see Lester Young (and his drumming brother Lee), Big Joe Turner, Billie Holiday, and T-Bone Walker all perform within a couple of blocks of each other on Central's busy promenade. In this lucrative segregated environment many musicians and lyricists broke new ground and established careers.

This black public sphere spawned all kinds of musical talent. In jazz alone LA has been home to Sonny Criss, Dexter Gordon, Red Callender, Gerald Wilson, Charles Mingus, Hampton Hawes, Ornette Coleman, Don Cherry, Billy Higgins, Horace Tapscott, Bobby Hutcherson, Freddie Hubbard, Ernie Andrews, Les McCann, Chet Baker, Art Pepper and (a figure later to become important for hiphop) Roy Ayers.

Los Angeles at that time was controlled by two musicians' unions. Local 47 was white, based in Hollywood, with a grip on the good paying studio jobs. Central Avenue was controlled by a strong black musicians' union, local 767, which ensured reasonable treatment for its many members from its office on Washington. It wasn't until 1953 that the unions integrated.

Central Avenue continued as the centre of black LA until the mid- to late fifties. It had been a popular part of the social map of Los Angeles for the Hollywood bohemian set. It was closed down by a combination of city legislation, a declining black economy and police intervention. The idea of races mixing in late-night enjoyment of African American music was too much for conservative city authorities that upheld 'red lining' (illegal zoning) and job discrimination. The integration of the two musicians' unions gave a few black musicians the chance to work uptown and the evacuation of musicians to New York (and residents to the west side) started a trend that led to its decline and eventual extinction in the sixties. What south central Los Angeles lost with Central Avenue was a locus for the black cultural, cross-generational experience. Since the mid-fifties this locus has been regained in small ways, but these moments are but flickering candles to remind us of the lighthouse that was Central Avenue.

Do not throw the donor card down on top of your ID
You never know when you ever and you never go when you might be

The LAPD might be greedy and may need a heart
Shoot a black man to dissect a body part
You ever wonder why they say freeze
This is a memo on the MO of the PIGees
Cryogenics in their clinics, have brains
Frozen for exposin' those on different mental planes
These are not the paranoid delusions of a rambling idiot
I need immediate, expediate release from those who are obedient
To the rule of breaking rules
Making tools for the undertaking
Schools of innocent lives, taken to survive
So do not throw your donor card down on top of your ID.

Mikah Nine of the Freestyle Fellowship freestyling on
Stretch Armstrong's radio show, July 1992

The Los Angeles Police Department (LAPD) has since its inception been the front line in the suppression of people of colour in this city. It is important to note, however, that the LAPD is but an armed wing of a legislative branch whose brutality against people of colour is equal even if they are less visible. In his essay on the history of social discontent and the LAPD, Martin Schiesl outlines how the LAPD went from being largely corrupt and inefficient in the late forties to being a force working on the military model after the appointment of Chief William H. Parker in 1950; it then developed into a modern autonomous army of occupation by the time of the takeover of Daryl Gates in 1978.

There have historically been three major grievances with the LAPD. First, there is the huge racial bias of the force. The 'monkeys in a Zoo' comments of Chief Parker after the Watts Rebellion of 1965, to the 'gorillas in the mist' comments after the Rodney King beating in 1991 are but verbal manifestations of a physical brutality that almost every person of colour has experienced in this city. Second, the LAPD has continuously gathered information about its constituency with more than simple crime prevention in mind. Many organizations set up to help the citizens of this city have suffered the disastrous consequences of police surveillance and infiltration directed by purely political interests. Third, the LAPD still is not answerable to any independent review body, and this causes tremendous problems in its management. That a city could end up paying for an ungoverned army of occupation seems unlikely, but the wild west of Hollywood pales in comparison to the unchecked outrages caused by the LAPD (see Appendix).

In 1940 there were sixty-four thousand blacks in the city; by 1950 the number had risen to one hundred and seventy thousand. By the early sixties this number had increased fourfold. Yet black Angelinos simply weren't reaping the kind of benefits their white neighbours enjoyed. But in the eyes of the city authorities, despite many, many warnings, everything was just fine.

The city of Los Angeles, he [Parker] assured a group of local journalists in the fall of 1963, would never become 'part of the battleground of the racial conflict that is raging in the United States today'. He told them that it was 'ten years ahead of other major metropolitan areas in assimilating the Negro minority'.

Martin Schliesl, *Twentieth Century Los Angeles, Power, Promotion and Social Conflict*, ed. Klein and Schliesl, 1990

The reality on the streets of black LA couldn't have been more different. The six hundred and fifty thousand blacks who lived in LA County were now almost entirely hemmed into the south central part of the city. One in four families lived below the poverty line and the opportunities for financial improvement were extremely limited. Public transportation in the south central area was bad at best. Police brutality was in evidence all over but in Watts it was appalling – sixty African Americans were killed by patrolmen between 1963 and 1965, twenty-five of them unarmed and twenty-seven shot in the back. One of the most outrageous of these events was the armed assault on a mosque in 1962. All of these conditions led to the outbreak of violence on the night of 11 August 1965.

After the summons of a young man on a drunk driving charge a crowd had gathered and a scuffle broke out between police and the crowd. By 17 August the riot/rebellion had been contained; it had covered 46 square miles and had left 34 dead, 1032 wounded and 3952 arrested. Local leaders quickly moved to find causes, setting up the McCone Commission. While the commission in its report did outline the social conditions that had led to the rioting, it sought to minimize their effect in favour of a 'criminal element' theory.

Hot rod policemen
　　Zipping through the ghetto streets in jetmobiles
Trampling niggers
Killing babies/Beating sisters/Into miscarriages . . .
　　Killing us whenever they want to.
Scared/Scared/Scared/Scared all the time.
Surrounded by guns in worse shape than South Africa
Brothers we better get hip and come off of this trip –
Warriors, come forth and lead our people to freedom
Like Nat Turner meant to do . . .
With an underground arsenal of terror
On those and anything in the way of our freedom
Kill/Kill/Kill
Until the sucker raises up off of you
And finds something better to do

Anthony Hamilton (Father Amdee), 'Kill',
Black Voices on the Streets of Watts, 1971

The Watts Rebellion became a model for the civil disturbances that wracked the United States through the sixties and into the early seventies. Los Angeles itself had not seen disturbances like this since the Zoot Suit Riots of the forties. East LA itself later felt the heat of resistance in the heady days surrounding the Chicano Moratorium of 1970. But the impact of political activism on the city was double-edged. It convinced liberal politicians that the menace presented by the city's minorities was palpable. This led to the increase in strength and efficiency of the LAPD. But these were also extraordinary times for the culture of the city.

Though a black public sphere on the Central Avenue model was no longer possible, the Watts Rebellion nevertheless spawned a cultural renaissance and a burgeoning avant-garde. Influenced by Sun Ra in late '59, Horace Tapscott founded the Arkestra. The Arkestra was a site for the collaboration of black artists across media. This provided the impetus for many other cultural organizations in the immediate post-'65 period. The Mafundi Institute, UGMA (Underground Musicians' Association, later to become Union of Gods, Musicians and Artists of Ascension) as well as the Black Panthers and US (United Slaves) were part of the vibrant cafe culture of south central, based in and around the Watts Happening Coffee House. In 1965 Bud Schulberg, a Hollywood philanthropist, set up the Watts Writers' Workshop.

This workshop showcased African American poets like Ojenke, Odie Hawkins, Eric Priestley, Kamau Daa'ood, K. Curtis Lyle, Quincey Troupe and the Watts Prophets. It also gave people with no formal training a chance to articulate their particular constituent needs – people like Alprentiss 'Bunchy' Carter, the former Slauson and Black Panther street poet, who was killed at UCLA in 1969.

To say that people had no formal training may be a little misleading, for on the streets of chocolate cities all over the US, there is a long and cherished oral tradition known as 'toastin', as well as the related practices, *boastin'*, *signifying* and *the dozens*.

> Toasts are a form of poetry recited by certain blacks – really a performance medium, widely known within a small (and probably disappearing) community and virtually unheard of outside of it. They are like jokes: no one knows who creates them, and everyone has their own versions . . . Though some toasts are pure boast or precept, the most common type is narrative – stories ranging from simple anecdote to highly elaborated, almost epic tales.
> *The Life, the Lore and Folk Poetry of the Black Hustler*, ed. Wepman, Newman and Binderman, 1976

Toasts come from 'the life', which is understood as the occupation of hustlers – people (generally men) who make their living and live a lifestyle related to illegal and semi-legal activities, prostitution, gambling and narcotics. The toasts collected in Wepman, Newman and Binderman's volume *The Life* are all recorded in prisons, but toasts could be heard in many private and public places in black America. The most famous toast is the Signifying

Monkey – a story, which has many versions, of the victory by trickery and deceit of the physically weaker monkey over the lion.

> The signifying monkey spied the lion one day
> And said, 'I heard something 'bout you down the way.
>
> 'There's a big motherfucker lives over there,
> And the way he talks would curl your hair.
>
> 'From what he says he can't be your friend,
> 'Cause he said if your two asses meet, yours is sure to bend,
>
> 'This burly motherfucker says your mammy's a whore
> And your sister turns tricks on the cabin floor
>
> 'And he talked about your wife in a hell of a way
> Said the whole jungle fucked her just the other day . . . '

This version is the Signifying Monkey was recorded in Attica Prison, New York in 1962. It was recited by an inmate from Harlem named Lou. However this toast could be heard all over the country – Father Amdee from the Watts Prophets tells me that this was the first poem he ever heard.

One characteristic of a toast is a flexible rhyming pattern, including mid-line rhymes and occasional triplets:

> That's me the mackman supreme,
> Rich whores cream, poor whores dream,
> Some say I'm the best pimp they ever seen.

But the most distinctive feature in the toast is the diction; it is vernacular poetry made from street language. The toast often contributes new phrases or words to the vernacular, as well as recording those that already exist.

The subjects of toasts are the con, the profession of 'turning out' whores, and tales of 'the life'. These stories are often related to the truth, but more often they are signifying. It seems ironic that the vernacular poetry of an oppressed people would be so concerned with the attributes of the wealthy – clothes, jewellery, cars and a sense of diminished necessity. Today the comic art of the dispossessed outrages with a show of being consumed by the signs of possession, distinguishing a new generation of popular culture with a frank acknowledgement of the importance of the commodity.

Within the Watts Writers' Workshop there were two distinct types of practices – one that was concerned with expanding the tradition of the toast, and another mainly concerned with finding verbal analogies for the instrumental experiments of John Coltrane, Archie

Shepp, Ornette Coleman, Horace Tapscott and Eric Dolphy. Both were associated with a radical political agenda, although approached from different angles. The unifying tenet of the workshop was a commitment to the possibilities of transforming spoken word poetry through performance.

The history of black poetry spoken to music prior to these experiments of the late sixties is largely undocumented. All such recordings are now extremely rare. Langston Hughes and James Baldwin have both committed themselves to vinyl, but perhaps the most outstanding example is Archie Shepp. Shepp, besides being an extraordinary horn player, is a fine poet. On his albums *Fire Music* and *Live from San Francisco* he manipulated his voice (as narrator and soloist) as an instrument, bringing an extra dimension to his formally advanced music. Charles Mingus produced one extraordinary album on Bethlehem Records called *Symposium on Jazz*, which employed actors to suggest the possibilities of the spoken word. The investigations on these albums were not continued and perhaps for this reason were forgotten. However, the most significant artist to pursue this genre up until the late sixties was Amiri Baraka. Baraka, who in the words of Donald Bakeer (a prominent south central writer and educator) 'taught us to be performance poets'. Through his understanding of the rudiments of both the music and poetry, Baraka forged several tough, inspiring records.

Among others doing similar work Oscar Brown Jr is important. His 1960 album *Sin and Soul* used street poetry over jazz in a way that transformed and reclaimed for new generations of African Americans poems like 'Work Song' and, strangely enough, the 'Signifying Monkey'. And the work in the thirties and forties of the lyrical wizard Slim Gaillard captured the babel in the street with nonsense/new language poetry. Recently, just before his death, Gaillard recorded with the Canadian/New York hiphop outfit the Dream Warriors. Many others have contributed, too many to detail, but the works of Babs Gonzalez, Scatman Cruthers, Jon Hendricks, Eddie Jefferson and Louis Jordan deserve special mention.

From the late sixties and early seventies came many fine artists of poetry to music, from the Last Poets, the Original Last Poets, Gil Scott-Heron, Brer Soul (Melvin Van Peebles), Nikki Giovanni, Stanley Crouch and the Watts Prophets. There are many other poets who never made it to vinyl and it is unfortunate that we have no record of their contribution outside what we hear about them through their peers.

What is so important about the Watts Prophets is that they took the African-American tradition of street language used in a formalized poetic way and brought it back to the street. While Quincey Troupe writes poetry that works well on paper and its links to the canon are visible, though the language is street language, the Watts Prophets came along and made this tradition work within popular settings – making poetry 'street' again. The Prophets employ a call-and-response format, generating many voices and characters, where poets such as Baraka remained one. The Watts Prophets' moral tales and dramas became very popular in the venues open to African American poets, from nightclubs to school halls to prisons.

After working on the compilation *Black Voices on the Streets of Watts*, Anthony Hamilton (Father Amdee) brought Otis O, Richard Dedeaux and Dee Dee MacNeil to ALA Records to record *Rappin' Black in a White World*. This album is a benchmark in the history of black music, if indeed a largely forgotten one. From the calls to action of 'Sell Your Soul' to the melancholic 'What is a Man' with Dee Dee MacNeil singing the chorus – *Rappin' Black* set out the themes of the music to come. There was a frankness and openness that was unique on wax at that time. In the censorship-ridden nineties we can appreciate their courage.

In New York, Jalal Nuridin, Omar Bin Hassan and Sulaiman El-Hadi put together the Last Poets who provided a New York analogue of the Watts Prophets. Even though they were unaware of each other until 1969, the Poets and the Prophets had a lot in common. What separates them is the different formal and political needs of their respective communities which still define the conceptual gap between east and west coasts in the music of today. Today both the Watts Prophets and the Last Poets can be found (sampled and preserved) on albums ranging from Def Jef's recent *Soul Food*, both Poor Righteous Teachers albums, DJ Quik, Too Short, Penthouse Players Clique, Tim Dogg and Tribe Called Quest's *Low End Theory*.

Their popularity in the early seventies brought the Watts Prophets (and the Last Poets) to the attention of the FBI. COINTELPRO (the counter intelligence programme) monitored black, Chicano and radical white groups. Many grass-roots organizations fell victim to its treacherous and unconstitutional espionage. The publicist at the Watts Writers' Workshop, Darthard Perry, a black student from Sacramento, was blackmailed into working for the FBI. He was not only a spy but a provocateur. He 'came in from the cold' in 1981 and, in an interview with black journalist Gil Noble, confessed everything. Perry effectively destroyed the career of the Watts Prophets.

Perry, however, was not unusual; many organizations at that time were infiltrated and divided or destroyed. In W. Churchill and J. Vander Wall's invaluable book *Agents of Repression: The FBI's Secret War Against the Black Panther Party and the American Indian Movement*, many pages are to given to describing the horrific revelations of Perry, Louis Tackwood (the Glass House Tapes) and Melvin 'Cotton' Smith. These men were paid with taxpayers' money to mislead and destroy legal, democratic organizations in south central and east Los Angeles. Perhaps the most caustic legacy of this era is the continuing and wrongful imprisonment of Geronimo Gi Jagga Pratt, the former military hero and Black Panther. As he enters his twentieth year of imprisonment (five in solitary), many continue to campaign for Pratt's release. The early deaths of Alprentiss 'Bunchy' Carter, John Huggins and Geronimo Pratt's (eight months pregnant) wife Sandra, can also be attributed to the Federal Bureau of Interference.

While many entertainers saw the possibilities for the spoken word music of the Prophets (including Quincy Jones, who used the group on his *Mellow Madness* album, performing a love poem), they were put off either by the volatility of the lyrics or by Perry's interventions. The Watts Prophets ended up as exclusively local celebrities, denied the national status that latter-day MCs would achieve.

Another milestone on the journey to hiphop is Melvin Van Peebles's 1970 masterpiece, *Sweet Sweetback's Badaaasss Song*.

> Sweetback defied the positive-image canon of Sidney Poitier, dealing openly with black sexuality, government sanctioned brutality, and the arbitrary violence of inner city life. Its refusal to compromise still sparks black artists from Ice Cube to Matty Rich.
>
> Nelson George, 'Buppies, B-boys, Baps and Bohos', *Village Voice*, 17 March 1992

Sweetback is the story of a black sex worker (performing stud), who, during an arrest, rebels and kills two cops to save a young black activist. He then goes on the run from Watts to the border and this chase basically occupies the last two-thirds of the film. Van Peebles made an avowedly popular film, but managed to bring his audience on a rollercoaster of formal experimentation, social realism and heavy down-home funk.

In 1980, Van Peebles explained the narrative strategy of his 1970 film:

> The reality is our people have been brainwashed with 'hip' music, the beautiful color, and the dancing images flickering across the screen. This is what they know as cinema. And this is where we must begin. We obviously cannot dwell there; but it's a point of departure . . . . That's what revolution is! It isn't everybody standing up there on an intellectual high. And it is not meeting people and starting from where they are not. It is starting from where they can see.
>
> quoted in Nelson George, *Village Voice*, 17 March 1992

The legacy of *Sweetback* is to be found in contemporary hiphop and black film, although the immediate product of the film's popularity was a series of inferior Hollywood pimp/ hustler films. These 'blaxploitation' films of the seventies proved that funding by an all-white industry was impossible without certain amputations even if the heart was sometimes left intact. These hearts kept pumping with a good supply of hard funk and soul; though the spirit of formal experimentation fostered by Van Peebles had been lost except for brief recurrences, like the still sequence in *Superfly*.

The *Sweetback* soundtrack album (Stax 1970) remains a monument to the possibilities of the collision of narrative sound, spoken word and fat beats (provided by Earth, Wind, & Fire). Van Peebles continued to experiment into the mid-seventies with this format and his efforts are preserved on a trilogy of records under the guise of Brer Soul. He also took this work on to Broadway with a pair of productions, *Ain't Supposed to Die a Natural Death* and *Don't Play Us Cheap* (both have accompanying soundtrack records).

The East Coast Connect

The story of DJ Kool Herc is well known. Herc was a Jamaican who arrived in New York in 1972 and originated a style of speaking over records he spun. What is important here is that – as pointed out by Steven Hager in his informative book *Hip-Hop: An Illustrated History, Rap Music and Graffiti* – Herc modelled himself on Jamaican toasting. Jamaican toasting is a form of speaking over dub (remixed instrumental) versions of records in a humorous and syncopated way. Jamaican toasting as Dick Hebdige points out was influenced by the rhyming style DJs and announcers broadcasting on the huge AM stations out of the southern United States, that could be heard in the Caribbean. Herc and several other DJs (Grandmaster Flash, Afrika Bambaataa, Grandwizard Theodore) at this time began throwing parties for young working-class blacks and Puerto Ricans, who later became known as B-boys in the different sections of the Bronx.

The south Bronx had been an area of affordable housing that contained many new immigrant groups as well as the expanding African American community from uptown. However by the late sixties it fell victim to the authoritative hand of Robert Moses who destroyed the vibrant social fabric of the borough with enormous and unpopular public works projects, most notably the Cross Bronx Expressway. From 1968 the Bronx witnessed the emergence of youth gangs in its housing projects and tenements, gangs that flourished due to declining economic circumstances. This led to the formation of the ninety-two-strong Bronx Youth Gang Task Force in 1969 from the ranks of the Bronx Police Department.

> During the early seventies life at the Bronx River changed dramatically. Since it was a stronghold for gang activity, the project was under constant police surveillance. Any teenager wearing engineer boots was likely to be stopped for grilling, which usually started with the question 'Are you a Spade or a Skull?' (the two largest gangs in the area). It was not unusual for fist fights to break out between the gang members and the police. Since the police were entirely white at the time, charges of police racism were rampant. Considering that newspaper stories from the time indicate that white gang members were seldom arrested, the charges may have had some foundation.
>
> Steven Hager, *Hip-Hop*, p. 7

But by the summer of 1972 the gangs of the Bronx had disintegrated and had been replaced by something else. In 1971 there had been an explosion of writing on the walls of the Bronx. Early pioneers included Taki 183, Super Kool 223, Lee 163d, Phase 2 and Tracy 168. This was the beginning of the social practice we now know as graffiti. There had always been writing on walls, but the hugely competitive, creative forces of the dispossessed on the streets of the Bronx in the early seventies created a new art form.

All the masters were working class offspring from working class neighborhoods like Washington Heights, West Bronx and Flatbush; the hardcore poor of the Lower East Side, South Bronx and Brownsville – those from homes where neither parent works – did not create ambitious graffiti. The masters were good kids whose parents worked for a living and participated in the American dream of becoming middle class. The bitterness and self recrimination that permeate the poor were absent from their environments. Among the black families it was not uncommon to find private houses, a car, color TV; in the Latino homes these articles were definite goals. High school and even college education were fostered aspirations.

This statement by Hugo Martinez, the sociology student from City College New York who founded the famous UGA (United Graffiti Artists) to foster the skills of the young artists, provides a backdrop from which to view early interpretations of hiphop culture, particularly the question of authenticity. It is easy to confuse legitimate prestige with access to resources. This question re-emerges in the musings over why, for example, relatively prosperous Long Island should emerge as a borough of hiphop repute as opposed to other areas. Or indeed, out of Los Angeles, why Compton?

In 1973 Kool Herc DJed his first party in the Bronx. Later that year, and with better equipment, Herc started to do a weekly show. Playing James Brown, Sly Stone and Rare Earth, doing shout-outs from the mic, and screaming 'Rock the house', Herc began to formulate what later became known as hiphop. He called his dancers B-boys.

With the gang situation cooling off, discos were starting to reopen. Everybody wanted to get into dancing again. But while most DJs played the same disco hits one heard on the radio, the music at the Hevalo [Herc had moved to this club later that year] was harder, funkier. Herc knew how to bring the crowd up to a frenzied peak and hold them there for hours. During these times, he seldom played an entire song. Instead he played the hottest segments of the song, which was often just a 30 second 'break' section – when the drums, bass, and rhythm guitar stripped the beat to its barest essence.

Steven Hager, *Hip-Hop*, p. 32

These 'break' (B-) dancers battled on the floor to see who could bust the most outrageous moves. They would dance solo or in crews and this was completely different from the coupling involved in disco dancing. Breaking advanced very quickly into an astonishing combination of gymnastics, jazz and kung-fu moves all held together by a pacing (up-rocking) to the beat that marked out the territory of the breaker.

Herc was in competition at this time from two other DJs. Grandmaster Flash was the inventor of the backspin – allowing for rapid and continuous play of the same micro segment or phrase of the record. (This found its analogue on the dance floor with corporeal backspins and headspins.) Afrika Bambaataa was a former Black Spade, community activist and master DJ who was whooping up crowds with records that nobody else would play, from TV tunes to rare funk and soul, mapping the new subculture on to a complex relation with the mainstream.

Influenced by James Brown, radio DJs and an obscure record called *Hustlers' Convention* by Lightnin' Rod, these proto-MCs put rhymes together over the music to keep the crowd dancing instead of just admiring the dexterity of the DJs. Many, it seems, found observing the turntable warfare of the DJs exhilarating and forgot to dance. 'You dip, dive and socialize. We're trying to make you realize. That we are qualified to rectify that burning . . . desire . . . to boogie,' Flash wrote and then had Cowboy and Melle intone at his shows. Before long, rhymers emerged, boasting, signifying and toasting – using absurd and humorous metaphors to describe their own skills and wit as well as the abilities of their DJs. MCs became celebrities and became as much a part of the show as the DJ and the breakin' crews. The art of bringing the crowd back to dancing drew on many traditions.

> I had learned to shoot pool
> Playin' hookie from school at the tender age of nine
> And by the time I was eleven
> I could pad roll seven and down me a whole quart of wine
> I was making it a point
> To smoke me a joint at least once during the course of a day
> And I was snortin' skag
> While other kids played tag and my elders went to church to pray
> Lightnin' Rod, 'Sport', *Hustlers' Convention*

The mystery character of *Hustlers' Convention* was none other than Jalal Nuridin of the Last Poets using an alias and performing 'prison' poetry over music provided by some members of Kool and the Gang. Unfortunately it is possible to read histories of hiphop (particularly in the press – but also from academia) that never mention the Watts Prophets or the Last Poets (or Nikki Giovanni, Gil Scott-Heron, Oscar Brown Jr, Slim Gaillard, Babs Gonzalez, Scatman Cruthers, Jon Hendricks or King Pleasure).

Herc, with the aid of Afrika Bambaataa, Grandmaster Flash and the inventor of scratching, Grandwizard Theodore, initiated a style of DJing that used disco styles of blending and running, but for new ends. By running a section or break from one record and cutting to the same section of the record on another turntable DJs created new music from the monolith of soul/R&B/disco. This homemade approach resembles the strategy of punk music at that time: breaking down the huge production aesthetic of theatre rock of the seventies, reducing rock music to its fundamentals.

From the slick productions of seventies' disco early hiphop plucked brief sections to be repeated and improvised over. Emphasizing the break simultaneously removes the treacle and bares the fundamental elements – tight, repeating drum patterns mixed with minimal bass and occasional skids, screeches or sighs of rhythm guitar or horns. On top of this is added the noise of the trick itself (scratching) simultaneously revealing and hiding the skill of the project. You have transformed the original. Sounds easy, doesn't it? This DIY reconstruction forced us to think of consumer goods in ways not recommended in the instruction manual.

> The thing that frightened people about hiphop was that they heard people enjoying rhythm for rhythm's sake. Hiphop lives in the world – not the world of music – that's why it is so revolutionary.
>
> Max Roach quoted by Greg Tate, *Flyboy*, p. 129

Fracture, rupture and interruption as well as the sheer reflexivity of enjoying the sound of a record being moved backwards and forwards rapidly (emulating first a percussion and later a solo instrument) became the materials of the hiphop DJ, all unveilings of the private vocabulary of the disco DJ. The sound of the disc being spun in reverse is common when cueing up a record – to hide the trick of the perfect segue the DJ rehearses the switch from one song to the next in his headphones. Hiphop DJs came along and revealed this screech, offering it as a sound to be savoured. This would celebrate the technical skills of the DJ but created a new task of finding records that were appropriate. By the late seventies the hiphop DJ had become not only a turntable gymnast and formidable soloist but a historian of hiphop and its varied lexicon.

As a young hiphop fan I broke more than one turntable attempting to scratch. When one considers that most records that I have scratched were hiphop vinyl, and that scratching actually damages the vinyl, it becomes clear that Grandwizard Theodore taught us to abuse our most highly prized possessions. He taught us the real possibilities of the commodity (its eventual unplayability/destruction) and made us appreciate its ephemerality (Theodore also led many of us to buy double copies of records).

DJs continually extend the music into other genres. Investigating jazz, soul, R&B, blues, salsa and country they cross into new cultural territories and histories. In return people all over the globe insert themselves into hiphop hybrids, changing the genealogy of the music and further expanding the range of the practice.

By 1979 Sylvia Robinson, a former 'soul talker', created Sugarhill Records and released 'Rapper's Delight'. Hiphop burst on to the mainstream with this single, and graffiti began to be exhibited downtown. Breakdancing – through the success of certain mainstream Hollywood movies – became a craze among the young all over the country. The international success of 'Rapper's Delight' sent everything through the roof – this new 'fad' bypassed its roots and catapulted an unknown group from New Jersey to prominence. But before long a lot of the early crews associated with Flash, Bam and Herc struck back and hiphop was formally unleashed on a surprised and relatively receptive world.

Westside Story

When we first came out here kids were doin' their own thing – it was called poppin'.
Crazy Legs, Rocksteady Crew, telephone interview, September 1992

Jimmie liked funk music. It was Crip music to him. He and Termite would listen to Funkadelic and practice poplock, the Crip dance, that required separate movements of all the parts of the body. Poplock was fun, but it was serious business if you wanted to be Crip. It was never done with girls . . . Suddenly Jimmie's body tensed. His muscles rippled. He ticked and wall walked in the pantomime poplock style unique to Crips. His body tensed and relaxed melding perfectly with the beat. It was like watching someone choreograph an epileptic fit. The other dancers stopped and watched Jimmie do more than dance. He was making a unique statement.

It was like destroying all the traditions of dance and recreating them in his own rebellious style. This dance was young. It was Los Angeles, and it was innovatively American. Flaco turned the music up higher.

Donald Bakeer, *Crips*, p. 100

'Rapper's Delight' by the Sugarhill Gang and 'King Tim III' by Fatback arrived on the West Coast, followed by tours by Afrika Bambaataa and his Soul Sonic Force in 1980, and the Rocksteady Crew in 1982. However, when the breakers arrived from New York they were greeted by a type of dancing that they had not seen before: popping and locking.

Locking is said to have been invented in 1972 in Los Angeles by a group called the Original Lockers. It was created out of a perversion of the Funky Chicken (by Rufus Thomas), a popular dance of the early seventies. Locking is named for the locking of the joints that characterize the dance. Its popularity is linked to the advent of gang culture in south central. Popping, on the other hand, is credited to *Soul Train* dancer Charlie Robot. In 1972, Robot developed a style of dancing based on the moves of a robot, although it is also quite obviously influenced by the street mime tradition. Robot's technique was slow and meditative, but a dancer from Oakland called Sen Robot modified the technique, speeding it up to disco tempo. Popping then started to become popular in northern California.

A dancer named Shabba Doo who was a member of the Original Lockers saw some street dancers in Fresno popping and he then brought the style to Los Angeles. Popping is typified by extraordinarily controlled body movement that mimics either animation or machine-like behaviour. Bakeer's 'choreographed epilepsy' description is quite fitting.

Popping and locking had subsided in popularity by the late seventies, but when breaking started to arrive from New York the tradition revived. The first breaker to turn up in Los Angeles is reportedly SugarPop, a breaker from Brooklyn who became a regular on the Venice boardwalk Hollywood Boulevard scene. The early eighties popularity of breaking – which became the umbrella term to describe the three types of dancing – can be largely attributed to the intervention of Hollywood. *Flashdance* and *Breakin'* and their independent (and superior) counterparts *Wild Style* and *Breakin and Entering* brought the new dance to the country and later the world. However, the meaning and history of the new scene as well as its links to the music, graffiti and black and Chicano (also Puerto Rican) youth culture were stripped away.

In 1982 an all-age club called Radio opened downtown that catered to the emerging culture. The DJs at Radio were Henry G, Evil E, DST, out from New York to work with Herbie Hancock on 'Rockit', Afrika Islam who had been the DJ for the Rocksteady Crew and had come out for the making of *Flashdance*, and local Chris (the Glove) Taylor. At Radio, a club based on the Roxy in New York, the LA sound began to emerge. Radio and later Radiotron are fondly remembered clubs on the LA scene, partly because they broke a lot of underground New York music to LA, but also because they catered to a large and diverse crowd in the years before hiphop became associated with gun play. Large park jams were possible, but only under the watchful eye of the city authorities (for example, the LA Street Scene). Public space is different in LA. Cruisin' in a kitted out ride (car) is a popular pastime. Graffiti are more common on the freeways than on public transport.

The early eighties also saw the emergence of Uncle Jam's Army (named after the Funkadelic album) which was a group of DJs and promoters led by Roger Clayton. They brought the music to the hood as opposed to trying to bring the hood downtown as Radio had sought to do. Uncle Jam's Army put on large shows and was essentially nomadic. Learning from the 'Chicano Woodstocks' (par Reuben Gueverra) that were being organized on the east side, they built flexibility into their events – this month they would be at the Sports Arena, next month the Convention Center. This is different from the Bronx scene where people were completely committed at first to single spots or hoods. Of course by the time of Uncle Jam's Army things had become more economically viable and hiphop could be mobile.

In LA rhymin' developed quickly in school yards, on buses and in lunchrooms with young MCs (masters of ceremonies) battling each other (challenging each other to rhyme better). Early battles in LA consisted of MCs rhyming over Sugarhill/Enjoy or Uni instrumental tracks in the same meter as the rhymers whose tracks they were, but changing the words in ways that described local situations or altered the meaning of the original in humorous ways – in much the same way as Toddy Tee and Mixmaster Spade's tapes were constructed. The hiphop aesthetic of making producers from consumers helped spawn LA's first indigenous hiphop rhymers. World on Wheels on Venice Boulevard, and Skateland in Compton, two roller rinks, were early developing grounds for these young 'microphone fiends' as well as recruiting grounds for the Mixmasters, a federation of mix DJs used by KDAY. Many MCs fondly remember the Friday-night competitions held at these venues and sponsored by KDAY, Lonzo Williams and Dr Dre.

By 1984, KDAY, through the influence of a new programmer, Greg Mack, became enamoured of the new music. Mack was more interested in breaking new music than in promoting hiphop per se – but he noticed that this new music could open up a sizeable audience that other stations didn't have. He brought a lot of new groups to LA from New York, including Run DMC, Doug E. Fresh, Whodini, Fat Boys and later LL Cool J, BDP and Public Enemy, and this had a profound effect.

Another crucial element in defining the LA sound was the electropop that had evolved out of a fascination with technology, fed by the new arcade games such as Space Invaders and Pacman with their electronic parps and squeeks, and also the surprising popularity of German band Kraftwerk. This moved the West Coast more than the raw funk/soul/reggae-influenced beats of the east, and led to the split between West Coast and East Coast that still lingers like the smell of a recently discharged weapon. East Coasters had the radical beats and respect but the West Coast had the record sales (and this continues as I write).

Early on the more commercial aspects of the music seemed dominant in LA. The popularity of Afrika Bambaataa and the Soul Sonic Force's 'Planet Rock', and the large spate of electropop offshoot groups passed in LA as hiphop. The community was the same as in New York, but the cutting edge of the music seemed to have been lost, in crossing the country, to commercialism. Part of this problem seems to have been access to recordings on the West Coast. Much of the early or old-school hiphop was recorded on independent labels (Uni, Sugarhill, Enjoy, Tuff City) which were hard to find.

This lack of access led to the development of a split in LA hiphop between those who had access and those who stayed with the electropop and West Coast funk. Those on the street who had access generally had it through New York relatives or friends. I've heard many an LA B-boy reminisce over his first time hearing an Ultramagnetic song or receiving his first Mr Magic, Marly Marl or Red Alert tape from New York radio. On the other hand I've heard MCs talk about how they never dug that underground shit like Ultramags and were weaned on Zapp, Parliament and Cameo. Neither camp is exclusive of the other, but from each arose a distinct musical legacy. The acknowledgement of an LA underground scene parallel with gangsta rap (with its feet in the funk legacy) has only recently come to public attention.

To further illustrate the difference between LA and New York at that time, let's look at two songs that were popular in LA in '85/6. First is 'Peter Piper', a classic New York B-boy cut from Run DMC, released in '86 from their album *Raising Hell* on Profile Records.

> Peter Piper picked peppers,
> But Run rocks rhymes,
> Now Humpty Dumpty fell down,
> That's his hard time,
> Now Jack was nimble, what, nimble,

And he was quick,
But Jam Master's much faster
But now Jack is on Jay's dick.

Now little Bo Peep cold lost her sheep,
And Rip Van Winkle fell the hell asleep,
While Alice's jumpin' in wonderland,
Jack's havin' Jill bumpin' in his hand,
And Jam Master Jay is takin' out that sound,
The turntables may wobble but they won't fall down . . .

The music is constructed through some classic turntable work by Jam Master Jay. He cuts, scratches and backspins the intro to Bob James's cover of the Paul Simon tune 'Take Me to the Mardi Gras' over an economic 808 drum track. The beauty of the whole effort is in its simplicity. Jay understands the use of the break, exploiting its silence to accentuate the rhymes. It has the feel of something created at a park jam and then recorded in one take. The rhyming is unforced, utilizing a call and response structure.

Moving to a West Coast example of a similar type jam from nine months later we find 'Cabbage Patch' by the World Class Wreckin Crew, released through Macola Records. Cabbage Patch is a dance not unlike the Bump, the Hustle, the Biz, the PeeWee Herman or the Steve Martin. It also uses 'Take Me to the Mardi Gras'. Contrary to Jay's use of the Bob James cover (which allows us to appreciate its complex percussion pattern), in 'Cabbage Patch' the melody of the bells is played on a keyboard using similar bell sounds. This is dropped in on one channel only; stripped of its percussion, it becomes one element in a complex of sounds. What replaces the sound of Jay's turntable wizardry is a heavily sequenced multi-layered track from the Linn SP1200 (sampling drum machine) of Dre and Yella. The drum sounds are electronic and are accompanied by the clicking, parping and popping typical of the West Coast sound of this period. Even another bell track is laid to offset the original Bob James track. The resulting track is heavy, complicated and ultimately not as catchy as Run DMC's classic.

The complexity of Dre and Yella's effort with its many percussive elements is closer to a big-band sound compared to the stripped-down funk of Run DMC. And the rhyming?

Went to a party in West LA
Wanna learn a new dance that's what you say,
Well here's a new dance that can't be matched,
So just step to the floor and do the cabbage patch,
When I got to the party it was half past nine,
Cold rockin to the rhythm of a B-boy rhyme,
When I stepped to the floor it was a total wreck,

Tried to do the wop and almost broke my neck . . .

While you're rockin' to the big beat drum,
Let us take a minute to tell you where we're from,
It's the West Coast city they call LA,
That's sunny California where the ballers play,
If you're not from here I'm'a let you know,
That we never ever have to worry 'bout snow,
So hit Venice Beach and put your mind at ease,
'Cos it's the middle of winter and it's eighty degrees,
Cruisin' down Crenshaw with the top pulled back,
Cold rockin' to the beat of the cabbage patch,
Gotta compact disc that's top of the line,
Twelve pitch EVs and a fresh Alpine,
With fresh Air Jordans and a Fila shirt,
Headed to your homies cos it's time to do some work,
Called him on the phone just to tell him I was near him,
Had to cut the sound system down so I could hear him,
The last song we did was called the Fly,
Didn't quite hit and I'll tell you why,
When we cut the song it sounded great,
Went to CBS got stuck in red tape,
Held us up kicked us in the butt,
So we said forget it, fire a rough crew cut,
Picked up a group and we were on our way,
Fresh homeboys called the CIA.

The difference in the rhyming style between songs is enormous. Shakespeare, Dre, Lonzo and Yella force out their formated lyric awkwardly. Each MC takes several bars and then passes on to the next – rarely do they accent each other's lines. This simplicity can be compared to the complexity of Run DMC's shorter but more sophisticated lyric.

Musically the Wreckin Cru was involved in leather and lace electropop, and wore maxi coats and lace gloves (and, rumours had it, make-up), as compared to the Adidas sweat suits and shell toes of Run DMC. Heavily influenced by Cameo, Prince and Zapp, these would be the groups the next generation of LA hiphoppers would disown.

If this early scene undermined LA's credibility, it also led to a certain autonomy, the kind that permitted the development of house music in Chicago and the bright moment that is Go-Go in DC. The World Class Wreckin Cru after the intervention of Eazy E would become Niggers With Attitude (Dre and Yella left Shakespeare and Lonzo) and the CIA mentioned in the last line of the song was Ice Cube and Jinx's first group with a third member, KD.

So You Wanna Be a Gangsta

The big break for LA came in 1987. LA was not the first city to have gangsta rap; Philadelphia's Schooly D is credited as the first hiphop gangsta, closely followed by KRS One and Scott La Rock of Boogie Down Productions (BDP) with their album *Criminal Minded*. However, with the media frenzy around the killing of a young Asian woman in Westwood (one of the city's nicer neighbourhoods on the west side) on 30 January 1988, LA's gangsta rap began to take all the prizes for authenticity. Captain Rapp had recorded 'Bad Times (I Can't Stand It)', a sort of West Coast bite of 'The Message' with its reversing of the title of the famous Chic track that was a staple of the commercial old school.

Ice T had always been fascinated with the player lifestyle and had named himself after the legendary pimp writer Iceberg Slim (whom he credits as his mentor in the sleeve notes to *Rhyme Pays*, his first LP). Iceberg Slim has written many books including the classic *Pimp*, and his 'political' book, *The Naked Soul of Iceberg Slim*. He has to date made one record, *Reflections*, released in 1976 on the ALA label. The album is basically four long dissertations delivered in Slim's wry monotone over musical accompaniment by the Red Holloway Quartet. On this short album Slim captures the allure and edge of the Life, though he was by '76 in many ways a relic. He was living as a writer, yet his voice contained the grit and toughness of his previous profession.

Ice T was part of the earlier electropop scene that centred around Radio and Uncle Jam's Army, the east side circuit with Tony (G) Gonzalez and a young Kid Frost, an electropop house jam scene with a primarily Chicano constituency. Though his early work was harder lyrically than that of his peers at Macola Records, it was still plagued by the up-tempo pippy beats (his 'Coldest Rap' is a good example of this). He was the 'star' of the documentary *Breaking and Entering*, the film about the burgeoning street dance scene in LA based around Radio. This led to a fictionalized Hollywood film called *Breakin'* in which Ice T ended up making a slightly embarrassing cameo appearance.

In 1986 Ice T recorded 'Six in the Morning', a classic West Coast gangsta cut with a B-boy twist. It comes from a time when the LAPD had been involved in many early-morning raids, arresting thousands of young people of colour, harassing them and then releasing uncharged ninety per cent of them. (Mike Davis estimates from currently available figures that two-thirds of 'younger black males' in Los Angeles have been arrested, picked up, and had their details taken since 1974.) 'Six' begins with an account of such a raid.

> Six in the mornin', police at my door,
> Fresh Adidas squeak across my bathroom floor,
> Out my back window I make my escape,
> Didn't even get a chance to take my old school tape,

Mad with no music, but happy to be free,
And the streets to a player is the place to be,
Got a knot in pocket weighin' at least a grand,
Gold around my neck, my pistols close at hand,
I'm a self made monster of the city streets,
Remotely controlled by hard hiphop beats,
Just livin' in the city is a serious task,
Didn't know what the cops wanted, didn't have time to ask . . . WORD

Seen my homeboys coolin' way way out,
Told um about my mornin' cold bugged um out,
Shot a little dice til my knees got sore,
Kicked around some stories about the night before,
Posse'd to the corner where the fly girls chill,
Threw some action at some freaks 'til one bitch got ill,
She started actin' stupid, simply would not quit,
As we walked over to her, hoe continued to speak,
So we beat the bitch down in the goddamn street,
Just livin' in the city is a serious task,
Bitch didn't know what hit her, didn't have time to ask . . . WORD

Continued to clock freaks with immense posteriors,
Rollin' in a blazer with Louie interior,
Solid gold the ride was raw,
Bust a left turn was on Crenshaw,
Sean E Sean was the driver, known to give freaks hell,
Had a beeper goin' off like a high school bell,
Looked in the mirror, what did we see,
Fuckin' blue lights LAPD,
Police searched our car, their day was made,
Found an Uzi, 44 and a hand grenade,
Threw us in the county high powered block,
No freaks to see, no beats to rock,
Didn't want trouble but shit had to fly,
Squabbled with a sucker, shanked 'em in the eye,
But livin' in the county is a serious task,
Nigga didn't know what happened, didn't have time to ask . . . WORD

Back on the streets after five and a deuce,
Seven years later but still had the juice,
My homeboy Hen Gee put me on the track,
Told me E's rollin' villain, BJ's got the sack,
Bruce is a giant, Nat C's clockin' dough,

> Be Bop's a pimp, my old freak's a hoe,
> The batteram's rollin', rock's the thing,
> Life has no meaning, money is king,
> Then he looked at me slowly, Hen had to grin,
> He said, man you got out early, we thought you got ten,
> Opened his safe, kicked me down cold cash . . .

Here T had managed to outline the events that made up the life of many LA street youth: police harassment, the arrival of rock cocaine and abusive stories about women. And T had found a meter that worked for the slow and stealthy pace of LA cruisin'. This meter would go on to be used by Eazy E on 'Boyz in the Hood'. This pace was more influenced by Schooly D's 'PSK' and 'Saturday Night' (similar narratives about the Philly player) than either the freestyle meter of New York or the electropop prevalent in LA.

When, in the fifth to last line of 'Six', T mentions 'batteram's rollin'', he not only refers to the new donation from the army to the LAPD, but to the popular hit by Compton original and West Coast enigma Toddy Tee. In 1985 Toddy and another infamous LA rhymer Mixmaster Spade had been swapping battle tapes among themselves in Compton. One night while watching the news on TV, Toddy had come up with an idea for a rhyme about the newly unveiled 'Batteram' and its pilot, Chief of Police Daryl Gates. The Batteram was an armoured vehicle for use in the 'war on drugs'. It was donated by the military to the LAPD to aid in the smashing down of the doors of crack houses, theoretically to prevent dealers from having the time to dispose of evidence. Toddy Tee's battle tape went on to recount a number of other stories relating to the proliferation of rock cocaine in Compton, rhymed over instrumentals of other people's and recorded through an echo box (in similar fashion to early Jamaican dub poets). The tape was phenomenally popular. It included 'Batteram' which is rhymed over the instrumental of the 'Rappin Duke', 'The Clucks Come Out at Night' rhymed over 'Freaks Come Out at Night' by Was Not Was (also covered by Whodini), 'Rockman, Rockman' rhymed over UTFO's 'Roxanne Roxanne'. The tape is incredibly raw, but through the rawness comes Toddy Tee's humour and acute observations.

> Yo Rockman I heard what you said,
> Talkin' too much shit about those baseheads,
> When Toddy Tee is rockin' the house,
> The police stop just to check me out,
> I was standin' on the corner, with some of my friends,
> Girl pulled up in a Mercedes Benz,
> So I rushed her and paid her no mind,
> She said can you break down to me in a rhyme,
> She said she wanted five-o,

And then half a track,
She said she didn't like it, so she tried to give it back,
And now she wants a quarter in exchange for her daughter,
I said now if I fuck her I might have to hit the border,
The girl is only twelve, I might end up in jail,
Doin' thirty years 'cos I made her pussy smell,
So I said can you be real,
You're sittin' here, tryin' to break a deal,
Here come the narc, baby please don't squeal,
I said I got some weed,
She said that that shit is old,
I said what do you like, she says the primo.

'Rockman' begins with Toddy asking, 'Lee, can you test the bass for me', a reference to the levels on the tape no doubt, but sure to be confused with another kind of 'free' base. This old school LA homemade tape is the prototype for the many acts to come on the West Coast scene. Its irreverence, crudeness and spontaneity still sounds fresh today. In terms of its sound it is the antecedent of many of today's platinum artists, from Too Short to DJ Quik.

Toddy Tee was finally discovered (apparently people came to Compton looking for the nineteen-year-old to sign him) and 'Batteram' was released as a single in 1986. It was hugely popular, but it didn't have the edge the earlier tape had.

New York, it's comin' . . . Detroit, it's comin' . . .
LA it's comin' . . . It's here,
The Batteram
Drug busters you better beware,
And don't turn your head as if you just don't care,
They say they got you in their hands and they don't need no proof,
They say they sick and tired of snatchin' down bars,
Cos with a tow truck it makes it real hard
And by the time they get in your pad
You done flushed down the toilet and now they're mad
So they mad as hell and they take you to jail
But you out the next minute cos you post bail
And on the very next day you say what the heck
You get a letter in the mail and it's a DA reject
And you jumpin' up and down cos there ain't no case
And to the police this is a waste
But rock man you'll see it soon
And you won't hear a snatch, you'll hear a boom.

Batteram

You were so high that your eyes was tight
And you didn't even notice the batteram lights
So go, when they said it was there,
You shook your head and said I don't care
Based out, without a doubt
When they said give up, you cussed um out,
And when your dope bustin' friends drove up in their cars,
You just stuck out your chest and acted real hard
You took off your Fila shirt and your Reebok shoes
And had the nerve to call the cops a bunch of fools
You called um pigs, sissies and even called um punks
While the batteram battery needed a jump
And by the time they got started, you fell to the floor
That's when the cops said they can't take no more
And you were so high, my little friend
That you didn't know your living room was in your den.

Batteram

So I sit at home about to eat dinner
I had a hard time at work and my day was gettin' thinner
My kids was in the room watchin' Mighty Mouse
And my wife was gettin' ready to leave the house
But as she opened the door, she seen a flare
It was an undercover cop standin' over there
So she hollered back to me, honey come and see
Just who this strange man could be
When I went to the door, I thought it was a thug
Cos he he kept askin' me to sell him drugs
So I said homeboy what you talkin' bout
You're mistakin my pad for a crack house
Oh I know to you we all look the same
But I'm not the one slangin 'caine
I worked nine to five, ain't a damned thing changed
And I don't have time for the hustler's game.

Batteram

Mayor of the city whatcha tryin' to do
They say they voted you in in '82
But on the next term, without no doubt
They say they gonna vote your jackass out
Because you must have been crazy or half way wack
To legalize somethin' that works like that

And the chief of police says he just might
Batterram each house he sees, on sight
Cos he says the rock man is takin' him for a fool
And for some damn reason it just ain't cool
When he drives down the street, I'll tell you the truth
He gets no respect, they call his force F Troop . . .

It is interesting to note that Toddy Tee's street tape is better remembered than the vinyl version. This must have proved to the young Eazy and Dre (as well as T) that popularity in the hood could be secured more easily with rawer, uncensored first-person cuts.

In 1986 Run DMC played in Long Beach at the Fresh Fest, which turned out to be a highly publicized public exhibition of gunplay by the resident Crips and some gathered youth of different affiliations. This sent signals all over the country. Then, the death of Karen Toshima by a stray bullet in Westwood in January of 1988 and the subsequent arrest and charging of Durrel Collins (an alleged gang member according to the *LA Times*), served notice to the population of LA of its problem with disenfranchised youth of colour. The controversy continued when three hundred extra LAPD officers were assigned to Westwood, enraging community leaders who had been vainly calling for help in south central both from the police department and the city authorities. But what clinched national acknowledgement of gang culture in LA was the controversy surrounding the film *Colors* by Dennis Hopper.

Hopper had been recruited by Sean Penn to direct an action movie to fulfil a contractual arrangement with his studio. Of course nobody banked on Hopper doing something so close to the political bone of the current climate in Los Angeles. But that fateful summer of 1988 he revealed to the world through a conventional 'buddy narrative' a hysterical view of LA's youth of colour. Hopper spent little time labouring over the possible social or economic reasons for their problems, instead opting for an anti-drug (crack) moral tale relating to these 'delinquents'. He ended up having to screen the movie for the police to prevent it from being banned by Assistant Chief Robert Vernon for fear of violence at public screenings.

This film will leave dead bodies from one end of this town to the other.
Wes McBride, president of the California Gang Investigators Association about
Colors, LA Herald Examiner, 20 March 1988

For government officials to say they were going to ban it in LA . . . What they are basically saying is that they have a police problem and they can't handle it. The gang thing is out of control – that's what my movie is saying. At the beginning we point out that there are 250 men and women working in law enforcement against 600 gangs with over 70,000 members. How can they possibly handle it?
Dennis Hopper, *LA Times*, 25 March 1988

You can be a movie star if you're a gang member.

> John Malone, Area Commander with the County Sheriff's Department, *LA Times*,
> 25 March 1988

The 'them' – what one local mayor calls 'the Viet Cong abroad in our society' – are the members of local Black gangs, segmented into several hundred fighting 'sets' while loosely aligned into two hostile super gangs, the Crips and the Bloods – universally distinguished, as every viewer of Dennis Hopper's *Colors* now knows, by their color coding of shoelaces, T-shirts and bandannas . . . Although gang cohorts are typically hardly more than high-school sophomores, local politicians frequently compare them to 'the murderous militias of Beirut'.

> Mike Davis, *City of Quartz*, p. 268

In *City of Quartz*, Mike Davis tells of the emergence of the first black youth gangs in Los Angeles as a defence against the reign of terror imposed by white thugs that spread southward along the Central Avenue corridor. In the social expansion of the fifties, the splits in LA youth groupings were generally along class lines: 'eastside' denoted a more blue-collar Chicano influence and the 'westside' a more peaceful, fun-loving car club-type atmosphere. However, the biggest enemies at this time for young blacks and Chicanos were the racially motivated manoeuvrings of Chief Parker's LAPD. It has always been in the interest of the police department to exaggerate the menace of the 'brown and black youth tribes' that ran rampant south of Wilshire, supposedly held back only by a staunch blue line. Indeed, as Mike Davis correctly notes, 'Parker's LAPD looked on the rehabilitation of gang youth in much the same way as the arms industry looks upon disarmament.'

> 'Yeh, son, your father was one of the youngest black freedom fighters in this city. We caused a lot of changes that week in August '65, and our message swept this country, the world. The black man would no longer accept oppression. Get your feet off our necks. Call off your police dogs or we'll meet you in the streets.
>
> 'A lot of people had to die to get the message across, but it brought everybody in the neighborhoods together . . . Gangbangers and gangsters all came together to fight the common enemy. Afterwards gangbanging kind of died. You had to be associated with some political organization, US v. the Panthers, Muslims, CORE, NAACP or something. We all had the same sign, then, the closed fist like this!'
>
> Donald Bakeer, *Crips*, p. 161.

The destruction of the black organizations that had sprung up after the Watts Rebellion of '65 by COINTELPRO in the late sixties/early seventies left a gap that would be filled by the advent of 'Crippin'' in the early seventies. Crippin' is the name taken by the founders of the now famous organization for their particularly menacing way of walking. It referred to 'crippled'. The mention of the word Crip in US cities today conjures up images of young black males riding shotgun with blue bandannas and khakis terrorizing their respective neighbourhoods with large-calibre automatic weapons.

According to Steven Hager, by 1972 south Bronx street gang activities had largely subsided due to the interest in graffiti. But 1972 was the year of the birth of the Crips along the Hoover Street corridor in south central Los Angeles. In opposition to the Crips, a confederation was begun between gangs from adjoining neighbourhoods, later to be known as the Bloods. For the youth of their respective constituencies these street federations serve many purposes, from surrogate families to employers. They, along with their older Chicano counterparts, have had a profound effect on the culture of Los Angeles: from the Chicano visual artists from the early seventies to the Hollywood representations of this lifestyle.

The escalation of youth violence of the mid-eighties is directly linked to the changing tide of cocaine importation into this country, from Miami to the overland routes through Mexico into southern California. This increased the economic stakes in Crip vs Blood turf wars to outrageous levels, although as any informed person could tell you, the community never saw any economic benefit. 'We didn't make AK 47s, we sure didn't fly to Colombia and bring the shit back, and look around you, does it look like this community is getting more prosperous?' as was once said to me. For black people, cocaine was merely salt on the festering wounds of economic neglect, the evaporation of manufacturing jobs and little or no political clout, despite an African-American mayor.

If Clinton ran in the 1992 presidential election in an attempt to prevent this generation from becoming the first to fare worse than their parents, his message seemed ironic in south central LA, where the last two generations have seen the evacuation of the middle class, and the departure of good jobs, leaving the boom industries of retailing crack cocaine and mortuary services. The public education system has all but collapsed and health services are beyond crisis point. When you add to this the effects of AIDS and the growing numbers incarcerated or those with dependencies, it makes a lot of sense to people on the ground that there is a conspiracy afoot. The structure of society quickly erodes when the only realistic prospect for the economic elevation of the individual remains participation in activities outside those sanctioned by the state or the private sector. Generations of ghetto youth have seen all their options evaporate. The gangs of south central are an outgrowth of these conditions.

LA's gangs have also produced some of the area's leading political activists. From Alprentiss 'Bunchy' Carter and Ron Wilkins to many of the outspoken rhymers of today, the necessity of resistance has forefronted many great brothers and sisters from the ranks of the so-called plague of youth gangs. A great many members of the Black Panthers, US

(United Slaves) and the Nation of Islam were (and remain) recruits from the ranks of LA's neighbourhood confederations.

> What would the Crips and Bloods say about the carnage if they could talk? It is, of course, a tactical absolute of 'anti- terrorism' – whether practiced in Belfast, Jerusalem or Los Angeles – to deny terrorism a public voice. Although terrorism is always portrayed precisely as inarticulate male violence, authorities expend enormous amounts of energy to protect us from its ravings even at the cost of censorship and restriction of free speech. Thus the LAPD has vehemently (and usually successfully) opposed attempts by social workers and community organizers to allow gang members to tell 'their side of the story'.
>
> Mike Davis, *City of Quartz*, p. 300

Mike Davis has accurately described the exclusion of these peoples from the mainstream media, but it is interesting to note that in blinkered Los Angeles as well as in Section 31 blighted Ireland, these communities have found other means to make their voices heard.

And when Davis laments the fact that today's generation 'flock to stadia' to hear Eazy E rap 'it's not about black or white but green' (meaning cash) while twenty years ago they would have gone to see Huey Newton, Stokely Carmichael or Eldridge Cleaver, perhaps he misses the possibility for discussion of these same older issues in new ways. For new generations the culture produced by the seeming hopelessness of the 'gangsta' lifestyle has become the social realism of the nineties.

It seems unfortunate that the left finds itself so radically polarized around the subject of this music, from the voyeuristic celebratory tones of the Socialist Worker and the RCP, so obviously eager to woo the African-American ghetto constituency, to the fear and loathing of the academic left, who have traditionally had problems with popular culture anyway. The former fringe groupings view the music as a window on the 'fourth world', focusing on the conventionally political groups and ignoring the history of the music and the black nationalist sentiments, as well as forgetting the commodity status of the genre. The academic left has traditionally been consumed exclusively with this, the commodity status of the music, especially in connection with hiphop's concern with male pleasures and accumulated wealth.

Instead of constructing an argument from specifics we are left to muse over often absurd generalities. Frank Kofsky's 1970 text still seems relevant.

> It would be extremely naive to think that any given set of purely musical innovations would suffice to emancipate black musicians from the grip of white entrepreneurial domination. To bring about a change of that magnitude would necessitate not only aesthetic revolution, but social upheaval as well . . . I, for one, am convinced that when it comes to the denouement, more than a few whites may find themselves on the 'wrong side' of the barricades simply because a Ray Charles or a Miles Davis has been giving them a changed perception of reality that, under

existing circumstances, could scarcely have been attained in any other way. If the traditional left in this country has fallen far short of its fundamental goal of imbuing white workers with a class wide consciousness, it cannot be said that Negro culture has failed to make its vivid imprint on those young whites lucky enough to have caught a taste of it.

Frank Kofsky, *Black Nationalism and the Revolution in Music*, pp. 60, 106

In 1986 a sixteen-year-old Ice Cube penned 'Boyz n the Hood'. The song was put together over a slow, heavy Run DMC-influenced track created by Dre and Yella with nasal lyrical whining by Eazy E. What made the song so popular was its frank depiction of the life of a young baller. As opposed to the cutesy meanderings of 'Cabbage Patch', 'Boyz' packs a punch in every couplet, making it a lyrical descendant of the original 'Batteram' tape. Also noticeable is its coherence compared to the awkwardness of Toddy Tee's amateur effort. The song has a rhymed hook and maintains a narrative intensity through it. The heavy reliance on street slang coupled with Eazy E's vocal credibility gave the song an irresistible edge.

> Cruisin' down the street in my 64,
> Jockin' the freaks, clockin' the dough,
> Went to the park to get the scoop,
> Knuckleheads out there shootin' some hoop,
> A car pulls up who can it be,
> A fresh El Camino rollin' Kilo G,
> Who rolled down the window and started to say,
> It's all about makin' that GTA.
>
> Cos the Boyz in the Hood are always hard,
> Come talkin' that trash and we'll pull your card,
> Knowin' nuthin' in life but to be legit,
> Don't quote me boy cos I ain't sayin' shit.
>
> Donald B in the place to give me the bass,
> Say my man JD is on free bass,
> The boy JD was a friend of mine,
> Til I caught him in my car tryin' to steal a Alpine
> Chased him up the street to call a truce
> The silly cluck head pulls out a deuce deuce
> Little did he know I had twelve gauge
> One sucker dead *LA Times* front page.
>
> Cos the Boyz . . .
>
> Bored as hell and I want to get ill
> So I went to a place where the homeboys chill,

The fellas out there makin' that dollar,
I pulled up in my six four Impala
They greet me with a forty and I started to drinkin',
And from the eight ball my breath started stinkin',
Left to get my girl to rock that body,
Before I left, I hit the Bacardi,
Went to her house to get her out of the pad,
Dumb ho said somethin' that make me mad,
She said somethin' that I couldn't believe,
So I grabbed the stupid bitch by her nappy ass weave,
She started talkin' shit wouldn't you know,
So I reached back like a pimp and slapped the hoe,
Her father jumped up and he started to shout,
So I threw a right cross, cold knocked him out.

Cos the Boyz . . .

I'm rollin' hard now under control,
Did wrap my six four around a telephone pole,
I looked at my car and said, Oh brother,
I'll throw it in the gutter and go buy another,
Walkin' home I see the G ride
Now Caddies drivin' Kilo G's on the side
As they busted a U, they got pulled over,
An undercover cop in a dark green Nova
Cad got beat for resistin' arrest,
Bust a pig in the head for rippin' his Guess,
Now G is caught for doin' the crime,
Fourth offence on the boil he'll do time.

Cos the Boyz . . .

I went to get them out but there was no bail,
The fellas caused a riot in the County Jail,
Two days later in Municipal Court,
Kilo G on trial, cold cut a fourth,
Obstruction of court said the judge
On a six year sentence the man wouldn't budge,
Bailiff came over to turn him in,
Kilo G looked up and gave a grin,
He yelled out fire and then came Suzy,
The bitch came in with a submachine Uzi,
The police shot her but didn't hurt her,
Both went up state for attempted murder.

Cos the Boyz etc . . .

The song showed a side of LA hiphop that hadn't been seen before, showing the B-boy in gangland, LA style. Eazy and Cube had created over Dre's beat a West Coast equivalent of Schooly D's 'PSK'. Both are simple rhymes over sparse drum patterns with prominent bell sounds; however, while 'PSK' is definitely from the early break beat tradition, 'Boyz' is a much slower, more menacing track. Dre had transformed the happy pippy beats of 'Cabbage Patch' into a grinding, authoritative, droning loop. He added the familiar boom of the 808 under his loop not only to give his creation more depth, but to give the track a cruisin' appeal. After all, what is the point of having a huge bass capacity in your trunk if you don't play music to test it? Dre to this day always judges his tracks by their qualities in his ride.

Another aspect of the track that merits notice is the long breaks between verses. Here Dre and Yella build up the menace of the sound by upping the tempo and dropping scratched segments of other records. Sections of Ice T can be heard along with the 'City of Compton' snatch from Ronnie Hudson's 'West Coast Poplock'. It gives the track a DJ edge, leaving the habits of the techno type spinning behind once and for all.

Eazy's strenuous delivery gave the lyrics a kind of ironic realism of which Ice T with his dramatic intonation at the time didn't seem capable. Myth has it that Eazy wasn't supposed to rhyme, but since the group that the song was written for – HBO, a long forgotten East Coast group – refused to do it 'because it was too West Coast', Eazy went in the vocal booth, cleared the studio and committed his incriminating voice to tape. As Jonathan Gold wrote of that voice in *LA Weekly* (5 May 1989), 'Eazy's rapping is a drawling blend of Woody Woodpecker and the vicious, whiskey-smooth tenor of Rakim.'

Eazy then fronted the money for the song to be pressed through the Macola pressing/distribution network and it hit the LA streets. KDAY put the song in rotation in mid-1987 and it stayed at number one on their call-in chart for four weeks. In the following months under the legendary umbrella of NWA, Eazy, Cube, Dre, Yella and Arabian Prince recorded 'Dopeman', a wry tale of the recurring crack dealer and '8 Ball', an ode to Olde English 800 (malt liquor), and other street classics. The only rhymer out on the West Coast doing underground music with a similar level of success at that time was Too Short, employing a limited vocabulary of the pimpsta lifestyle and heavy bass loops reminiscent structurally of dub.

NWA's first album was an unauthorized bootleg pressed by Macola. It sold thousands of copies, staying on the *Billboard* black album chart for almost a year. There was litigation but the growing army of fans didn't care. The album is embarrassing at times, but the tracks by Eazy and NWA make it quite clear why their product did so well in relation to that of their peers.

NWA proved with Ruthless Records in LA in '87, as Malcolm McLaren, Roger Armstrong and Ted Carroll had in London in 1976 and Sylvia Robinson (Sugarhill) and Bobby Robinson (Enjoy) in New York in 1979, that it was still possible to do records for under a thousand bucks and sell millions. It could be argued that the success of Ruthless wouldn't have been possible without the prowess of Eazy E. The Gordon Gekko of Compton managed to turn a cottage industry into a multi-million-dollar business overnight, while still maintaining control. He eventually severed ties with the Macola distribution network and moved to Priority Records. He refused to deal with major labels because of the delay involved in putting records out. Both Dre and Eazy understood that cutting the lag time from production to release was crucial if records were to move.

> Yeah, Priority could put out records quickly, but Macola could put them out overnight. I liked working with Brian Turner, I considered him a partner . . . the majors were full of shit, I couldn't deal with them, now in many ways it feels like I had predicted the future. What with the 'Cop Killer' [Ice T] fiasco, everybody's coming back to the independent route. The speed thing is important but we also got the creative freedom and solid distribution too.
>
> Eazy E, phone conversation with author, 10 December 1992

Dre in many ways became the West Coast Marly Marl, lending his Midas touch to many records, shows and radio programmes. His ruff, bass heavy, funk oriented style became known and respected across the country. He produced a plethora of records in Los Angeles in the following three years, including a solo effort by Eazy, a novelty record for JJ Fad, DOC's first album and an R&B album for Michel'le. Within a year of signing a distribution deal with Priority, Eazy's Ruthless records had sold eight million.

> . . . the Los Angeles based group NWA [. . .] shook the shit out of East Coast rappers and fans alike with *Straight Outta Compton*. That record not only put listeners within point blank range of LA gang mentality, but it did so non judgmentally, without any sense of moral distance, going so far on some tracks as to use black on black violence as the metaphoric base for some of the group's boasting. In a music built on revenge fantasies and sensationalism, NWA brought reality closer to the foreground. As the gunshots echo from West to East, out here LA gang violence sounds like nothing but black genocide turned in on itself. To hear a group endorse and uphold it with relish not only seemed shocking but intolerable, if not inhuman. Yet what they put to the test was the argument that rap was the voice of black Americans who had no voice elsewhere. If the mentality NWA spoke out of prevailed in their area, and rap music was reality music, why shouldn't their music bear a one on one relation to their social context?
>
> Greg Tate, 'Manchild at Large', *Village Voice*, 11 September 1990

The proposition that NWA are reality rappers has in many ways clouded the debate. NWA were primarily interested in selling records; this has to be understood first. In a highly calculated move based on the continuing longevity of Dolemite, Blowfly, Iceberg Slim, Richard Pryor, Redd Foxx's adult entertainment and many popular African American film characters, Eazy and Cube chose a participatory style of narrative. To be non- judgmental meant creating a gang called NWA. To uninitiated listeners and later viewers the idea of Niggers With Attitude would appear to be their worst fears come to life. But to those aware of the codifications and theatricality the whole charade would be a tragic comedy of everyday life with its inside jokes and malice. To view this performance as a transparent window on the thoughts and words of day-to-day south central is profoundly limiting, but it was a marketing strategy that worked perfectly.

NWA placed themselves on the hiphop map with authenticity, capturing the aggression and anger of the streets of south central in their intonation and timbre. This places the listener in an intimate position relative to their rhymes. Ice T sounds like a narrator by comparison. It is like hearing Albert Ayler and Wynton Marsalis; while they may play the same melody the way of performing it can be entirely different.

> We're telling the real story of what it's like living in places like Compton. We're giving the fans reality. We're like reporters. We give them the truth. People where we come from hear so many lies that that the truth stands out like a sore thumb.
>
> Eazy E, quoted in Mike Davis, *City of Quartz*, p. 86

Eazy's sore thumb of course is protruding from a hand that has more than one finger in Hollywood, yet another in black nationalism and its pinky caressing the asphalt tops of Compton, Central, Imperial and Crenshaw boulevards. Compton was almost an arbitrary choice – it could have been Watts, Long Beach, Lynwood, Downey or Willowbrook. But there had always been a strong local following for hiphop in Compton since the Wreckin Cru days. Dre and Yella spun with Lonzo at a club there called Eve's After Dark, which is where Davy D brought scratching to LA, by teaching Yella to scratch. And they had always sold a lot of records at the Compton Swapmeet.

But hiphop Compton, according to Eazy, was created as a reply to the construction of the south Bronx/Queensbridge nexus in New York. If locally it served notice in the community in which Eazy and Dre sold their Macola-pressed records (not to mention the potential play action on KDAY), nationally, or at least on the East Coast, it was an attempt to figure Los Angeles on the map of hiphop. After the album had gone double platinum Compton would be as well known a city in hiphop as either Queens or the Bronx.

However, to credit NWA alone with bringing LA to the mainstream would be a mistake, for pursuing their own path at the same time were King Tee, Pooh and Bobcat. Bobcat and Pooh early on had been to New York working with LL – Pooh had hooked up the beat for 'Jack the Ripper', an all-time 'dis' classic – and King T was formulating styles of rhyming here on the West Coast while many were still bound to the monotone gangsta rolling format. Close on the tail of NWA were Compton's Most Wanted, Above the Law and a slew of gangsta rhymers all exporting south central imagery to hiphop listeners worldwide.

A critical factor in the rise of south central hiphop was the crest of the KDAY wave. Greg Mack turned the marginal R&B station into the sixth most-listened-to station in Los Angeles. Mack conceived a format that took chances with its playlist. He built strong album tracks or B-sides into prime-time programming, featuring fifteen-minute mixes during drive time and running a club circuit that brought in acts from New York when they had only one single out. Mack pioneered the promotional tour, the main way hiphop fans see live music from outside their own scene. The promo tour is a series of club dates put together by the record company or management company to showcase a new act. The group travels the length of the country performing their single and perhaps two other songs at nightclubs. Generally the record company pays their expenses and the band appears free.

Most importantly Mack was firmly committed to playing and showcasing local talent. 'The one thing we would do is play a marginal LA record before a slightly better New York one,' said Mack in an interview. KDAY not only broke music to black Los Angeles but black Los Angeles broke records to it. 'Boyz n the Hood' is a good example of this: 'I knew Eazy and all those guys, but when we heard the record we were like er... it's OK. But then, anytime you went somewhere, that's all you heard. So we asked them to clean it up a little bit. They did and Bam! Hottest record on radio.' No other station had either the commitment to or the impact on the youth of south central as KDAY, quite apart from its influence on the varied and cross-cultural audience that hiphop was building in LA.

> As a hitmaking machine, KDAY had been the most influential black AM station in the nation; as a social force, it had aired both anti-gangbanging symposia chaired by Barry White and the Sunday night sermons of Louis Farrakhan; as a muse, it spurred the early careers of nearly every rap star to come out of the West Coast: Ice T, NWA, Tone Loc, MC Hammer, Ice Cube, Young MC. As a dance party, it ruled Saturday night. KDAY broadcast Crenshaw High sporting events, and was always running live feeds from things like the all-black Bill Picket Rodeo or the opening of a new fried chicken franchise in Inglewood. It was inconceivable that a rapper would swing through town and not drop by the station.
>
> Jonathan Gold, *LA Style*, October 1991, p. 184

Mack set up a retail store and his own record label – Mackdaddy Records – to complete the loop from artist through radio play to the consumer. Although the label released a number of classic LA cuts (including King Tee's 'Bass' and Payback's 'A Mother'), it is probably best remembered for the compilation *What Does It All Mean*, distributed through Motown. This compilation, similar to those released by Macola Records (*NWA and the Posse* and *The Posse Two*), had first efforts by the late MC Trouble, the Throwdown Twins, latter-day producer Epic and a young David Faustino (Bud Bundy from a network TV show *Married with Children*).

In March 1991, KDAY, the most significant radio station in recent LA history, fell victim to a system geared to homogeneity. It was bought by Fred Sands, a realtor and close friend of George Bush, for $7.2 million. He changed it into a business news station. Crude, raw, youth stories from LA had been replaced on 1580AM with the coded drone of Wall Street figures. New hiphop releases were now denied any airplay in the city as KGFJ flatly refused to take the kind of chances that KDAY had. Jonathan Gold claims that LA hiphop became more hardcore after this point; and many groups discontinued making radio-friendly versions of their material. In the eyes of many the closing of KDAY constitutes a violent crime against the youth community of LA, although very little protest was heard at the time of its closure.

Beware of the Black Fist

It has been said many times in many places that freedom is a road seldom travelled by the multitudes. But we would like to invite some of you to come, and go with us and perhaps you'll see a side of life that you've never seen before. I'm the son of a bad . . .

The Barkays recorded live at the LA Coliseum, 20 August 1972 (the seventh anniversary of the Watts Rebellion) compiled on the Wattsstax double album, later sampled by Public Enemy, 'Show 'em Watcha Got', *It Takes a Nation of Millions*, 1988

. . . I find myself in a somewhat problematic position because my own image appears now and then in visual evocations of this nationalist impulse that fuel the advocacy of revolutionary change in contemporary hiphop culture. These days, young people who were not even born when I was arrested often approach me with expressions of awe and disbelief. On the one hand, it is inspiring to discover a measure of historical awareness that, in our youth, my generation often lacked. But it is also unsettling. Because I know that almost inevitably my image is associated with a certain representation of black nationalism that privileges those particular nationalisms with which some of us were locked in constant battle.

Angela Y. Davis, 'Black Nationalism', *Black Popular Culture*, p. 323

If 1988 is remembered for the dawn of Los Angeles gangsta rap, it was also the year of the radicalization of political content in the music. Second albums by Boogie Down Productions (BDP) and Public Enemy (PE) set the tone followed by the efforts of the Jungle Brothers, Eric B. and Rakim and Big Daddy Kane. The socio-economic ripples of Chuck D and Kris Parker's (KRS One) rhetoric have turned into veritable tidal waves of influence on hiphop in the ensuing years.

In his book *Rap Attack*, David Toop outlines in detail the history of 'message rap'. Going

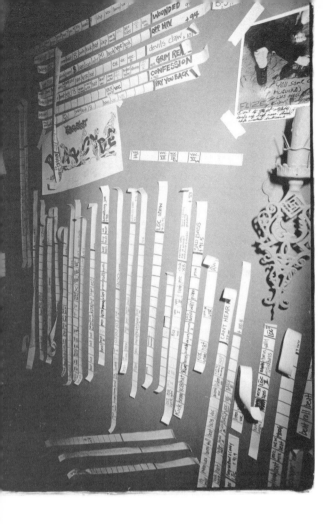

Track Assignment tape at Delicious Vinyl studios, Hollywood, 1992.

**Breakers at a West Coast Rock Steady
meeting in the Hiphop Shop, Hollywood,
1992.**

Technics 1200 turntable photographed in El
Paso, Texas, at a College Boys show, 1992.

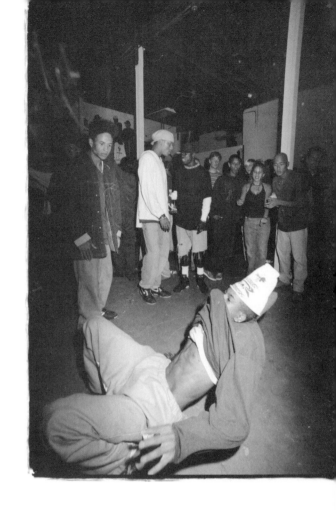

Breaker at Brass, Hollywood, 1991.

Grandmaster Caz rhymes while Def Jef and
Prince Whipper Whip watch and Marques
Wyatt spins, Brass, Hollywood, 1991.

Ganjah K's lyric sheets at Hollywood Sound
studios, Hollywood, 1993.

Crowd at outdoor hiphop event hosted by
the Hiphop Shop, Fairfax High School,
Hollywood, 1992.

J Smoov at the Good Life, South Central
Los Angeles, 1991.

back to H. Rap Brown and Amiri Baraka, the Last Poets and Gil Scott-Heron, Toop establishes the tradition of direct social content in rhyme. However, it is with disdain that he tells of the trend that Grandmaster Flash set off with the popularity of 'The Message'. Before 'The Message' there had been a number of attempts at inserting social relevance into the music, such as the well-remembered 'How We Gonna Make the Black Nation Rise' by Brother D, imploring its listeners to become aware of the impending genocide of the black race:

> The Ku Klux Klan is on the loose,
> Training their kids on machine gun use,
> The story might give you stomach cramps,
> Like America's got concentration camps.

But 'The Message' with its infectious refrain 'Don't push me 'cos I'm close to the edge, I'm tryin' not to lose my head, ha, ha, haha, It's like a jungle sometimes', spread all over the globe with a ferocity that led to a litany of message raps varying in quality and sincerity. One of these records was LA's first rhyme on wax since the Watts Prophets, 'Badd Times' by Captain Rapp.

Even this early, the contradictions of mainstream, socially committed hiphop are obvious to Toop: 'The contradictions of a money-minded craze for gory social realism and criticism of the Reagan Administration, with its callous cutbacks in social programs, are hard to resolve. The juxtapositions of protests about rape victims with rampant machismo or hard-times lyrics sung by kids in expensive leather outfits and gold chains can be hard to stomach' (p. 124). By 1987 the cutbacks had become more callous, and the social realism got gorier. A second term of Reagan at that time was about as welcome in hiphop America as David Duke at an NAACP meeting.

Both PE and BDP put out classic first albums. To this day, *Yo Bum Rush the Show* (PE) is a benchmark for its gruff, uncompromising tracks. The Bomb Squad took the funky tracks of Jam Master Jay and turned them on their head. It was as though suddenly shakin' your ass wasn't enough – the music in some way needed to be analogous to the nervous rush of living in America's decaying urban centres. Messrs Shocklee, Sadler, Rubin and Ryder snared the energy of punk, mixed in the tonal experiments of sixties avant-garde jazz and then turned this veritable weapon on largely unsuspecting B-boys.

Harry Allen maintains that formally experimental hiphop shouldn't lean on comparisons to the jazz before it, or indeed any of the other musical forms that it has been compared to. While Allen is correct, it is also true that the music has learnt from work done elsewhere. And Allen is obviously aware of the rearguard action the music is fighting with a 'third stream' mentality.

If *Yo . . .* is a classic of B-boy experimentation, it also reflects a burgeoning of black pride and the spirit of resistance. On the track 'Rightstarter (Message to the Blackman)' Chuck yells:

> You spend a buck in the 80s – what you get is a preacher
> Forgivin' this torture to the system that brought cha
> I'm on a mission you got that right
> Addin' fuel to the fire – punch to the fight
> Many have forgotten what we came here for
> Never knew or had a clue – so you're on the floor
> Just growin' not knowin' about your past
> Now you're lookin' pretty stupid while you're shakin' your ass.
>
> Mind over matter – mouth in motion
> Can't deny it cause I'll never be quiet
> Let's start this right . . .
>
> Yes you if I bore you – I won't ignore you
> I'm saying things that they say I'm not supposed to
> Give you pride that you might not find
> If you're blind about your past then I'll point behind
> Kings queens warriors lovers
> People proud – sisters and brothers
> It's the biggest fear – suckers get tears
> When we can top their best idea.
>
> Our solution – mind revolution
> Mind over matter – mouth in motion
> Corners don't sell it – no you can't buy it
> Can't defy it cause I'll never be quiet
> Let's start this right . . .

Public Enemy here served notice that they were not taking prisoners on their journey through B-land (B-movies Schooly D had called them) to being industry legends of the nineties.

In 1988 when *It Takes a Nation of Millions* was released, PE aligned their music with the political struggle of its community of origin. While 'The Message' and 'Boyz in the Hood' might tell you what the problems were, PE started the finger pointing and it hurt – the FBI, the CIA, the government, the whole system was at fault.

Public Enemy's project leaps backwards to the continuum of resistance from Frederick Douglass, Nat Turner through the W.E.B. Du Bois/Booker T. debates to Malcolm, Martin, Stokely, Huey and Angela through to Elijah Muhammad and his successor Louis Farrakhan while catapulting us forward with the most sophisticated sound collages on wax. To do this justice it is necessary to examine closely one track. 'Show 'em Watcha Got' is a good example, for its simplicity and because of Greg Tate's eloquent writing on the song. (Also at the time of going to press its main sample has been used in two hit singles – N2 Deep's 'Back to the Hotel' and Wreckx n Effect's 'Rump Shaker', which have emptied the horn loop of its expressiveness – such are the perils of commercialism.)

> Since we are not only dealing with regenerated sound here but regenerated meaning, what was heard 20 years ago as as expression has now become rhetorical device, a trope. Making old records talk via scratching and sampling is fundamental to hiphop. But where we've heard rare grooves recycled for parodic effect or shock value ad nauseum, on 'Show 'Em . . .' PE manages something more sublime . . .
>
> Greg Tate, 'Manchild at Large', *Village Voice*, 11 September 1990, p. 124

This sublimity is due largely to the horn sample (from the La Fayette Afro Rock *Malik* album from 1976) that runs looped through the song. DJ Shadow from Davis, California assures me that the 'Shocklees really sweetened it up'. (The Shocklees are renowned for never being happy with a straight sound, always fattening, filtering or thining their samples.) This horn stab, when contextualized by the opening phrase from the *Wattsstax Soundtrack* (quoted above) becomes simultaneously a melancholic ode and call to attention. Then Chuck and Flav's war chants kick in, 'Public enemy number one' followed by 'Show 'em Whatcha Got' acting both as a station identification and statement of purpose. Then with the final sample of Sister Eva Mohammed's powerful litany of leaders – 'The same God inspired Marcus Garvey, Rosa Parks, Steven Biko, Martin Luther King, Malcolm X, Nelson Mandela, Winnie Mandela (stay strong sister)' which concludes with the 'Join me and welcome, listen clearly' – we are left with no doubt as to what is at stake on the album.

This literal act of insertion by Public Enemy into the tradition of black resistance collapses the boundary between popular culture and politics. While Archie Shepp might write 'Malcolm, Malcolm, Semper Malcolm' or Emmery Lee Joseph Evans Jr could put 'Part E,S' on wax in 1970,

> . . . Yeh in the ghetto,
> Where niggers fine vine, but ain't got a dime,
> To defend Panthers against crime . . .
> Let H Rap rap,
> Let Huey duey,
> Let Bobby Seale deal,
> Let Dizzy Gillespie.
>
> *Black Voices on the Streets of Watts*

Public Enemy had set themselves up as the 'martyr . . . missionary . . . prophets' crossing the traditional boundary between commentator and participant. Both Shepp and the Watts Prophets see themselves as griots, while PE proclaim their own status as warriors/leaders. Characteristically, instead of a live vocal for their war chants they sampled themselves from their first album. This further confuses the categorical status not only of PE but also the historical material. Intentional static on the track acts as not only a signifier of age and authenticity (horn sample, Wattsstax and Sister Eva Mohammed), but of illicitness. The net effect is meditationary.

> To articulate the past historically does not mean to recognize 'the way it really was' [Ranke]. It means to seize hold of a memory as it flashes up at a moment of danger. Historical materialism wishes to retain that image of the past which unexpectedly appears to man at a moment of danger. This danger affects both the content of the tradition and its receivers. The same threat hangs over both; that of becoming a tool of the ruling class. In every era the attempt must be made anew to wrest tradition away from a conformism that is about to overpower it. The Messiah comes not only as a redeemer but as the subduer of the Antichrist. Only that historian will have the gift of fanning the spark of hope in the past who is convinced that even the dead will not be safe from the enemy if he wins. And this enemy has not ceased to win.
>
> Walter Benjamin

In 1988, recovering from the death of his DJ, Scott La Rock, KRS One released the second album from their group, Boogie Down Productions (BDP). It was entitled *By Any Means Necessary* after the famous Malcolm X adage. This album was also to expand the social vocabulary of hiphop.

Two years earlier KRS and Scott put out *Criminal Minded* on B-Boy Records. *Criminal Minded* is far more sparse than anything provided by PE, but it has a funky range (with heavy Jamaican influence) that keeps it a dance-floor staple to this day. The main difference between KRS and Chuck is in delivery. While PE had employed traditional oratory and court jester traditions, KRS had developed his own oratory through styling and harmonizing. Tracks like 'South Bronx' and 'The Bridge is Over' (a rebuttal of MC Shan's claims regarding the Queensbridge Projects: 'The Bridge') are classics for their style and the simple economy of their lyrics. Take 'South Bronx', for instance:

> Now way back in the days when hiphop began,
> With Coke La Rock, Kool Herc and then Bamm,
> B-boys ran to the latest jam,
> But when it got shot up they ran home and said damn
> There's got to be a better way to hear our music everyday,
> Peoples gettin' blown away but come outside anyway,
> Let's try it again, outside, cedar park power from the street lights made the place dark,
> But yo they didn't care they turned out,
> I know a few people know what I'm talkin' about.

> Remember Bronx River rollin' thick,
> Cool DJ Red Alert and Chuck Chillout on the mix
> When Afrika Islam was rockin' the jams,
> On the other side of town was a kid named Flash,
> Patterson and Millbrook projects,
> Cassanova all over ya know ya couldn't stop it,
> The Nine Lives Crew, the Cypress Boys,
> The Real Rock Steady takin' out these toys,
> As odd as it looked as odd as it seems,
> I didn't hear a peep from Queens,
> From '76 to 1980 the dreads in Brooklyn was crazy
> You couldn't bring out your set with no hiphop
> Because the pistols would go [sound of gunshot]
> Because why don't wise up
> And show all the people you are wack,
> Instead of tryin' to take out LL,
> Why don't you take your homeboys off the crack,
> 'Cos if you don't, well then their nerves will become shot,
> And that will leave the job up to my own Scott La Rock,
> And he's from . . . South Bronx, South South Bronx . . .

KRS plunges us down the (memory) lane to the days of park jams in the south Bronx, disses both Brooklyn and Queens and provides us with a lesson in syncopation and breath control. If Chuck D is the orator and Flavor Flav the jester, KRS is the styler. If Chuck had learnt from the legacy of Adam Clayton Powell, Malcolm and Louis Farrakhan, and Flav is an imagined meeting between Dolemite and Busy Bee, then KRS is like a freeway collision between Melle Mel and Miles.

KRS also wrote a remarkable ode to his nine millimetre, '9mm', which acted as catalyst for further rhyming classified by the inadequate umbrella term of 'gangsta rap'. On the cover of *Criminal Minded* was a picture of Scott and KRS brandishing a shotgun, a pistol and a hand grenade, looking after business. Two years later KRS re-emerged on the cover of *By Any Means Necessary* with a gun 'lookin' out the window like Malcolm'. The gun play of *Criminal Minded* had been subsumed into the highly charged reconstruction of the famous Malcolm X photo. The wax inside the controversial cover continued the minimal beats from the first album, but the lyrical flow was now directed at society at large. It was as though both KRS and BDP figured out that there was now a bigger public at stake and in the process enlarged their statements for the now larger context. In 'Stop the Violence', BDP warned:

> Time and time again as I pick up the pen,
> As my thoughts emerge these are those words,

I glance at the paper to know what's goin' on
Someone's doing wrong the story goes on
Mary Lou just had a baby, someone else decapitated,
The dramas of the world shouldn't keep us so frustrated
I look, but it doesn't coincide with my books
Social studies will not speak upon political crooks
It's just the presidents, all the money they spent
All the things that they invent
And how their house is so immaculate
They make missiles while families eat gristle
Then they get upset when the press blows the whistle
Phone calls are made profiles are kept low
You tamper with some jobs, now the press is controlled,
Not only newspapers but every single station
You only get to hear the president is on vacation
But stay calm there's no need for alarm
You say goodbye to your Mom
And you're off to Vietnam
You shoot to kill, you come home and you're a veteran
But how many veterans are out there peddling
There's no tellin', cos they continue sellin'
As quiet as it's kept, I won't go into depth
You can talk about Nigeria, people used to laugh at ya
Now I look, I see USA for Africa?!

What's the solution to stop all the confusion
Rewrite the Constitution,
Change the drug which you are usin',
Rewrite the Constitution or the Emancipation Proclamation
We fight inflation
But the President is still on vacation . . .

In effect KRS moves from orator through joker as a styler, taking the listener through explanations of his last album, condom awareness, hiphop history lessons, and (with an irreverent approach) the government.

In many ways 1988 proved to be a fortuitous year for reawakening the sleeping giant of minority resistance in the US. While gang hysteria swept Los Angeles, Oliver North became a national icon, the nightmare of Reaganomics was entering its next phase with the disastrous victory of the Bush-whacker. Through the Iran/Contra hearings came the leaked rumours of the Federal Emergency Management Agency's Rex 84 plan, an update of the King Alfred Plan, the dreaded plot to incarcerate all people of colour and their sympathizers in the event of widespread civil disturbance. This obliterated the late seventies from view and provided an unobstructed view of late sixties' radicalism from a peculiarly dark perspective. Realization of the impact of the Counter Intelligence programme had hit home.

Less influential but none the less significant contributions to this process arrived from Schooly D, the 'Saturday Night' bad boy, now screaming 'Don't call me nigger, whitey', the Jungle Brothers were proclaiming 'Black is Black' (sampling Lightnin' Rod) and asking (after Marvin), 'What's Goin' On?', Big Daddy Kane was sending words to the motherland and De La Soul were 'Plug Tunin''. It made sense at that historical juncture for many artists to reach for cultural and social references in their music; radicalization seemed most appropriate.

By the time *Straight Outta Compton* came out there already was an established frame of politicized music. This is perhaps the most important aspect of all four of the above albums. These records also determined the entrance into hiphop of non-African American subjects. While non-African-American people, particularly Puerto Ricans, have been involved in hiphop from the word go, it took until 1990 for Chicanos, Caucasians and numerous other groups to start to rhyme about their constituent needs. PE and BDP had shown that it was possible to talk about social, cultural and political problems without falling into the 'USA for Africa' trap.

Kid Frost (Mexican-American) and the Boo Yaa Tribe (Samoan-American), the first groups from LA that weren't African-American to get national attention, had been rhyming before '88, but they came to prominence in the broadened field of hiphop's cultural nationalism. Certainly it can be argued that it may not have been possible for Kid Frost to make 'La Raza' without PE, but too many forget that Chicanos had been involved in the culture from Herc's debut as DJ.

Music of the Tense Present

Well what happens is like, right now rap had evolved into like real difficulty music, you know where style is definitely of the essence, you know everybody can't sound the same, while there are certain rules, certain universal laws that can't be broken, you maintain certain hiphop tenets and you break all the rest of the rules – you know it's like that, it's all love . . .

Mikah Nine from the Freestyle Fellowship to Bobbito on Stretch Armstrong's Show on the Columbia University Radio Station, New York, July 1992

During 1989 and 1990 hiphop on the West Coast began to diversify. Gangsta oriented hiphop continued to thrive and, through its commercial success, facilitated the emergence of many other artists, styles and subjectivities. Ice T's Rhyme Syndicate project is a good example of this, as well as Eazy's Ruthless signings.

Following the success of his first album (*Rhyme Pays*) and the runaway success of his *Colors* (the title track of the film), Ice T set up Rhyme Syndicate Productions. It was a production company run by Afrika Islam and T to spotlight and manage the careers of a number of rhymers that had been involved on the scene. A number of West Coast MCs were first committed to vinyl on their compilation album *Syndication*, through Warner Records, although the majority of the acts on the compilation were immigrants from New York, like Ice T himself. The locals on the album were T.D.F., Low Profile (WC and Alladin), Nat the Cat and our old friend Toddy Tee while the sunshine men from the east were Spinmasters (Henry G and Evil E, two brothers of Latin descent from Brooklyn), Everlast (soon to become the bald-headed Irish American rhymer), Domination, Bango, Mixmaster Quick, Donald D and the appropriately named Bronx Style Bob. Another artist associated with the Syndicate who was signed at this time was the invincible Divine Styler and the Scheme Team (Cockni O Dire, Aday, Kalonee and Brandon). T then took a number of the crew to Europe on tour. In the end most of the artists on the commercially successful compilation ended up being signed to Warner Music on their own.

By now more labels were taking chances with what would otherwise have been considered marginal records. The pop success that Delicious Vinyl had with Young MC ('Bust a Move') and Tone Loc ('Wild Thing'), was unprecedented and led to more West Coast acts being signed. New producers like the Dust Brothers, Wolf and Epic, Grandmixxer Muggs, Sir Jinx and Tony G all contributed new sounds and feels to the cacophony of beats while the 'gangsta' sound maintained its hegemony on LA's streets. Despite this commercial success, respect was slow in coming for the artists and producers from the East Coast hiphop intelligentsia.

In 1990, Ice Cube began to collaborate with New York. Certainly artists from both the coasts had been on record together before. Afrika Islam produced Ice T, Prince Paul had produced LA/New York outfit 7A3, and both Bobcat and DJ Pooh had East Coast production credits, but Cube's idea was more ambitious. He sought to bring the gangsta style of rhyming from the west to the apocalyptic beats of the Bomb Squad (Public Enemy's distinctive production unit) of the east.

In mid-1989, Cube had split from NWA in a disagreement over creative control and (needless to say) money. He had always been considered the best writer in the group, having penned the early classics, but many doubted that he could continue with such a high-profile career without Dre's beats or Eazy's business acumen. But Cube didn't even flinch. In taking the production of his first solo effort to New York, he attempted not only to build a solo career but to raise the standard of street rap. He succeeded and managed to ruffle a few feathers along the way. The product of this collaboration is his 1990 album *Amerikkka's Most Wanted*.

Amerikkka's Most Wanted is a more biting, critical and conceptually complex album than *Straight Outta Compton*. Understanding that NWA had reached a semantic limit on 'Fuck tha

Police', he sought to retrench and investigate the situations that led to this impasse. Switching from humorous toasts on 'Gangsta Fairytale' to open debate with the opposite sex (represented by a debuting YoYo) on 'It's a Man's World' to political rhetoric PE style (with Chuck D) on 'Endangered Species' and 'The Bomb', Cube expanded the vocabulary of the LA street style to match the sophistication of his New York peers while maintaining his LA gangster persona. In naming his album after the influential crime show Cube signalled the arrival of a new kind of visibility for black inner-city youth on tabloid news shows that conjured visions of an endemically criminal population in every major city.

Amerikkka's . . . sought to give a face to this criminal underclass and this face was to be the furrow-browed, jherri-curled, beanie-clad face of Cube himself. Cube to this day is the foremost hiphop meta-critic, providing listeners not only with stories, but potential criticism of his practice from different perspectives coupled with acute usage of media voice-overs. If NWA *knew* that there was a bigger audience out there Cube *incorporates* this audience's views of him. Cube was probably the first artist out here to experiment fully with the political and commercial punch of what he was creating.

The record begins with Cube being led to the electric chair and when asked by the warden if he has any last words he shouts, 'Yeah, fuck all y'all'. From there the Bomb Squad collages, contemporary, historical, fictional and documentary sound meshes, following an anti-hiphop DJ from a fictional radio station with a female anchor woman talking about the imminent destruction of black males. It is as if Cube and the Bomb Squad realize that for African Americans the past is tenuous, the future is in question and all that is left is a present; this present is a collision of many pasts and futures, both real and imagined, and, above all, this present is tense.

> At the bottom of the news tonight, there's been a new animal aimed at the direction of falling off the face of the earth. Yes, young black teenagers are reported to be the oldest and the newest creatures added to the endangered species list. As of now the government has not made steps to preserve the blacks; when asked why, a top law official added, because they make good game.
>
> Insert from *Amerikkka's Most Wanted*

> Yeah, boyee. This is work booty music in a big way. Great, Chuck D, Hank and Keith Shocklee, and Eric Sadler gave *Amerikkka's Most Wanted* the kick that was sorely missed on *Fear of A Black Planet* (the third PE album). This is straight up hard edged warrior music. Like the beats of African pre-battle ceremonies, it either makes you want to dance into oblivion or go off and bumrush somebody.
>
> Joan Morgan, 'The Nigga Ya Love to Hate', *Village Voice*, 17 June 1990

> This music is rage; it is completely demanding of anyone who hears it. It is like a baby crying: you can't ignore it. I know those people have problems but this is like uncontrolled anger. Please turn it down.
>
> The author's building manager

'Once Upon a Time in the Projects' brings the listener on a visit to the forgotten public housing projects of the inner city to pick up a date. The smells, sounds and perils (including his false arrest) are spelled out dramatically, leaving the listener slumped in empathy. Cube, of course, never satisfied with listener empathy, bellows, 'Don't fuck with a bitch from the projects.' Ironically on *Amerikkka* Cube had chosen to bring a microphone rocking female on deck, a young woman named YoYo. He had effectively upped the stakes. Cube, like many rhymers that year, had shaken the expression of fear and melancholy from the music in favour of raw rage. He continues in this fashion as do the many that have succeeded him.

LA was now at the forefront of attention, with many labels interested in tapping into the commercial success of Cube, NWA and Ice T. In that year many Los Angeles groups were signed or recorded albums. Obviously it was becoming harder to follow the initial impact of NWA, but none the less solid albums were being committed to vinyl. Comptons Most Wanted, Above the Law, Capital Punishment Organization, King Tee, Boo Yaa Tribe, Kid Frost, Mellow Man Ace, D.O.C., Low Profile (later to become WC and the Maad Circle), Everlast (later to become House of Pain), Divine Styler and YoYo all contributed to the choir of voices emanating from LA's growing hiphop constituency.

Kid Frost and Boo Yaa are Chicano and Samoan respectively, with lyrics and stories similar to those of the black rhymers that had preceded them in the public eye. Boo Yaa (which is a slang equivalent to the discharge of a shotgun) were graduates from the poplocker school of LA hiphop, growing up in the south-eastern part of the city among both Chicanos and blacks. Sons of a preacher, the Boo Yaas had experienced the influence of African American music by being in the choir. And with their experience of growing up in the barrio they brought a new sensibility to rhyming.

Frost was an old school LA rhymer who had never achieved commercial success until he reworked an El Chicano song from the early seventies ('Viva La Tirado') with Tony G, and turned it into '(Viva) La Raza', a 'Chicano pride' song. This success can be attributed not only to the coming home of the large Chicano audience that had been part of the early electropop days, but that had veered off in the mid-eighties into a retreat to oldies and funk/ disco, but also as a result of the growing constituency for the politically viable hiphop that Public Enemy and Boogie Down Productions had produced. It is as though the more nationalist hiphop had become the more other subjectivities began to see its use.

The irony of course is that 'Viva La Tirado' was written by Gerald Wilson, a Los Angeles-based African-American big-band leader and Central Avenue veteran, active from the forties until the present. He had written it as a tribute to a Mexican bullfighter he admired, and it was then covered by El Chicano. El Chicano were previously named the VIPs, but in the politicized days of the early seventies in east Los they changed their name. So Frost's Chicano anthem contains within it all the ethnic complexity that hiphop itself even in its most nationalist forms displays. Frost's first album (*Hispanic Causing Panic*) is marked by an extensive use of Spanglish in rhyme, Spanglish being the term used to describe the combination of Mexican and English slang spoken in the barrios of Los – it is also the title of the classic old school cut by Spanish Fly on Enjoy Records.

Instrumental to both the Boo Yaa album and Kid Frost's success was the musical knowledge of veteranos Tony G and Skatemaster Tate. Tony G had been a member of the Mixmasters with Dre, Bobcat and Yella as well as being a finalist in the New Music Seminar DJ mix contest. Skatemaster Tate is a Cubano from Los Angeles, who has perhaps the best collection of rare soul, funk and jazz on the West Coast. He is a veteran skater, punker, DJ and hipster on the uptown scene.

The theoretical importance of the expansion of hiphop into a voice for many different subjectivities – women, Chicano, Cubano, Asian, Irish, gay and all the variants covered by black, Jamaican, Dominican, etc – is twofold: first it brings the struggle of African-Americans to many new ears, thereby providing a new perspective on one's own problems. Second it may be possible that through the hiphop model we may find the 'real' world music, not the decontextualized, badly curated 'objects' of Paul Simon or Peter Gabriel's colonialist vision. Both Gabriel and Simon flirt with nostalgic views of the Third World, but the grunge thrown up in every country that has heard what Bambaataa, Flash, Herc and Theodore created back in the seventies provides us with active participatory models for future musics, musics that will conjure both specific histories and bumping goulashes.

In 1988, Nelson George had written that hiphop had gone national, but it hadn't yet gone regional. By this he meant that while hiphop had spread its audience all over the country, the rest of the country was not making hiphop on a par with the music coming from the three boroughs of New York. Between 1988 and 1992 a lot had changed: Los Angeles had developed not just a regional sound equal to that of Miami or DC but led the field in the expanded field of multiracial hiphop.

By 1992 hiphop has expanded in its influence in this country to an enormous degree. Sista Souljah's comments became an issue in the most recent presidential election; hiphop-influenced clothing has crashed on to the fashion scene from Macy's to couture; *Yo MTV Raps* is the highest rated show on MTV; Cube, PE, Ice T and KRS One are nationally recognized figures appearing on nationwide talk shows and opinion sections; Oliver North, Charlton Heston, Jesse Helms, presidents Bush and Clinton have all spoken out against rap lifestyle and several court cases have involved hiphop artists, from the obscenity case against Two Live Crew to the sampling cases against Biz Markie, De La Soul and the Beastie Boys to the murder trial of Mac Dre in the San Francisco Bay Area. The Simon Weisenthal Center tried to boycott Cube, Public Enemy boycotted Arizona and the Police Association tried to lobby the shareholders of Warner Records to force Ice T to remove 'Cop Killer' from the *Bodycount* album in the summer of 1992. To cap it all, virtually every record company involved in hiphop has refused to release or distribute the second album by Paris, *Sleeping with the Enemy*, because of its inclusion of a revenge fantasy song called 'Bush Killa'. These suggest the varied ways that hiphop has become headline news. The underground culture initiated in the tough Bronx of the early seventies has arrived on to centre stage USA.

In Los Angeles the last days of 1989 provided a confirmation of the reputation for gang violence that the public had come to expect from the music. At an Ice Cube, Poor Righteous Teachers, Too Short, YoYo concert in Anaheim, the restless crowd that had been kept waiting outside (holding their eighteen-dollar tickets) long after the beginning of the show, erupted into open gunplay. A sixteen-year-old girl was critically wounded in the stomach. KDAY (in its final days) was quick to remind the offenders of the nice time awaiting them in the Federal Penitentiary.

Hiphop entering its third decade has expanded its field of reference and influence while continuing to explore and redefine that which is unique to it. The new school culturalism of the late eighties typified by De La Soul, the Jungle Brothers, X Clan and Poor Righteous Teachers seems to have been superseded by old school revivalism best typified by second albums from Brand Nubian and A Tribe Called Quest as well as the highly influential debut from LA's own Cypress Hill.

Cypress Hill have achieved a unique status within hiphop: they have successfully married old school sensibility (styling, harmonizing, straight beats and hooks) to LA gangsta chic. This is done through a combination of south-east LA Latin lingo performed in a nasal tone heavily indebted to Ramelzee, New York-style beats with references to the classic old school documentary *Wild Style*, and homage to California's largest cash crop, marijuana. Their debut, eponymous album released through Sony Records on Ruff House has gone on to be perhaps the most influential record of the early nineties.

Cypress Hill is Grandmixxer Muggs, B-Real and Sen Dogg – an Italian, a Mexican and a Cubano from Southgate, a predominantly Chicano neighbourhood in south-east Los Angeles adjacent to Compton. Both Sen and Muggs have family connections to New York while B Real is an LA native. Cypress articulate through an extension of old school sensibility rather than as an imitation of it. Perhaps the best example of this is on the B-side of their first single, the classic 'How I Could Just Kill a Man'.

The track is a treatment of Lowell Fulsom's famous 'Tramp'. Several artists had used the Fulsom sample before this (including De La Soul), but Muggs had managed to maintain the song's raw blues feel. (Fulsom, interestingly, is a part Native American part African American blues singer who still plays in LA today.) The lyrics are delivered in a nasal drawl by the blunted B-Real. The final verse concludes,

> It's gonna be a long time,
> Before I finish, one of the many missions,
> That I had to establish,

To light my spliff, excite your whiff,
Ignites it,
If you ain't down bullshit,

Say some punk tried to get you for your idol,
Would you call me one time and play the role model,
No, I think ya'd play like a thug,
Next year the shot of a magnum slug, comin',
Comin' at cha,
Ya know I'm gonna gat cha,
How do you know where I'm at,
When you haven't been where I been,
Understand where I'm comin' from,
When you're up on the hill in your big home,
I'm out here riskin' my dome,
Just for a bucket or a fast ducket,
Just to stay alive I gotta say fuck it.

Here is something you can't understand,
How I could just kill a man . . . (repeated)

The song was a runaway success, breaking the group almost immediately to a national audience, something that hadn't happened to an LA act so quickly before. The group's reliance on a return to basics format, in the face of a sea of politically rhetorical music or eclectic hippy-hop, reawakened people to the fact that what was special about the culture was its ability to laugh in the face of adversity. Cypress effectively became smirking stoned rhymers in the face of a difficult recession. They finally put an end to the question mark over West Coast hiphop and simultaneously reminded the hiphop nation of the contribution of Chicanos.

Within months Muggs had set up the Soul Assasins, a production unit which would incorporate first House of Pain and then FunkDoobiest. House of Pain in the summer of 1992, through their monster hit, 'Jump Around' and their *Fine Malt Lyrics* album, would reinvent white ethnicity in music.

Simultaneous with the rise of Cypress Hill was the emergence of a vibrant freestyling culture in Los Angeles, which led to the return of the missing links of hiphop culture in LA, dancing and graffiti. Instrumental in the consolidation of freestyling culture in south central is the Good Life, a health food store with a small stage area that on Thursday nights is transformed into an arena for the exchange of styles, ideas and skills. It is fitting that in its publicity the Good Life compares itself to both a radio station and Harlem's Apollo Theatre.

To visit the Good Life is to visit the core of the music. After being greeted by B Hall (the godmother of the renewed culture in south central and a veteran community activist) what one experiences, among the wheatgrass and the natural drinks, is both a continuum for tradition and a forum for new ideas. The Good Life provides a space for the discussion of everyday life, politics and fun. Here hiphop for LA's next generation is created and disputed. While a number of groups and individuals have emerged from the Good Life – Freestyle Fellowship, Urban Prop, Sin, Big Al, Menace II Society, Volume 10, Ganjah K, Wolf, Nigga Fish, Funky Trend, Pigeon John, Hiphop Clan, Tres Loc, Figures of Speach and Capital AK to name a few – the most significant aspect of the place is its attempt to reinvent a public space for youth of colour in that area of the city.

The sound of freestylin' (rapping from the head) over breakbeats (continuous beats made by alternation from turntable to turntable) found at a park jam or freestyle session, is only now beginning to be explored in the studio. Old school records like those of Grandmaster Flash or Treacherous Three were usually constructed by replaying (using a live group) the music, and carefully laying the vocal track on top of it. This became the model for the transfer of the music to vinyl. In the late eighties however, with the advent of advanced sampling technology, the earlier format of improvisational rhyming over a break began to be re-explored. While the turntable skills had become automated (instead of using turntables the break could be sequenced and replayed through a drum machine), the feel of vocals done in one take began to re-emerge.

In hiphop, there is a profound aural difference between a freestyle and a formated rap. Freestylin', whether it has been transcribed to a steno pad or not, is created improvisation-ally to the beat; breath control, intonation, iambic pentameter and tuning are the defining characteristics. The freestyler often makes conceptual (narrative) leaps. Here is an example of a freestyle rhyme from the Freestyle Fellowship, the first group from the creative hotbed the Good Life to become visible to the mainstream.

> Would you like to be a part of my fantasy
> Fantasy, insanity, vanity, family,
> Can it be, can it be, it'll be great,
> We can break all laws of gravity,
> Make room we'll fly to the moon,
> On a boom, we can let it get better
> Get etiquette, adequate that'll get sloppy
> Ten four, ya copy, big jalopy
> Poppy seed popper, floppy teeny bopper hoppy,
> Hyped my squad to Gods of the mic,
> So play Vanilla, hamma shamma lamma
> Ding dong, Killa slam or plan a pop song,
> Cut,
> But I like break beats and
> Beatin' on the wall of the bathroom

> The B-boy – B-boy forever.
>
> Aceyalone of Freestyle Fellowship, 'My Fantasy',
> *To Whom It May Concern*, 1991

Acey plays with the sound of the words achieving a free association that is both challenging and open. It is reminiscent of early hiphop, if more conceptually complex.

A formated rap is one that is written, while listening to the beat, but the primary space of the creative process is the steno pad as opposed to the freestyle session. The performance of the rhyme usually takes place for the first time in the studio.

> Little boys and girls they all love me,
> Come and sit on the lap of ICE,
> And let me tell you a story or two,
> About a punk ass nigga I knew,
> Named Jack, he wasn't that nimble wasn't that quick,
> Jumped over a candlestick and burnt his dick,
> Ran up the street 'cos he was pipin' hot,
> Met a bitch named Jill on the bus stop,
> Dropped a line or two and he had the ho,
> At that type of shit he's a pro,
> So Jack and Jill went up the hill to take a nap,
> Young bitch gave him the clap . . .
>
> Ice Cube, 'Gangsta Fairytale', *Amerikkka's Most Wanted*

Cube is in pursuit of the comedic, parodic narrative rather than in the possible percussion-ism of Acey's verbal assault. Cube obviously rounds out his rhymes in the studio and probably improvises in the process, as indeed Aceyalone commits his rhymes to paper to help him memorize them, but their writing styles are almost completely different. The formated rhyme is more the legacy of the Watts Prophets, the Last Poets and Gil Scott-Heron going back to both the oratory tradition and toasting, whereas freestylin' is the legacy of the Furious Five, Melle Mel, Grandmaster Caz, Prince Whipper Whip, Busy Bee, the Treacherous Three, Jekyll and Hyde with links back to scatting.

Traditionally LA has been known for its reliance on the formated tradition. A formated rhyme at its best can tell a story in a gritty, journalistic or first-person way. On Cube's *Death Certificate*, on a track called 'Alive on Arrival', talking first-person about being shot and brought to Martin Luther King Hospital, he rhymes:

> I need to see an MD
> an y'all muthafuckers givin' me the third degree
> Look at the waitin' room
> it's filled to the rim

like the County jail gang room
Nobody gettin' help
Since we po' the hospital it move slow
Now I'm laid out
People steppin' over me to get closer to the TV
Just like a piece of dogshit
now I die on this nappy ass carpet
One hour done pass –
done watched two episodes of M*A*S*H
And when I'm almost through
They call my name and put me in ICU
Half way dead no respect and handcuffed to the bed

Cube relishes capturing the sights, smells and sounds of MLK trauma centre, colliding the tradition of the documentary with the humour of the boast and its first-person narration. Whether we choose to find Cube's opinions upsetting, enlightening or (as many did) dangerous, we cannot refute his skill. Cube flexes – putting in words in ways other rappers wouldn't attempt, like a trumpet lilting and then parping, squeaking but following and re-creating the beat. Most writers missed this legacy in the deluge of critical writing about *Death Certificate*.

At this point I should recap. While the black community is definitely the community of origin of the music, the B-boy/girl lifestyle is a product of and a response to integration. The culture of the gang, the culture of the vato, the pachuco and the westie, euro-disco, skate culture, house, rastafarianism and Islam all contribute to the vocabulary of hiphop, but the B-boy is more or less independent of these. Here the notion of culture is important, for hiphop learns and borrows from not only different musics but different lifestyles. The recent rise in Islamic hiphop might be taken as an example. The conventions of happy life in the suburbs are what is avoided, and all that stands in opposition to them is celebrated. This may somewhat explain its popularity among the community that fifteen years ago would have been listening to punk rock. However, when your options are working for minimum wage at McDonalds or putting work in for the local locs, producing hiphop can be viewed not just as a style, pose or haircut but as a tool for survival.

In 1993 it has become exceedingly difficult to talk about hiphop as a unitary phenomenon. Too many writers have addressed hiphop as one thing or as a singular set of voices. It is a number of different ideas, lifestyles, subjectivities gathered together around a shared concept of the possibilities of communication through the African art of rhyming over beats. Those horrified or frightened by hiphop misogyny, homophobia or intolerance should pause before generalizing. Hiphop is a forum born out of call-and-response, and more than any other popular cultural form has the ability to self-correct. There are feminist, lesbian, gay and even anti-ageist rhymes. Hiphop is discursive and the debate is not over.

If rap itself as a word means anything it connotes 'talking'; this is its usage in African-American slang. Ironically, however, within street language 'rap' also means ' a criminal charge', and as we head towards the end of the century the interchangeability of these terms has become *de rigueur* for the establishment.

In conclusion I will say this. Hiphop in LA today is a community of bedrooms, occasional open mikes and airwaves. In homes all over the city people gather around turntables, record collections, SP1200s and MPC60s and conjure worlds that intersect with and absorb reality. Connected by a network of tapes, hard to find samples, a nomadic and often underground club scene, and places like the open mike at the Good Life, different perspectives are shared, microphone techniques are invented and beatbrokers collage new soundtracks for urban survival.

HIPHOP CHICANO

A Separate but Parallel Story

Raegan Kelly

What's up Homie? Don't you know me?
Si mon.
Ain't you the brother of the mas chingon?
Straight up, and I'm down with the Raza
Kid Frost got my back
BooYaa's en la casa
Cause every day things get a little crazier
As I step to the microphone area
First I call my city
Puro Los Angeles
[lights up & cops a hit] Yeah homes
That's what the ganga says . . .

Cypress Hill, 'Latin Lingo'

Laying claim to the gangsta persona is a favourite theme in hiphop. Reading the wax, Toddy Tee, Schooly D, and NWA get major props . . . but for the concepts of *carnelismo, calo* terminology (homeboy, OG, etc), the pachuco/cholo/gangsta style of dress, and the lowered ride, proper respect is due the *varrio*.

Chicano gangs, or 'street syndicates', have been a fact of life in LA since the early 1930s (some claim earlier); accordingly their history, memory, and culture are long and strong. Defined by Martin Sanchez Jankowski as (roughly) adaptational organizations whose primary goal is survival through self-reliance,[1] 'gang youth', while always a target of the media and law enforcement, have become, in LA at least, social pariahs without peer. To take pride visibly in this position is one way of inverting it, but the presence of colours, oversized Dickies, pendeltons, street lingo and fire power within the language and style of hiphop is only in small part fantasy-fulfilment – many of those who talk the talk have walked the walk.

Parallelling the development of gang culture were the rise of the lowrider and the zoot suiter in LA. In the *varrio*, self-reliance and brown pride go hand in hand, and a large percentage of brown hiphop integrates commentary on race and cultural difference into straightforward narratives of life on the streets. Sen Dogg of Cypress Hill exemplifies the West Coast B-boy in 'Latin Lingo' – he declares his homies, his Raza, his hood, LA hiphop (and, of course, a phat blunt) in a particularly West Coast combination of English, *pachuquismo*, and hiphop slang. Both linguistically and stylistically, aspects of the West Coast gangsta, whether it be Kid Frost, Ganxsta Ridd (of the Boo Yaa Tribe) or Ice Cube in a pendelton, Dickies and a lowered '63 S.S., originated with *pachucos* and Zoot Suiters of 1940s *varrios* of east Los Angeles.

Like the 'Teddy Boy' of Harlem, the *pachuco* was the ultimate expression of cultural resistance, anarchy, and (in)difference in the North American south west of the 1940s. Generally identified as Chicano gang members (although most were not)[2] *pachucos* sported pompadours, wide-shouldered extra-long fingertip coats, high waisted 'drape' pants with pegged ankles and reat pleats, wide-brimmed hats, long watch chains, and *fileros*. Much has been written in detail about the 'Zoot Suit Riots' that took place in Los Angeles in 1943, but what matters is precisely what caused civilians and sailors to roam the streets in mobs looking for young Chicanos to beat down. In *The Zoot-Suit Riots*, Mauricio Mazon describes their hatred as being comprised of a mixture of patriotic fervour and fear (mixed with envy) of difference, and of themselves.

To the good citizens of LA, '[Zoot Suiters] seemed to be simply marking time while the rest of the country intensified the war effort.'[3] *Pachucos* openly smoked marijuana, spoke their own tongue, had their own style of music, dance and dress. Most infuriating, however, was that *pachucos* and zoot suiters spent so much time developing their own insular culture while good 'patriotic' Americans built bombers 9-to-5 and went off to war. *Pachucos* didn't have a good 'work ethic'. They didn't seem to care, had their own set of priorities, and this pissed people off. (The attacks weren't completely symbolic, of course – it was around this time that the California Youth Authority camps were established, and an increasingly militant approach to law enforcement in Los Angeles was adopted.[4]

The Lowered Ride

Although the east side of Los Angeles was generally regarded as being overrun by gangs, violence, and an undocumented workforce,[5] what was to become one of the largest *varrios* in the south west had its own fast developing political, musical and street culture. In the early fifties a 'basic car plan' was initiated by the First Street Merchants and the sheriff's department, and the tradition of car clubs began among east Los Angeles youth.[6] Originally designed to provide an alternative to gangs, car clubs became a focal point for social life in the *varrio*, providing a place to work, hang out, listen to music, gain knowledge of self-expression and cultural identity through the arte of car customizing.

Chicanos have been customizing cars since the forties. The concept of a fully customized car, top to bottom, front to back, inside and out, took years to develop, but from the very beginning it was treated as an art form. Generally starting with a used American standard, a clay model, and much ingenuity and love, customizers take bits and pieces off different automobiles out of scrap yards, alter them and put them together to create a totally new and unique car. Bill Hines is one of *Lowrider* magazine's 'Legends of Lowriding'; his first custom was a '41 Buick convertible with 'chopped top' and a Cadillac front end. Known to some as the 'King of Lead' for his ability totally to rework a body with a lead paddle and a spray gun, he was also one of the first to design a hydraulic lift system for raising and lowering custom cars (using modified aircraft landing gear parts), California-style, in 1964. (The first lifted custom was purportedly done by the Aguirres of San Bernardino, CA, on a 1956 Corvette).[7] Hydraulics served a dual function – to raise a lowered vehicle for driving long distances (protect the underside), and to keep the cops away (riding too slow was a ticketable offence). 'I remember a guy with this candy turquoise '63 Ford . . . that wanted to fool the cops. So, he had me juice it in front and back. He'd cruise with it laid until the cops spotted him. They couldn't figure it out. They didn't know what a lift was.'[8]

To drive a beautifully customized ride low and slow down one of LA's main thoroughfares is an expression of pride, pride in being different, taking one's time, being Chicano. Jesse Valdez, another of the original lowriders and former leader of one of LA's best-known car clubs, The Imperials, remembers the heyday of lowriding: 'In '66, '67, '68 – we'd cruise Downey, Paramount, Whittier. That's when everybody was lowriding; Chicanos, black guys, white guys.'[9] Whittier Boulevard, a unifying site for east LA through to the mid-seventies, was the site of the Eastside Blowouts, the Chicano political protests of '71–2; it provided a focal point for the *muralista* movement of the same time and Luis Valdez's 1979 movie *Boulevard Nights*. (Valdez's film, a classic Hollywood document of *varrio* street life in LA, opened ironically just after the boulevard was permanently closed to cruisers.) Favourites of the car culture tended to be instrumentals with sparse lyrics and heavy basslines – 'Whittier Boulevard' by Thee Midniters, 'Lowrider' by WAR (previously Señor Soul), 'More Bounce' by Zapp.

Latin Lingo

Calo is the privileged language of the Mexican-American barrio . . . (It) was neither a *pachuco* nor a new world contribution. Calo has its ancient roots buried deeply in the fertile gypsy tongue (Calé, Romano, Zincalo and Calogitano . . .) . . . fractured in spelling, crippled in meaning; mutilated French, English, Italian, and the dead languages of Latin, Greek, and Hebrew, plus medieval Moorish. Calo, originally *Zincalo*, was the idiom of the Spanish Gypsies – one of the many minorities in Spain. The *conquistadores* brought Calo to the New World. Already identified by the upper classes as the argot of the criminal, the poor, and the uneducated, Calo and its variants became well known to the conquered Indian . . . .

Mauricio Mazon, The Zoot-Suit Riots, p. 3

To followers of scat and the spoken-word traditions of jazz and bebop, Calo probably sounds little different than the jive scat of Cab Calloway or the inverted *Vout* language of Slim Gaillard. In some ways today it operates much like early hepster phraseology – hip Calo terms like homeboy and loc have completely penetrated hiphop and gang culture. But for the *pachucos* of the forties and in the *varrios* of today, Calo is also an important way to mark cultural difference/peripherality through language. Frequently referred to as 'Spanglish' (half English, half Spanish) Calo is in fact a tongue all its own, a 'living language' whose words and meanings change from location to location and person to person.

> Muy Loco, Crazy
> Ever since I come from Mexico
> I don't want to do the Mambono
> All I want to do is go go go
> When the crazy band she starts to blow
> All the *señoritas* say to me
> Come on Pancho dance with me
> Pancho Pancho don't go to the Rancho
> Til you do the Pancho Rock with me
>
> Lalo Guerrero and His Orchestra, 'Pancho Rock'

The great Latin bandleader Lalo Guerrero was one of the first to incorporate Calo into the Los Angeles club scene in the forties. *Pachuco* and zoot cultures gravitated towards the big-band sound, which Guerrero fused with the structures of swing and rumba in songs like 'Chuco Suave', 'Marijuana Boogie', and 'Vamos a bailar'.[10] Another Calo favourite was the Don Tosti band's 'Pachuco Boogie', characterized by Johnny Otis as Chicano Jump Blues, 'which consisted of a jump type shuffle with either Raul [Diaz] or Don [Tosti] rapping in Calo about getting ready to go out on a date. Very funny stuff and another candidate for the title of the first rap record.'[11]

Through the fifties and sixties east Los Angeles developed an active recording and club scene, which, as Steven Loza explains in *Barrio Rhythm*, 'was integrally related to the black music experience, for musical as well as economic reasons'.[12] The influence went both ways, and in 1952 African American saxophonist Chuck Higgins released the hit single 'Pachuco Hop'. Loza quotes Ruben Guevara's description of the east LA music scene in the late fifties and early sixties at El Monte Legion Stadium, which reads like an early description of

Go-Go: 'A lot of Anglo kids copied not only the styles (hair, dress) but the dances, the most popular of which were the Pachuco Hop, Hully Gully, and the Corrido Rock . . . the Corrido was the wildest, sort of an early form of slam dancing. Two or three lines would form, people arm in arm, each line consisting of 150 to 250 people. With the band blasting away at breakneck rocking tempo, the lines took four steps forward and four steps back, eventually slamming into each other (but making sure that no one got hurt) . . . After the dance, it was out to the parking lot for the grand finale. Where's the party? *Quien tiene pisto? Mota?* Who's got the booze? Weed? Rumours would fly as to which gangs were going to throw *chingasos* – come to blows. The Jesters Car Club from Boyle Heights, which dominated the Eastside, would parade around the parking lot in their lavender, maroon or gray primered cars, wearing T-Timer shades (blue or green coloured glasses in square wire frames) . . . '[13]

Latin and Afro-Cuban rhythms seem to have penetrated the early hiphop scene at least a decade before we hear any bilingual or Calo phraseology. In the early seventies, at the same time as lowriders in Califas were bumpin' the sounds of Tierra, Señor Soul, and Rulie Garcia and the East LA Congregation, Jimmy Castor was creating hiphop beats in New York using a fusion of 'one-chord riffing, a Sly Stone pop bridge, fuzz guitar, timbales breaks, and an idealistic lyric applicable to any emergent movement . . . '.[14] David Toop credits Jimmy Castor with being a hiphop innovator, at the centre of the Latin soul movement in the sixties and highly influenced by Latin masters like Cal Tjader, Chano Pozo, and Tito Puente.[15] Seven years later Afrika Bambaataa would redefine 'influence', straight cutting Slim Gaillard's unique *Vout* lyrics into the mix.

In *Hip-Hop: The Illustrated History*, Steven Hager describes the early tagging and writing scene in 1970s New York as being racially integrated: the first tagger on record, Taki 183, was Greek; the second, Julio 204, was Chicano; and Tracy 168, a young white kid living in Black Spades territory, founded one of the scene's largest crews, 'Wanted', in 1972.[16] The internationally known Lee Quinones and Lady Pink (stars of *Wild Style*)[17] were both Puerto Rican, as were the members of the all-time great breaking group, the Rock Steady Crew.

In the Bronx, funk and early hiphop entered the already hot Puerto Rican street and dance scene around 1977–8, with members of the Zulu Nation schooling Puerto Ricans in the ways of breakdancing and Puerto Rican DJs like Charlie Chase spinning funk and sporting early B-boy styles at their then disco-dominated block parties.[18] Rammelzee ('Ramm-elevation-Z – Z being a symbol of energy which flows in two directions)[19] and RubyD, recently dubbed the Puerto Rican Old School by West Coast Puerto Rican funkster Son Doobie of Funkdoobiest, rocked the mike all over NYC. The 1983 hit 'Beat Bop' (Rammelzee vs. K-Rob) showcases what Rammelzee is known best for – what he dubbed 'slanguage',[20] an ingenious combination of freestyle metaphor and over-the-top hiphop drops delivered in the Shake Up King's particular nasal drawl:

Just groovin' like a sage y'all
Break it up, yeah, yeah, stage y'all
Like a roller coaster ride that can make ya bump
Groovin with the rhythm as you shake yer rump – rock rock ya don't stop
You got it now baby – ya don't stop
Just hiphop the day, yeah doobie doo
Yeah scoobie doo, whatcha wanna do crew?
Just freak it, ya baby, just freak up, ya ya baby
Drink it up here, I know my dear
I can rock you out this atmosphere
Like a gangster prankster, number one bankster
Got much cash to make you thank ya
Rock on to the break a dawn – Keep it on now keep it on
I know Zee Zee that can rock quick
Like a high kind a class
Hand yer rhythm to the stick . . .

'Beat Bop', Rammelzee vs. K-Rob

In 1980 a young Samoan dancer named SugarPop would move west from the streets of New York to bring breaking to the poplockers of south central, Venice and Hollywood in Los Angeles. One of the groups SugarPop encountered was the Blue City Crew, a group of Samoan poplockers coming out of Carson in south LA. In Topper Carew's movie *Breakin and Entering* about the early eighties breaking scene in LA, the crew talks about how the advent of street dancing correlated with a drop in gangbanging in the hoods and *varrios* of LA – homies were taking their battles to the dance floor. 'In LA it ain't like that . . . If you got the moves, you can hold down. That's all it is.'

It was also around this time that hiphop started to penetrate the LA Chicano dance scene. In the mid- to late seventies Chicanos were throwing giant dance parties at Will Rogers State Beach, Devonshire Downs and in parks and roller rinks in the San Fernando Valley, complete with battling mobile DJs, hundreds of Curwen Vegas, MCs to keep the crowd hyped and, of course, circling helicopters. Precursors of today's massive rave scene (which are approximately 75 per cent Chicano in Los Angeles), the music of choice at these parties was alternative/new wave, disco, and early techno-based hiphop (Egyptian Lover, Magic Mike, Melle Mel, Grandmaster Flash). Due to popular demand, in 1983–4 Uncle Jam's Army set up special Valley-side gigs at the Sherman Square roller rink in Sherman Oaks. Young Chicano, Latino, and Samoan MCs, many of them former dancers, were working their way through the LA house party scene at this time, but one of the earliest to make it to wax was Arthur Molina, Jr (aka Kid Frost) in 1984 with the single 'Rough Cut'. The music, written by David Storrs of Electrobeat Records (the same Storrs who wrote the music for Ice T's 'Body Rock'),[21] has a decidedly early West Coast flavour, but lyrically the song bears a strong resemblance to Run DMC's 'It's Like That', also released in 1984.

Sometimes you wait around
Rockin' cold hard streets
People strugglin' hard
Just tryin to make ends meet
I just stand tough
hold down my feet
Never understand the meaning
of the word Defeat
So you see it's like that
And that's the way it is
But when I'm on the microphone, it goes something like this:
Body breakin' Booty shakin'
Good money for the makin'
You just put it in my pocket
Cause you know I got talent
It's Rough, it's Tough
Let me see if you can handle my stuff
It's Rough Rough Rough Rough Rough . . .

Kid Frost, 'Rough Cut'

The earliest bilingual hiphop song that I've heard on record is out of New York – Carlos T (aka Spanish Fly) and the Terrible Two's hit 'Spanglish'.[22] Rapping over a classic Grandmaster Flash beat the Terrible Two dominate the song in English, with Carlos T coming in short and fast. 'This is the way we harmonize, everybody, everybody, I said Danse funky danse, y que danse, todo mundo, todo mundo.'

In 1989 the Cuban-born Mellow Man Ace kicked bilingual lyrics throughout his album *Escape from Havana*, generally alternating line for line between English and Spanish, as in 'Mentirosa', or verse for verse, as he does in 'Rap Guanco', over the Kool and the Gang bassline from Lightnin' Rod's[23] cut 'Sport' on the *Hustlers' Convention* album of 1973:

. . . I'm the lyrical, miracle founder of the talk style
Put together intelligently wild
And what I came up with is called Rap Guanco
Different than house, nothing like GoGo
And if you're wonderin' damn how'd he start this
Well, last year I opened my own market
Cause it was time for somethin' new to come along and I thought
A bilingual single, that can't go wrong . . .
. . .
Ahora si que vengo   [And now yes I'm coming]
Sabroso si caliente . . .   [Flavor very hot] . . .

Mellow Man Ace, 'Rap Guanco'

A year later, Kid Frost hit the streets with his classic adaptation of the Gerald Wilson/El Chicano tune 'Viva La Tirado',[24] 'La Raza', matching in syntax and lingo the Pachuco street slang (Calo) of east LA.

> Quevo
> Aqui'stoy MC Kid Frost
> *Yo estoy jefe*   [I am in charge]
> My *cabron* is the big boss
> My *cuete* is loaded   [pistol/rod]
> It's full of *balas*   [bullets]
> I'll put it in your face
> And you won't say *nada*.   [nothing]
> *Vatos, cholos*, call us what you will   [Chicano homeboys, lowriders]
> You say we are assassins,
> Train ourselves to kill
> It's in our blood to be an Aztec warrior
> Go to any extreme
> And hold to no barriers
> Chicano and I'm brown and proud
> Want this *chingaso*?   [smack, wack, as in 'beat down']
> Si mon I said let's get down
> . . .
> The foreign tongue I'm speaking is known as Calo
> *Y sabes que, loco?*   [And you know what, loc?]
> *Yo estoy malo*   [I am mean/bad]
> *Tu no sabes que* I think your brain is hollow?   [Don't you know that . . .]
> . . .
> And so I look and I laugh and say *Que pasa*?   [What's happening?]
> Yeah, this is for La Raza.
>
> Kid Frost, 'La Raza', *Hispanic Causing Panic*

'La Raza' is important for several reasons. It marks a radical change in Kid Frost's work – the distance between the non-committal 'So rough, so tough' of 'Rough Cut' and 'It's in our blood to be an Aztec warrior/Go to any extreme . . . ' marks a change in consciousness, at least of his perception of hiphop as a language of consciousness. Frost's use of Calo is an appeal to the authenticity of the streets and the *pachuco* lifestyle, but within the context of the song it is also a nod to Chicano pride, as is the claim 'Chicano and I'm brown and proud'. The term Chicano, derived from *mechicano* and once considered derogatory and indicative of lower-class standing, applies to all people of Mexican descent/all people of indigenous descent. To call yourself Chicano is to claim La Raza, to locate your origin within the struggle of a people for land and for cultural, political and economic self-determination.

Also, Frost's use of an El Chicano hit, as opposed to the less culturally specific beat of 'Rough Cut', is a nod to the *veteranos* (who to this day remain partial to Oldies over hiphop).

The early nineties have been watershed years for Chicano hiphoppers – a peak moment being the 1991 release of Cypress Hill's first album. Showcasing the combined talents of Mellow Man Ace's brother Sen Dogg, B-Real, DJ Muggs, *Cypress Hill* integrates the best of Rammelzee's hiphop tricknology, the Calo rap of Don Tosti and Raul Diaz, bad-ass West Coast gangsta mythology, humour, and trademark beats.

> Gangsta Rid, What's up Y'all?
> 'It's a tribe thing . . .'
> . . .
> 'Hey where you from homies?'
> It's on
> He sees 'em reach for his gun
> Buckshot to the dome
> He jumps in the bomb
> Homies in tha back but she just wants to go home
> But he trips to the store
> Homeboy needs a 40
> White boy's at the counter
> Thinkin' 'O Lordy Lordy'
> Pushin' on the button
> Panickin' for nuttin'
> Pigs on the way
> Hey yo he smells bacon . . .
> . . .
> Scooby doo y'all, scooby doo y'all
> A scooby doo y'all
> A doobie doobie doo y'all . . .
>
> Cypress Hill, *Hole in the Head*, 1991

It's a Tribe Thing

I am a revolutionary . . . because creating life amid death is a revolutionary act. Just as building nationalism in an era of imperialism is a life-giving act . . . We are an awakening people, an emerging nation, a new breed.

Carlos Muñoz, Jr, *Youth Identity, Power*, p. 76

Corky Gonzales's Crusade for Justice in 1969 brought people from every corner of the *varrio* together in the name of self-determination and La Raza. One of the concepts put forth during the course of the conference was that Chicano students, needing 'revolutionary role models, would do well to emulate their brothers and sisters in the streets, the *vatos locos* of the *varrio*. *Carnelismo*, or the code of absolute love in Chicano gangs, was to be adopted by radical student nationalists as the locus of their developing ideology.[25]

The Chicano hiphop that has made it to wax in the last two years frequently assimilates some combination of street mentality and nationalist politics, whether it be as simple as giving the nod to brown pride, or as complex as the cultural nationalism of Aztlan Underground. The gangsta presently dominates brown hiphop, good examples being Proper Dos (west LA), RPM (Valley), Street Mentality (Pico/Union), The Mexicanz (Long Beach) and Brown Town (east LA), to name a few. The music: generally simple beats, frequently scary, down with ganga, *rucas* and *cuetes*, sometimes intentionally educational, and occasionally hilarious. Groups like Of Mexican Descent represent a new generation of lyrical wizards, working in two tongues, with breath control, and kicking knowledge of self.

Cypress Hill are at the centre of one of LA's finer hiphop posses, the Soul Assassins. The more recent group Funkdoobiest (consisting of Puerto Rican and Sioux MCs and a Mexican DJ) are down, as well as the Irish American group House of Pain, and allied are the Samoan brothers of the Boo Yaa Tribe, Mellow Man Ace, and Kid Frost. For me, the Soul Assassins represent some of the most radical (and difficult) aspects of living in Los Angeles. On one hand they describe the celebration of difference through hiphop (and the fierce potential in collaboration and in the music), on the other, their lyrics frequently demarcate territorial and personal boundaries (BOOM-in-your-face). But at its most elemental, the beats of hiphop are about walking all over those boundaries with no apologies.

Out of the east we've heard from groups like the Puerto Rican Powerrule (New York), and Fat Joe the Gangsta (Bronx), there's a Brewley MC in Puerto Rico, and reggae español posses in Panama and Mexico, but brown hiphop seems to be coming to fruition on the West Coast. Although the Latin Alliance project didn't hold, hopefully the concept was not outmoded but a little ahead of its time. In a city where 10 per cent of the world's population of El Salvadorans lives around MacArthur Park (downtown), the possibilities for cross-cultural collaboration and unity seem, well, massive. And with cats like Kid Frost, Cypress, AUG, Proper Dos, and OMD sharpening their skills in every corner of LA, hiphop is where to make it happen. After all, it still remains true that (referring back to the Samoan brother from Carson City) in LA hiphop if you are down, you can hold down.

Special Thanks to Bulldog and Tate

Notes

1. Martin Sanchez Jankowski, *Islands in the Street*, Berkeley, Los Angeles and Oxford 1991, pp. 25–7.
2. Mauricio Mazon, *The Zoot-Suit Riots; The Psychology of Symbolic Annihilation*, Austin, 1984, p. 5.

3. Ibid, p. 9.
4. Ibid, p. 108.
5. Steven Loza, *Barrio Rhythm; Mexican American Music in Los Angeles*, Urbana and Chicago, 1993, p. 42.
6. Ibid.
7. Dick DeLoach, 'Bill Hines: The King of Lead', *Lowrider Magazine*, April 1992, p. 52.
8. Ibid, p. 53
9. Dick DeLoach, 'Jesse Valdez and Gypsy Rose', *Lowrider Magazine*, October 1992, p. 56.
10. *Barrio Rhythm*, p. 71.
11. Ibid, p. 81.
12. Ibid.
13. Ibid., p. 83.
14. David Toop, *Rap Attack 2: African Rap to Global Hip Hop*, London and New York, 1991, p. 22.
15. Ibid, p. 24.
16. Steven Hager, *Hip-Hop: The Illustrated History*, p. 21.
17. *Wild Style*, Charlie Ahearn, 1981. A 35mm rap-umentary about the early integration of the different elements of hiphop culture in New York. Also starring Fred Braithwaite and Patty Astor.
18. *An Illustrated History of Hip Hop*, p. 81.
19. *Rap Attack 2*, p. 122.
20. Ibid.
21. Billy Jam, liner notes on *West Coast Rap, The First Dynasty, Vol. 2*, 1992, Rhino Records.
22. On *Greatest Hits of the Zulu Nation*, circa 1982.
23. AKA Jalal of the Last Poets.
24. See Introduction for details and history.
25. Carlos Muñoz, Jr, *Youth, Identity, Power: The Chicano*, Verso, 1989, p. 76.

Further Reading

Rodolfo F. Acuna, *A Community Under Siege: A Chronicle of Chicanos East of the Los Angeles River; 1945–1975*. Monograph no. 11/Chicano Studies Research Center Publications, Los Angeles: University of California 1984.

Rodolfo F. Acuna, *Occupied America; A History of Chicanos*, New York: HarperCollins 1988.

Dick DeLoach, 'Bill Hines: The King of Lead', *Lowrider Magazine* 14, 1992, pp. 52–3.

Dick DeLoach, 'Jesse Valdez and Gypsy Rose', *Lowrider Magazine* 14, 1992, pp. 56–8.

Willard Gingerich, 'Aspects of Prose Style in Three Chicano Novels: *Pocho, Bless Me, Ultima* and *The Road to Tamazunchale* in ed. Jacob Ornstein-Galicia, *Form and Function in Chicano English*, Rowley, Massachusetts: Newbury House 1994.

Steven Hager, *Hip-Hop: The Illustrated History, Rap Music and Graffiti*, New York: St Martin's Press, 1984.

Martin Sanchez Jankowski, *Islands in the Street*, Berkeley, Los Angeles and Oxford: University of California Press 1991.

George Lipsitz, *Time Passages; Collective Memory and American Popular Culture*, Minneapolis: University of Minnesota Press 1990.

Steven Loza, *Barrio Rhythm: Mexican American Music in Los Angeles*, Urbana and Chicago: University of Illinois Press 1993.

Mauricio Mazon, *The Zoot-Suit Riots; The Psychology of Symbolic Annihilation*, Austin: University of Texas Press 1984.

Carlos Muñoz Jr, *Youth, Identity, Power; The Chicano Movement*, London and New York: Verso 1989.

Harry Polkinhorn, Alfredo Velasco and Mal Lambert, *El Libro De Calo; Pachuco Slang Dictionary*, San Diego: Atticus Press 1983.

Stan Steiner, *La Raza: The Mexican Americans*, New York, Evanston, and London: Harper & Row 1970.

David Toop, *Rap Attack 2: African Rap to Global Hip Hop*, London and New York: Serpent's Tail 1991.

THE INTERVIEWS

ROY PORTER

Roy Porter is an LA music legend, a survivor. Born in Colorado Springs, he came to Los Angeles in 1944 in time to be part of the first generation of LA boppers. He began by playing with Howard McGhee. Later, after drumming on Charlie Parker's early Dial recordings, he set up his own big band. He played with everybody from Perez Prado to Charles Mingus and gave Eric Dolphy his first opportunity to blow. Dealing with drug addiction through the late fifties, he disappeared from the scene but returned in the late sixties with his Soundmachine, a short-lived combo that recorded some outrageously funky material. In the nineties Roy Porter reached his seventieth birthday and his work is still being heard either through sampling or reissues. He has also published an autobiography entitled *There and Back*. This interview took place at Porter's south central home in November of 1991.

Roy Porter: When I first got to New York I was playin' swing drums with a band at the Apollo Theatre. When I went down to Minton's Playhouse one night I heard a drummer by the name of Kenny Clarke – they called him 'Klook'. I heard this drummer doin' some stuff and I'm thinkin', 'Look at this cat, he's doin' somethin' different.' But it was years later that it came to me that that was the first time that I heard a 'bomb' drop. That's what you call a 'bomb': the way he was doin' it. Then I heard Max [Roach] and, uh, when I heard Max, the way he dropped a 'bomb' was . . . (he imitates a drum . . . dee bop dee bop slapping on his knee) . . . and I thought, 'Man, this is somethin' different.'

    Now a 'bomb' is nothin' but an accent the way I would do it, either from a snare drum to the bass, or from the tom-toms, or from two tom-toms with a 'flam' effect. A 'flam' effect is like . . . (vedumppp, he mouths the noise of a 'flam' effect) that's the idea. The records that you hear me on, the way I drop my bombs, mine exploded, that's what I would call it, 'cause of the 'flam' effect.

Brian Cross: Is that why they said it was like closin' doors?

RP: Yeah, you've heard about it.

BC: Is that the key to bebop drummin' at the time?

RP: At the time . . . now see I'm gonna talk to ya now. There's some great drummers 'cause I hear somethin' and like something everybody does. If it ain't no more than the way they hold their sticks or the way they sit at the drums, everybody's got somethin'. But Max Roach, to me, now he is the ultimate. Now maybe I'm touched but Kenny Clarke was bad, and my idols like Sidney Catlett, Shadow Wilson, Jo Jones, Buddy Rich, they were all bad, but Max did somethin' that others didn't do.

. . . See now if you tell Max to play three bars and one quarter, that's what he's gonna play and know what he's doin'. He ain't like Art Blakey. But he got them great big hands, great big arms, he was a powerhouse. He played from the gut, the soul, from the muscle, and he had a thunderous thing goin' on the drums. But technicality-wise Max Roach was a monster, and still is to me the ultimate bebop drummer. Some things I tried to play like Max but I wasn't tryin' to be no Max Roach and I never studied either, so there wasn't no way for me to play like Max. So I went on to play whatever it was that I wanted to play. That's why Howard [McGhee] said to me, 'Well man, you do whatever you feel and well, you know what you're doin', just don't fuck up' (he laughs).

BC: That was the transition then, from swing drums to bebop drums – that you could keep the 'meter' but could go off and do other things so long as you didn't throw off anybody else?

RP: Right, don't get in the way of anybody in their solos. Goose 'em but stay behind 'em and push 'em. Goose 'em, bump 'em with a bomb. Goose 'em here if he gets to playin' real good like uh, Dexter Gordon did on 'Blowin' the Blues Away' with Billy Eckstine's big band, you understand?

Drums are supposed to be back there played, you know. I like drum solos and all like that, but I was a drummer that sat back there and kept that 'meter' time goin' and kicked that soloist in the ass with a 'bomb'. We call it kickin' him in his ass with a 'bomb'. You know, to make him blow. It's left up to the drummer to give him the inspiration to keep goin', you understand? And that's what I would try to do. 'Cause I got these little hands and all that stuff, I get tired playin' solos; I wasn't what you call no solo drummer, no way, man. 'Cause I would sit back there and, uh, make ya move, and if you couldn't play in front of me, then you couldn't play. No brag, just fact.

There's a difference, drummers today. I hear a lot of drummers who are bad, a dime a dozen, bad motherfuckers they played their ass off. But they haven't had that experience of playin' bebop. They should've played with the masters where the masters were playin' solos and jammin' and shit and then they'll learn how to play behind soloists, not just playin' all themselves, not just thinkin' about what *they're* playin'. When you was playin' with the masters in those days, you had to complement what they were playin'. That was the difference between back then and today. The guys today who think they're great, they're good. They're great, but then they get them attitudes, I don't like them young people's attitudes, 'cause they don't know where the fuck it's comin' from. It came from people like Art Blakey, Max Roach, Shadow Wilson, go way back. If it hadn't been for those people, these people wouldn't know what to do. Somewhere along the line I got lucky, I got in there some kinda way. So they used call me 'that old bomb dropper' or 'that old door slammin' muthafucker'.

BC: What was it like goin' down Central Avenue and playin' down there?

RP: Oh shit! I first got out here in 1944 so I was stayin' with my half sister on my father's side. I was doin' gardening work with an old man, a friend of the family. I said I'd like to get over there on the Red Car – it would take you over to Santa Monica and that's the only way you could get over there, and got downtown and would change from downtown to the U-Car that started out on 5th Street and curved around 6th Street [and] ran into Central.

BC: Where did it start?

RP: Central started on 5th Street, keeps goin' from 6th Street on down clear on out to 108th and Central Avenue. I guess they call it the ghetto now, it was a monster then, but I guess it's the ghetto now. But it started down Central Avenue and I was on the street car man and uh, all the clubs man, had jukeboxes that played 78s. The street cars, goin' down the street: one club here, two, three clubs on one block and the war was just winding down, soldiers, sailors, the streets were packed . . . and you hear this music, man. 'After Hours' by Erskine Hawkins, next club you hear Joe Liggins and the Honeydrippers with 'I Got a Right to Cry'; those were the big hits at the time. Mostly these are blues, no jazz or nothin' like that. All down Central they were playin' rhythm and blues. Wasn't no rock'n'roll, they kept it race records see. That shit you go out to Hollywood and hear. It wasn't for blacks.

BC: From what I can tell from reading about it, Central was prosperous.

RP: It was, I'm tellin' ya. And at the time, in the forties, the Dunbar Hotel, and it didn't stop there it continued on down to 108th way out to Watts. Black neighbourhoods, where black people made their mistakes . . . Dunbar Hotel was owned by blacks. Now the little downbeat club where I played was owned by whites but it was run by blacks you know. See so I'm sayin' they had their own mortuary, grocery store, Lincoln Theater, hotels, Clark Hotel on Washington, nice black hotel, on down to the Dunbar, we talkin' about the east side now: Central Avenue, '44 through '49, and it was over in round '50. I left here in '50 to go to San Francisco. But the heyday was during that time and before that. I talk about '44 'cause that's when I came out here, is when bebop started. The type of music we were playin' I call it revolutionary.

BC: When you went down there first, that would've been during the war, so a lot of hip cats would wear zoot suits?

RP: The peg legged pants, and what you call them, wing tip shoes, white and black and white and brown, but that style is back now, so yeah, that's what these dudes were wearin'. And they were sharp. Money, yeah, plenty of money, shipyards were open, plenty of money, you had your pimps over there on Central, black girls and white girls . . . I'm just tellin' you how it was. And us musicians we had to fight them broads off with sticks – black or white – because we were doin' somethin' new, any one you want man, 'cause they would be like, 'I don't know what these muthafuckers are playin' but goddamn it's somethin'. They must be doin' somethin'.'

Finally, it took a long while for them to catch on to bebop. The hard core beboppers out here at that time, the innovators before Bird came out here [were] Dexter Gordon, Howard McGhee, Wardell Gray, Teddy Edwards, Hampton Hawes, a drummer by the name of Chuck Thompson, a piano player (called) Jimmy Bond, he was a catalyst. The hard ones, the ones musicians would sit around and learn. Before Bird got out here, and after Bird got out here . . . whew! . . . and I happen to be one of the dudes who got to play on most of his shit.

BC: How come Bird came out here?

RP: He came out here with Dizzy. LA at that time was a mecca that was very enticing 'cause it had Central Avenue. You know Lana Turner and Ava Gardner – they were slummin' comin' to the black neighbourhoods, them fine bitches, Dizzy came out here, Ray Brown, Will Jackson, they didn't accept bebop like Diz wanted them to accept it out here, but we were out here all the time, we worked all the time.

BC: How did you get hooked up with the rerelease project?

RP: Mike McFadden of Groove Merchant record store and Luv 'n' Haight records. In regards to the *In the Groove* album, he said he was from Frisco and I told him where he could get 'em. And he bought the last 200 of them, sold them out and then we got together and he wanted to know what else I had. So I let him hear 'Funky Twitch' which is off another album, and from that he was interested in 'Party Time' and 'Jessica' which was on the album. I was very surprised that it happened, on a 'hipster' label twenty years later. I thought it was over.

BC: What were you listening to when you were doing the Soundmachine stuff?

RP: I was listening to a lot of different stuff: Blood Sweat and Tears, those white cats. Of course you can't forget George Clinton and James Brown and a lot of jazz stuff.

BC: How did you feel about being sampled?

RP: I felt honoured, I mean I don't know nothin' about no hiphop but it was nice to have my rhythm tracks used and they threw in a little Kool and the Gang; it was nice. I called them up and they were real nice about it.

**Two B-boys at United Nations, Downtown
Los Angeles, 1991.**

**Alladin spins at Stanky Booty, Hollywood,
1992.**

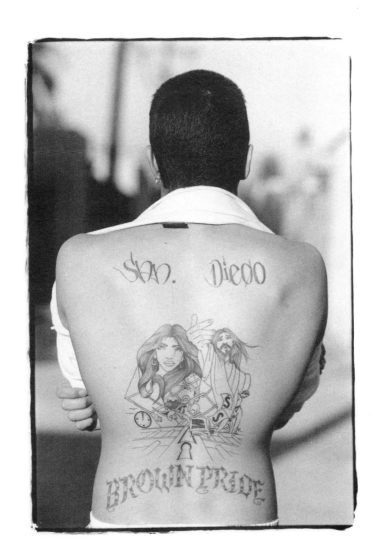

Blue's tattoo, Venice, 1992.

Muggs at the Palladium, Hollywood, 1992.

Cube receives mike backstage at the Palladium, Hollywood, 1992.

Dat Nigga Daz and C-Stylz of the Dogg
Pound, west Los Angeles, 1993.

**Suggah B blows up while T-Love watches
on The Soul Spot, Hollywood, 1992.**

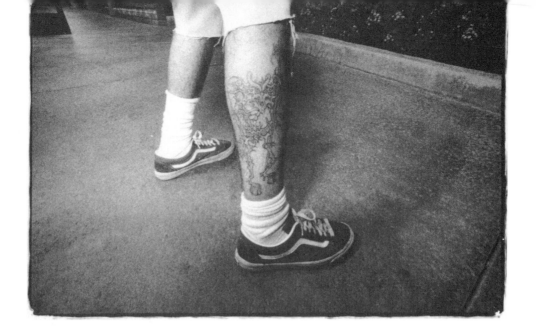

Ben's tattoo.

**Uncle Jam's Army reunion, The Palace,
Hollywood, 1991.**

**Note given to photographer at Uncle Jam's
Army Reunion, 1991.**

HORACE TAPSCOTT AND JMD

Horace Tapscott is a jazz enigma in Los Angeles. He is a strongly community based, uncompromising artist who has been involved in the Black Arts movement since the early fifties. His Arkestra (evoking both ark and orchestra) was a seedbed for many of the city's musicians, poets and actors. Horace himself is a quiet, humble and humorous man which often makes one forget his fierce piano style and his outspoken view on race. This interview took place at Horace's Leimert Park home with his son-in-law JMD (Darryl Moore) of the Underground Railroad, one of LA's foremost live jazz hiphop outfits.

Brian Cross: You remember Central Avenue?
Horace Tapscott: Yes, I was there. I lived on 20th and Naomi. East of Central. They had an African-American music union back in those days, Local 767. It was on Central where the Santa Monica Freeway now crosses it. I spent every day down there, you know, growing up down there. Me, Frank Morgan, Eric Dolphy, when Mingus was getting started . . . That was when I was about from thirteen to seventeen.
BC: The unions were separate in those days, Local 47 for whites and . . .
HT: It was all racist, of course, everyone was aware of it and it wasn't a big thing. You knew it was racist, but that was what you had to do. But all those big time Hollywood musicians and stars would come down on Central. This happened until 1951, when they merged the unions. The jobs didn't get any better for us, though. But see on Central Avenue when there was segregated unions all of the hipper jobs were on Central Avenue, in the night clubs. Me and the younger cats who weren't old enough would be sneaking in the night clubs. Gerald Wilson would let us in to see his band, Lionel Hampton, Duke Ellington, Count Basie would all sit down and talk to the young musicians. We could ask questions, you know, it was a rich situation for the music in the forties up until the merger. Then a number of laws started to change. You know they closed up Central Avenue downtown because of the mixture of the races. You know when those female movie stars

started coming to Central all kinds of laws would start being implemented. All of a sudden everybody was in the wrong place, ya dig. They shut it down from Washington and Central on down to Slauson, one at a time.

You know when I came up if you played drums or the blues after ten o'clock at night you had committed a crime. It was race music in them days. The young white kids weren't allowed to sing the blues, 'cause that was sinful. Even in the black community some of the more spiritual people considered it sin music, they wouldn't let you play it on Sunday. The music was saying so much that it upset everybody. It all began that way with the blues. That's what rap is today.

When I was growin' up before I came to California, in Houston, Texas up until 1943, my mother was a jazz musician and she accepted people like Floyd Dixon and Amos Milburn into her house. To see the music turn through all these years, to be a part of it you become very silent because you don't know what to say next. In the early years you could talk about the music and tell it came from here and that this is why it was said and done. You know the blues and the spirituals, same chord changes, it's just the wording is different, 'Musician' was a magic word in those days, you might even get fed with the preacher in people's house on Sundays.

We benefited from the education that integration ended up giving us but the down side was . . . you know the song 'Louie, Louie'? I was in high school with the writer; he wrote it in 1950. We have Alumni Dances at Jefferson High and he was there one time and he said, 'Hey Horace, I finally got my money.' He is fifty-nine and he wrote it when he was seventeen, 'Louie, Louie'. My man still lives over here. It takes them so long to accept it. Any time the music changed in this country it came out of the black community. So much of that is not visible to people; man, they don't know where the music came from. We got to set the record straight. So much has been lost. Anytime anything radical comes out in this country it has to do with race and hatred. Any time there's a new approach to the music by black musicians, there's hatred.

BC: Just to go back for a second, how did you decide on the piano?

HT: When I came out the womb it was all set up. My Mama had a big ol' piano inside the door and when you came in her house you had to play the piano. So she set me down when I was six. From then on she stayed on my case. All the other kids went to football games on Sunday, I went to concerts – I used to have to practise six hours a day, on three instruments, piano, trombone and baritone horn. It was part of my lifestyle.

When I first came to California, got off the train at Union Station and the first thing I saw was City Hall and all that. Then we got in the car and went down Central to my house, with the suitcases in the car and my Mom said, 'Pull over here.' I thought we were at my house and she took me out of the car and brought me to the barber shop and introduced me to my first music teacher. The first person I met was my music teacher . . . before I even saw my house. That should let you know what was important to my mother. But from when I went to the musicians' union I had so many teachers, a few main mentors but a lot of teachers.

BC: Talk about the splits in jazz, from swing to bop and then from cool and hard bop to free.

HT: Well they are the same kind of split. The bebop had to do with dope and women and crazy dudes with crazy talk. Dizzy Gillespie and Babs Gonzales had a lot to do with the slang. When I did that record with JMD and the Freestyle Fellowship, I was talking to the rappers and I spoke to them about this stuff and they went to look it up. They thought it was their fathers started this rap but it was their grandfathers. Louis Jordan was the father of all this. Listen to that stuff, man.

BC: But the thing I don't understand is, in jazz history Louis Jordan is the last artist you hear about before bop. It's like he gets bracketed into late swing . . .

HT: Well, that's where the problem starts, bracketing. All these cats were together, man. The writers started splitting them up. I am a witness. On Central Avenue all these guys were together, just rapping and talking. They would always be talking about the racial stuff, that was the main part of our community. They didn't dream that stuff up. It came from their experiences.

We got started on the free jazz out here in '59, tryin' to get a point over about what's really happenin'. A lot of cats didn't like the Arkestra because it was far out but it wasn't: Fletcher Henderson was doing the same thing before I was born. But it was kept quiet. I just wanted to straighten the record out. So the music became a message, a pipeline, by bringing all the arts together. So you know these fellas from Watts came along and said we have some poetry here. Boom, the Watts Prophets. Then we had these women called Sapphire Streaky also doing the poetry. Three women talking about black women's perspectives using all the foul language, man. It was like that then, we played the dozens and started putting rhythms and rhymes to it, a lot of teeth got knocked out but it was heaven . . . . Have you ever driven down Central, Brian? From where to where?

BC: Yeah, well I started one day the whole day. I stopped like every block, just to see where everything was; I started 5th Street downtown, 'cause I figured that's where the trolley started. I just drove the whole way to Compton pretty much.

HT: Yeah, when you drove down from 6th Street, when you got to Washington, that's where it all began – Washington and Central down at the Clark Hotel. Me and my wife used to walk past it on Central (when I) was fourteen years old . . . Art Tatum and Bill Douglass and Rick Gamon would be playin' and the hotel would be empty, so they would be playin' to us, you know . . . and they was just, the day was just that loose. 'Cross (the) street Billie Holiday would be at a little old hotel messin' around with somebody else, they'd be walking the streets a lot . . . yeah it was really comfortable, you wouldn't even think about it, it was just goin' on – you'd see all the cats playin', they'd just be playin', that's all I knew mostly were the players.

BC: It seems to me that that emphasis on learning an instrument when you are really young seems to have fallen away – why?

JMD: That's simple, it's money, 'cause in school they used to give you instruments like they give you books. Everybody on my street had an instrument and when they cut down all the funds in the schools, you couldn't have [one]. Sometimes they would give you teachers in school and you'd have a private instructor, then they would just give you your instrument. But they cut the money right when I was getting out of school, and then rap started getting bigger, because kids didn't have instruments, so the best way to channel their creativity was writing down lyrics and saying them; didn't cost money and didn't cost nothing to be a DJ either.

It was pure economics, 'cause everybody wanted to play. I think if they hadn't cut down on the schools there would be a lot more musicians. It's just fortunate or unfortunate depending on how you look at it that all these kids with talent, kids like Mikah Nine [from the Freestyle Fellowship], [are] musicians trapped in the body of a rapper – Mike's come a long way on the trumpet in a short time, just imagine if he'd had the trumpet in his hand since he was nine, he'd probably be the next Freddie Hubbard. But the only creative outlet kids got now is to write a rhyme, you can always sing in the hall or the shower. The city ran out of money, and rap gets bigger and bigger and bigger . . .

BC: That seems to be the way it's gone.

HT: Well, a lot of that has to do with electronics. Machines comin' in. A lot of young folks don't have to practise, just push a few buttons and things happen. Then there's the selected few that did it anyway, that's who you hear now, the younger cats in their early twenties who were fortunate to be in that kind of community where the music was passed on to them – they've done wonders, they rerecorded old things, and added something else to it. But the fact of it is they came out of a thinking area where they think manually to do things rather than having it done electronically – it's very easy to learn [the] rudiments on your drums if you push a button and it keeps happening. There's a place for everything; however, some of the basic things cannot be changed at this point in time . . . . The things I feel about electronic instruments, it has nothing to do with the instrument, it has to do with the person who's playing it. They should start by practising, if you learn on the instrument, then you can play the electronic.

BC: It seems too that a lot of what got lost, which is what the Fellowship is workin' on, if you had a place where people could play together, like the musicians' union, where you have young people playing with older people – if you take away that place, then you lose a lot of the exchange . . . . Improvisation, free exchange is lost when you take the live aspect out. But it's comin' back too. That's the thing with electronics, it changes how the music is made, but . . .

HT: Well economically too Brian, it puts a lot of cats out of work. That's the worst part. Technically, you say, hey we can beat the price, and that's what you were just wondering on the improvisational part, and that's with these movies where two people will be in there makin' movie soundtracks. If you are a musician you know and it just drives you crazy, you remember when there were all live people, playing the dickens out of the music.

BC: Seems there's a lot less people able to make a livelihood out of hiphop. It's not like there's several different levels, now you make a lot of money or nothing. A lot of that has to do with integration too. Like the argument is made by Nelson George about the Negro leagues. They had a whole sector of people employed with black owned black run teams, but when they integrated you have a few players make a lot of money, but you've lost the infrastructure.

HT: That's it, it's all racial, it all comes from the top, and it's all splintering things behind it. . . . The idea is to be recognizable as an African American who has made a contribution toward the goldness that comes out of this country: you had a great part in it, each race had a great part in this country and should be recognized for that contribution to this big bowl of soup as they call it. And that's where the word 'respect' comes to mind. You begin to respect the people better, just offering different creative things to the community in which you live. Those people start being recognized to the point where they are utilized and can function within that community, but you have to have a certain kind of control over what it is that you do and where you're at. Otherwise you get this splintering. All of a sudden Hollywood wants to get a hold of it, then it becomes something else, you know?

Like you say, the only money you can make is big money, or no money, you dig. And all the younger cats are racing to 'let me be number one this week'. The whole essence of things is lost: I thought you were going to write me four bars, 'cause you love the music, or dance 'cause you love to, but now you trying to be number one so it's gonna be a hit or so and so.

BC: How did you put the Arkestra together?

HT: I put it together out of necessity, for the music and the art. We did it to be informative as well as play music for the young people of the community. They didn't have to play an instrument, they could sing and dance and act, that kind of thing. Our thing was to tell the truth about everything that we knew, that all the things we were taught previously, they were lies. We could prove it, some of the old people that had been around could come and talk to the youngsters and then we'd play . . .

We pulled the Arkestra together on the other hand 'cause the music was changin' up. A lot of youngsters was comin' in 1957 and '58 and didn't have no place to play, no venues at all. You could come to this house and play, you could spend 24 hours if you liked learning the art . . . whether you were a musician or whatever. People became very intimate and spiritual. People follow music, it opens things up, people listen to a drummer, they listen to it and it gets their attention. You have these concerts and we'd utilize the media to our own purpose. Understanding what our community was and how we was working in it, if you didn't realize this man then you was just a stump. People were hanging out like they wanted to be together, so we started out a 35-piece group, 35 guys the first time, in this house on

56th Street and Figueroa, then there was another house, we started doing original music. They come out of the black community, black writers and things. It didn't really have any straight-in, downright military purpose, it played many parts, it brought people together and helped them relaxing from going wild cause they had a place to talk and meet people, and concentrate on creating things together now . . . It was that kind of thing built over a period of 25 to 30 years . . .

BC: What was UGMA?

HT: The first thing was Underground Musicians Association, then as the years went on it changed to UGMAA, the Union of God's Musicians and Artists Ascension, and that was all of the artists.

BC: So a lot of accounts of that history say that the main boom for cultural activity happened after '65. Is that true?

HT: They just noticed it then, 'cause in '61 and '62 we were giving free breakfasts out in Watts. The Black Panthers, the US group (Ron Karenga's), all these groups were in the community, functioned in various ways for blacks, we were the only music they had, was the Arkestra. We played at all their things, there was tribal things every now and then. But the Arkestra would bring them together, let's put it like that. It would bring all the people together and they would start realizing other things. We were part of the whole motion, the movement that started out here, in fact some of the beginners of it.

We had a place out in Watts to do it in, and we continued in the church house; before that we went to Whitney High School, we spent time over there . . . had functions there all the time, this is all in 1963, '64. We were blamed for beginning the insurrection in 1965, out on 163rd Street 'cause of the music we were playing. People were dancing in the streets and singing our music, the police would come up and take the microphone and say, 'I want them downtown to hear and see how this begun.' A cop came up to me in the coffeehouse and started saying, 'Stop the band. Stop the music.' I said, 'What?' More music came up, and he said, 'Stop the goddamn music.' They had pregnant women standing against the wall with their hands up. So we were blamed. Meanwhile down at the park, there it began. The so-called riots began down there.

And the music kept playin', so naturally we got the union informed that we were a nationalist band. Sometime when the Arkestra would go to South Park on 51st and Avalon, the union – this is how integration started acting up – the Local 47 started coming into the community. Years before that I had gone down to Local 47 and said, 'Hey man, bring the music into the community. We could provide funds for the musicians and all that.' After the riots (so-called) happened, the Local 47 had a big mix band down at South Park. We were down at the Malcolm X Center, the Arkestra, you dig, on Broadway, me and my bass player David Bryant went down to South Park to listen and see what was happening, and the president of the union at the time waved to me, ran over and said, 'Horace, why it's you.' And this was on a Sunday, we left and went back to the Malcolm X and meanwhile the

Black Panthers came in and ran the band off the stage, and said, 'Get out of here! Where's the Arkestra?!'

On Monday the president called my house and said I hadn't paid my dues and they suspended me, and you know none of the cats of my band were in the union. The president called me and said, 'You done got the job out there on Sunday', and I said, 'I'm not in the union.' He said: 'Don't worry about it'; I said: 'None of my band is in the union.' He said: 'Don't worry about it.' We didn't go down there to do that. I just came and checked it out, but some of these Panthers went off, two of 'em had guns. They didn't shoot nobody, but they got up on the mike and naturally the cats left. It was just that we had so much motion in the community, almost everything functioned where the music was at. We did work for free. Of course, some of these cats we had work for free to help, they got in positions, and they started hiring somebody else, you dig? You didn't even exist no more for some reason.

All kinds of things came out of the black community. We showcased it 'cause it was radical and it was necessary. Nowadays you can turn on the radio and the television and see some of the things that were started then . . . There were no gangbangers, few guns. Every time people would get together and they had a difference, they'd be dancing it off. It was very different times as far as folks becoming aware. Once people can see and hear and feel something that comes from them, there's no point in worrying about whether you're number one, 'cause you're always gonna be there. In their minds, you just there now. Might not be musician, but they were raised on the music, they don't have to wear it on their shoulders, they lived it, it's a day to day thing. That's the part that makes you feel that it was all worth it, you know what I'm saying?

I feel really bad that a lot of these kids are doing creative things and they think the people they doing it for care for them. And in two years they either busted or dead or on the streets, 'cause they out of their pocket now, now all the fighting in the trenches has been done. Now the jump-on-the-bandwagon people come along and scoop up what they want, and all the functions that's supposed to come from within the community is outside control of it. That sickens me . . . Mickey Stevenson, one of the Motown producers of the sixties and seventies, says we would have been insultin' somebody's intelligence makin' these albums that they let through nowadays. I left the scene working in the studios et cetera 'cause it took away certain things that I believed in.

JMD: One time when you invited me and Nilijah to come see you at Catalinas, we was having a good old time. You blew up, typical Horace show. I just looked at Ni and she just burst into tears, crying, 'Muthafucker is a genius, ain't nobody gives him the credit he deserves', and she was right. 'My father walks around Crenshaw, everybody know my father.' Except for here in America. You know. And that kind of jacked her up on me: 'I don't want you to sell out, but I don't want you to – I want you to be able to make a living.' I mean she boo-hooed all the way home. 'I won't compromise, we can be poor too.'

BC: . . . The statistics I have read from just '60 to '65, the number of people that got shot in the back, is unbelievable.

JMD: Yeah, if you ran you was guilty. My mother always said don't run . . .

HT: . . . Then there was Chief Parker [of the Los Angeles Police Department]. Nija's Mama refused to work when he was in the hospital, she was a nurse. He was in there bleeding, and she said let him die, she refused to do anything to help him. There was a cat and his wife going to the hospital one day, on Avalon. The police pulled him over, took his gun out. The guy said, 'I'm taking my wife to the hospital.' And they shot the guy. Talkin' about how his gun hit the window and went off accidentally, that was the first insurrection before '65, that's when everyone was upset and the police was in trouble . . . they finally said 'Later'. The police stopped coming in the neighbourhood after a while 'cause the snipers started – they'd just shoot you man, they'd come out BANG! Not 'Halt', but BANG! They used to be recruited in the newspapers from Mississippi, the white officers. Big old ad, in Mississippi police offices. To come here to LA.

BC: The thing about Parker is they say he made it [the LAPD] into this military regime . . .

HT: It was. It is . . . On 56th Street, I would leave my house, and the car was following me everywhere. They came to my door one day, in Hawaiian shirts and black sunglasses, and I had been out all night, and I was on my way to the pad, and I drive by and see these two white cats on my doorstep, and she looks at me like that. I kept on driving, I didn't come home for two days . . . anything like that to get you down. I been working with the Panthers, gonna be under surveillance, they saw what we was talking about, every time we would go to a college an insurrection would happen . . . So I was under the gun for a long time, couldn't work anywhere, strange things would happen with the mail. They used to try to plant things on you, and come bust you. 'Cause once you get involved with the community and people started listening to you, then you become dangerous. Blow you away man . . .

. . . We have the community marching band, got all kind of drums in it, this marching band will have the conga drums in it. We thinking along the fact that it should have at least eight trumpets, four tubas, and a flatbed to roll in after the soloist, a bass player. Yeah it's all planned now, we got two pieces already. That's how it seems to be planned, something for every aspect of the black community, someone doing poetry, and dances, all in one parade. Number of drum and bugle corps . . . I remember parades in the black community when I was a kid, I got so excited, only I used to run when I heard the drums in the far distance, boom boom boom, I'd run in the house, my sister would come and get me from under the bed, I'd say, here come the drums.

JMD: That's how I started man, I used to march in the Compton Scorpios. I couldn't even play, I had a drum set, but I was still unco-ordinated, to learn how to march and play, that's when the shit started comin' together. I could just play beats, but marching and doing steps and playin', that let me know what the real funk was about. It was just us and the drill team, we used to win first place and if we didn't get first place we started cryin' 'cause we were just that bad, man. We were the baddest of the bad little marching bands.

BC: That's where jazz came from too, from marching bands, right?

HT: How I heard it was, wherever they had the slaves at, they threw the old beat-up horns at 'em, old beat-up brass things that wasn't no good, to the slaves . . .

BC: After the civil war apparently there was an abundance of instruments from their marching bands [the armies].

HT: There was an abundance of a lot of things. Louisiana, Georgia, we do know it was in the south, we do know that's where it began. Louis Armstrong asks where did jazz begin? It came out of the uterus, it just began, I don't know. All I know is I enjoy playin' it.

KAMAU DAA'OOD

Kamau Daa'ood is a performance poet and community arts activist. He was an active member of the Watts Writers' Workshop and UGMAA. Currently he is part of the black arts revival centred around the Leimert Park district on Crenshaw Boulevard. With prolific jazz drummer Billy Higgins he founded the World Stage which is a store-front performance gallery dedicated to providing a venue for the development of jazz and poetry. He also owns Final Vinyl, a great resource store also in Leimert which has become a popular haunt for jazz lovers and hiphop producers. This interview took place at the World Stage in 1992.

Brian Cross: Talk a little bit about the Watts Writers' Workshop.
Kamau Daa'ood: I got involved with the Workshop when I was about 18 years old . . . I had seen this play by Leroi Jones, Amiri Biraka called *Black Mass* on Broadway Boulevard in LA [during] my senior year in high school and it really kind of turned me around . . . I was sitting on the side and there was a red light on the other side of Baraka – and he was reading and spit was flying from his mouth it looked like fire coming from his mouth . . . There was a programme I saw on TV about the Workshop, and it had Ojenke, Eric Priestley, Emmery Evans and K. Curtis Lyle in it . . . So eventually I found they had a branch on the west side, and one in Watts . . . I met people like Otis [Smith] of the Watts Prophets who was very instrumental in encouraging me along. Ojenke was really the cat, like a horn player tries to play like Trane – Ojenke had that influence on me . . .

There were two basic styles of poetry developing at that time: one centred around rhyme, bluesy, out of the tradition of Langston Hughes; the other school leaned more towards imagery, phrase lines of poetry more like a saxophone solo, out of the tradition of Amiri Baraka. I wanted my work to sound like Coltrane riffs and sheets of sound. All the work at that time was fiery social commentary, we were all on a mission to bring light to the minds.

The first time I read was at South Park. Ted, Lena Horne's son, had seen me with some work and asked me to come on stage and read. Horace Tapscott and the full Arkestra were playing 'Equinox' by John Coltrane behind the work, it was a heck of a debut. That was probably 1969.

BC: Where was the jazz scene located at that time, was it Central?

KD: Central Avenue was gone by the late sixties. There were a few clubs left in the community, Marty's on the Hill, Memory Lane, Parisian Room, The Tropicana, The IT Club and a few others. We had to go out of the community more and more to hear our music, The Lighthouse, Troubadour, Shelly's Manne Hole. The Society for the Preservation of Black Music was started by John Carter, Horace Tapscott and UGMAA. The Society would put on these last Sunday of the month concerts featuring local talent at Foshay Junior High School.

The arts were very much integrated at the time, you had dancers, voices, I used to read my poetry in the context of the Arkestra really as another soloist. The tenor player might take a solo, then I might take a solo, it would be that context and it was good training, 'cause very seldom was it a rehearsed kind of situation. Like many times Horace would be playing and he would look at me and I gotta find something that's appropriate, like waiting for the water to be just right. It was improvisation, words changed from what was written on the page, emphasis changed according to what needed to be emphasized at the time.

It was a great experience, I met a lot of wonderful people. That's what is so beautiful about the community creative process, the people involved have a tendency to teach others through their example and that there are other ways of approaching this life, other than the cubical kind of perspective that is for us. There are very few settings where the young can meet with the older and share information, and I think it has a lot to do with the kind of mindset the media has placed us all in . . . that's a difference now.

BC: I often think how different hiphop would be if we had a Central Avenue, or an UGMAA, a public sphere . . .

KD: I read this article once, and they were talking about how a lot of older people think the younger generation has let them down, dropped the torch, and the young lady was saying, 'Y'all didn't pass no torch in the first place.' And that's the problem I think, it's that gap that happened. A lot of young people think they had to develop in a vacuum. It's not always easy when you have to start from scratch to do something . . . scratch [laughs]. But I think hiphop would be much more different in that there would be a lot more depth to it – its complexities in terms of its polyrhythms and its mastery of that, even its complexities in terms of rhymes – it could take that to another level . . .

BC: But even its ability to refer, it seems to stop around 1970, with sampling . . .

KD: You can't really separate what was happening with the art from the times. The country was in a state of rebellion, revolution on an outward and an inward level. A lot of shackles that bound people were broken away from them. They began to discover their bodies. The whole beginning of this multiculturalism began in that period in terms of even being aware of other cultures, dibbing and dallying in other thoughts, a lot of that took place in the early sixties. Things got out of hand as well, the powers that be took a whole other approach in terms of regaining control, the powers that be determined that this would never happen again. They went into their think tanks and figured out how to ensure that. Everything from this chemical warfare of drugs that has plagued the community to the gang situation to the AIDS epidemic, there would be no more explosions, only implosions. That's just the reality as far as I am concerned.

BC: What do you remember of COINTELPRO?

KD: There was a struggle to regain control, and control anything that did not fit in the status quo. The Panthers, any civil rights organization, and I guess because of the truth and the hardness and the reality painting that was taking place in the black arts movement at the time, the Workshop was moved on. We might be naive about the powers of the arts, but the establishment is not. They know the power of the art.

There is a reason why the radio programming changed drastically. There was a time you could hear anything, but about '72 to '73, the whole approach started to change. I think one of the things is they really started to understand the media. They understood that one of [the] reasons why things spread so fast across the country is they were being covered by the media, so they stopped reporting things the way they did before. Things were played down . . .

BC: So let's talk about your own work since then.

KD: Until now I mean there really wasn't a serious place for a word musician. Back then you had a lot of poets across the country. The main thing that the poets did is they published little broadsides, and there were a lot of poetry readings. But these artists have lives that must be supported, and there were very few ways that serious artists could make a living at what they did. I'm talking about wordsmiths, those that had savvy, played the school thing and taught. There were a few luminaries who could make a living through publishing, and then there were those who aligned themselves with the music . . .

When I was eighteen, poets Fatisha, Odie Hawkins, Emmery Evans and I were approached by Laugh Records (ALA Records) about doing an album. They were trying to capitalize off of the success of the Last Poets. Me and Fatisha had the attorney check out the contract and basically we would have been selling ourselves into slavery so the day before we were supposed to go in we backed out. They called in Ed Bereal who was a dramatist – he had a mean group called the Bodacious Bouguerillas, a guerilla theatre group, street theatre – and Father Amdee (Anthony Hamilton), and that's how *Black Voices on the Streets of Watts* got recorded. They had offered us a hundred dollars and for 18-year-olds that was a little bit of change. And the way it was set up and they still try to do it, they charge all the cost of the album to the artist, and once that money is recouped from the sales, then the artist can begin to get a percentage. And if their album fails the artist ends up owing the company money, and the contract had us locked in for seven years, and we were so uncompromising, we really missed a lot of opportunity being such purists. Around that time I got a call from Umar from the Last Poets asking me to join them but I wasn't willing to leave LA.

At this stage in my life I see my work as healing, mending psyches through the arts, [to] create space for this to happen, the ritual space of performance, the classroom, the one on one magic, the World Stage. To produce, to perform, to educate. Always try to remember that the healer must first heal thyself, a constant struggle. After all the bullshit has past, it's about life and the human potential, our relations with each other, our relationship with the Creator. It ain't about money or *stardumb*. It's about truth and dignity and the sacredness of breathing. You struggle to make music of your moments.

BC: So how did you get involved with Billy Higgins?

KD: I stayed involved with the Arkestra for years, the Pan African People's Arkestra. I continued to do readings at colleges, I aligned myself with musicians and all of that; as an artist I had to stay involved whenever I could. But it's hard to make a living, especially if you don't fit into the role of the starving weird artist dope fiend crazy. I grounded myself in what I was taught in the Arkestra. The idea of the community artist is really a noble concept, you serve the community rather than star status, you really serve people. I believe the work I have done here has really been appreciated. I have learned things.

I did hundreds of readings and performed with numerous bands, we built a community centre called the Gathering, food co-ops, not funded, alternative schools for the children, supported by the artists, by the concerts and the readings and the theatre. Later I started working with the jazz festivals at the Watts Towers, I was one of the founders of the Drum festivals down there. It's like trying to write poetry in between the exhale and the inhale. I teach occasionally, I taught at CSUN (California State University at Northridge), at Otis Parsons, places like that . . .

If we were gearing our stuff towards the coffins made in Hollywood, doors would have opened up, but we were pointing to the sores in society, the inequities, we spoke of Allah. Always this alternative approach and world view that was being put forth, so why in the hell would somebody finance an alternative view to theirs?

I met Billy Higgins on this journey. Billy is a light, a globe traveller collecting rhythms of the world in his heart. They radiate in his smile. It is through our experiences that our spirits shape. We founded the World Ṣtage: Performance Gallery, a place where the community deposits its laughter and tears and transforms them into music and poetry. It has become a vital force in the creative community of south central. Thoughts are things when you begin to think a certain way, you begin to gravitate and other things begin to gravitate towards you. You begin to seek, you begin to find. That's why artists need to watch their lyrics, the word can heal and the word can cause disease. A lot of these cats be throwing out concepts and they really don't know the power.

Back in the sixties there was bloodshed and people were willing to die for their beliefs and although when I look back a lot of that was irrational madness, but the heart was pure, [compared] to today where I think a lot of people talk a good game, but I don't think they really believe what they say. They would not stand behind what they say with their lives, there was a lot of good people that ended up in jail and dead for what they said.

WATTS PROPHETS

The Watts Prophets (Anthony Hamilton – Amdee – Richard Dedeaux and Otis Smith) in many ways provided the inspiration for this book. They are the godfathers of Los Angeles hiphop. I was introduced to Amdee by Roni Walters, a young African American clothing designer who sat in on the first interview. The Prophets have re-formed since this first meeting with Amdee and are finally beginning to get the kind of respect they deserve. They recorded one album as the Watts Prophets called *Rappin' Black in a White World* and did several other projects including a song on Quincy Jones's *Mellow Madness* album and an interlude to Don Cherry's *Multikulti* album. The second interview took place in late 1992, in my apartment.

Part One

Roni Walters: *Rappin' Black in a White World*, how long did that take to record?
Amdee: One take, that was one take. We were ready when we went into the studio. We had over 35 different presentations. We went into the poverty programme and the community centres during the day, and working clubs actively every night. We played in clubs where they had wire protecting us, we would do poetry anywhere. I remember one time, there was about 10,000 people at Oceanview Park and we were supposed to do poetry, and these were the things that let us know rap music could really touch people – there were pit bulls fighting, barbecues et cetera, and it was lively, so the guy was like, 'We're going to put you guys over in this little auditorium over here, 'cause nobody wants to listen to poetry right now.' And we said, 'Oh man, with all these people here, just give us the microphone and the stage and let us worry about that.' We got up and about the middle of the first poem they stopped the dogs fighting and the whole park became quiet and set there and listened to about an hour presentation of our poetry.

So we knew clearly what the effects of rap was going to be. We realized that disco music was drowning out spoken word, was drowning out the word and we had a saying, 'First came the word, not a song, not an instrument, first was the word and they would always go back to the word.' That was our intention, we wanted to bring the word back out in front, and that could have been the influence of the fifties and sixties music, where there was plenty of pretty music, but you could always understand what was being said.

All the things we did, we did for the benefit of the community, we didn't do a play just to do a play, we did it to raise the consciousness of the community. And that was sort of the spirit of the sixties, we did a lot of right things and we did a lot of wrong things during the sixties. One of the wrong things that we did is the constant building of hostility and the constant blaming of whitey for our problems. That day is long gone. If we feel like we are a slave than we are a slave by choice, we have to take care of our own thing. We got into a civil rights syndrome, that is really more destructive today than it is constructive. We're the people that say be free, but Clarence Thomas is not free to be himself, because he is not into the civil rights thing. We have a group of black leaders who are beggars who have failed miserably. Any person who calls himself a black leader today should be ashamed. Where has he led us? We're last in everything except crime on earth, we're a wonderful people and we could pull out of this, but we have to turn to ourselves. If you asked the average black person who was the last person to do him a goddamned dirty lick it was another black person. We're not saying there isn't racism, there is, but we all know that. It's up to this generation to move it a step further. People would be surprised to hear the Watts Prophets today, as we may seem to be ultra conservative. The other day a brother came up to me and said, 'Welcome King and Queen' to my wife and I said, 'Maybe we used to be Kings and Queens before, and maybe we will be again, but today we're last in everything.' And he had to say, 'Yeah you're right, brother.' We've got to stop playing with our destiny. I have a poem 'Clowns All Around'; we're turning black into materiality, clothing, hair, shoes, rap, but these aren't the things that feed our children and send them to school. We need to have individual accomplishment to have group unity.

I wrote a poem the other day:

> Be collective when you can, take a stand
> Most important be your own woman and man.
> And keep your destiny in your hand
> Look first to yourself for wealth . . .

After the '65 riots, Budd Schulberg came to Watts and established the Watts Writers' Workshop. I came to the workshop in 1966, and there were so many writers and poets there and such large requests from all over the country for writers from the Watts area to go and speak and do their poetry that writers began to go out in groups; four or five writers would go together, two sisters, two brothers and from that the Watts Prophets formed. Richard,

Otis and myself started going together. At the beginning we didn't care much for each other's poetry. Richard Dedeaux was a Louisiana creole and wrote poems like 'What Color is Black?' while Otis Smith, who was from the deep South, took black in a very serious way. And here I'm from the city, I am sort of between all of it. But we started reading together and people started requesting us.

We entered a talent show at the Inner City Cultural Center. We took second place in the show, but just before we went out, they asked us our name. We looked at each other and said 'I don't know' and a girl who was standing there waiting to read poetry said, 'Well you guys are the Watts Prophets.' And from that day on we took that name. And we began to read all over the country. We had requests from Harvard, all over . . .

But there was always something holding it back. It finally came out in the end. Just like whenever black people have introduced something new in the field of music, like when jazz came out they fought it, when bebop came out they fought it, when rhythm and blues came out they fought it, and when rap came out they fought it. I'll just give you some proof of how viciously they fought rap: it is the issue of *Mother Jones* magazine called 'The Meanest Dirtiest Trickster Ever'. This is a picture of the man I hired as the Watts Prophets PR man, Darthard Perry. He destroyed the careers of a great many writers in the workshop. Like the Watts Prophets.

Brian Cross: Why do you think this guy set out to single-handedly destroy the careers of everybody involved?

A: A network of informants were sent to the community right after the Watts Riots, right after the sixties.

BC: Were they put there by the FBI or by Parker?

A: By the Federal Bureau of Investigation. They were harassing and destroying black organizations all over America.

BC: So it would be consistent with what was happening to the Panthers?

A: There you go. Well, the same things were happening to us, the cultural organizations. This man kept telling us that he was telling the FBI that we were nothing but a workshop; there was nothing there but poets, singers, writers, and actors, we didn't have any guns, we weren't planning a revolution. And it was really. It was a workshop like I guess will never be seen again. It was like a hospital Bud Schulberg had brought to the midst of a bunch of hungry deprived artists. You'd see them walk in there head down in a dejected state and after a couple of weeks you'd see them, holding their head high with a smile on their face, feeling they were somebody.

That's what happened to me. I didn't know I was a writer. But I always would write on little pieces of paper and then just throw them away. I didn't know what, I just wrote and threw them away. In 1966 I had just gotten out of prison and was looking for a job, so I used to go to the poverty programme every morning. And I'd be scribbling and throwing it away. There was a writer there who has about 13 novels out now, Odie Hawkins. He was picking up the little pieces of paper, and one day he finally stopped me and says, 'Hey man, so you're a writer?' And I said, 'Oh no, I'm an eighth grade drop-out and I can't spell.' And he said, 'Man, you're a poet.' He asked me to come up to the Watts Writers' Workshop. At that time I was in between going back to drugs and the streets because things weren't working out. That's what I meant when I said this place was a hospital. I asked him, 'You all have anything to eat over there?' You know, that's really the reason I went to the class.

So I read some of the stuff I had scribbled on the pieces of paper and the class really loved it. And from there a poem, really I could say a poem saved my life, because from that poem I realized I could do something. I had something inside of me. And then I started writing and then on to the Watts Prophets.

BC: So was it Dee Dee MacNeil who put the music to the poetry?

A: We always had music, we'd play with drums et cetera, but with Dee Dee she brought a fresher approach, more knowledge about music, how to mix it up. She had been under contract with Motown as a songwriter, had written 'What is a Man?' for the Four Tops' songs for Diana Ross, she wrote Rita Marley's biggest hit 'The Beauty of Jah's Plan'. We heard her playing a tune for a play called *The Iron Hand of Nat Turner* and the tune was called 'Black in a White World' and we said, 'We want that girl in our group.'

RW: Is she still writing?

A: Yes. She's in the clubs. In all the jazz clubs, Dee Dee is well known. When she stopped performing with the Watts Prophets, she started singing, so now that's what she does. She mixes poetry with her act. She is really the mother of all the women rappers. She was the first one to rap.

What made the Watts Prophets so different was that we were so visual. Each poem was to us a complete play and each poet contributed to that. We didn't just stand on stage or walk back and forth like they are doing now, we would act it out. If I was talking about the drug addict or drunk, well one of the poets would be drunk and the other would be nodding, and then they would say things that would help push the point. We took this concept we had stumbled on so seriously that we moved in together, and for over two years all we did was poetry every way you can imagine.

The Last Poets' album came out a little before ours, but we didn't know anything about the Last Poets and they didn't know anything about us. They were as far east as you can get and we were as far as you can go west. And this seemed to be growing in the ghettos of America at the time.

RW: When did the Last Poets and the Watts Prophets finally meet?

A: At a performance at USC [University of Southern California]. I am trying to get the tape of that performance right now. It's the only time the Last Poets and the WPs were together, and if you could see that tape, you could really see the foundation of where rap is today. The style of the Last Poets is more like Umar from New York, where as you see coming out of Compton, Eazy E is more the Watts Prophets, more my style in particular.

RW: When was the last gig you guys performed?

A: '79, '80 somewhere around there, that was the last performance. But we stayed together for 14 years, and we were faithful. We didn't know what was happening to us. At first, we began to notice all of our opportunities falling through, after the first four or five years. Then we began to say things to each other like, 'Hey man, you shouldn't have said that poem, "Ask not what you can do for your country". That's causing trouble, that's the President of the US, don't say that poem anymore.' And the other poet would say, 'Well I'm free to say what I want to say.' So we began to have these kind of little bickerings. Then, after we'd solved that, we began to say things to each other like, 'Hey man you ought to take that cussing out, you know there's too much cussing, that's what turning people off.' And so we took the cursing out. Then we said, 'Hey man, let's stop saying black, let's try and be more universal.' And we began to argue over stuff like that. Because we knew something was wrong but we thought it was us. We couldn't understand it when we had a standing ovation every reading . . .

We were approached to change our style. Laugh Records came to us and said: 'Look, you guys have a multi-million-dollar art form here, you don't realize what you've got, we could all be rich, but this is what we want you guys to do: we want you to put a little disco music to that' – that's right, disco – 'and we want you guys to start dancing' – exactly what the rappers are doing today. 'We want you to take that black stuff out; make sure you take that out, and dance.' We were furious, we were poets and that's what we told them, 'Look, we're poets.'

We got in a big argument with Laugh Records, because it was a blue label, Richard Pryor and Pigmeat Markham were on that label – we told them we're not comedians, you gotta do something, so the record company started this subsidiary called ALA records in order to release our albums.

We used to go to the prisons to read poetry. This one time we went to San Quentin and we asked to visit the brothers in the hole, the isolated ones. We were sitting at a table across from each other, and there was a guard standing about three feet from us – we had to hold an interview that way. These brothers, when they sat down set this package right on the table and during the interview whispered, 'Would you take some poetry out for us?' With the guard right there, I just nodded my head and when I got up to go I picked up the package and took it out. This led to a KCET-aired film called *Victory Will Be My Moan* by Sue Booker. And in it you'll see us doing poetry from behind bars similar to what Eazy E did in some of his videos. It won several awards.

Part Two

Brian Cross: I want to fill some things in. What were you doing before the Watts Prophets, Otis?

Otis Smith: I was just starting a family, I had a job at one time, a local job, I worked for Bob Glover; that was about it as far as jobs go. I had been writing for a while, that was the attraction to the Watts Prophets when they started up. I never showed my writing to anyone, I just wrote. I was writing and then when the workshop started up I started going, and then after the riots everybody had classes. Screen Writers Guild had a class, KCET had a class. I started taking all of them, writing classes, I got involved. Then out of the workshop, I met Richard and Amdee.

Amdee: I first met you through Mafundi.

OS: George Bolin, but everybody was always into everybody else 'cause it was so close. The workshop was about to open at that time.

BC: And what was Mafundi?

OS: Mafundi was like the workshop in that it was a kinda artistic institution.

A: It was a Watts happening coffee house, that's where Watts Writers' Workshop grew out of. It's where the Mafundi Institute grew out of, that's where all the –

Richard Dedeaux: It was the Mafundi Coffee House. There was us. There was the Panthers. They was right all next to each other on 103rd.

OS: There was a guy by the name of George Bolin, who was a poet too. He said, 'You two should get to know each other', and he was referring to Amdee. It was a couple of months before we finally got to meet. By that time the workshop was happening, and out of that, first time I saw them was in a play.

RD: *Finder's Keepers.*

A: *Losers Weepers*, yes.

OS: That was when some of the TV people like NBC was giving some of the people a little play, primarily Harry Dolan.

RD: We all come from different directions. When I came to the Watts Writers' Workshop I had been to the Committee in Hollywood. I studied under Farrell Perry for a while. Then I went to the Cellar Theater on Vermont, and then I hooked up with this Irish Repertory Theater. I saw the ad in the paper. It was the Donnybrook Players, and I stayed with them with Behan – what's his name? Yeah, we did *Shadow of a Gunman* and *Molly Brian* and that was a lot of fun. We used to go across the street to the Irish bar on 6th and Vermont, right across from the theatre, and they taught me how the Irish . . . Well, we all had the same problem, 'cause [of] the English – but any way, we all ended up at the workshop. I was mainly into acting. I had written two plays and I was interested in gettin' that started. I ended up gettin' involved with the Watts Writers' Workshop. Anthony was teaching the workshop then, and I was in the actors' workshop, when Ted Lange came in. We had a hell of a theatre, which is another story.

OS: The workshop at that time was very much alive. People was comin' from everywhere. Whites was comin', blacks was comin', it was alive. My first real introduction to theatre was . . . there used to be a theatre right on Fountain, I'm sure it's gone – but I remember sittin'

112

there. It was primarily a white theatre. It was a white play. I was makin' up things in my head, not writing them, but it fired me up, the poet was born.

BC: Which poets were at the workshop then?

A: Ojenke, Eric Priestley, Johnny Scott, Eric Sherman, James Tomas Jackson, K. Curtis Lyle, Quincy Troupe.

RD: A Latino brother, let's not forget him.

A: Lee Omas, Gurl McGee, these were all real great poets. Alprentiss 'Bunchy' Carter never came to the Watts Writers' Workshop, [but] I knew him. He was a Black Panther and he was really one of the first LA street poets, bar none. He had a form of rapping, it was his street poetry. He was close maybe to the Slausons, that's where he came from. His mother lives right there down the street from David Moseley, which is in Watts. He had some very fiery poetry. He had his own style, and he did it on the street corners, he didn't do a lot of readings; he was the kind of guy who would jump out of his car and slap the pimp. Tell the hos, run 'em all off the corner . . .

But then there's something else about that, about Watts and rap. Watts has always been [a] very very vocal community. Maxine Waters is a rapper. People that come from out there talk good, I don't know why, those people have always been very, very vocal, and it's always been a rapping thing. A very vocal community and you saw on that Watts album (OFTB). They always say the wrong thing, 'Chief Gates, muthafuck you!' This is the kind of shit, the kind of boldness, people from out there could rap. They always had that.

BC: So when was the first time you guys performed together?

OS: 1970, '71.

A: We had been going around not as the Watts Prophets around '68, reading together. Otis came to the workshop a little later than the rest of us.

OS: Helen performed with us for a while. We started playing a lot of places. She was married at the time, was a real estate broker. She quit. She was much more politically aware, lived in Baldwin Hills at the time.

BC: What about Dee Dee [MacNeil]?

A: Her and Jean and – who died – were sitting at the piano doing *Black in a White World* which was a play and she told us she wasn't a singer and we told her she was a singer. We started going to her house and encouraging her.

OS: We were doing the colleges in the day and clubs at night. We started doing shows, we was like the talk –

A: John Daniels had a great deal to do with us. He was the one who saw what we could do. He watched us, he videoed us, twenty years ago, the first video. And he told us get out there and act, get rid of the paper. Richard had a lot of the acting skills . . .

OS: Once I went out and had red ink and red light, so I realized I had to memorize my poems.

A: I insisted on having the paper.

OS: Yeah, but he would go out and the paper would be upside down.

RD: He started writing the poems all up and down his arm.

A: That's true, I still do it.

RD: We did sixteen weeks at Mavericks; that was before the album. We changed the whole atmosphere there, Richard Pryor –

OS: George Clinton and the Funkadelics, I remember that so well. They were different, one of them had a red underwear suit, they ripped the place up.

A: And then John didn't pay them so they robbed the place, but then they had them back!

BC: The first album came out in '70, was that before the Watts Prophets?

A: Yeah, but the Watts Prophets were in existence. I came down to the studio, and I said I have a group, the Watts Prophets. He said we'll cut this one then we'll cut that one, so we came down to Maverick Flats and we cut it. Odie Hawkins was my teacher and the one who discovered me as a writer. He had a group called the Bodacious Bouguerillas . . . which was one of the greatest guerilla theatre groups ever.

RD: At the workshop we did several plays and –

A: Then he brought community television there. KCET did community news in south central, big cameras, rolling things. Richard made 'em bring two cameras to Broadway in Watts, and all the community stuff was filmed there.

RD: Which is where *Victory Will Be My Moan* came from, our first documentary. We shot it in San Quentin.

OS: We had problems all the way with this trip. When we got to San Francisco, they didn't want us to have a rental car. The prison didn't want us to come, but we performed . . .

A: We did prison after prison after prison, the fed, the pen and the juveniles. When we started poetry it was our idea to take poetry to the schools, breakfast in the schools, Headstart, all those were Black Panther ideas.

OS: At the time we was doing poetry, we did prisons, nightclubs, schools, worked with the Panthers, the Red Cross, they all called on us, the Boy Scouts. We went to a men's club and they said you guys is the greatest thing we ever seen.

A: We did poverty shows, with five or six people in the projects, to auditoriums. We'd do our shit, sit down and talk to them, then do some more poetry. The celebrities would be just sitting there frozen. We took pictures with James Earl Jones, Quincy Jones, but strangely those pictures disappeared –

OS: I imagine some of those people got the pictures but never brought them out.

A: From the very beginning we tried to incorporate the music; we used to listen to instrumentals, and then we started playing with whoever was there, bass, drummers, whoever, guitar and drums, whatever was there. Whoever wanted to sit in, oooh ooooh oooh, the drummers on that album were good. Odie Hawkins had played a long time. The bass player on the first album was good. He was well known on Central Avenue for playing with Sonny Criss. I think he was playing at that time.

OS: Everybody saw us, Jim Brown, everybody saw us, we were shocking – the CIA and all these other people were out there. We were saying things about the system, we were so out there. The Last Poets were saying things about black on black, but we were just addressing everything [yet] now we're not really remembered.

BC: But a lot of people do remember, that is proved because of sampling. But even DJ Quik was saying that he remembers he was scared when he heard you guys. Quik of all people.

A: We scared a lot of people.

OS: Some of the bourgeois liked it, but they didn't want to say they liked it in the suburbs.

A: I did my poetry to nothing but a black audience once, a 'bougie' audience, and they were like what do you mean by that, honkie and stuff? I was mad. I was like what do you mean, what do I mean? We read once at Loyola Marymount which is where the black doctors and lawyers go and this girl stood up and said condescendingly, 'There is some people here call themselves poets.' But everybody had started leaving the auditorium.

OS: I remember James Baldwin and stuff listening. They was froze. By any poet out of the Watts Workshop, we had become an ensemble.

A: People said it's not just what you guys say, it's how you look, the background voices.

BC: Amdee, you said the first poem you ever heard was 'Signifying Monkey', is that true for the rest of you?

OS: No, I grew up in the south, and they had segregated schools there, so you were constantly getting introduced to black history. My teacher, her name was Miss Whitwell, introduced us to a lot of the black arts. My poets was like Paul Dunbar and Langston Hughes, and James Weldon Johnson and Claude McKay, they was common. That's why when I came to LA and I was coming to my adulthood and they were talking about Black History month, it really didn't make no difference to me. I was performing poetry when I was a little kid and another poet I heard which really wasn't a black poet was Rudyard Kipling, the poem 'If'. I performed 'The Creation', I was a little prayerboy and they would take me from church to church and you'd do a poem and you'd pray. I did a lot of other things like 'The Little Brown Baby with Sparkling Eyes', lies lies.

RD: I was influenced by not only the black writers that Otis was talking about but Kenneth Patchen, Rod McKuen, and I always had hope in my poetry; it was real interesting, see, when I went to the Watts Writers' Workshop. I did my poetry there, because I had been with the Donnybrook Players. So when I took my work to the workshop Ojenke and them was the ones that was evaluating the players. They was like man, this ain't black enough, you got to get more vicious than this, so I took it to the white community and they was like man you gotta soften this up it's too vicious. So I was like always toeing that line.

BC: Had you heard prison poetry at that time?

RD: Oh, yeah. See what was happening at the workshop was there was only one flavour of poetry at the workshop. I was some kind of a 'can we get along' poet, Otis was the love poet and Amdee was the street one.

A: When I was at the workshop, I didn't really know what happened until about a year ago. I was in this class [and] I met a girl named Royleen, who told me that she was studying English at UCLA. She remembered me from the workshop. When I started at the workshop, I didn't know anything about poetry, about structure or anything like that, I just started writing it the way I felt it, but when I came to the class, she said that I didn't know what was happening but they did. I began to change all of their writings; I wasn't the teacher, I was the student, and she said that they began to wonder, how the hell did you rhyme canary with – or something like that, my rhymes wasn't the normal thing.

OS: I had people say that too. One of the things was the imagery that you was using. Like I had this poem called the 'The Pimp': 'Like the engine of my heart come pushing through the deep freeze of my frame, my blood is like ice water in my veins.' And they was like, how can you use that kind of imagery?

RD: Well the diversity of the Watts Prophets, Anthony has always been the fire of the group, and Otis is the love poet of the group, and I'm always trying to find some good in all this bullshit. One day we were having problems with that. They was trying to get me to have some fire, and Harry Dolan sat us down and explained it's the diversity of the group that makes us unique in the first place. You can always be the most popular by coming up with the most hate. So we tried to work it. Anthony would go out there and talk about tearing up the world and we'd try to put it back together in some way.

A: And we even have trouble with that today, 'cause today all they want is that vicious type poetry, they won't allow us to –

BC: It's mainly Amdee's voice that gets sampled.

A: Yeah, it's not that I write any better than anybody in the group. It's the viciousness of it, the topics and the way I say it.

RD: There's many times I thought about coming on that way, hearing the applause and I'm talking about 'maybe a change is overdue' and he's like –

OS: And I can recall too that whatever emotion I felt, I would write it. But I learned very quickly that they wouldn't take it all. The first time I did 'Hey World', they was like what the hell you talking about? I would express myself and I learned poems that wasn't really hardcore. People couldn't take it. But for myself I still wrote it and I think I like what it's done for me. It allowed me to maintain a certain balance I appreciate, 'cause after a while you write a lot of the anger out and after a while you don't have the same fire you did when you were twenty years old. You got families and stuff and you get into another flavour, and one of the things about today is they want you to be the way you were at twenty. They don't want you to grow old [so] that you're a father, a grandfather. The rhymers today are gonna change. It'll probably be easier for them 'cause there are so many of them, a whole school, plus their audience will be changing with them.

A: Where I put value in words for the first time was in the insane asylum, that's where I first realized the value of words. But when I first felt the impact of words was one night at

Mavericks Flat, I did a poem: 'Dig sisters in wigs and homemade eyelashes, what's your trip, you say you black and you proud when you in a crowd, when you home alone, many false things you put on, hot fire to the brain blue in the eyes, what's your thing, are you ashamed of what you had when you came.' And when I said 'came', a wig hit me in the face. A sister stood up, and she was a cool sister – not the type to do this – she started crying and she came up on the stage and took the mic and said, 'I'm black just like you, I got a wig and I'm not ashamed of it.' And she was crying and Dee was like, 'We're gonna get killed, you've done it.' There was a thousand people there. That's when I learned the impact of words and I had to be careful. My intention never was to hurt, and I never did that poem again. I just wanted to help, and I saw that I hurt.

OS: It's difficult for someone no matter how brilliant or talented they may be to have the wisdom and experience of a forty-year-old man, when you're twenty. And similarly it is very difficult for forty-year-olds to have the desire and outlook of a twenty-year-old.

A: I was always into spiritual things. Richard and I went to Shelly's Manne Hole one night, all three of us then. We went to see Roland Kirk. We was the only black folks in there, and he said, 'Baby, I'm gonna play a tune for you all and it's called blackness. I ain't gonna play nothing but the black keys on the piano.' He was playing horns and all this stuff, and all of a sudden, he just leapt up, he took all his instruments and started throwing all his instruments into the back of the baby grand piano, and then he took the chair and started smashing, and we just jumped up – he was having a hard time 'cause he was blind – so we ran up.

OS: And this lady thought we was gonna stop him.

A: And we ran up there and helped him. We were just wrassling, smashed the chair until it was just splinters. The manager was like 'Goddamn it', he never forgot that. Rahsaan (Roland Kirk) was like, 'Don't be mad at me baby, I'm just a old blind man.' And he said to us, 'Where you all goin', I'm going with y'all.' Marvin Gaye – once Richard wrote an introduction for Marvin Gaye and it was so bad, that when he came out on stage he ran back off and said, 'Who the fuck are you guys, give me your phone number right now!'

A: The *Black Voices* album was a direct response to the Last Poets. Laugh Records (ALA Records) heard about this album when it first came out. The Last Poets we had heard of were the original Last Poets, but we were already the Watts Prophets at that time. We were already doing our thing. The Last Poets got an album out before we did, we wasn't on that yet. So when *Black Voices* was done I said, 'I'm in a poetry group, you got to hear us', and when he did he recorded us like that. We did one album *Hey World* after *Rappin' Black*, but it never came out.

OS: I was like let's do it ourselves. That was about '73, '74; we needed to be more organized, we only took it to two people and they said no.

What it's doing to me is, there is an awakening, an awakening process, people are starting to become aware of what is being said, for their own purpose and understanding. But it's a slow movement, with all the gangsta rap (and it's pretty interesting to see who's promoting that over conscious rap), they totally divert the whole purpose of what that is doing, but I'd say in a couple of years that's the only rap (conscious) that will matter to people. Drug dealers will say, yeah, we are poisoning our people, gangbangers — yeah, we are killing our own, they will realize, they will hear what they are doing. We just trying to let them know, 'cause even you have the bourgeois black on the hill with their house and cars and they think they made it, they're safe, but they're in the same situation as we all are. They might take out the gangster during the day, but the government is going to get the bourgeois black at night . . . .

Michael Mixxin' Moor is a pioneer DJ/activist from Los Angeles.

The real thing that got me into hiphop was KSPB, this high school station out of Pebble Beach. They had this thing called 'Super Soul Sunday'; they had this guy called Cool P, originally he came in on the afternoons when he was a junior, and he used to rock all the hiphop shit. He used to play shit like 'That's the Joint'. He used to play the Disco Four, all the old Sugarhill and Enjoy shit, Treacherous Three, Crash Crew, whatever it was he'd play that shit. I met up with Cool P and we were cool. I started buying records from him and ended up on 'Super Soul Sunday' in 1984. It was not entirely hiphop, it was everything. We didn't really get service so anything you wanted to play you had to buy. That carried on until 1985, on Sunday nights, it was almost an entirely hiphop show. I graduated and went to Loyola, and then I had to go through the whole waiting game. They had a funk show that played a little hiphop, I used to hang out and people would come through. King Ad Rock came way back in the day when the Beasties had that 'Beastie Groove' record out. That's the first place I heard 'Public Enemy No. 1', this photographer named Glen Friedman brought it on demo tape. So eventually I got there in '88 when KDAY was still on the air. Now new shows have popped up, Fly ID has come and gone, Michael Moor been around, he's been doin' his stuff, but I guess on the consistent hiphop, straightforward music – that edge – that's me. That's my story.

Mike Nardone is the host of the longest-running hiphop show on radio in LA, the 'We Came from Beyond' show on KXLU. He is a B-boy premier and his show has helped the careers of many well-known LA groups.

OLD SCHOOL ROUNDTABLE

(WITH G MONEY AND CHINO)

The Old School Roundtable was an attempt to reconstruct some sense of what it was like for the first generation of hiphoppers in LA. It happened in late July 1992 at my apartment and after some initial reservations people began to talk.

Cast of characters: (in order of appearance)

Chino (CH): Old school LA B-boy of Korean descent who was raised in South America; he currently works for Def American Records.
Rudy Pardee (R): Old school rhymer with the LA Dream Team.
Flash (F): Old school DJ who had just put together a collection of early West Coast hiphop for Rhino Records.
Captain Rapp (Rapp): Old school rhymer, most famous for 'Badd Times (I Can't Stand It)'.
Lonzo (L): Old school rhymer, DJ, manager, promoter and member of the World Class Wreckin Cru.
Lovin' C (LC): Old school poplocker and rhymer, member of the Rappers Rapp Group with DJ Flash.
Michael Mixxin Moor (MMM): Old school DJ and mixer, he currently has a radio show on KCRW which combines his special brand of speeches, news footage and mixes of new hiphop.
G Money (G$): LA hiphop impresario and promoter. He runs the Hiphop One Network, a free information line for the LA hiphop nation.
Cli N Tel (CL): Old school LA rhymer, member of the Wreckin Cru, currently a member of crew called UMA (Union of Mother Afrika).

CH: Let's start by getting everybody's individual story on how it all happened.

Rapp: Back then it was the East Coast, West Coast thing.

L: Egypt [Egyptian Lover] went down to New York, right, and we called him on the phone and he said, 'Aww baby, they're gonna boo you', and we were like, aw shit, so we went down to the Palladium and there were about three to four thousand people down there, we nervous, so I decided to cut my act down to one song, 'Turn Out the Lights', which was a big song at the time – they were playin' it on WBLS, we did our thing. That's when I was in my muscle man mode. I was kind of buff, they loved it, I was the hero. We didn't have a problem . . .

LC: I went to New York and went looking for NWA's album, I didn't find not one West Coast record out there. The only one they were talking about was Ice T.

MMM: I was in New York and when I came out there wasn't nobody mixin' out here. I was comin' back and forth, around '79 and I started mixin' on KDAY and KJLH, around '80, and by the time I left everybody was mixin'. Everybody started bringin' records back, people would say, 'What you got is what you got.' I saw people like Lonzo and I was like, 'I wanna do that.' Saw the two turntables, then in New York I saw mixing and thought, 'This'll make me the shit!' So I was always gettin' my cues from NY, only to get people to look up to me out here. 'Cause when I started there wasn't nobody to look up to, they was like MCs, you know they couldn't mix to save their lives, like Uncle Jam's and shit . . . . What Lonzo was doing was givin' us all something to shoot for.

G$: When did Uncle Jam's Army get going?

L: UJA didn't officially start until 1983. Roger Clayton and I used to do parties together back in '76 to '77. And I was a DJ, he was a promoter. My company was Disco Construction, his thing was Unique Dreams. This was before they had 1200s, so I was a bad cat, I had two matching turntables. I hold the arm up 'cause the arm wouldn't move by itself, two matching Sanyo belt drive turntables, semi-automatic, so we would make it out to the middle, and it would go back over, alright. So all that mixin' was out, you had to warm it up to get it going, alright. Cue it up and let it roll for a minute. I had the original coffin back in 1976, they didn't make a disco mixer, only thing you could buy was a Numark or a Cerwin-Vega, and that was six hundred bucks, and I was only makin' fifty a gig, so how could I afford one? Anyway, me and Roger had the Alpine gig in Torrance, we did that for like two years every other Friday off and on. We went our two separate ways. I was luggin' equipment and he was collecting money every night, so there was an imbalance here. So he went off and started Uncle Jam's Army . . .

MMM: Also tell them how there was other promoters too, like Starship.

L: I was IP's boy, International Promotions out of Long Beach, two brothers, hotel promoters mostly.

CL: Didn't they do the Shrine Auditorium at one point?

L: Eventually they worked their way up to it, but I don't think it was IP. We all got together and formed UPA (United Promotions Association), and we all got together with the

Convention Center and we hired Mike to DJ. This time I was doin' the club, everybody was like chillin' out. Everybody made money, so we was like ahh, forget the DJing, we'll go and do this here.

CL: So you guys all came together at the Sports Arena?

MMM: See they was all doin' gigs down at the schools in south central, makin' fifty and one hundred dollars a gig, and I was like, damn what's up. So I got smart and started to move my shit elsewhere and make some money. We decided to build the biggest sound empire . . .

L: Right, 'cause we did the clubs for about two years, and it was on the decline, 'cept Eve's After Dark. That was like the Krush Groove of the West Coast, okay. Everybody came there . . . it was hard. I hired Kurtis Blow to come to the club, and he brought Davy D, and he taught Yella how to scratch, and that brought scratchin' to the West Coast. Few months later I brought in Run DMC who brought in Jam Master Jay, also who taught my boys, most of my rappers.

R: You brought LL Cool J out here.

L: Right. Me and Rad Mack.

CL: That was his first appearance and he got booed. At Dudos in Compton, Central and 125th. I had started out with Disco Daddy, and Disco Daddy was managing a little group that me and my cousin had, and we were goin' around doin' talent shows and shit . . . One week I heard Lonzo talkin' about a talent show at Eve's After Dark. Was Dre there too?

L: Dre just got there . . .

CL: Me and my buddy was like, 'Hey that sound pretty good.' So all that week we worked on this routine, this thing called the Snake Box. That Saturday we called you, and you said go ahead man and do your thing. I showed up with Joe Cooley, we'd done house parties and stuff like that in Compton, so I'd just get up and say stuff to get the crowd goin', freestylin', I didn't have no routine. So I just said, fuck it, I'll get the crowd goin', so I got up there and did 'Yes, yes, muthafuck it.' All that kind of stuff, got the crowd goin', won the contest, and Lonzo was like, 'Hey man, come on back later this week.' . . .

R: So that's how Wreckin Cru started . . .

L: . . . My Company was called Disco Construction. We built the parties mobile-style, right, then my two boys Eric and Charles would come in and tear the shit down. So we got nicknamed the Wreckin Cru.

MMM: Then disco played out.

L: Right, so then I had to change my name from Disco Lonzo to Lonzo. They were the guys that tore down the equipment, but when we moved into the club they weren't tearin' nothin' down so I made them a sub-entity of the club. You come to Eve's After Dark, you hang out with the Wreckin Cru, everybody had jackets and the whole nine yards. Actually the Wreckin Cru, they couldn't rap a gift, so I was looking for some guys to come on and –

R: So the Wreckin Cru was like a posse.

L: It was about fifteen cats. The club was having some legal problems with the Sheriff's

Department, was in the process of being shut down, and so I was looking for something else. Hiphop was jumpin' off real well on the East Coast, so I figured it was only a matter of time before it hit the West Coast. So I told the fellas we're going to put together a little package real quick, and we'll be ready to roll, okay . . . so that's when we cut our first record, we started doing Dudos over in Compton, then our second record.

R: So, how did you know who was goin' to be the formal members of the Wreckin Cru when you had fifteen guys?

L: Yella was a DJ, Dr Dre was a DJ. I can't DJ, nor am I one of the greatest rappers, everybody knows, so I sat back and said I'm just gonna be a member of the group, and finance everything. So I needed a good rapper to front the group, and that's when I met Mark (Cli N Tel).

CH: What was the first ever piece of LA vinyl?

F: 'Gigolo Rap', 1981.

L: We was doing Dudos every week and also we were doing the KDAY mixmaster show, 'Traffic Jams'.

Rapp: Don't you think the people in New York supported the rappers? Here it wasn't like that. You were like isolated, you were by yourself . . . I remember the days of going to Uncle Jam's Army, I would have to fight to get to the microphone. Everybody knew me, but I'd get there and I'd fall in line . . .

MMM: That was a clique too. Even me, I used to be one of the major players, when they moved to the Sports Arena, everybody had all the equipment. We was the ones makin' sure they could do their show when Afrika Islam came out here. When Run DMC came out we was doin' Eve's After Dark on a larger scale, and it was too big for them, it was too big . . . I remember seeing a poster at that hiphop shop that says 'KDAY and Avalon Attractions'. That's when I knew the shit was fucked up because we lost control.

L: But you know what killed all that though? Gangbanging, because it got to the point where you couldn't do none of that stuff no more, everything would turn into . . .

Brian Cross: About what time was that?

L: '85 to '86. We would put a thousand to fifteen hundred people in the Biltmore, people would go in, have a good time, no problem, but nowadays you can't put . . .

BC: It's all the techno and rave kids that can have the big jams, but hiphop can't do it.

L: Hiphop is killing itself. Because the hiphop generation cannot seem to put aside their personal problems to deal with a mass of people . . .

CL: I also think it's about responsibility, material you rap about, you bring out, at least to try to wake someone up or force them to think . . .

L: I think it's right here, the only problem I have with that is so many of your white companies are controlled by white people . . . I tried to do my positive thing, they'd say oh no Alonzo, that stuff is good, but do some more love stuff, do some more dance stuff, so here you are, you're tryin' to take your black ideas.

Rapp: Your pro-blackness.

L: Your pro-blackness. To a white company they don't want to hear that, 'cause that's not what's sellin' to them – you talk about shootin' somebody, you almost have to sell out to buy in . . . . The Wreckin Cru at that time, we were one of the first rap groups to get a major record deal.

CL: That was right around the time when I left. Right. In fact, you gave me the contract.

L: From CBS.

R: You all beat us? 'Cause we went to CBS.

L: We all went to CBS the same day, saw the same guy – you guys (the Dream Team) were at three o'clock, Bobby Jimmy was at three-thirty, we were at four. We got the deal, they signed us first, no problem . . .

R: They didn't like us.

Rapp: Lonzo's a better talker.

L: They gave us a deal, tell us we had full control, right. First of all we did the album in such a slick way, it pissed 'em off. Wreckin Cru just came off tour, I had some dollars . . . they gave us a ten-thousand-dollar advance, everybody got kicked off, we went into the studio, bought a whole system, which was the shit at the time, did all the pre-production at my house, went to the studio and cut the album. Financed it myself. They wouldn't give us the budget until January 1, January 15 we delivered the album. We got a cheque for seventy-five thousand, which is totally unheard of, they thought we was goin' to use live musicians and all that, so they were pissed off: 'You just took one hundred thousand dollars from us.' We fell into a political thing. Before they would accept the album, they told us to change two songs. At this time Jessie Johnson's 'Freeworld' was a cut; they told us go back, listen and do something more like that, and if you listen to 'Fly', it ain't nothing but 'Freeworld' with some new lyrics. So we cut the album . . . we had to convert it before we got paid. They made sure we had something that they could sell to the masses so they thought, which was the worst thing we could have done career-wise. On top of that our executive producer Mark Leonardo left the company. Second of all, I cut the deal myself, I didn't have no manager.

BC: Could you explain about the Macola [Records] thing?

L: First of all, Macola was financially the worst thing that happened to any artist that walked in the door, but exposure-wise, there's never been a system better. If you had anything that sounded like music, he [Donald Miller] would put it out for you, he would turn it into wax. It might not sell, and if it did, you probably wouldn't see no money, but you probably got some gigs, notoriety. Macola was a prototype of the company to come [but] he had one problem: he didn't like to give away no money. Wreckin Cru got paid some of the money that was due to them, Dream Team got paid some of the money that was due to them. Only reason we got paid was because we done sold so many records you couldn't tell us we didn't make no money. This was before we was really gangstas, so [when] we did our first album we got twenty thousand. Shit that was a lot of money.

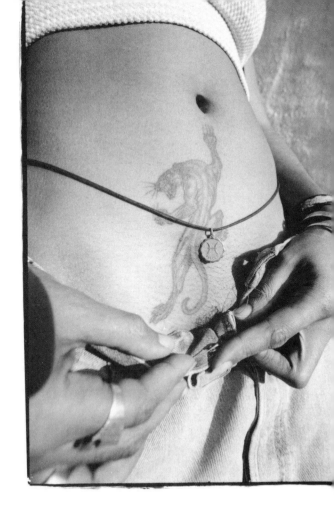

Medussa's tattoo, 1993.

Daggs at Public Enemy show, Palladium, Hollywood, 1992.

Gettin' open at the Good Life, south central
Los Angeles, 1991.

Bus Stop relaxing on video shoot for OFTB,
Nickerson Gardens, Watts, 1992.

**Alim and King Dizmost rip shit at Rudolfo's,
Los Feliz, 1993.**

**Tre from the Pharcyde at the Mayan,
downtown Los Angeles, 1992.**

**Crowd at Freestyle Fellowship/Pharcyde
show, Music Machine, west LA, 1992.**

Mikah Nine gets open in front of the
Underground Railroad, Fais Do Do, Los
Angeles, 1992.

**Heavyweight session Pharcyde Manor,
south central Los Angeles, 1992.**

Crowd at Jimmy Jam's birthday party, Strip Club, Hollywood, 1992.

**Heavyweight session Pharcyde Manor,
south central Los Angeles, 1992.**

R: That was when niggas was really excited about making records.

L: We never had a contract with Macola, I never signed shit at Macola. Macola didn't give contracts 'til like 1989, you went in, gave your tape, he'd give it to Jeb Tequila. Jeb Tequila would take it to the processing room, you'd talk to Jane at the front desk, call in later, get your record number, go in and pick up a couple of hundred records. You never had to give him money for the records.

My thing was I had worked with enough distributors, I knew I could go around, shop my own stuff and put the money in my own pocket. I had a street network, working with guys like Swampdog; he taught me how to deal with distributors and do that thing so we could always generate some money. I have never received a royalty cheque from Macola. When 'Turn Out the Lights' came out, I must have made twenty to thirty thousand selling them to distributors, 'cause Don [Miller] was so crooked he would feel guilty sometimes – when he went out of business in 1990 he gave me all my catalogue.

L: Before Macola was doin' rap he was doin' country and western . . .

L: He was doin' Mexican records . . . but he wasn't makin' no money. Roger Clayton is the one who turned me on to Macola. He was doin' 'Yes, Yes, Yes'. I was still pressing my records over at Bill Smith's in El Segundo, and it got to the point where most people don't realize, if you have a hit record out and no money, that's really a curse; everybody wants you to give them credit, but they aren't givin' you no credit. So you're standin' there with two hundred dollars and you sellin' one thousand records a week. It's hard to go cash and carry, and Macola was the first one to say, I'll take your record, they treat you so nice and shit, we didn't know.

R: We really didn't care, we wanted a record out.

L: There was nobody we could go to and ask questions. When I was first sellin' records out of the back of my car, I would go to a record store and ask them, what you give me for it . . .

R: You gotta understand that Donald Miller's white, he got some black guys comin' in here, turnin' out makin' a lot of money. 'Egypt Egypt' was really what got him excited, it was sellin'; here comes some more black guys comin' in here, Wreckin Cru, they made it easy for us 'cause I didn't have to deal with none of that stuff . . .

MMM: 'Jawbreaker' blew up . . . I ain't talking about 'Rockberry (Jam)', I thought 'Rockberry' was better than 'Dream Team's in the House' which was like a smash. It was a good record, you had all the commercial mainstream – it wasn't really KDAY, it was like down the middle, as soon as POWER 106 came out, they started pluggin' it . . .

CL: They played that song so much you could really say it helped to get POWER 106 known . . .

R: We had 106, KGFJ, KJLH, KDAY, and KROQ.

Rapp: First rap to play on KROQ . . .

R: Right, and that song got us as the first West Coast group on the New York Fresh Fest Tour . . .

L: We hated you muthafuckers for that, we hated you all man . . .

F: I wanna hear now how the Dream Team came about man, what's up?

R: Alright man what can I tell you all. Came from Cleveland in '83, fall of '83, worked at World on Wheels, managed for a while before I started DJing, worked hard. At that time I was in the record pool, recording with Tracy (Ice T) and Foot.

Rapp: You know I thought you guys lived here, man (Dream Team) . . .

R: When I came here, I came here because I was a drummer, I used to play in a jazz band, we used to play the bar called the Kiniman Grill in Ohio, and they came out here, so when I finally came out here I worked at Wendy's . . .

Rapp: What was you doin' at Wendy's, man?

R: I was managing . . .

Rapp: I thought you'd be managing fries man . . .

R: Naw, I was the manager of the place, and that's how I met Snake. Snake came in for an interview and I hired him. We got to talking and I found out he'd been doing things with DJing so I invited him to do some things with the Dream Team, go around to the schools and what not, that was the same time as that 'Fruit Fly' . . . he had made a record and I went to Tracy and said, 'That dude made a record, I want to make a record.' And Tracy said, 'You better stop laggin'.' About a month after we had had this conversation I went back to Tracy and asked him how I could get with it, he introduced me to a guy that was takin' up the music business. I talked to him about twenty times on the phone, found Macola the same way, the Egypt label, called Macola and said yo man let's do it, and that's how it was.

Rapp: Did you guys get taken care of though, somewhat?

R: No. We got a little money . . .

Rapp: That's why I didn't think it was worth it gettin' ripped off, I didn't want to make anybody rich and not get paid.

R: But see the only thing you guys don't realize is that if I had to do it again, I'd do it the same way. I do have to give Don credit, because if he hadn't done it I don't know how I would have ever made record number one . . .

Rapp: The resources were there, we just did not know where to go get at it.

L: We didn't know jackshit about the record business, all we knew is that the records were made out of wax . . .

F: We were just a bunch of DJs, basically . . .

L: You look at guys like myself, they didn't even have disco mixers like I said . . . I met Roger, he used to come to my parties and DJ and shit, I had my little hat with my light on the top and that was my thing. I was more an entertainer DJ, the thought of mixin' was the farthest thing from my mind. Just keep 'em going, don't want no dead air. I was trained through radio, I went to broadcasting school so I didn't want any dead air. Mixin' em together was unheard of, I was lucky just to have them there.

MMM: And one was faded out and the other in.

R: And if you was lucky you might catch it on beat.

L: Technology was not even ready to accommodate us at the time.

F: A Realistic Radio Shack mixer.

MMM: We didn't have what the big boys had, if you did go to a big disco, they did have all of that fly shit, we just didn't have it, we couldn't afford it.

L: It was special order shit though. The disco was just hittin'. It hadn't hit the black clubs yet, they was still playin' the jukebox, right. When I walked in to a club four years after I'd been DJing to more than one hundred dollars a night, they thought I was from Mars. 'What you want, a hundred bucks? For what, you just a DJ.'

When I first got into radio, I got a scholarship from Gardena High School to go to a broadcast school owned by Don Tracy and Jay Rich, 1975, LA Broadcasting School. I never wanted to go to radio 'cause, fuck, I got a lisp, fuck that. After I heard myself on tape I was embarrassed, so I figure I could be a club DJ. I didn't have to say nothing, I could do a little rap, I was trying to be like Montague, right, we used to go over to the little sock hop over in Compton, and they had Montague and a couple of other cats . . .

CL: Montague was the brother did 'Burn Baby Burn' [catchphrase of soul radio DJ the Magnificent Montague which became a symbol of, and synonymous with, the Watts Rebellion].

L: I figured I could charge a dollar a head, borrow a couple a speakers, 'cause my entire DJ set was two components, speakers on top you had to drop the record down and the arm came over and shit, you grab one of them and it broke so I had to use the eight track, with a forty-five on top . . . play the eight track with the headphone right, so when you got to the song you put that song out, but then you got replace and pop it in, make your record jump . . . there was no record players designed for DJs, there was nothing BPMs [beats per minute] – what the fuck was a BPM? I didn't find out about BPMs till I was working in the record shop. That's when Roger and me, my job was packing records, Roger was selling it. So I had one client always bought records from me, he was a DJ in Las Vegas, he told me about BPMs. He showed me how to count 'em and shit, but he didn't tell me you had to have 1200s to do it. You can't count BPMs on a belt drive turntable, it will not work, okay, they got too much play in the damn thing . . . My thing was rhymin', okay, I was Disco Alonzo: 'Give you a double dose of disco dynamite, stick it in your ear and blow your mind.'

LC: Woo, that's some corny old shit.

L: Yeah, but we did that shit and we was bad. When Chic first came out with 'Good Times' and I was able to say a rhyme for eight bars over that shit, people stopped dancing.

MMM: That was the first dance I ever gave. I had only seen DJ but I had never done it and I was like Lonzo was on the mike there and talking and I was like, let me get on there. I was in awe.

L: You walking through the crowd, you had a girl, maxicoat, DJs was cool. We was like super slide gangsters. My thing was Disco Alonzo Millionaire DJ; we had no money, making $75 a night, wasn't till 1974 till things started getting good. I was making alright because I was working so much 'cause there wasn't that many guys around. Just me and George, nobody could afford George. I was $75 Alonzo, for $75 I would do your reception, your funeral, picnic, whatever, so I'd DJ all day for a family picnic. I'd pick it up, dust it off and go to a dance all smelly and funky, one hundred and seventy five a day was good for then. Making one hundred and sixty a week slinging records on the phone, then make two hundred playing them on the weekend. Then you had guys like Michael and shit coming up and mixing and then I couldn't pay on the big hotel gigs any more 'cause you got these young fuckers comin' up. You had to have skills now. I was a personality, that's all you had to be was a personality, Funky Damon was a personality, Brother Love, we all competed for the gigs, only reason I would get them was I had two speakers of my own so I didn't have to charge 'em for rental. I was one of the original mobile cats, but it was all shit, so plus, I could talk, loved it especially and weddings and stuff. Then I have my own club a year later and I look up and people are no longer talking, in fact, shut the fuck up and mix. And I never learned to mix.

MMM: That's when I first started to scratch and people looked at me like I was crazy, so I thought I'll just leave this alone for a while, and keep mixin'.

L: In fact, we was pissed, you tryin' to scratch, muthafuckers like 'What the fuck is he doin'?' These dudes I had hired are like Mike be fuckin' with records and shit he don't know what he's doin'.

R: They never like nothing they ain't used to.

MMM: That was cool because see in New York you make the breaks long.

CL: Yella and Dre used to take those breakbeats and mix 'em down long so then I could rap over them.

BC: Well, what happens when it goes from the pimp role to the straight hardcore banger role, in '84 and '85; how did that come about?

CH: I first noticed LA banger rap with 'Boyz n the Hood' and I think Schooly D kind of brought that out here.

L: When Wreckin Cru first started off, I refused to walk out on stage wearin' tennis shoes, fuck that.

R: Y'all were wearin' makeup.

CL: Let's get this shit cleared up right now, the Wreckin Cru did not wear no makeup. No.

L: I'll tell you, on the first album cover, Shirley dressed up me, Dre and Yella; 'member Shirley, the big fat girl that Dre had the crush on? And she put some eyeliner on right here, the Prince shot, but I refused to let us on stage wearin' tennis shoes . . . Run DMC came to the club, and we had spent a gang of money on some uniforms, hard but flashy hard like the Temptations and Soul Sonic Force, so [when] Run DMC come to LA they got on tennis shoes, no laces, some black Levi's, with their hats turned around backwards. Run DMC went from, they was at Eve's After Dark that fall, the next April they was the booyaa shot, double up bam having it, so Dre and Yella got discouraged, were like we're not spending this money, but I was like we are the World Class Wreckin Cru, so soon as Cli N Tel left the group, got a contract with CBS, got zapped from CBS, went back to Macola, still claimin' the World Class image. Our contract was up in November of '87; we did 'Cabbage Patch', 'House Calls' . . . 'Fly' was on CBS. Eazy E had been doing demos in my studio all along. When 'Boyz n the Hood' first came out, nobody wanted to touch it.

CL: I think I heard it on KDAY for the first time, and I was like goddamn, that voice they're scratching in there sounds familiar. Shit, that's my voice they're scratchin' in there . . .

L: Who's that gangster out of New York, big killer with the gold teeth – yeah, Just Ice, that's when I really noticed the image of rap starting to change . . . Run DMC had already proved that this image of rap could sell, Dre and them wanted to be on that same trip and abandoned the World Class image – which I have to say Hammer picked up two years later and made about a billion dollars off it.

F: Isn't that the truth?

BC: By that time the big shows are over ('88 to '89), but what happened to change that? What happened that the gangs are starting to take over?

CL: You got to look at the sociology of what's going on. Drugs were starting to come into the community more, crack around the same time, brothers start claimin' the territory more seriously to sell they dope and all that. So naturally, if they controlled a certain territory and some dance crew tried to bring a bunch of people from another hood in for a party, well that's violating they space, so they gonna cause a problem at the show.

MMM: Yeah, 'cause the last Uncle Jam's show I remember at the Sports Arena, they cancelled, I took my wife's little sister to the Run DMC show, but to see the tears in her eyes when they cancelled it, I was like, this little girl was eleven years old. So we sold all our equipment, and started concentrating on radio (while) the rest of us just started makin' records.

CL: What I did after I left the Cru was work with Unknown DJ for a bit, worked with Ice T on 'Doggin' tha Wax', did the Big Beat for a bit, you know WC and Unknown and Tony G. In '88 I got a little deal on Sutra, the same label as the Fat Boys did but they were going down so, at this time, 'It's Time to Jam' [Sweet Sensation – up-tempo club music known as 'Latin hiphop'] was getting played a lot on KIIS AM: 'we like the cars that go boom' and I was with Sutra for about a year after which I figured out they wouldn't sell shit.

Rapp: So scandalous how they was doin' it. They told me to fly out to WWRL, and WBLS, Mr Magic, it was a head thing. You know I'm in NY, but it wasn't nothin', 'cause I took Kim with me to NY, and we was goin' to perform 'Bad Times' and shit, and the scheduling was crazy, crazy, you're not even goin' to sleep. They tryin' to juice you for everything, day after day to do all this stuff. Now that I know how to do it, it's a whole different thing. I looked for the guy to get paid, and he says I need to talk to you, house only gettin' this much so we gonna pay you half and I remember sayin', look man I came all the way out here to do this, two brothers I ain't never seen them, and I said until you get my money you ain't goin' nowhere. I had told my little brother I was gonna do this for him, you know how the story goes, and they're gonna give me half, close to around Christmas time, and I had no manager. They sent me a round-trip ticket and that's it – nobody waiting there for me. Just catch a cab and come up to the radio station. Those three days taught me more than anything, if you gotta little hole in your game then bam, that's it.

L: The industry preys on young dumb folk, they don't want cats like us in the industry. I'm considered very dangerous. You go to Macola, need a manager, and they be hovering, waiting for you at the door, the same dudes as now . . .

R: Same devils handlin' NWA, Jerry Heller, 'No Vaseline' [Ice Cube song about the break-up with NWA and Jerry Heller], he managed me first.

L: First they had Egypt, then you guys . . . they'd hover around Macola's door, as soon as you had a contract they jumped all over your ass. They'd sit in the lobby, you'd get a contract, come out all ego, they'd want twenty five per cent.

BC: So Macola's gettin' 20 per cent, Jerry Heller's got 25 per cent, and supposedly you're getting 50 per cent, but . . .

L: But after you split it and pay everybody you got shit. When we got the CBS deal, Dream Team was on one side of the fence, Wreckin Cru was on the other . . .

R: We got signed the next week, CBS didn't want us, so we went to MCA.

L: We were so confused, half the group was bein' influenced by Shirley, I was bein' influenced by Swampdog, so we had a lot of confusion. We were on our first tour, tour bus cost thirty-five hundred dollars. CBS just called right before the tour, a tour of Mississippi. We had internal problems, bullshit tour. Did the deal with CBS, and shortly after that I hired Jerry Heller.

R: So Heller didn't get you the deal.

L: No, I got that myself. He got pissed off 'cause he wanted 25 per cent. Management team had Wreckin Cru and Dream Team, they made money off Dream Team, but they hadn't made no money with Wreckin Cru.

R: We had $125,000 and I gave Mory 25 per cent 'cause he got the deal, that's okay, that's normal.

L: I have a problem with that there, management fees, if a real manager took 15 to 20 per cent of the net, that would be okay, but they take it up front, 20 per cent of the gross. So they profit as much as we do. You expense to me, then I got expenses to pay, you gotta be concerned, and he's got his money up front before I even made a dollar.

Rapp: But see if you got a manager who's your manager, who cares about managing, but we had dudes who really didn't know what they were doin', taking too much off the jump, didn't give a damn. They thought we was a bunch of dumb niggers . . . and to tell you the truth, we were! That's all. I was at Motown once, and I had heard Mike, he was having auditions at his house, the Motown guy was talkin' we goin' to do this for you. I knew he could tell I didn't have no money, I was smilin' the whole time, cause he's mentioning we goin' to do this for you you're going to have limos, and you know what, you're goin to be a star. You ain't got no lawyer, you walk out the door, and they're goin, 'Sucka, dumb nigger.' Even now in 1992, there's a whole lot of brothers out there rappin', and they awesome, and they're gettin' beat by the same thing, same old thing.

MMM: The old schoolers got to take it back. What we all had goin' is out of our control now. And we refused to do the hard layman's work to take it back. You should have never been controlled by Jerry Heller. If you went to MCA, you should have had a label deal, where you could have brought other cats in . . . I wanna lay something down, we gotta tell these young cats. This kid is gonna get ganked. Don't play yourself against your own people with the corporate people . . .

CL: I'm trying to tell you if you're gonna make your money, you're gonna get played.

BC: It seems to me the answer is black-owned, black-run record companies et cetera, but whenever that question comes up in relation to LA, everybody asks how did KDAY go out the window. KDAY set a precedent, it was the first 24-7 radio station that played that kind of music.

L: But you got the same thing that's always been in effect: Ice T don't like Ice Cube who don't like Hammer who can't stand Sir Mixalot. We know guys who could have gone to the bank and bought KDAY collectively, Hammer could have bought it hisself, but divide and conquer . . .

MMM: You got people tellin' these dudes what to do, Ice Cube got this kid, this white kid workin' promotions for Street Knowledge, that's foul, that's foul . . . ain't there a good enough black dude in the community could have done the job?

L: We tried it with West Coast, it was the best idea since sliced bread, four independently owned, independently run black companies. I don't think I am prejudiced, but history speaks for itself: you gotta go to the white man to get your records, you gotta go to white people to distribute 'em and wait for them to pay you, you still have no control.

G$: Ice T sold straight underground.

MMM: Yeah but he didn't blow up until he signed the big deal.

CL: The question is how as black people can we best maintain control of the record industry, and yes we may have to negotiate, but we have to do it from a position of strength, and what kind of power do we have that can equal theirs?

Rapp: We got our talent.

MMM: There's a whole new crop of people, we have to take this situation and set up a plan, cause this rave shit is exactly what we used to do.

L: Problem is that everything that is done is always done west of Wilshire or in Hollywood, okay, that's what really pisses me off. There's no place in the hood . . . We need a network of stores. But there's always the problem that the record industry is so unstable that they don't want to give credit, loans to it.

BC: But it is always said that Macola generated enough money so that Ruthless could get going . . . Luke Skyywalker as well.

L: I never sold dope. When Eazy E came to me, I put him into the game of how to make it happen. I'm not saying I'm the greatest cat in the world or nothing. He can attest to it. When Eric came to me, he had a pile of money as big as this bowl. When Eric started rapping it was a big joke, a big joke. Ice Cube would come into the studio trying to perfect his rap style. I got Ice Cube his very first deal, he got signed to CBS before we did. When Eric came around he had no intention of being a record company. When Jerry Heller signed him up with a record deal at Macola, nobody had any idea he was going to be anything. I had to turn him on to all my connections. The reason why Dre and I are not tight to this day, when I bought my BMW, Dre wanted my RX7, okay. So he co-signed for the vehicle, I was taking notes for it out of his CBS money weekly. Each of 'em got about fifteen thousand, but each owed me about two or three thousand because I was payin' out of my own pocket before that. Everybody got five thousand on Tuesday, Thursday they came back broke.

CL: Let's just say they didn't spend their money wisely.

L: A month goes by and nobody got money but Lonzo, and Lonzo got a house and a BMW. 'Lonzo's fuckin' me.' Dre gets tickets up the ass, somebody breaks the back window, steals the radio, steals the car, it ends up in the pound, and I'm still paying notes. Dre ends up in jail, we ain't doing nothing, just sitting at home getting fat. Talking about what we used to do. I put up half his bail, now he owes me plus the car note. Couple months later, I'm as low as whale shit, you know, skatin' on thin ice, we ain't gettin' fat no more, we missin' meals like a muthafucker . . . he calls for help, for bail, I can't, so he calls Eazy up, Eazy gets him out of jail, in exchange for some record cuts. So Eazy comes to me and buys studio time. To get his car out of the pound, Dre does more cuts, and I'm in debt, plus we ain't makin' no money. Attitude starts flyin', we do 'Cabbage Patch', we doin' a little bit, World on Wheels, little local shit, little Mexican shots in Santa Ana, then Macola calls and says we owe him sixty five thousand.

F: That's Macola man, you owe him now. I owe him ten Gs and I don't feel bad.

L: All our records and we can't get paid now, so he kept all the money from 'Cabbage Patch', and he didn't manage shit. Go in the studio August of '87, cut 'Turn Out the Lights', Eazy's in Dre's ear, come with me come with me. I had done Michel'le a year before that, a little chubby kid with a black tooth cause it had died or something when she was a kid, the tooth had died, so if you noticed she never smiled. Mona Lisa's going on tour back in Boston, I want to make a record, I call Michel'le she had never made a record in her life, she's a chocolate shake eatin' muthafucker, alright . . . she gotta have two chocolate shakes, so we doin' the demos in the studio and she says, 'Alonzo, I gotta have some money to get my teeth fixed.' She was working at the May Company in the Fox Hills Mall. So I paid her so she could get her some teeth, so baby got her teeth jumpin' off, we go back to the studio, Dre doesn't want to use the bitch . . . I went into dictatorship, we gonna use her, she finally does the shit.

We put the record out, Macola doesn't do shit with 'Turn Out the Lights', as you know the playlists freeze in November. We have a meeting with Dre and they say if I don't get money they out. Macola gives me back my thousand dollars, they think I'm collecting royalties, everybody's fuck you, fuck you, fuck you. 'Turn Out the Lights' blows up in February and I got no band. Jerry Heller's in their ear. If you ever read anything about Eazy, Dre or Yella, you'll never read anything about World Class Wreckin Cru.

TODDY TEE

Toddy Tee is an LA old school original. His seminal 'Batteram' tape is possibly one of the most influential underground tapes ever produced in hiphop. Today Toddy lives in the San Bernadino area. This interview took place in his mother's home in Compton. Also in attendance is Big Boy, an LA hiphop impresario.

Brian Cross: So when did you get into it?
Toddy Tee: I started doing stuff in high school. I was into it always, but once I graduated in '83, me and Mixmaster Spade used to DJ parties. We would DJ together, but when we were doing tapes we would DJ against each other, trying to see who had the best street tapes, right? Spade was with everybody, everybody had Spade tapes in Compton, just everybody. So at the time I was DJing, then I was writing raps and saying them. I really didn't want to be a rapper. I wanted to be a cop, a fireman or a hitman. I don't know, I was fascinated by either of the three, but it didn't turn out that way, and I don't want to be a cop or a fireman nowadays.

Anyway, what happened, Spade was making a tape and he was bragging, and I said, man, I'll go home and make a tape, it'll be the hardest street tape. So I went home and made the 'Batteram' street tape. That was like the OG before the record one, and shit man, that tape was, you'd be surprised where that tape was. I got famous off that tape, didn't make no records, just street tapes. Everybody had that tape, record shops, bootlegs. We just rapped about what was going on, crack heads, but we called them cluck heads. So I made that tape and everybody like, 'Man, he done roast you on that one, Spade.' I got record companies hunting me down, trying to figure out who was making them tapes, so I hooked up with a independent record company a friend had. It was cool. Then we came up with the first 'Batteram', it was the first hit on the West Coast, as far as rap . . . no no no I take that back, I think they had 'Dream Team in the House'. When we came right by we shot straight through the West Coast to San Francisco and stuff. I done did a lot of tours with Zapp, Klymaxx, Fat

Boys. I was on tour with a lot of groups, Doug E Fresh, Slick Rick, '85, '86, and the beginning of '87. Then we came out with 'Just Say No', which did the same thing. We would always get the radio stations, we never really *Billboard*-ed. But we got good, 'cause then it was like me and you having a record company and putting stuff out, but it was showing up all over the place. It was nice, it was fun.

Big Boy: How did you and Spade get out, together and stuff?

TT: One day I was in the studio, and Spade had been in a car wreck or something so he was in a wheelchair for a minute. So I went to see him. We was tellin' jokes. I was like damn we should put this on record, so my other buddy Mixmaster Ken and Baby Charles was writing a rap. So we just wheeled him up to the studio. Yeah, that's when we did that one, that's when everybody started getting with us. Dre and them were like, 'Damn these cats from the street.' We rapping about drugs and everything else instead of 'throw that in' and all that type of music. So then I hooked up with Ice T. Me and him did stuff. I got records of me working with him, you know rappin' with 'Iceberg' and all that stuff. I discovered (MC) Trouble, I got her her first thing at Motown. I did her first song and they had a controversy thing where I basically got the deal, and everybody else took over. That's what you get when you don't sign nothing, and me and her were stuck in the middle so we decided it was best to leave it alone.

BC: Was it the success of the street tape 'Batteram' that made you decide to go on rapping?

TT: No, it took them a while to get them to get me to make a record, 'cause for a while I didn't want to do it. It was the street tape that really got it pumping, 'cause I spoke to Greg Mack and he said, 'Dang man we been waiting on this a long time.' But he said, 'This ain't the version.' And I said no, 'cause somebody had given him the street tape but he couldn't use it 'cause of all the cursing and stuff on it. That was off the Rapping Duke, his 'Die Hard' one. I don't know man, at first I started taking it as a joke, until doing the tours, 'cause the 'Batteram' got so popular so quick and requested so often I was like damn.

BC: How did you come up with 'Batteram' first day, man?

TT: I think I was watching it on the news, when they was raiding people.

BC: 'Cause the song lasted longer than the 'Batteram', right?

BB: That was like the theme song in Detroit.

TT: Matter of fact I was watching the news and making the tape. But I was actually just hearing the music and just watching the TV, and I was mixing the Rapping Duke, then I just came up with that one. Then I took a whole bunch of other songs. 'Batteram' was nice, but after a while the people you be dealing with, you don't want to get involved any more. I wanted to get out there and learn the business part, that's why I said Ice T would be my last thing. 'Cause everybody can rap, but that ain't really happening. The girls and all that, that was fine. Nowadays it's a little more dangerous. But anyway, I just decided to do my own album, do it my own way, instead of going to a production company with somebody. It's gonna be just me and the record company.

BB: I remember back in the day with the gangsta tapes, we used to sit back in the car and try to analyse, like what the hell does this mean?

TT: Yeah, we used to make up words, like cluckhead and now everybody say it . . .

BC: You must have tripped out when 'Boyz n the Hood' came out.

TT: Naw, you know why, 'cause I already knew it was more like a copy type thing, but I don't really get into that, 'cause I figure if one person gets really large they can help others to get up in the business. Ice had 'Six in the Morning' and all that and I liked Ice's stuff, but everybody after us started gettin' street. Now if somebody would tell us they were doing street before we were I want to know what they were saying 'cause I ain't heard it – nothing about dope, nothin' about cluckheads, nothin' about nothin'. As far as straight streets and somebody smokin' and gettin' smoked, in fact Spade had a tape with Ren rappin' just like him all the way through it. Everybody was bustin' up. One night we see him, we was teasing him he couldn't deny it cause we had the tape. Spade starts this, 'Y'all wanted to be like me, you know it.' That's like a trend thing, when you got a neighbourhood, when somebody is rappin', everybody got their tape, somebody gonna want to sound like them.

Now when I listen to a tape, I don't want to sound like nobody. Now there [is] just a lot of competition. I don't worry about it. I like a lot of the new rappers. I buy their tapes to support them, especially if they from Compton. Out here I think we dominating rap now, Compton is a fuckin' rap capital, the sound is so clear here.

BC: Why Compton?

TT: Because Compton had so many rappers that hit. Watts didn't really have no rappers, they gettin' 'em now. I know OFTB (Operation From The Bottom). But the biggest names in LA was the Dream Team and Ice T. But what Compton had, seemed like a new group popped up every two months. One of the baddest engineers we used to work with was this dude named Vadjeck, he understood rap. You give him a tape, say, 'Man I'm going to McDonald's to get something to eat, you want something?' He say, 'Naw, take your time.' By the time you come back, Vadjeck done change the drums, the hi hats –

BB: Where's he at now?

TT: I don't know, a lot of us stopped working with him 'cause he took so damn long, we started gettin' around engineers that fix five songs in one night. Vadjeck could only fix one song in one night.

BB: Back in the day he was on everything.

TT: Vadjeck was hard . . . his girlfriend says something . . . oh yeah, she says he's a nasty man. She met him. He's a flirt, man. Pooh was good, King Tee used to just crack me up, the only cat you'd go to a show he wouldn't even finish the concert, he'd just start baggin'. He say 'Forget it', or forget the words, and every time I used to get on stage I'd say, please don't do like Tee, don't forget. Tila (King Tee) said, 'Man I heard your album was pretty hard.' Shocked me 'cause I ain't did it, and after that he says somebody told him. I was sellin' tapes, by the end of the week, I would have a gang of money, we could have bought condos or something. Somebody told me the original street version of the tape is still at VIP Records, they used to bootleg them suckers.

BB: Anyone dis you back then?

TT: Always got props from people. They never really did that.

BB: How do you feel about people always giving props to old school East Coast rappers like Caz who haven't even been in the studio in a long time but never to West Coast pioneers . . .

TT: The West Coast don't even have any pioneers . . . if you ask a real straight up rapper from Compton they'd say Todd and Spade, but I don't want to be called a pioneer 'cause that makes me feel old, and I ain't that old!!

. . . It's been cool, though, rap is cool, sometimes it's slow, sometimes they say you're wack, sometimes they say you're cool. I done had so many rumours about me. They say I been in jail, I went for three days in '85. They say I still in there, or he based out smoking, he blew up a McDonald's, they just be giving me credit for things I haven't done.

BOO YAA TRIBE

The Samoan Boo Yaa Tribe are synonymous with hiphop in Los Angeles. They appeared as poppers in the early documentary *Breakin and Entering* and have released one album on Island and recently a single on Hollywood Basic. This interview took place in the shade in the backyard of their Silverlake home.

Brian Cross: So you want to tell me a little bit how the band started?

Godfather: Basically as kids growing up my father was a minister and he put the seed in us to play instruments and that's really where we started. We learned to play instruments in church, and we grew up with War and Sly and George Clinton and James Brown, and lovin' funk, we always said we wanted to have a band. Ganxsta Ridd was always saying we were gonna come up through rap, we didn't have any money so that seemed the way to go . . .

Ridd: I was gangsta rappin' before almost anybody out here, we just didn't have no money, maybe if we was sellin' dope and all of that, to make a record like other groups, I don't want to say no names.

GF: Ice T heard Ridd rappin' back in the day and he did 'Squeeze the Trigger'.

Ridd: I was all gangsta, my style was county jackets, I was rappin from the B-boy perspective.

GF: So we decided what is Boo Yaa, we figured our signature would be our rhymes and our harmony, and Ridd was take no prisoners, when you hear a heavy metal track with rap it brings out a craziness in people; if you been to live concerts, it's a whole different feel. That's what we like.

Ridd: That's what I like about the new rule, if you gonna do rap you gotta do it live, if you trackin', you gotta put trackin', 'cause Boo Yaa is always live . . .

GF: In rap we're to the point where we have to depend on samples, we have to depend on the hits of the seventies, we want to make music that kids in future generations will want to sample. That's what was weird for us 'cause people would look at us funny, like Parliament was before its time, we're before our time because people can't understand us, they think we're wrestlers or something.

We're doing funk of another kind, the new funksters, Parliament of another time. New pioneers – people freak out, where the hell did these Samoans learn how to play funk? Being from LA you grow up in the neighbourhood and that's all you hear. You grow up loving that music, the Delfonics, all the Motown stuff, the Dells, and that's where we get our harmonies from, instead of taking it to the new style, we take it to the War style. It all melts, two different tenors, a baritone, writing from the heart; if we write a song and if we don't feel it, we don't do it . . . When we first came into this business, we came in standing alone, all we knew was the street, in the street it's our homeboys against them. We called the stage the boulevard.

Ridd: And the microphone was the gun, you don't carry a gun unless you can use it, that was our whole mentality.

GF: But that was way before NWA came out with that on your back B-boy shit. We didn't know about the business, they released our record in the nineties even though it was an '89 record . . . It's a dirty business man, you gotta watch out. My first manager was so lazy, an armchair manager. It happened to Boo Yaa, we gonna be around ten years from now, we want to be respected for our music, not that we started the gangsta style.

Ridd: Our lyrics are still hard 'cause that's all Boo Yaa, that's all we know, we can't sing about flowers and things and love, you know, the closest to a love song we get is about our moms . . . We don't dis ladies, we don't call 'em bitches, and we don't have any problems with ladies, you know. They call 'em bitches cause they can't get 'em.

GF: Our people respect our women. That's just something we were raised with, if someone disrespected my momma I'd be like I'm gonna take your head off. We don't even have to cuss to get our message across.

Red: We let our image speak for itself, people see us they know. Our crowds don't even move 'cause they are so shocked, we take our hair down and let it go . . . the whole crowd goes crazy.

BC: What's cool is in Europe they don't even know that there is a big community of Samoans in LA.

GF: I know when we go to Europe they're like, what are you, Hawaiians? We are the only Samoan act to ever go to the theatres; we feel sometimes that we're the blacks in the business, they treat us like we're blacks now, the way it is now you make it what you want it to be. There was this one guy didn't want to play us on the radio cause of the one song 'Psyko Funk'.

Ridd: He looked up at me all surprised, sayin' you're not even black, they think that. You don't have to judge me 'cause of the colour of our skin, Boo Yaa Tribe just went psycho 'cause they wouldn't let us in. A lot of black DJs thought we were dissin' them. We grew up with blacks – how could we be dissin' them?

GF: It isn't about a black or white thing, it's about a minority thing, we all have to get together, that's why we got together with Ice T so we could show . . . on one song we got three black guys (Ice Cube, Ice T, King Tee), Samoan and a Hispanic (Kid Frost). That is why we got the song 'Brother to Brother', stop killing each other.

Ridd: They wanted to use that song in *Boyz in the Hood*, that movie came out and all of a sudden you got all the media there, all the camera guys at the opening waiting for something to happen. It's real sad, you got *Terminator* opening down the street and nobody is *there*. The killing has nothing to do with the music; you get in the mood, but you don't get in the mood to kill somebody, people love it, you can't stop rap. What are they gonna do? Are they gonna take all these rappers and put them back on the streets to sell drugs?

GF: Yeah rap is the best thing that ever happened to us, I don't know what we'd be doing.

Ridd: That's why this whole censorship thing bothers me . . . all that is bullshit, where does Boo Yaa go from here with no rap? I'd blame them if they banned rap and kill the muthafuckers. We'd be on the streets sellin' dope or in jail.

GF: We respect rap groups who stay right there with what they believe in, KRS One, Chuck D. We believe in family. The Boo Yaa Tribe is all about music, we are a band and we do make music.

BC: So do you think Boo Yaa is a product of LA more than anything?

Ridd: Oh yeah the whole thing, we were born out here; we blame our parents for bringing us here, 'cause if we were on the island of Samoa we'd probably be gospel singers. You just never know, it's just the environment that you're in. I'm not blaming the environment, it's what you make it. Like my mom when I got out of jail: I went back to the street, my mom thought it was my friends. She sent me to Hawaii, and I started banging there, so I realized I had to change myself, to grow up. If everybody took the time to watch their family, their little brothers, help them grow up.

GF: My father always says to blame the parents, it's the upbringing.

Ridd: When we were growing up we were the worst, the whole city was terrified of us. When we were on the street we'd kick up dust with anyone. If you sweat a little girl in our family, man we would go to your house and wreck everything and break anyone that was inside.

GF: But the thing is we grew up and helped all these people in our family. Now our dad is proud of us, but he never told us to go get a job.

Red: They believed in us, we wanted to make music, they supported us. They knew one day we could be good people.

GF: 'Cause being the sons of a minister we were the worst ones.

Ridd: Our ballad, 'Mommie Dearest', the song is like an apology to every mom from the kids for bringing them bad times.

GF: My mom went through a lot for us, going through court and when we were locked up, when I was in jail. Nobody visited us, only my mom and my brothers; she was hurt, so we wrote this song saying we want to give her the world. We've got seven boys and one sister, and on top of that we have family and friends living with us. My mom worked and my dad was a minister and she took care of all of us, she never once said go get a job, we played football, not once did she say hey get on. Her sisters would say they're all bad, and she'd say leave my boys alone, they're my boys.

Ridd: Every tear that falls, it makes my heart burn,
You brought me in this world, I still haven't learned,
I keep trying as long as I live,
The way you raised me, I must learn to give,
You used to tell me to stay away from my friends,
If I follow them you may never see me again,
So here moms, this song's for you,
For all the hard times I put you through.

GF: So what did we learn today? Boo Yaa's a band, Boo Yaa makes music and Boo Yaa's a strong family.

Well . . . I remember Ice T, he wasn't really out, I remember him trying to flow to Art of Noise, breaking and stuff like that. I got Run DMC's first time on air doing the KDAY show, I got the tapes; it's funny — that was big then. I also got GI Joe raps and stuff, it's wack but it's funny. I remember things getting shut down, parking lot shootings and stuff, Run DMC cancelling their last concert . . . But KDAY was the thing we all listened to.

In terms of an LA or a West Coast sound, I think it's not really in terms of that, but west is comin' up, people who come out of YPA (Youth for Positive Alternatives) and the Good Life. But I think it's more in terms of styling, cause east or west everyone's trying to battle everyone. The only way things will turn out best for hiphop is if everybody in the industry joined up or something, meet up somewheres . . . With this rave stuff going on it's like so separated, us being in the hiphop scene, only thing we have to look forward to is Thursdays at the Good Life and shows . . . .

Of Mexican Descent are new school Chicano rhymers from Los Angeles.

GREG MACK

Greg Mack was the programme director responsible for making KDAY the first hiphop radio station in the country. This interview was done in his north Hollywood home.

Brian Cross: Where are you from?

Greg Mack: I'm from Van Owenstein, Texas, a suburb of Dallas. I came to LA July 30th of 1983. I was working at Magic102 in Houston and our 'competition', a guy named Jim Maddox, sent my tape out here to get me out of the picture. So they called me out of the blue, we want you to come work for us, they treated me great, at KDAY. They were playing a lot of pop and R&B. In Houston we didn't play hardly any rap, maybe three or four times a day. But when I got to KDAY, about a month after they wanted to make some changes, our goal was to be KGFJ who was ruling at the time, so they made me music director. When I moved out here I was living with my mom in south central, so I would open my window and hear all the booming systems, all they were listening to rap. I asked my cousin and he said they all listened to KGFJ 'cause they were the only ones that played rap.

KDAY wasn't designed to be a rap station, I wanted it to be a hit station, play the hits. We called the record stores, tallying up the requests, and started playing rap mainly in the evenings. Then we put on the Mixmaster shows which went really well because the Wreckin Cru had gotten big and Dr Dre and Yella were the original mixmasters. That had to be in '83 . . . I mean probably around September, October, and so that really took off. We got Tommy Boy records behind us, the Mixmaster show ratings went through the roof. Saturday night, one Saturday night we got a 22 share in the books, which in LA is just outrageous; it was the number one listened to show in the whole city even next to KIIS and Power and all that.

We started to expand the rap records that were hitting real good, the LA Dream Team was real hot, we broke Salt-n-Pepa 'Push It', we broke Lisa Lisa and Cult Jam's 'I Wonder if I Take You Home'. That was probably our biggest key, we would break things nobody else would touch. Also around that time a man named Russell Simmons was starting to come up, and he used to fly up from New York. And he said: 'Greg, let's build something here, let's bring LL Cool J out.' We broke Run DMC, Whodini, the Fat Boys. We eventually ended up calling our station the Hitbreakers, we break the hits. It also tied in with the fact that [when] breakdancing came in, we gave out breaking boards [pieces of cardboard for putting on the ground to breakdance on] with KDAY on them. Ice T used to do a club with us called Radio.

BC: Radiotron?

GM: Radio, they used to call it Radiotron but someone else owned the name so they changed it. That was Ice T and Henry G and Evil E and Afrika Islam. We were always somewhere, we would do noon dances at school with the kids, we created an underground culture. The big chains didn't want to buy rap up so the 'Mom and Pop stores' were making a killing, as well a lot of the local rappers wouldn't get touched by New York so we gave them a chance. And at the same time they were pushing our numbers up. It was a whole vibe. Uncle Jam's Army was already in effect when I got here – they could get thousands of kids instantly; there was another one [called] Ultrawave, all the dances in the city they controlled, so we had to tie in with them.

I came up with the name Mack's Marines. Bobcat said don't do that, call yourselves Mixmasters, so that's how the Mixmasters came about. We were originally gonna sign him as our official DJ, but he wanted a big contract, but we got some of the best DJs in the city doing try-outs and stuff. Dre and Yella were the first ones, their careers just skyrocketed. So we had Tony Gonzales, Joe Cooley, Jammin Gemini, M Walk, Ralph M, Coolio. I couldn't keep DJs 'cause we were losing them right and left to rappers. Each one of them would do an hour separately, we'd be there from six in the evening till three in the morning. We didn't even edit, if they had a skip or a cuss word we had to do the whole thing over again . . . it was very carefully planned, we wrote the whole thing out. We would play some street stuff, but we tried to keep it mainstream. We would do a lot of scratching, we came in second at the New Music Seminar three years in a row . . . every year they would just rip us off.

BC: Would you say there was a different sound come out of LA than from the East Coast?

GM: No question about it. West Coast was more musical, New York more rhythmic beat wise, at first the West Coast was like, ehhh, too techno beats, fast, but with Eazy comin' up, it changed things a little bit. The east started paying more attention, then we had Tone Loc, Young MC and Hammer.

BC: So how did the West Coast make the transformation from pippy beats to the street sound?

GM: The East Coast guys got more props but the West Coast sold all the records, so Russell started getting a lot of West Coast producers to mix his stuff, the LA Posse, Bobcat, Kurtis Blow moved out here, Heavy D has moved out here, a lot of them had girlfriends out here. At the same time as that was going on, Luke Skyywalker made a niche for himself with the 808 sound, most of the 2 Live Crew was from Riverside, so the West Coast started getting some respect. You couldn't sell too many records of course, if you sell too much they think you've sold out; that's the funny thing about hiphop, very few rappers can get away with hitting it big.

Getting back to KDAY, it was never intended to be a rap station, we were not a rap station from '83; '88 we were 40 per cent rap, with the rest hits and R&B, but for the last two years they decided to go rap 100 per cent and the station took a nose dive. They had to have a balance, but that was their idea. KDAY was very balanced, we only played rap in the evenings . . . it was perceived as a rap station 'cause it played rap when no one else would, but it was balanced. My theory with playing local rappers was I would rather play a mediocre West Coast rapper than a hit from the east, 'cause the West Coast rapper would say KDAY is the shit all over the streets, and with the kids you gotta be a hit.

But the adults would listen to us because we didn't play just rap, and we also played album cuts, [while] the other stations won't touch those, even today. Songs such as 'Do Me Baby', you couldn't play that on the radio, we would. Let me tell you something, there's a big market for a KDAY-type station right now, and any station that did it right would blow up. A lot of the stations won't play rap cause the advertisers won't fund it. You can't just play all rap and expect to win.

What happened was the last two years KDAY was on I had resigned as music director to do a couple of albums, and they didn't understand what I had been doing. They believed the myth that we were a rap station, so they went for it, and just like every music, there are wack rap records, and they just started playing everything, and they lost it. I think it was 95 per cent rap.

BC: Why don't you think the people in the industry bought the station?

GM: I don't think they realized what the loss would mean, 'cause I went to all of 'em. I went to Russell, buy this and get it on the right track, plus a lot of them were scared. They do a personal background check on the owners of radio stations for FCC purposes and a lot of these kids got started by dealing dope, so a lot of them couldn't have withstood the background check. Then after it happened they were like, God I wish we had done it. I would love to buy it, I think KDAY could still be here today. There's a huge market for it, at KDAY we had 40 per cent black listeners, the rest were white and Chicano. I'd go to UCLA and all you'd see is white guys bumpin' rap in their jeeps.

BC: So how did you first notice the effect of the trouble?

GM: When big concerts would come into town there would be big trouble, and I think the straw that broke the camel's back was that Run DMC Long Beach show, which I was at. That was the worst I've ever seen in my life, it was bad. I was MCing it, and what had happened was, they let a lot of gangs in from different areas. Security isn't hip to colours, there were little fights in the beginning. Then this guy threw this other guy right over the balcony on to the stage while Whodini was performing, so they got up on the stage trying to talk to the guy, next thing you know a whole section was running, gangs were hittin' people, grabbing gold chains, beating people. I had this girl group with me at the time out there, I asked security to help me get these girls, security was hiding in the back. I got the girls, ran to the car, there was a Crip next to me getting his shotgun, getting ready to do God knows what. As we were leaving I saw cop cars and helicopters, on the news people were leaving all covered with blood. It was the last rap show ever in Long Beach, and Run DMC of course got blamed, even though they didn't even get to play. Everywhere they tried, things would just get messed up. There was always something, it just died out, so the only thing we would do is World on Wheels. I remember doing a show with Force MDs, it was sold out and raining, everybody was standing out in the rain; there was something about that place, people had a respect for it.

We used to do Skateland USA (in Compton). We and Lonzo used to do Dudos in Compton, we used to put some acts in there: New Edition, LL and Run and all of those people. The thing was if you did it in a certain area, gangs from outside that area wouldn't normally come, if you do it in [a] neutral area they all come. [But] they raised the insurance so high no one can afford it.

AFRIKA ISLAM

Afrika Islam is an old schooler from New York, best known in Los Angeles for producing Ice T and for his clubs Water the Bush and United Nations. He is credited with bringing Afrika Bambaataa's Zulu Nation to Los Angeles. This interview was done in Islam's Hollywood home in late October 1992.

Brian Cross: When did you first come out here?
Afrika Islam: On tour I probably first came out here on the Soul Sonic tour in '80, then in '82 I came with Rock Steady for the making of *Flashdance*. I came back out for that movie *Breakin*, me and Ice T were in *Breakin* together. Then I started doing the clubs, I first did the Radio. Me, DST and Chris the Glove [Taylor] were the DJs. We used to fly back and forth, we did Power Tools, we did Rhythm Lounge, then, um, Seventh Grade, then I came out for a while and stayed and did Performance, Red Square, Peace Posse, Shake Shack. I played a lot of the underground clubs basically. It started like from '82 on, but I never stayed out here more than three months. I used to stay with Ice T and Alex [KK], who owned Radio. I was staying with Ice in '87, we had gone to New York got signed to Sire, came back and worked on the record (*Rhyme Pays*) and then it was just a process of going on tour, coming back. I met a girl out here, fell in love then stayed for a few. Now I guess I've been here for two and a half years with an address, stayed.
BC: What about hiphop out here back then?
AI: The only hiphop I think that you could see, was poppin' and lockin'. That's documented in that movie *Breakin and Entering*, it shows Sugarpops, Poppin Pete, Skeeter Rabbit, the Trons; that was the scene. Venice Beach had an outdoor scene, which Ice was down with himself. The only other scene I saw out here was more like the funk scene – that was Uncle Jam's Army, and the other underground scene was Rhythm Lounge. Those are the only scenes I knew. Breakers and graffiti artists that had just came out in the galleries and stuff, there wasn't really a scene. Radio established the club to do it.

It was an underground club downtown, there was nothing but rock and roll and oldies at that time club-wise. This was the first underground where you could go with free beer and psychedelic movie sets, oil paintings, body paintings, exclusively hiphop and funk music being played with a 99 per cent white and international crowd. The only ones that were black being those who were involved in hiphop. Soul Sonic Force, Ice T, a lot of those groups came out. It was invented by AJ and KK, and it was modelled on the Roxy in NY to make what happened out here sort of like what happened in NY. After Radio there was like the Dirt Box that inhabited the same sort of principle.

BC: What about the Radiotron?

AI: Two different clubs, the Radio and Radiotron. Radiotron was like a little bebop club for hiphoppers. Radio was like a breakin' club with industry people coolin', the trendy crowd used to hang out there. That's where the East Coast people would come and hang out, since hiphop wasn't being played on the radio – there's no reason to send for groups – so the only thing that hit LA was the Fresh Fest, Kurtis Blow, Davy D, Whodini, Run DMC, Grandmaster Flash and the Furious Five, Rock Steady Breakers of course. The only time rap got played out here was late eighties on KDAY. '86 to '87 really began with Ice T, he was fundamental at that time, 'cause Ice was a Zulu King. He was made one by Bambaataa, early in the game, he was direct friends with Moe Dee, Grandmaster Caz, Melle Mel, Whipper Whip, they taught Ice what it was to be a hiphopper, not a rapper, and he adopted the lifestyle . . . The next eventual step for anybody is to make a record. His first was called 'Winter Madness', then 'Doggin' tha Wax', it set a trend – he did a gangsta type rap. That shit was unheard of in NY, they was doing everything from party raps to the message-type raps, but he was early in the game for beating somebody up on a record. Now it's the trend.

BC: Can you talk about bringing Zulu out here?

AI: Zulu was out here in '82, it started with the breakers and the graffiti artists. Anybody in Radio was considered part of the Zulu Nation, it was part of that peace ideology: people came down to funk, listen to music, hang out and go home. No violence, man. AJ, Ice and KK were hardcore Zulus, AJ was a painter, KK was a engineer, the DJs were all Zulu, myself, DST, Chris the Glove, that's how it happened.

BC: What did Zulu mean?

AI: Peace, authorization perpetuated in the ideology of peace and discovering the truth at any instance. Actually the ideology of the nation is knowledge, wisdom, understanding, peace, justice and equality. And that criteria is really searching for the truth in any manifestation possible, and through the music of hiphop and lifestyle and culture is where we express it. That's how it is, it's evident in this house.

BC: You grew up in the Bronx, right? Are there conditions hiphop grew out of?

AI: It grew up out of the ghetto.

BC: Geographically the Bronx is different than LA.

AI: It's a lot smaller, you took the bus and met people at high school, the gangs were like [a] territorial situation, the gangs, the Black Spades, were basically based after, like either [a] semi-black liberation army, somewhere between the Black Panthers and a motorcycle gang without motorcycles. So they dwelled in the projects. My father Afrika Bambaataa put it together as he started putting together the ideology of Zulu – which is based on the Zulu warriors of Africa fighting the British to maintain their own sovereignty. So he united the Black Spades, being the largest gang, with other gangs to form an organization. Originally the Zulu Nation was called the Organization, which was basically dancers coming together for peaceful parties. The party people outweighed the gangsters, so you had more of a fun atmosphere than a gangster atmosphere and that spread throughout NY city. That force was huge as a money-making project, records were being made, people were getting fame, getting respected, so as your appearance got better, you could search for truth and avoid violence cause you were a somebody, you were a Melle Mel or a Davy D – you were a somebody.

My first battle: I battled Break Out and Baron at a Funky Four plus One show. I was with Raheem and Busy Bee, they were my MCs, and I was the DJ. I actually have my first flyer right there (points to the wall) November 4 1977. DJs battled then, one played an hour, the next played an hour, and whoever rocked the crowd more won. I was a dancer to begin with, I was the 13th member of the Zulu Kings and we used to dance with groups like Kool Herc and the Herculords, Smoke had the Smokey dancers, so when we met up, the Zulu Kings were notorious, there were Zulu Queens, Zulu Hustlers, then came the Rock Steady Crew after the Zulu Kings. I started writing rhymes for the Soul Sonic Force, then the Cosmic Force and then I started DJing. There were two sons of Afrika Bambaataa at the time, me and Afrika Bamboo. Afrika Bamboo started to go into his own and I became the only son; I was the military part of the nation.

I invented the chapters, the council, and started structuring the military formations of all the Zulu chapters that were around. So I was like the Malcolm X if Afrika Bambaataa was Elijah Muhammad. I grew up in that sense, but at the same time I was a DJ. 1977 was my first official real battle, from there I went to Broadway International which was my first real downtown performance, where DJ Hollywood and Eddie Cheeba played, and from there in 1978 I hit, um, I was all over the world. From 1982 to 1985 I was DJing at the Roxy, me and DJ Red Alert and Donald D for like three and a half years. I was the first hiphop DJ on the radio. The show was called the 'Zulu Beats', we played everything from demo tapes to live performances, 1982 to '85. It was authentic, real hiphop, cause I knew the lifestyle, I lived it. WHBI, myself, Mister Magic, Earl Chin and Gil Bailey, they played reggae and me and Mister Magic played hiphop. After that I joined a group called the Supreme Team, which eventually became the Supreme Team with Malcolm McLaren but we were a radio show before we were anything and I branched off and did 'Zulu Beats' and they branched off and did Supreme Team. That's how it started.

BC: When did you meet Ice T?

AI: Afrika Bambaataa said yo, you should meet him, he's a down brother. I met him, went to Radiotron, and we became instant friends from then on. He was rhymin', DJing, dancing, I met him and the Blue City Strutters – that is the Boo Yaa now. Then Pop and Pete Taco who taught Michael Jackson to do all his shit, I met 'em all. I had already had a gold record ('Planet Rock') before I came to California. I had already been to Tokyo, France, Russia, and then to come to LA, it was just bikinis on Venice beach and shit. So I was like, damn, this is kind of a nice place, you weren't thinking about money, you were thinking about women and smoking some indica. But yeah, we became automatic friends. We would talk about Iceberg Slim and the military life, plus he (Ice T) always stood up for his friends. I always stood up for the Spades, he stood up for the Crips. He showed me how to make and manage money, and I showed him how to live hiphop. The Rhyme Syndicate is an example of the West Coast Zulu Nation, that's all it is.

G BONE

Greg (G Bone) is an LA B-boy par excellence. He is most remembered for starting and running Ultrawave which was the younger west-side equivalent of Uncle Jam's Army. This interview took place at his mother's house in the Crenshaw district in the autumn of 1992.

G Bone: Okay, me and a guy named Roddy Rod and a guy named Rick Rock, we started up our own little DJ company with Radio Shack equipment and two Technics belt-driven 1200s turntables and just got out there doing parties for no money. Well, for about 60 dollars a gig. We used to work at the Fox Hills Mall selling pets at the Pet Store and there was a Radio Shack in there too. We used to go to all the big dances at the Convention Center, the Sports Arena, a place called the Ritz which much later became the Playpen, when Uncle Jam's took it over. Uncle Jam's Army, Party Lot Promotions and a guy named Ricky Hilly with RH Productions were the main promoters and I went to high school with RH. They were the guys, but I was a pop locker so there was no way.
Brian Cross: What year were you poppin'?
GB: '78, '79, who was out then was the LA Lockers, Shabba Doo and, um, Rerun that used to be on *What's Happening*, and these guys from Long Beach called the Electric Boogalooers. Pop locking came from Oakland to Long Beach then it hit LA, by the time it got to NY it was old out here.

   . . . Anyway after I got out of high school, working at Fox Hills [I] must have been making minimum wage, about three dollars then, we came up with the DJ idea – this little 14-year-old Rick Rock came out with us – we started buyin' records from Music Plus with our whole paycheques. People had a lot of houseparties back then, 'cause gangstas were really looked upon as a joke, it hadn't hit yet, there was no such thing as drive-bys.

   My uncle gave me an old station wagon, before that we took the bus – the economy was on the rise in the mid-eighties so more people had cars – anyway, we were hittin' the scene. Michael Moor was DJing at the Bitten Apple; hearin' him on the radio mix in the early eighties was a big influence, we would listen to him and DJ Tee and go buy the records and try to mix them. We were basically not really makin' any money. All we had was two speakers, Acculab speakers and a home amp with tubes and a Radio Shack mixer that didn't have crossfaders. They made it with buttons.

There were these guys on the east side, off Vernon and Ascot, called Knights of the Turntable that knew some girls over on our side of town . . . Whenever these girls would have parties in Baldwin Hills, they would get these guys to DJ. It was like in Youth Groups and stuff, but that was our turf. So we started competing, and then you had the next level of guys called Baldwin Hills Productions, and they were getting a lot of gigs too. We weren't able to step to them yet because they had nice equipment from RH.

Music Masters was our name. We started meeting the Knights and going to their parties. The Knights were the Wiz, Darnell Adams, the Warlock, that was Darnell Adams, and they had a little brother called Rod Adams, Boulevard Rod, he was only 14 and he could really mix real good. The older two guys, brothers were into programming and blending. While Rod and Rick Rock and myself were into rocking the mike our style was kind of different. Finally we said to the Knights, we're not going to get anywhere doing this, let's hook up and go after Baldwin Hills Productions, 'cause they were much bigger and they had the more lucrative jobs. So we came up with Ultrawave Productions as a name for both the crews.

So the first dance we did, we gave a dance around the corner on Vineyard Park in the gym. We xeroxed flyers, they said Ultrawave and about thirty people showed up, which was okay considering, you know. Anyway Baldwin Hills Productions came down and dissed us . . . we havin' a ball though, but as it turned out, those thirty people happened to be key party people, a buzz happened, and we started getting gigs.

They did everything up on Ladera, where black people with a little money live, not like in 'the Jungle', but up in the hills on both sides of La Brea. So in order to squash us before we got too big, they called the DJ showdown, at St Bernardette's Parish up in Baldwin Hills. We rehearsed for about a week and we came up with some rap routines and some crazy turntable antics, and we turned them out 'cause we did a performance. Warlock did a rap: 'Ultrawave is in the house where we belong, so Baldwin Hills pack up your shit and go home.' There was a couple of nuns there, they were bopping their heads, the crowd's yellin' Ultrawave so we got all the gigs, and Ricky Hilly started letting us use his equipment. So now we're into '83 and Ultrawave was running the west side as far as house parties was concerned. We jumped from 60 to 150 dollars a gig, it was a big thing, we wanted to be independent. After a while over little bullshit things, we fell out.

BC: Talk about the Nissan Truck phenomenon.

GB: It was a valley thing at that point, white boys in the valley had them. You've seen that magazine *Truckin*, well they had taken from the lowrider thing to a Valley Truck thing. Right before the summer of '85, there was this dealer named Benzo Al; he had a lot of money, and he had a Nissan truck hooked up, as people would see him they would start picking 'em up. It wasn't unusual to see those trucks in the Valley, but the white kids would usually have older trucks, Al had a new Nissan. I think he pretty much brought it to the hood. By the summer of '85 or '86 if you had a truck with sounds under the tarp, you was on. That's why they made that law that you could get arrested for parading without a licence.

. . . By the summer of '85 Uncle Jam's Army had all but folded, so we had a lot to do with getting Crenshaw going. Everybody was comin' down in those days. LA Dream Team came down after their second record, 'Dream Team's in the House'. They were all jherri curled, and we were all flattops and shit, not the jherri curl thing. One night Rollin 60s came down to crash, but we took care of it. We pushed the name of the organization and the DJs, that is the way the Hispanics were doing it, and that's the way Uncle Jam's Army did it. Then this guy came up to me called Bandstand Sam, he wanted a shout out for the Bandstand Boys, so we shouted him and all his crew got hyped. Then Ultrawaves wanted me to shout. They were these guys that set up for me in exchange for not paying in and juice everywhere in town. In clubs and to eat; it was that big. Then came the Dapper Girls, they were fine Ladera babes, talkin' can you say we're in the house . . . then we had the Ultra Girls, they would just stay live at the party. Then there was Kevvy Kev who was in the Marines, he was stationed in the Philippines with some other Marines from New York. He would do this chant: 'The roof, the roof, the roof is on fire, we don't need no water let the muthafucker burn, burn, muthafucker burn' . . . he started saying that at my club. It caught on. The whole crowd would do it.

When the record came out by Rockmaster Scott and the Dynamic Three or somethin' – everybody thought it was us, but we didn't make it up. There was a lot of crews at that time like the Glitter Girls and the Georgie Boys . . . everybody was now part of a crew, the Romeo Boys, everybody . . . So Ricky said it's time to jump to the next level. Ricky called this guy named Ansel, who used to manage UJA, and he managed to get us the Veterans' Auditorium. So we gave a dance at Veterans' Auditorium, had about 800 people. Had all these dance groups were comin' up, Groover Girls, Groovers, Love Nuts, Love Boys . . . so I said let's just have a dance show. We invited some people from KDAY and some of the record companies. Twice a month we gave a dance at the Veterans' Auditorium, fifteen hundred to two thousand kids, especially on the holidays. All the holidays.

Ricky being the devout Catholic that he was said it was time to give something back to the community. I was pretty wild and I didn't think it mattered, but he taught me a lesson. So he had me doing some fundraisers, did Special Olympics for free, and I got into it. We had a huge party with (canned) food as the admission, we had cameras shooting the thing, trophies for the best dancers. We did everything, and had no problems, not one shooting, we had undercover security and they would be all over a fight immediately. Our format was hiphop, fast songs, then finish the night with some oldies to slow them down, calm them down.

BC: So it's '86 and you've had no trouble at all?

GB: Not really. Nothing.

BC: Had you noticed a rise in gang activity?

GB: We got dissed by Ice T for that, on 'You Played Yourself', 'no beepers no hats', talking about a dress code. But that's how we did it, no gangsters, people on the west side didn't wear big ropes or khakies, or if they did they would be tappered or beepers or hats. Not that we didn't want dealers to dance, but we didn't want it in our scene . . . we kept the gangs out, 'cause that's all it took – one shot, one stabbing. Our manager got 20 per cent to take care of all that at the door, I had ulcers behind that shit.

We folded in '88 because these other dance promoters started coming out. There was a stabbing at a Hispanic wedding at the Veterans' Auditorium. The people getting married were two 18-year-olds, so they cancelled all events for teenagers. That was in Christmas of '87, the day before our dance. I fell out with my partner and that was the last Ultrawave dance. Now everybody's waiting for the reunion. That's the whole story.

**KDAY, Crenshaw Boulevard, south central
Los Angeles, 1991.**

Uncle Jam's Army reunion, the Palace, Hollywood, 1992.

Cokni O Dire tries to make a beat using the
radio at the Heavyweight session, Pharcyde
Manor, south central Los Angeles, 1992.

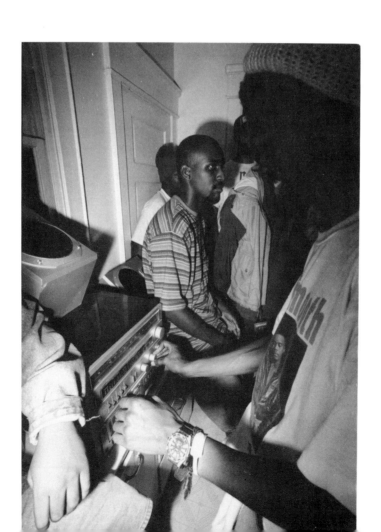

**King Dizmost grabs the open mike at
Stanky Booty, Hollywood, 1992.**

Cash Flex spins at the Airstyle brothers
booth, Crenshaw Mall, south central
Los Angeles, 1992.

Lisa Loc gets open at Jimmy Jam's birthday party, Strip Club, Hollywood, 1992.

The Attic, south central Los Angeles, 1992.

DJ spins at the Attic, south central Los
Angeles, 1992.

MATT ROBINSON

Matt Robinson is a hiphop club promoter. He has also managed several groups, secured a production deal and DJed for Bill Clinton. He has been instrumental in bringing hiphop uptown to Hollywood and the vanilla suburbs.

Brian Cross: What's your first memory of hiphop in LA?
Matt Robinson: The spot called the Rhythm Lounge, the spot that Matt Dyke used to play at, in '82, '83, somewhere. This kid named Solomon was running it, it was a real art school crew fusing in the hiphop that was coming in from NY with old soul and funk records, a concept that has been played to death out here since then. But you know, it was better than the Bay City Rollers. I was going to school in NY at the time and I almost didn't want to go 'cause the shit was so much fun to me at the time . . . I was just a hiphop fanatic, going to the Roxy every night, seeing Cold Crush and Fearless Four, even New Edition, that summer was just my first taste. The LA Dream Team came up with some shit, I hated it and my boys from NY would snap out on that and I was like, I'm not playin' that. I came back from NY in '85, '86. KDAY was just in effect, but in Hollywood you weren't getting much, I think Skateland and World on Wheels were in effect, but out here there was nothing. Some of the underground kids on the west side were starting to mix shit up, like Matt Dyke started Power Tools right about then. He mixed shit up, hiphop and soul and rock all together.

I got back from NY and started to lie and tell people I was a DJ and shit, we started a thing called Funky Reggae. We opened it in somebody's loft, playing reggae instead of rock. I was really into the dancehall scene in NY: on one corner a kid would have his box playing Run DMC and on the other would be Yellowman and I knew shit had to click 'cause it was the same identical brother, just one was from the West Indies and the other from Brooklyn . . . Chicken Chest was all out and we just wanted to take it to another level. Matt was getting into the rock thing, and there were pockets developing where punk was riding, after [the Clash's] *Sandinista*, TSOL, the locals like Fear was out and wrecking shit, punk rock kids were starting to link on to hiphop. I knew all those kids 'cause I was with it myself. The first show, Lyor Cohen – manages a lot of Rush's shit – put Run DMC on with the Circle Jerks or some shit like that and everyone loved 'em. They started to realize the crossover appeal . . .

By '86 to '87 we started rocking the Funky Reggae, the concept was to move it from place to place every week. I was the musical person, and my partner Shawn MacPherson had crazy promotion skills: he used to go downtown and get Funky Reggae whistles and little plastic dinosaurs, put 'em on the invitations, on and on, the kids would roll in. We had everyone from EU playing at the spot on the GoGo tip, Spike Lee had his birthday party there, Yellowman came in and rocked some shit and of course every local reggae MC. Public Enemy came in at 2:15 one morning and rocked the shit, took it over. But the scene was still very infantile in the late eighties, I still think the shit is infantile compared to where it could go.

It went from Funky Reggae, then we did some real quote unquote Hollywood shit. My partner Shawn, who now owns Smalls, well we started getting mad press, Mike Tyson, Eddie Murphy started showing up, and we were thrown into this scene that I didn't really want: the highbrow crowd with knuckleheads; it was real crossover. Sean Penn and Emilio Estevez dancing and shit, so then we did some shit like El Dorado, downtown, star search for sure. I'm not trying to disrespect that scene, but I was starting to purposefully play softer tunes, when I really wanted to play Spoonie Gee so as not to upset the rhinestone cowboy kids. Then I said fuck it and started Peace Posse . . .

Shawn was burnt out. Funky Reggae was at this spot called Osco's; it got really really violent. On Sunday nights gangs would have their parties, kids was getting shot up frequently, people started coming 'cause they thought Osco's was booming. They couldn't understand the reggae, Crips would try and stake out their territory. So I did Peace Posse. Downstairs there was a jazz lounge, the third floor was a reggae room, the second floor was mad hiphop shit, and the top floor was just a cool out spot for kids just to flow. It was at the Variety Arts Center, it got closed down 'cause of some shit that went down with the Boo Yaa Tribe.

We were packing in fifteen hundred kids, then one night someone pulled Roscoe from the Boo Yaa Tribe's braids. I didn't know that he was in Boo Yaa. Anyway he took the kid down. I had made this rule that anybody gets in a fight ain't coming back next time, having come from so much violence. So they came around next week nine or ten strong and I told security, yo tell 'em they can't come in, and he was like, you tell 'em that shit . . . I was like, I ain't sayin' shit. Meanwhile they got pissed because we waited to tell them until they got to the front of the line. They said, (if) we don't get in no one gets in, then they blocked off the door. We had a crowd in the street. I didn't know them kids, my security got soft as fuck . . . everybody backed off. Out of some act of insanity I decided to step to the Godfather (leader of Boo Yaa), I said yo one of your kids got in a fight last week and they can't come in, and he gave me this look. For the first time in my life I really thought death was imminent. I was like, stop, the cops pulled up, and wouldn't even fuck with 'em. So I snuck in the side door and shut up the club, but Boo Yaa were still standing there.

I was doing production [for Island] a few years later and suddenly these two family vans pull up and all of a sudden these kids get out of the van. Oh shit, this is not gonna be good. Chris Blackwell [president of Island Records] is gonna be looking at me. But we both had equal fear; they were afraid I would fuck the deal with Island. They were looking at me with very strict eyes like yo, you ain't sayin' shit. I was afraid for my life, and after that I was like yo, you all should come to the club. The guest list will be smooth and shit and we could have a lot of fun, and they all broke [into] grins. Afterwards Godfather put his arm around me, told me hey, you looked out for us, we know what went down back then, but you look out for Boo Yaa, Boo Yaa look out for you. He said we'll come down and security will be perfect, nothing will go wrong, and he looked at me and said but why are you so fucking crazy? Why did you step to me like that, we was that close to killing you man, and I said I was just protecting my business. Shit, that was some panicky shit.

From Peace Posse, we moved to a Mexican restaurant called Mariscos, and right then [Afrika Islam's] Water the Bush started jumping off. I was starting to do records, trying to wean myself out of club promotion, I had too many lawsuits and run-ins with fire marshals. I was kind of burn on it you know. I was doing low profile shit that was kind of fly, but when I seen Water the Bush it reminded me of the Funky Reggae days. It was bumpin'. They had successfully tapped into the urban scene while pulling in the suburban crowd, it was cool to see it go down.

BC: What happened in the transformation from pre-NWA to that sound?

MR: I was really devoted to the art of East Coast hiphop as a DJ at the time. I wouldn't be caught dead dropping Egyptian Lover, you know. I blocked that shit, jherri curl hiphop, but you couldn't deny Eazy and all that shit 'cause they were so hard, it was they own shit. They aren't as skilful as East Coast kids, but the East Coast recognized the West Coast for the first time. Then, bam! Ice Cube and all of a sudden there was respect, they stopped sayin', what you got a jherri curl detector at your club. They started playin' their shit cut with fly West Coast shit. Dre and Yella was the first kids to get mad respect from the knucklehead B-boys in NY . . .

BC: So do you think there's such a thing as a West Coast sound?

MR: I don't think it's been defined yet. There was one they've been trying to forget.

BC: At 135 beats per minute.

MR: Kill that shit – I think we're in the process of defining one, between Pharcyde, Freestyle Fellowship, the next Cypress Hill. I think the Beasties' last one [*Check Your Head*] is a West Coast record; they been here for several years. It was done with live West Coast musicians, there's a feel to it . . . it's so weird cause the West Coast was originally defined by the Beach Boys and the Ventures, but that shit has just evaporated. The beach kids listen to hiphop now. The problems with the club scene blowing up here is a problem with the police, they look at the kids as an army against them. With the history of fights, the fights from before, people get paranoid, the security and police throwing shit – even during the gang truce now, the cops are setting 'em up, just like in South Africa with the ANC and Zulus going up against the police-backed Inkatha – it's fucked . . .

Death Certificate *was a cool record, it was basic West Coast, me, Bobcat and Rashad, then Jinx did cuts, a whole little crew in itself came together to produce that album. It's LA, it's got its own little flavour, classical shit, from the 'Nigga You Love to Hate' to 'Bird in the Hand', you'll never have another record like* Death Certificate. *We figured people would get upset, if you tell the truth people get upset. As long as you talk about black-on-black crime it's okay. You tell something the brothers need to know and people say wait a minute you can't be doing that. But you always steppin' on somebody's toes when you steppin'. That record was not for them to like, it was for them to listen to and learn . . .*

DJ Pooh is a prolific producer from Los Angeles. He recently set up his own record label, The Bomb Records, whose first release is *Sickinnahead* by Threat.

Well, people are kind of afraid of us, since what happened to Ice T and stuff with 'Cop Killer', people don't really want to take a chance with what we're saying . . . that gets you a lot of publicity, they might have to pull us off, we're too hardcore. We're not going to change our style though, we're hardcore because that matches the reality of the situation, our situation . . .

Criminal Mindead are Chicano rappers from the San Fernando Valley.

ICE T

Ice T has released five albums (*Rhyme Pays*, *Power*, *Iceberg*, *OG* and *Home Invasion*) and been involved with several soundtracks (*Colors*, *New Jack City* and *Trespass*). He has been an outspoken leader in the hiphop community and is revered for his independent thinking. He was the centre of the biggest censorship scandal to hit the United States in recent years in 1992 with his speed metal group Bodycount and a song called 'Cop Killer'. In 1993 he was dropped by his label (Sire, distributed by Time-Warner) over the artwork to his current solo album, yet he rebounded by setting up Rhyme Syndicate Records and distributing the record through Priority.

Brian Cross: What was the first hiphop you heard?
Ice T: Well, the first hiphop music I actually heard was the Sugarhill Gang, with somebody on a record actually rhymin', I learned about rhymin' when I saw the old Dolemite movies, but I started to say rhymes when I was in the gangs, when I was gangbangin' I would make up rhymes, gang rhymes. I could tell you one later . . . do you want me to say one?
BC: Yeah . . .
Ice: Okay, this is a gang rhyme I would say, before I knew what rap was . . .

> Strollin' through the city in the middle of the night,
> Niggas on my left and niggas on my right,
> Yo I cr-cr-cr-cripped every nigga I see,
> If you bad enough come fuck with me,
> Seen another nigga, I said crip again,
> He said fuck a crip nigga this is brim,
> So he pulled out the roscoe, Roscoe said crack
> I looked again nigga was shootin' back,
> So he fell to the ground and I aimed for his head,

One more shot the nigga was dead.
So I walked over to him, took his gun,
Spit in his face, and began to run.
So if you see anotha nigga layin' dead in the street,
In a puddle of blood to his head to his feet.
Hope it's time all you suckas get hip,
Fuck a brim nigga this is crip.

So those are like gang rhymes, here go one . . .

Rollin' to a party on a Saturday night,
I left this pad down and out for a fight.
Had on my waistline leather and my Levi's cuffed,
And under the coat I knew I was buff,
'Cause I was drivin' that iron gettin' ready for the set,
And I was packin' my punch, nigga never forget.
The ring in my ear was hangin' halfway to the floor,
And I was so tired I walked sideways out the door.
My ride was lifted front side and rear,
Glass was all tinted wasn't none of it clear,
It was cratered down with col' ass pearl,
Deepest tuck in the God damn world.
I had quadrophonic headphones with the tone to be fixed,
Under the seat I had 30 odd 6.
On the way to the party I was scrappin' and hoppin',
'Cause I knew by the end of the night there was gonna be some poppin'.
Got to the set I just let it lay on the ground,
And the Buddahs came to check it out from Chinatown.
When I fell in the party there was niggas for days.
And I was lookin' crazy in some hella-fied ways.
I just walked to the corner and listened to them talk,
And on the first James Brown record I jumped up and did the Crip walk.
Now I was walkin' so hard couldn't nobody compete,
I was about to turn out the party with my God damn feet.
Some nigga got out of line,
His nose, my fist had no trouble to find,
After drivin' the iron so hard all that day,
I drove his face in one hell-uva way,
But his partners fell out and so did mine,
The punchin' went on for quite a long time,
But then all of a sudden I heard some poppin',

I knew not too soon this fight would be stoppin'.
I seen 22s, 38s, and a forty-five.
And knew not too much would be left alive.
Niggas broke out in a God damn rage,
I even think I seen a sawed-off gauge,
But homie I was sent from hell not heaven,
I broke out with the chrome plated 357.
The name of the game is simply survival,
And in the night time you're dead on arrival.
Me and my partners we was gone like the wind,
The police came and blamed it on the crips and the brims.
Some niggas knew in the corner and the dark.
Them crazy niggas eyein' tryin' to part,
They go by the name of Burnett, Zel, and Tre,
They belong to an assoc. called the EPA.

The Eliminators Pimp Assoc. So, this shit . . . I got millions of 'em, I used to say these when I was in the gang, so niggas was just like . . . 'Oh! shit, say some of them rhymes' so I also learned how to quote words from Iceberg Slim.

BC: Where did you hear about Robert Beck aka Iceberg Slim?

Ice: They're street books. Niggas would come to school with them in their back pockets, and I would read 'em and think, 'Oh my God, it's the phattest shit in the world', because it's exactly what hardcore rap is: it's the lingo, it's the life, it's the whole life we live. So I started readin' it, and I used to quote his words . . . I would go to school and say this shit and the girls would go crazy! All the rhymin' I would do, I would call it Iceberg, Iceberg Slim, so my homies would be like . . . 'Hey man, say some more of that Ice shit' 'cause my name was Tracy, but they would call me 'Crazy Tre', so they changed that to 'T'; they'd say, 'Say some more of that Ice shit T'. Get it? Ice T? . . . that's how I got my name.

But I rapped, but I never thought of puttin' it to no music . . . so, um, I went into the army 'cause I had gotten my girlfriend pregnant when I was in the tenth grade, I mean she was in tenth grade and I was in twelfth. So I told her look, I gotta do somethin' I gotta get some responsibility. So, uh, I went in the army doin' four years and heard 'Rapper's Delight' and immediately turned it over and tried to rap, but I couldn't cause 'Rapper's Delight' was beat oriented and my raps you see ain't beat orientated they more like hustler's rhymes. So that's when I first heard it and first tried to do it.

BC: There is a difference between, in *Breakin and Entering*, where you're comin' from and what you're talkin' about as opposed to *Wild Style*. For one, it's not to the beat and two, it's more like the 'pimp and hustler' thing as opposed to the B-boy, even though you got that too.

Ice: Well, I'll tell you the truth: durin' *Breakin and Entering* and even *Breakin* I was really fakin' it. I didn't know what rap was and was attempting to be a rapper, and I was listenin' to NY rap and attempting to rap about that particular type of shit. It wasn't me, that's where the grey area was in my career; it's kinda like, 'Well, Ice, you were in these movies and shit', but I really wasn't a rapper and I was tryin' to be one, but I thought you had to rap about rockin' a party, but in true fact I had never rocked a party. We weren't livin' in hiphop culture, hiphop started in NY. They had graffiti artists, breakdancers, we didn't have any of that, we had gangs.

So when I was in gangs and when I was in the army and shit, I was out here stealin' and gangbangin', and pimpin' women, and hangin' out with drug dealers, so . . . I'm pimpin' and doin' that shit, then I'd go into a club dressed like a breakdancer and tryin' to rap and my boys was like, 'Hey man, you gotta rap about what we do, do some of that gangsta shit' – my boys didn't really like that shit. They wanted me to rap about the gangsta shit . . . when I was into gangs, at that time, it wasn't about makin' money, it was about standin' on the corner, lookin' ill and fightin', no dope. The hustlers were the ones, the players. They were the ones who were makin' money, the niggas that was wearin' fly clothes and they hair was smooth, and shit like that. We used to go get the guns from the gangbangers and the gangbangers looked up to us, so . . . my boys was like, 'Yo man, why don't you say some of them rhymes', meaning like the ones I just said. I thought nobody wanted to hear that shit, and they was like, 'They do man, they do'. So this is when I'm doin' records like 'Doggin' tha Wax' and 'Ya Don't Quit'. If you listen to those raps, they sound like NY battle raps, you know, just screamin' about rappers and rappin'.

Even on 'Doggin' tha Wax' it was extremely violent. I remember when I turned it into a radio station they was like, 'Oh, we can't play this' and I was like, 'Why?' and they said because 53 times you said you'll murder somebody on this record. You don't rap about takin' the mike, you talk about murderin'. I was like: 'Look, that's what hardcore is to me; you know other rappers are talkin' about, "I'll break ya like a pencil" and I'm like, "I'll shoot you in your muthafuckin' head".' I was really into the violence rather than the other rappers who were fantasizing about violence. So we come up with this song called 'Six in the Morning' which was a B-side! Now the only record that was out similar to it, and I gotta give credit for it, was Schoolly D, he had a song called 'PSK'. Now the only difference between 'PSK' and 'Six in the Morning' is 'PSK' is vague. The eerie thing about 'Six in the Morning' is that the records were done near the same time and I never heard 'PSK' and we used the same vocal style, the same shit, and my boys called me up sayin': 'There's a boy in Philly bittin' your style.' And I thought, how is he bittin' my style? I thought, fuck it, it's a fuckin' coincidence and whatever, so that was cool but then it wasn't 'cause Cube came out with 'Boyz n the Hood'. He told me though, he called me up and said, 'Yo, I made a record just like "Six in the Morning".' Me and him bein' such goods friends, it was like a 'friendly bite' kinda like, not like I'm gonna rip you off, like one of your best friends talkin' about look at this book I wrote and you're like damn . . . looks just like what I just wrote, but he's like 'what do you think about it' and I was like 'okay, cool' . . . We made 'Six in the Morning' and shit hit the fan.

That song turned out to be my identity. Everybody's like, there it is. It was the first record to be heard about havin' a gun, bein' chased by the cops, killed niggas at the end, um . . . I was like, you know, fuck it, if that's what muthafuckas want I can do that, that's easy for me to do that shit. That's my life. It's like if you made eggs every mornin' and one day someone said, hey you should sell these eggs. To me my life was so involved in that drama every day, it was easy.

[Uncle Jam's Army, Radio, The Workshop on 95th and Western] I rapped at all these clubs, and when I first started niggas tried to diss like, 'ah, you tryin' to do that NY shit' and nobody was really into rap out here. So I hooked up with Grandmaster Caz, 'cause him and Afrika Islam would fly out here and perform, and Caz was the one who told me, 'cause I told them I was tryin' to rap, and Caz said: 'Look man, stick with this shit, 'cause it's gonna blow up and when it does you'll be on top but if you fuck around and slip, somebody is gonna take your position. Stay down with it and it'll happen.' Now, when I worked on *Breakin* I worked with this white dude named David Storks who produced some of the breakin' records and he started a label and he was hooked up with Kid Frost. So me and Kid Frost turned out to be good friends and we would do shows together, car shows. We would perform all over, in Bell, and Southgate, Montebello, because the SpinMasters, Evil E and Henry G were from Brooklyn and they came out here and they were doin' NY beats and brought them to LA. So I met them at a club and they were really cool about it and they were like, 'Look we're out here from NY and if you ever want to hook up we're down.' Straight up, no bullshit. Glove was not really my DJ, he was like the club DJ, I didn't really have a DJ, so I hooked up with the SpinMasters and I would go to their parties in east LA in garages and houses and I would perform with them, and uh . . . Evil would just spin, or Henry, and then they would spin for me, put on some breaks.

I was tryin' to get them a record deal. An unknown named Andre Manyel who now has the label Compton's Most Wanted is on, he ran a label called Technohop, and he was like you can't make a rap record from LA and I was like, yes we can and I said let's put out SpinMasters' record, 'cause I was tryin' to help them out, and he was like nah, man, and I said fuck it, so I did 'Ya Don't Quit'. That was back at the time when all the records had Inspector Gadget and shit so we used that Bugs Bunny shit (he hums the melody) and we were like, alright at that time everybody was usin' cartoon hooks. So we did that, and it sold so I was like, okay c'mon now, let's do the SpinMasters and he was like, 'Nah, man let's do another "Ya Don't Quit"; 'cause he was thinkin' about the money. I went to NY tryin' to push 'Six in the Mornin' with Islam and Islam was connected to a dude named Ralph Cooper whose Dad ran the Apollo. Ralph Cooper had a deal goin' with Sire Records which was a compilation deal with Melle Mel, Grandmaster Caz, Bronx Style Bob, myself and Donald D.

He threw me on there because of Islam, but what ended up happenin' was Donald was still signed to a label 'cause he had a record called 'Girls' and he had a group called the B-Boys. Matter of fact, Donald was the one who said '1, 2, 3, break' and, 'Rock the house ya'll' Mel was still signed to Sugarhill; Caz still had a problem with Tuff City and Bob never had a record out and I was the only one who wasn't signed and had a record out. So Sire said 'let's sign Ice', not because I was good, but just because I was easy to get. So I kinda lucked the fuck out and got a record deal and I think the smartest thing, the thing I knew, that it wasn't because I was good . . . I was lucky.

BC: The transition from earlier LA, where the popular records like Egyptian Lover, and all that and the clubs, Toddy T made that tape, you had 'Six in the Morning', Ice Cube had 'Boyz n the Hood' and it was still underground and it didn't really happen till '88, between the Fresh Fest in '86 and up to '88 when that girl was killed in Westwood. That was when people were like, Oh, there's something going on in LA, every week there's something in the news about it, then *Colors* came out . . . it's authentic to be from LA, it's hard now, it's not all jherri curls and up-tempo beats . . .

Ice: Right, there was all that right. I went to NY and I tried to bail out on stage, throwin' money and shit, telephones, and kids in NY were like, 'Damn, there's people in LA like you?' So, I spent a lot of time tryin' to beat down that image. Sometimes I look back on those days and think 'damn', LA was changin'; it wasn't just the music, people were startin' to understand rap 'cause people weren't really into it. They just had an attitude about it because it was from NY we jumped off, Eazy and them jumped off with 'Dope Man' which [was] a major record, then *Colors* jumped off, then uh . . . another thing jumped off out here that a lot of people don't know about. *Colors* man, I went on the Dope Jam Tour, when we used to tour NWA used to come on tour with us . . . There was Biz and Kool Moe Dee, BDP, Doug E. Fresh and Eric B. & Rakim. We came out and had a police car and wrecked shit, and that was the first time on a grand scale LA had a tour, you know. We were representing LA, and we didn't even have no songs, you know we only had one album, we had *Rhyme Pays* and um, fuckin' *Colors* and we came out on *Colors* and we just came out and wrecked shit. From that point on, LA was really considered somethin', it was kinda like that tour, I put the nail in the wood and NWA just came out and was like 'boom' and just drove that shit in with *Straight Outta Compton* and it was on.

I'll tell ya what is really with this whole West Coast thing, if you really, really, really break it down there's NWA and there's me. Tone Loc did his thang, Young MC did his thang, and then you got NWA who turned into Dre, who turned into Eazy, who turned into Ren, who turned into Cube, then you got . . . I mean the only new thing is Cypress [Hill], ya know and Kid Frost. I mean LA is really, for a city with this many muthafuckers in it, there's still very few rap groups who can go gold in LA with hardcore rap. You have to have a certain sense of credibility involved in it, that makes somebody believe you, because the gangbangers out there . . . they know what's real so they kinda like, sizin' up a tape and they don't want to hear it. You're gonna hear a lot of underground hardcore tapes, but the groups that sell it,

Too Short, um . . . I can still sell a few tapes . . . Cube, Dre, Geto Boys, it's hard to go gold or platinum with this shit cause muthafuckers gotta believe you.

BC: The thing that trips me out about it is, it's like for a form of music, even compared to jazz and shit, rap has been set up in such a way from the corporate level down it's not really set up as a career. They're really thinkin', even for you to be around after five records that's really unusual in hiphop.

Ice: Word!

BC: Most of the time it seems as if record companies want one album, they'll pump you for a couple of singles, maybe a second album and if that doesn't work it's like 'see ya' and . . .

Ice: Well, with me it's different 'cause I never let the corporation push me to that 'big' record. See I've never had a platinum album . . . but I made personal attempts not to go pop . . . . If you fuck around with corporate shit . . . Oh shit, they'll be like, well we could get blasé blase to come in here and produce this and get on the radio and you say, Yeah! . . . I'll go that route, and it don't work, because the term 'pop' means 'popular'; that what you're doin' is popular at this particular time, popular at that moment, you've done something that's popular, that also means that like what's popular this year may not be popular to wear next year. It's hard to stay popular . . .

I would never like to get myself into a mode where, if I had a very big single, I would be terrified, I would be like, 'Uh, how do I follow that shit.' It would be nice to sell a record but . . . you don't know man, we go into the studio, and we say literally we want to lose one hundred thousand fans this year, how are we gonna lose 'em, we're gonna talk shit about this, we're gonna solidify my audience find out what they're afraid of. I'll give you an example: last year on *OG* we didn't mess with no women, so I get these reports: 'Oh Ice T, you've decided to leave the women alone.' Okay, so I'll think I don't want you to buy my record if you think I'm gonna leave the women alone 'cause I'm gonna fuck with some women on this album. You know, I'm gonna do what the fuck I wanna do, so if that's why you like me now, then sorry! I don't really give a fuck. I always said if I can sell those hundred thousand records then I'll always have a nice income and now that I have my own label it's cool. Rappers aren't in control of their careers.

BC: One thing that struck me about your voice as opposed to like Cube, or Kool G Rap, is . . . do you have the Iceberg Slim record?

Ice: Yeah.

BC: It reminds me, like very smooth and . . .

Ice: One thing about me is I can talk the hard shit, but I'm not afraid to show you my vulnerable side, 'cause I'm more concerned about being a real person, than being this image of Ice T. That's why I made records like 'Shit Hits the Fan' 'cause one lady heard that record and she said: 'Well, Ice T, that's a ploy, what you're trying to tell women is this, is how to get things.' But I'm thinkin', look, we did all the fuck records, the wipe my dick on the curtain, we've done all that so I'm tryin' to do a different realm of the sex rhyme; like, you know when a guy goes out with a girl he always comes back with some story. And really I made that record after I saw the movie *Boomerang*, you know, I thought I'm gonna have a girl play me, you know she does me and then jets out, she's got the car and she's got it down, basically she knows what the fuck is up. You know in other words, move towards real. I know as far as my career [is concerned] I know I couldn't really blow it outta the water any more. In other words, amplify, the only hope I have really in my career is to go deeper. If I'm gonna deal in drugs get into the depth of it, take you into a more darker circle of it . . .

BC: It seems like hiphop has always been based around authenticity, how down you are, or on the other hand with new school hiphop it's been construed that if you didn't live in like the projects, if you didn't live in Compton then you're not authentic, or if you didn't live in Brooklyn or whatever . . .

Ice: I understand exactly. I'm one of the ones who will let you know that, it's got nothing to do with where you live or any of that shit, it's who you are. Anytime you interview somebody and they sit up there the whole time and act hard it's fake, it's fake. The person to be afraid of isn't the guy who will act tough, it's the guy who will show you pictures of his kid . . . chill out, laugh, show you pictures of his birthday, then take a dinner fork and pull your fuckin' eye out your head then continue the conversation. Me, myself, I guess it works against me sometimes; I think since I'm not so concerned with acting hard, that makes people think I'm soft. 'Cause I will get on TV and have a nice conversation, but to me it's like these people are the people who can be fooled for the unreal. See, massive America will see you act crazy and they'll just assume you're crazy, and my shit isn't made for those people. My shit is made for people in the prisons, it's for the muthafuckers who have been through the shit. It's beyond the invincible shit. I think that is one of the areas that I'm willing to reach in that a lot of other hardcore rappers won't.

BC: Is there any other medium which has represented the gangsta lifestyle besides hiphop?

Ice: Well, West Coast rap is really the book on it, but from my perspective that's for them to do. I was a gangbanger and I can rap about it, but when you hear Eiht and them from Compton's Most Wanted, they doin' gangbangin' rap. I don't do that, I do hustler rap. I was ahead of my time with the gangbangin' rap, so eventually the gangbangers will turn into hustlers. The only one who does the gangsta rap shit harder than me, I'm willing to admit, is Scarface, but Scarface doesn't claim to be no gangbanger, he's just a straight hustler and he's got it down. He's one of my favourite muthafuckers.

Now brothers are more toned down, drivin' Lexus and shit. You never see the hustlers, really; once you become a hustler you lose contact with your hood as far as love, meaning you still love your peoples but you don't wanna live in the hood no more. See, a gangbanger has determined that his hood is worth dyin' for, a hustler wants to live in Beverly Hills. The hustler mentality clicks on, and you start to say fuck this street. A lot of hustlers that are there don't rest they heads in LA, they'll be up here someplace, and they'll come into LA, sell dope and leave. I remember when I was gangbangin' the players stepped to me and they was like, 'You stupid man, check out this Rolex, what do you know about a Rolex nigga, Louis nigga, Louis Vuitton.' And I would be like, 'What's this . . . it's a bag nigga.' And they'll be like, 'Naw, it's Louis Vuitton nigga.' My buddy rolled up in a Benz, you know Benz, everybody wanted Cadillacs and Lowriders. 'Benz, muthafucker, this is class, we goin' to play tennis muthafucka,' and I'd be like 'tennis?' and they'd be like, 'Yeah, tennis nigga, see when these muthafuckas play tennis they put they wallets down, so you know we just get the credit card numbers and boom, we on our way to Vegas gonna do a little somethin' out there then go to Miami,' and the hood is just behind you. That's why when muthafuckas come to me and say, 'Ice, you live way up there on the hill, how are you in contact with the hood?' and I'm like, 'I've been outta the hood for a long time, I never wanted to live in the hood, the hood isn't a place you live in by choice unless you dumb, you live in there because your mama didn't have enough money to live elsewhere.' Now a lot of muthafuckers is runnin' around sayin', 'man, I don't wear no gold' and I'll be like, 'you don't wear gold cause you got robbed, muthafucka' . . . you don't wear gold. Hustlers always wore gold and diamonds nigga, my hair will always be long and I will always be this way, 'cause this is who I am. People will tell me like, 'Oh you got nice furniture and shit,' and I'm thinkin' I always knew what fly shit was. I have a lot of pride in the fact that I put finesse in my game. That is where when you read Iceberg Slim you know it's all about ghetto finesse. You hit this level of, I wanna dine and eat with captains and admirals and be at the spot with fine hos, and you know, all that 'ol gangsta shit like standin' on the corner drinkin' a forty, I'm tryin' to drink Dom nigga. My boys used to call me from jail and be say to me: 'You Ice man, this ain't no place for no player, they got ten blue rags up in this muthafucker, they don't know nothin' about no Gucci and shit they be G-in' in here.' I don't want to do that. I understand the gang mentality totally, but there's an elevation that happens. I be seein' new Gs and they make they money and they sag, with corduroys and a silk shirt, they still ain't got it yet. Some of my buddies came over here, you'd swear they was all doctors, lawyers, record execs and just be fly.

That's what I'm about. I ain't tryin' to go back that route 'cause hustlers have learned to become invisible. You can see the gangbangers and the workin' brothers and OG's who are still bangin' never learned to put no finesse in they game, and they found a home in those streets. Ain't nothing fly about that. Players always want the finest shit, that's it. That's people's new shit, about me: 'Oh Ice T got all this money now, he ain't in contact with the hood' . . . Shit, I'm more in contact with the hood than ever, you could not pick one kid outta the hood that wouldn't want to live here. I'm tryin' to turn this into the 'black' neighbourhood. We're from earth, ya dig, not from no hood. Every week I have my homies up here just chillin' . . . I learned early in the game, with the money I would be able to help, and insulate myself from the police. I also knew that I could get it without sellin' out, if I had talent. As long as I don't have to hurt nobody or sell my soul.

BC: Did what happened at Warner Brothers leave a bad taste in your mouth?

Ice: It's a point at Warner if you're runnin' an agenda that's counter to the system, eventually you're gonna run into a situation where they're gonna say, 'We don't want you to do this,' and you say, 'I gotta,' and you just have to be prepared for that break.

BC: For the amount of money that Warner made off Ice T?

Ice: They should've stayed down with me?

BC: It's not like you have a retirement plan.

Ice: The only thing you got is the rights to your records. I don't hold anything against them man, it's business. I'm a shrewd enough businessman to know that if I have someone in my camp causing problems you gotta break 'em off. I was costing them money. About 120 million dollars got caught up in that twist. I gained out of it too, though: I was committed to three more albums [and] I got out of that. I had enough business sense to make my own label. I'm a pull through, I ain't goin' nowhere. A hustler can make anything outta anything. What you see here is me, not Warner Brothers. I invested it. There's just as many games on the illegal side of the fence as there are in the legit side of the fence. I'm not fuckin' around. Now, my objective is to get my homies out.

BC: It seems hiphop has provided the antidote for the whole phenomenon of poor-bashing, because even in the media it's factual, dramatizations of everything. Hand-held cameras and even in the show *Cops*, everybody the police officer runs into is a criminal. They never show the court scenes. I mean the guy who was arrested for assault, it doesn't show that maybe the reason why is because the man he assaulted was comin' at him with a twelve gauge. The whole shit that went down with you and Sista Souljah, somebody had finally realized the shit you were sayin' was maybe . . .

Ice: These politicians, they have advisers, they don't say anything if it's not all planned out. They're playin' chess, more than we are, you know we're just artists. So first you gotta ask yourself, who is listenin' to this tape? Who brought this to Clinton? So somebody said this is a way you can attack this girl, and say what you want. Flipped the script. They wanted to pull my record to look good and get the press off they back, but the minute I pulled the record the media was right back on they ass.

BC: The way it seemed to me was everybody was lookin' at the cops like oh, they're just doin' their job? But they have this propaganda machine, tellin' you what's goin' on . . .

Ice: You're right, without rap there's no voice back at the machine.

KID FROST

Kid Frost can be credited as the first Chicano nationalist of hiphop. Although Puerto Ricans had rhymed in 'Spanglish' since the late seventies, Frost called attention to his heritage in a way that wasn't necessary in the naive days of the old school. Frost has released two albums through Virgin Records and worked on the soundtrack to the Edward James Olmos film *American Me*. This interview took place at his manager's office in the fall of 1992.

Brian Cross: Do you want to talk about the early stuff, I think it was called like . . .

Kid Frost: 'Terminator' . . . yeah the whole Kid Frost thing started in '79, everybody had started breaking and we got into that popping thing. We were going everywhere with Boogaloo Shrimp and all those kids. Then I heard 'The Message' from Grandmaster Flash and when I heard that it was like a turn around for me. So I had to start kicking lyrics out there. Ever since then my stuff has been real reality based. Everybody was talking about partying and stuff and we were taking it into the streets. In '81 I cut my first record on wax called 'Rough Cut' on the label that me and Ice T had come up with . . . it wasn't really for money or nothing, it was to get something on wax and put it out. So that's how we got started. Then we started doing backyard parties in Pico Rivera, east LA, Whittier, all these areas and really the whole San Gabriel Valley, and nobody else was doing it, nobody else was rapping or doing backyard parties and stuff . . .

BC: Were you involved with Uncle Jam's Army?

KF: Yeah I did some shows with UJA, I opened up for Run DMC at the Sports Arena, with Greg, Egyptian Lover. At the same time Low Rider was already doing car shows and stuff so I was into the cars and stuff way before it even was brought in, when they just had regular bands like El Chicano. We were the first rappers to hit the car shows anywhere, Kid Frost. That was the Bug show and Custom Car show and that was I think in '82 in San Bernardino. It was a big show and people were just amazed that somebody was rapping, because they had heard it but they had never seen it live. I seen the audience that I had was a pretty predominately Hispanic audience so I saw that and started going towards them more.

The other rap groups that were coming out in the San Gabriel Valley trying to get paid did not pay dues, they just came out and boom, back in the days you had to battle, go places, Santa Fe Springs and battle Kenny Rock. They had to go over here and battle these kids, but there was no Mexican rappers out, just me rapping against blacks, battling against black groups. It was a lot more challenging for them to see and get literally ripped up by a Mexican rapper and a lot of them couldn't deal with that. So a lot of the jealousy came in and they started putting salt in my shit, but it would just make us come away and start writing crazier shit and about that time I dropped 'Terminator' on wax and it was cool. Nobody else was really on wax and it was cool to be blowing out discs and stuff, 'cause to go to a backyard party and being on wax I was getting all kinds of respect. Plus I had Ice T with me and we were literally doing shows everywhere. I would literally pay Ice T fifty bucks to ride the Greyhound to come do a show in Fresno and so we would all be on the bus together.

BC: Can you talk about the Long Beach Arena? People say that was a turning point for LA, big shows on the wane, signalled the transfer of LA hiphop from electro pop to gangster, leaner, funky, raw: more sampled . . .

KF: I think that the Wreckin Cru had a lot to do with putting the techno stuff out there. Everybody was amazed at the amount of equipment they would use. Dre and Yella had definitely hooked into something at that time. The kids were really popping and going towards that Kraftwerk, 'Planet Rock' Bambaataa thing and so what they were doing was trying to make that techno punk thing over here in LA. So by the time the music came all the way to LA it had really changed, it wasn't as cool and it wasn't as hard. But I think what really made everybody go back into the sound was that everybody started finding their roots, where they were from. We started going into El Chicano, Santana, early 1960s TexMex. The sound that we knew and that all the Chicanos had loved for years, but nobody knew how to incorporate it with rap. So when we were hooking up, Tony G was like: 'We got to fuse this together somehow. I don't know if it's going to work right away, I don't know if everybody's going to jump on it, but let's try it man, we ain't got nothing to lose.'

And that's how it kind of happened, the birth of going towards live percussion and keeping that Latin roots in there – keeping Latin flavour in there. You had a little bit of technology, you had the drum machine which got a little better and everybody was taking snips and learning how to sample instead of going into the studio and making something from scratch. It went from the Dr Rhythm drum machine to the 707s to the 909s to the 808. Then everybody started going to where they were getting old songs, bringing them back and taking little snips and tidbits off of other little breaks and it was like who can get creative and who can get that hard.

BC: If you would agree that there is a West Coast sound a lot of people would say that it has to do with the car, and that heavy heavy bass sound . . .

KF: That heavy heavy bass sound believe it or not started out in the Bay Area. It started out in Concord with the Concord Stereo; they're the ones that really started hyping it up. The lowriders, definitely the Chicanos are the ones that started the big boom system. I mean, everybody knows that they started lowriders and everything: you know it wasn't a mixed culture, it was Mexicans everything. Those Mexicans are in lowriders, those Mexicans, and it turned into styles where everybody wanted to have a system more louder than the next guy so the amps came in, and once that happened the explosion of the big boom system happened. But there was no boom systems in New York at that time.

Over here in LA the only pedestrians they have is walking from their car, over here everybody is on the solo creep, everybody is doing their own thing in their own little world in the car pumping their music. It just goes along, the whole thing with style, everybody wants to get over on the next guy, have their own little thing going, and that's how the cars came in and more rap came to be listened to by Mexicans and Chicanos. Before it was more separated, the blacks listened to rap and Mexicans listened to the Nancy Martinez, Shannon, you know 'Let the Music Play', they wasn't really listening to hiphop until the emergence of the gangsta rap.

BC: Do you think it's surprising that it took so long for a Chicano scene to break in LA? Considering the amount of Puerto Ricans involved in NY from the beginning.

KF: It didn't so much surprise me, but what it is, is that the raps that they were writing up there in NY, were novelty. It was too happy bullshit, nobody was going to take [it] that serious, even the same case with 'Menti Rosa' [big 1990 hit for Mellow Man Ace], I feel like it was that same novelty happy, let's get paid and let's exploit this bitch – who's a liar and all that. That whole thing is, well, when you got people out there in the Hispanic community, I think that Hispanics are a lot more serious than a lot of the other races out there and that's not saying that oh we're stronger or better, but they frown on a lot of things in the Hispanic community. We don't have real strong role models, we don't have the Michael Jordans or the Magic Johnsons, our role models are thumpers, you know what I mean? Our role models are [the boxers] Julio Cesar Chavez or Macho Camacho, we don't have real strong . . . you know, Che Guevara and the Brown Berets and stuff like that. But we don't have nothing where we have somebody that Hispanics all look up to. So when you say something negative they come and they get you man. They watching you.

Knowing all that, we really had to be cool with how we came out. We had to be cool knowing our Spanish, cool with the lyrical content. I never, never on any record disrespected women or somebody's mother 'cause that's not done in the Hispanic community. Anybody that does that on wax, like Gerardo when he came and disrespected those parents on that record, that's frowned upon, man. Hey, you can't be doin' that shit, right away he don't get no respect 'cause people frown on that bullshit. Because they don't want to hear it. So with that I just like let it be known that I ain't out to waste my record company's money on bullshit. Especially when I could be talking about reality and what's going on.

It's a big myth, from what people hear off these NWA, Eazy E, records they think right away that's the way south central is but in reality it's two races tryin' to live together. I mean, first of all Los Angeles is predominantly Hispanic, so for them not to have Latin rappers, or not to have rappers kicking Spanish flavours, it doesn't make sense. There's so many kids out there that are Hispanic, listening to rap. So now they have something they can relate to, whether it be Kid Frost, Lighter Shade of Brown, Proper Dos, any groups like that, Brown Town. There is a new merge of Latin rap flooding the market. It could hurt us or help us and just boost it up, so we're really still in pioneering stages of Latin rap, the emerging of it.

In fact if I was to go to jail right now I wouldn't be allowed to talk to blacks. I would have to go with my homeboys and kick it with the Mexicans; they would be like, Frost, you gotta hang with us you can't be hangin' with them or else we ain't gonna be there if you need us. So it's like, there's a lot of things in the street that people don't realize . . . When you make these gangsta raps and you make these reality-based things, then you got to be ready to go out on the street and deal with the bullshit that goes along with it. Whether it be muthafuckers out there trying to test you from every hood. West Coast right now homes we roll so thick. I'll take 'em out, except for Boo Yaa, I wouldn't mess with those muthafuckers, any other crew, any other crew I'll take 'em out, dude. That's not fuckin' talkin' rap, that's talkin' out there in the street, in the world. Anybody fuckin' ever cross me like that in this whole world shit'll just spin cause I've got a reputation so big and got backup so thick, them muthafuckers call me on the phone when they got a gig with me to make sure I ain't got no beef. Because they the ones goin' to be gettin' some shit. When I said in 'La Raza' if it gets out of hand I know some Mafioso straight up, it wasn't like saying, I was talking out my ass, they wouldn't let me come out and say dang he's talking about us, he's talking Mafia shit. The Maravillas and the White Fences and the gangs in LA have been out way before the Crips and Bloods, so it's kind of funny for them to have a truce and shit, they ain't been out that long, just twenty years.

BC: Does it trip you out . . .

KF: That groups like NWA came out and stole Chicano culture and stuff? Pendeltons and shit . . .

BC: Yeah, yeah, you look at *Boyz n the Hood* and see Cube in a lowrider, or even Kriss Kross – that's even cheesier.

KF: Oh yeah that's really cheesy man, the lowrider shit and you know they shipped it from out here, took it back east and you know the maintenance ain't done right. People ain't got that car right, but because it's something that they think, 'Oh, let's exploit a lowrider.' Then you got these guys who are like, 'Oh, well, Detroit's black and that's the motor city so for blacks to be lowriders is no big thing.' But they don't understand that we've always been stripped of our culture, and we've always been stripped of our heritage and our background; it ain't nothin' new. But they don't lowride like Chicanos lowride and they don't hook up their cars like we do, you can tell the difference right off the bat. You could put a

Chicano's lowrider right there and tell how much cleaner, how much more fresh it is right off the bat, than a black dude's lowrider. There are a lot of lowriders out there who are black that are bad, but it's not the same, man . . . I even had to put some in the video, because it's easy to come out rhymin' 'Cruisin' down the street in my 64', and not even own one. Drivin' around in a BMW, and I've got a 64 [Chevy Impala – classic lowrider car] and I cruise around in it, but I ain't exploiting it 'cause everybody already knows the time.

. . . Chicanos have always been shunned, in TV they always make us play thugs or gangsters, they never give us roles that are strong, and this is LA, Hollywood is where they make the shit.

BC: In Arizona you have a more *norteno* cowboy flavour as opposed to the cholo thing. Does that affect your show?

KF: Yeah, well not really so much in Texas, but in Arizona 'cause it really is a racist spot. They suppress the Hispanics into confined areas where they know that if anything goes down they can go in and zero in on that shit and lock it down. Texas is not really like that. They call Texas, Chuco Texas, they got Puchucos, they're different. But I remember I had cousins in El Paso and shit and I would go down and take my style. That's when the hushpuppies were in and I was teachin' em how to be gangsters, showin 'em what's up . . . . It's no different, I could have come out and said this is for east LA and the song would have been no different . . . But I didn't want to, I wanted to say the *raza*, the race, all of us as a whole. It's said how a lot of these Chicano families moved to these cities for cheap manual labour and it's really fucked up 'cause their roots aren't really nowhere; here's work so here's where you're going to live. They don't have a foundation for the family, because of manual labour. To get Mexicans it's a lot cheaper to get them to do the fucked up work.

BC: Have you played in Mexico City?

KF: Yeah, I played a fuckin' bullfighting ring, thirty two thousand people in Mexico City. It was intense because the people in the back, they had to make the speakers half go this way and half go that, and they put a revolving stage – it was crazy. They just literally just ripped me up . . . I've been to Chile and I've already pushed a real strong thing there. 'La Raza' was big, not so much in the clubs, 'cause they got the techno thing crazy right now. It's gonna be hard for a Cuban group like Cypress Hill to really break out in Mexico City because the Cubans and Mexicans don't really get along like they should. Like the Latin Alliance project where we tried to bring everybody together but no one accepted it because everybody's superior, the Dominicans don't get along with the Puerto Ricans, Puerto Ricans don't get along with Cubans who don't get along with Mexicans and the list goes on and on. It was sad because here in LA it was hard to be mellow. People would say to me don't get along with the Cubans, don't you know in jail they got em all PC'd upstairs along with the fags and shit, because in the population someone's shanking 'em. It's not something that we can control and it's not something the government can control, it's just how the races feel about each other. Maybe if we start getting in there and letting 'em see things might change, but I don't see it happening. I've tried to make strong changes and I tried to tell Latins to unite, [but] muthafuckers just don't do it, they don't listen sometimes.

BC: One thing I wanted to ask, what is it with the Chicano/oldies thing?

KF: First thing, everybody started advancing, and everybody started going into newer things, but Chicanos are really fond of memories, *los recuerdos*. What they remember of what their moms taught 'em and what their dads teach 'em and all of that. East LA is not like fast, but we want to advance and go to the higher level, but after we do all of that, they're more kick back. They want to kick with their girlie, so they want to listen to music and think of memories and drink and think about the old days when they were with their parents . . . That's how the oldies started. Parents would tell 'em, oh well, we used to listen to the Vanguards and we used to listen to Brenton Wood and Mary Wells and all that. Everybody else overlooked 'em while the Chicanos just kicked with 'em. You play rap for some of the hardcore Chicanos, even some of my homeboys, and they say why you wanna rap ese, fuckin' blacks' homes, fuckin' *mietas*? And I say my rap is gonna be for the Chicanos' homes about *raza* and shit and they're like, oh, *orale* and when they heard my shit come out they were like, dang. So I incorporated the oldies into my sound cause I know how deep the oldies are. People like Thin Line and Smiling Faces, Bill Withers – we used them 'cause I knew it would be a lot easier for them to listen to the stories, like I did with 'Ain't no Sunshine'. They can go, oh, he's talking about us, eh? Some of the younger kids'll hear oldies and say that sounds like Kid Frost, 'cause it passed 'em by; they were into Boy George and shit.

BC: Tate was saying it was like a family thing, all the generations can listen to it. Sampling is beginning to introduce the music to a whole generation of kids . . . they go back and get the original of 'Cruisin', or 'Viva La Tirado', El Chicano . . . that's why all this shit about sampling is fucked up.

KF: Exactly, they're trying to make us go back to phase two of the techno, Dre and shit, make everybody make their own shit up, and it's like yo man, the foundation, those roots are what inspired me to go into the music in the first place.

DR DRE

Dr Dre is singlehandedly given credit for formulating the transition musically from up-tempo electrofunk to slow-tempo gangsta lean. He has a notorious reputation for trouble, having been involved in an assault case with television presenter Dee Barnes and several other less publicized incidents. He broke from NWA after their *Efil 4 Zaggin* album in a problem over finances and creative control with Eazy E. From there Dre went on to form Death Row Records and recorded his first solo album, *The Chronic*, with the assistance of Snoop Doggy Dogg. At the time of going to press this album has sold close to three million copies. This interview was done at Solar Studios during the recording of *The Chronic* in the fall of 1992.

Brian Cross: What were you doing before the World Class Wreckin Cru?
Dr Dre: DJing. I was mainly DJing high schools' parties, mobile DJ. I was playin' early hiphop, whatever was hittin' at the time, a lot of P-Funk stuff, Zapp, all that shit.
BC: What were you listening to when Lonzo put the Wreckin Cru together?
DD: Pretty much the same shit. But all that shit was wack, I wasn't in the driver seat then, I was 17, I put my two cents in and they would be like, yo man, we don't want to do that. I was like, okay fuck it, I'll go with the flow, I was just tryin' to get in there and make a little money, you know. But when I got a chance to do my own stuff, producing you see what turned out, NWA. I just sat in the studio, I used to make these mix tapes; I had a four track over in the garage in the hood in Compton. That's how I learned how to use the board and everything. From the four track I advanced to the eight track and then fucking around in a little demo studio we had, using the money we had from DJing we bought a few things for a little twelve track studio. I started fucking around with some beats.
BC: So 'Boyz n the Hood' was the first track you would have done?
DD: By myself? Yeah, see with the four track, the Wreckin Cru was a DJ crew. In Eve's After Dark, I would make tracks in the back and play 'em on the weekends just to see how it would

do. With 'Boyz' I decided I wanted to do something on my own outside of the Wreckin Cru, right. I didn't have no ins, I didn't have no money, but I had the talent. So I said let me find me a group to produce and somebody with some money to back 'em. I called Eazy who I knew, called another friend named Laylaw. They come over and I told them I want to sign this group from New York, and I had Ice Cube write this song for these guys 'cause I didn't like the way they wrote songs. However they could rhyme, so we got everyone together and they were like, 'Yo man we ain't gonna do this song, this is some West Coast shit.' So they left and Laylaw was like, 'Yo, I'm out of here,' so it was just me and Eazy in the studio, with a little eight track. And so I told him to do the song and that's how 'Boyz n the Hood' came about.

BC: How did you know Cube?

DD: He lived about two houses down from my mom, somewhere 115th and Van Ness. Jinx, that's my cousin, I was staying with him for a little while.

BC: How did you make the transformation from Egypt to . . .

DD: It wasn't really a transition, it was what I wanted to do in the first place. This is how Cube started rapping matter of fact, they had a little group back then called CIA: him, Jinx, and this other kid named Darrell (KD). I was like you gotta do some shit that's gonna be funny, but have it hardcore if you want to entertain people and stuff. I would tell them to re-do popular songs like 'My Adidas'; they would re-do the song to the same music but make it real dirty, like funny, so the crowd got all into it.

BC: Were you listening to much East Coast hiphop at that time?

DD: They still didn't touch what I wanted to touch. The East Coast had some shit that I liked, but I wanted to do some hardcore shit. People like listening to Richard Pryor and Dolemite, the hardcore shit. The stuff you couldn't hear on the radio at that time . . . I wanted to make people go: 'Oh shit, I can't believe he's sayin' that shit.' I wanted to go all the way left, everybody trying to do this black power and shit, so I was like let's give 'em an alternative, nigger, niggernigger niggernigger fuck this fuck that bitch bitch bitch bitch suck my dick, all this kind of shit, you know what I'm saying.

BC: Did you trip when it hit big?

DD: Yeah, we was just sellin' 'em out the trunk, trying to make money, we sold close to ten thousand records right out the car before we got signed. It ain't about who's the hardest, it's about who makes the best record, as a matter of fact it ain't even about that, it's about who sells the most records. It's not about I'm harder than you, it's about record sales.

BC: Did you put the sound together from lowrider?

DD: Yeah definitely, I make the shit for people to bump in their cars, I don't make it for clubs; if you play it, cool. I don't make it for radio, I don't give a fuck about the radio, TV, nothing like that, I make it for people to play in their cars. The reason being is that you listen to music in your car more than anything. You in your car all the time, the first thing you do is turn on the radio, so that's how I figure. When I do a mix, the first thing I do is go down and see how it sounds in the car. I was using an 808 and synthesizers and of course the

SP1200 the whole time, but I wasn't into using other people's music, I wasn't hip to it. I would listen to it for ideas, but then I got into it. But now, I'm trying to get out of it.

BC: From day one on the West Coast people seemed to have been slower to use samples.

DD: I mean if I can get away with not using other people's music I'll do it, I'll replay it and shit, if I can replay it, if I can't, I'll use a sample.

BC: How many tracks will you use on a song?

DD: The early stuff was eight track, then twenty-four. The NWA album was twenty-four track, but the singles before that was in the garage.

BC: Talk about KDAY and the mixmasters.

DD: Yeah that's cool. I got hooked up through Greg Mack; he had heard the tapes I was doing on the street, so me and him got together. At first it was just fifteen minutes every day on his show at five o'clock called the 'Traffic Jam'. I did like fifty mixes for him. Then it just got to where I was too busy and he started bringing the mixmasters in. That must have been in '85. Roughly.

BC: Did the KDAY thing help out?

DD: Definitely, helped me out producing. Those mixes were wild, each like a little record. KDAY was the shit, they put a lot of people on the map, they definitely put NWA on the map.

BC: How did you react when white kids in the suburbs started bumping gangsta shit?

DD: That tripped me out, that bugged me the fuck out. If the shit is good, people are going to listen to it, no matter what colour you are. It bugged me out the first time I saw that shit.

BC: What kind of funk do you listen to man?

DD: George Clinton, Zapp, let me think, Sly, Bootsie of course, George Clinton has definitely been strongest.

BC: How do you put the tracks together?

DD: Smoke a little bit of the chronic, start fucking around with the drums. My boy Colin plays the shit out of a bass, fuck around with some bass lines, lay it down, lay a track on top of that, maybe Snoop or DOC or RBX, somebody is in there, layin' some rhymes down, put this together and boom, we gotta song.

BC: Why do you think it was Compton, rather than Watts or . . .

DD: It's not really a matter of where people come from, it's a matter of talent. I could have been from fuckin' Missouri, I would have been doing the same shit. There's some people in Watts bumpin' some good shit. Watts just hasn't been discovered yet.

BC: The Bronx/Compton configuration interests me not 'cause of Tim Dogg but because these turned out to be the two cities of hiphop and I'm trying to figure out why . . .

DD: But you gotta think about it. We came out with Compton, the NWA thing, so every time somebody sees Compton they gonna buy that shit just 'cause of the name, whether they from there or not. Compton exists in many ways in the music to sell records.

BC: Want to say something about the Dee Barnes thing?

DD: I didn't do it. She said I threw her down a flight of stairs, then I stomped her and beat her ass. All we had was a little argument and my boy got me out of there. She had an eighty-dollar doctor bill – checkups can cost more than that – she went to work the next day. So she calls me and says like that was fucked up, 'I'm gonna get you, you do some records for me and I'll forget about it.' I called her a week later, her manager says we want you to do four songs for Dee Barnes's album *Body and Soul*, without your name. I said okay and signed the contract. Then the NWA album came out went to number one; she called and said, 'I want a million dollars.' I said fuck you, she said alright your ass is going to court. It went to court, but the civil thing hasn't went, she lost her job, she lost her lawyer. I ain't gonna sweat that shit. That shit is two years old, and it's probably gonna flare up again when my album comes out.

BC: Do you want to see what has been written before it goes to print?

DD: You can say whatever the fuck you want, there's no way you gonna hurt my reputation, I'm already a bad boy.

EAZY E

There isn't a lot that you say about Eazy that hasn't been said already. His nasal voice is eerie. He is very short. Not much is known about where he comes from. He has a notorious reputation for being a shrewd if often underhanded businessman. He is very conscious of his image. He is also a very friendly and disarming person. This interview was done at the Woodland Hills offices of his record company in the fall of 1992.

Brian Cross: What is your first memory of hiphop in Los Angeles?

Eazy E: I remember all the Uncle Jam's Army and everything but it just seemed like it was just that techno, you know, the fast stuff. It just seemed like there weren't really no hiphop. I remember the Dream Team, but I wouldn't call that hiphop either.

BC: Talk about the establishment of NWA.

EE: Figure you got Dre as the producer and me. We came up with the name and then we added Ice Cube and Yella. We came up with a name to shock ya. You couldn't really tell us what to do and what not to do. So together, I had Ren, he wanted to do his little solo thing, so I put him in the group and it just happened. We never did anything we didn't want to do. We did what everybody else was scared to do, like 'Fuck tha Police'. Before that everybody was doing their own thing. Ice Cube was in another group, Ren was doing his little thing, Yella and Dre was in Wreckin Cru at the time. They left all that.

BC: What about the first album?

EE: NWA and the Posse? That wasn't really a NWA album, that was just a bunch of artists that they had on different . . . it was like a compilation. And I guess they just used NWA to sell it, you know.

BC: Was that sanctioned by you?

EE: He [Donald Miller] just threw that together hisself, just to make some money. Macola had a lot of big people over there at one time but he just ended up fucking everybody. He had Two Live Crew, Hammer, Timex Social Club, us, and a couple of other different groups. Just imagine if he had us still, he coulda did something really. But he was always slippin' shit out the back door.

BC: Tell me about Ruthless.

EE: I had my own little label over there, my jackets, and shit. Went over to Priority who didn't really have anything at the time but the California Raisins, so we did Ruthless/ Priority. Then I started doing other deals with like Atlantic, Atco, CBS, MCA, a lot of deals, then I got another deal with Giant records. But here I am the president, owner, everything, no partners.

BC: What are your views on self-determination, either from a business or cultural perspective?

EE: You mean more black record companies? Yeah, if they know what they be doing. A lot of people don't know what they be doing. Imagine if there was one black record company, one major company and everyone went over there – imagine how powerful that would be? People have power and they don't even know they have it. 'Cause a lot of the records put out are black rap, R&B, if you take all that away and build one big black owned and run company it would fuck everybody else off. A lot of people don't trust black people. A lot of black people steal, it's sad but it's true. Fuck this black–white thing. I can trust my manager, he won't run off with half my money on the road and shit.

BC: What about the effect of a white suburban listening audience?

EE: They like listening to that 'I don't give a fuck' attitude, the Guns N' Roses attitude. They buy something like 70 per cent of our stuff. They wanna really learn what's going on in different parts of the neighbourhoods, they wanna be down, just like I want to be down too.

BC: How do you put together a group like NWA when nobody else is doing anything like that?

EE: We just wanted to do something new and different and talk about what we wanted to talk about, like dick sucking, we wanted to talk about that. Like people say, well you can't talk about dick sucking, or this or that in order to get this deal. I be like fuck the deal, I'll just wait. I'd rather take nothing and do what I want to do, than take a lot and do what they want to do. That's why we never signed with any major label. We wanted to do some shit that would just shock everybody, that we could relate to, and obviously everybody else could relate to. We just did it.

BC: Lonzo talked about you having all this money and stealing from Dre and Yella.

EE: Oh that bullshit he talkin'? Me and Dre was buddies from way back. We used to DJ and shit. I had money, and Dre said, 'Why don't you start a label?' So I did. Lonzo had a little studio in the back of his house, he probably told me some shit how to do this and that. He had Ice Cube, 'cause they had a little group called the Stereo Crew at the time. Yella and Dre and him were in the Wreckin Cru, but they were doin' all this work, and he used to give 'em like peanuts. Dre had a fucked up car, he gave 'em like twenty-five dollars a week. Him and Yella were producing bootlegs and shit all the time, he used to give Cube and Jinx twenty-five dollars a week between them. From watching him fuck everybody over I learned that what you do is you take care of 'em, and they'll be cool to you. Dre goes to jail, I call Lonzo, to tell him to get him out of jail. Lonzo says, 'I ain't got no money.' So I go and get him out on a nine-hundred-dollar bail. I was like fuck that shit, he can't even get you out of jail, you and Yella doin' all the work and shit. He probably introduced me to somebody. My manager was his manager. One day I met with him on the side, Lonzo tryin' to get a cut and shit. But you see him, where he is now and you see me where I am now? If Lonzo wasn't so fucked up he wouldn't be where he is now, or trying to do this, or whatever.

BC: What did you do before hiphop? I saw you say you were a pharmacist?

EE: I don't really give a shit, they wouldn't know if I was telling the truth or not. Yeah I used to sell drugs. And if I wasn't doing what I'm doing now I'd probably be in jail or dead. Dead or in jail. Lonzo had more than me at the beginning, he had a house and a car, and thought he was the shit. If he wasn't so fucked up, he'd probably be right along now. Lonzo's a fuckin' loser. That fuckin' lipstick and lace and boxers and shit didn't last too long. Trying to sound like Cameo, it was hittin' back then, but you can't do it nowadays. Lonzo even had Michel'le, you know something was wrong. You can't have somebody blowing up and getting on the radio, then give them a hundred dollars. Damn, when Michel'le came out and her record was doing good, this muthafucker tried to rerelease 'Turn Out the Lights'.

BC: Why do you think West Coast rap hasn't got the respect?

EE: Some of the West Coast does get the respect and some doesn't. I mean, 'cause the dudes figure, they used to hear the Dream Team, Wreckin Cru, what the fuck is this, you could get some oldies and sample 'em and shit, but they be doing dee dee dee, all this crazy electronic shit. And half the artists come out now, they don't want to hear that shit. But groups like NWA, Ice Cube, Ice T, they get respect. Then you got groups that are comin' up like Cypress Hill and House of Pain, all them get respect. This fast, fast dancing shit, they don't want to hear that shit, I don't want to hear that shit.

BC: Want to talk about the Ice Cube break up?

EE: What about it? He wanted to do his own thing. That's really all I got to say. Everybody wanted to do their own thing, I was doing my own thing. We talk once in a while.

BC: No bad blood about what went down on both records?

EE: Nah. That's business. If it was personal you would know about it.

BC: What about the white management, livin' in Riverside thing. Do you care?

EE: Not really. I don't know anybody in Riverside, let alone live there. The only thing that got me was 'Eazy's dick smells like MC Ren's shit'. How would you know what my dick smells like? I mean shit, how did Cube know, you know? Not unless my nuts was on your chin, and my dick is in your mouth. That's all I got to say.

BC: Are you a Republican?

EE: Hell no, I don't give a shit really. How could I do a song like 'Fuck the Police' and be a Republican? I guess you can really, but I don't even vote. I just went 'cause those muthafuckers sent me an invitation. They pulled my name off the computer 'cause I give a lot of money to charities and stuff. Soon as I got there CBS and other news stations were all there askin' how you guys gonna let him get in here. It was a whole big mess, on every station. I just wanted to go, see what they was talking about, just to see. I get home, everybody was like, 'Oh so you're a Republican, blah blah.' Hell no, I ain't no Republican. They was talking about the fuckin' war and how this and how that, it was bullshit.

BC: What will Eazy E be doing at 40?

EE: I don't know. I wish I had me a big company, as big as Motown, my own. Doing everything, distribution, pressing, everything.

ICE CUBE

Ice Cube is Los Angeles' most famous hiphop son. Formerly of NWA and now the head of a multi-million-dollar operation, Street Knowledge, he is the image of success without sellout. Enough has been said about his ability and vision as a rhymer; however, Cube now has a film career, appearing in *Boyz n the Hood* by John Singleton and *Trespass* by Walter Hill. The following interviews were done in October of 1991 over the phone while Cube was in Atlanta filming *Trespass* and in November 1992 just before the release of his latest album *The Predator* at his office in south central.

Part One

Brian Cross: So when did you start rappin'?

Ice Cube: In the ninth grade. I went to Western, then I went to Taft High School.

BC: What are your first memories of LA hiphop?

IC: My first memories was people like Egyptian Lover, Dream Team, World Class Wreckin Cru, early Ice T, see if I can remember that far back . . .

BC: On the subject of 'Black Korea', I'm sorry if you've been asked this question a million times, but anyway, a lot of people have said Koreans are as exploited by the system as blacks and that unity is really what is needed. What do you think about that?

IC: Unity is what's needed . . . where?

BC: From the working-class community, across racial barriers basically.

IC: I mean that'd be cool if they wanted unity. Black people for years have been pro-unity, wanting to blend in, wanting to fit in, wanting to do the same as whites and things but it's been a fistfight the whole way, so you gotta come to the conclusion that everybody don't want to unite and then . . .

BC: Did you write the song after Latasha Harlins?

IC: Way before that.

BC: So what did you think after that happened?

IC: It just proved my point, and then peoples sayin', I don't wish things to happen, but it did, and the shit is on a collision course like a train, right?

BC: I agree and I think it's interesting that you wrote the song before [the] Latasha Harlins murder. You know Bradley endorsed a plan a couple of days ago by the Korean shop owners' association to create a hundred new jobs in south central for black young kids in Korean-run liquor stores. Do you think that will make a difference?

IC: It's cool but we're lookin' for their respect, you know what I'm sayin'? You keep the same personnel that are in your business, just respect the people that come in and shop there. 'Cause we put these people's kids through college, they been there for fifteen years in the neighbourhood, all we want is some respect when we come into the store. You can create a hundred new jobs, you can create two new jobs, we still gonna demand that respect. I'm beginning to think that they're sympathizing with the people that disrespect the black community, and fuck how we think, fuck how we feel, you know what I mean?

BC: What did you think about the fact that those tracks aren't going to be released in Britain?

IC: I hate it. It's like I really feel like calling up Island and telling them they can go just fuck theyself. We all fight censorship, censorship is all around, it's not just rap music it's who-ever they can get into this graph, but then Island, before they even get a response from Europe, they gotta be hypocrites. Whenever censorship come on they gotta keep they mouths shut, if any of Island's artists get censored they shouldn't have a damned thing to say, they wouldn't support nobody . . .

BC: Some critics have said that what motivates your music is the documentary impulse. Is that how you write, do you keep a notebook?

IC: No I don't keep a notebook. Some things I write. Not all my things you can take to heart, some of my records are entertainment. You can take my political commentaries and my involvement seriously but I don't walk around looking for shit as it happens, I speak on it after I notice it, you know what I'm sayin'?

BC: But it seems to me that the songs with the closest details of your surroundings seem to be the ones that piss most people off, which I think is kinda interesting. Michelle Wallace, she is an African-American writer from New York, says the reason that rap doesn't have what would be called love songs, is that the relationship between the sexes in black America has reached a sort of all-time low. What do you think?

IC: Well you know that's true, but anyway we got enough R&B muthafuckers, we got enough of that, that's all they singin' about. Could a rapper do a love song better than Luther? But why even step to that, we beyond that, we thinkin' about different things. Why isn't the bond strong in the black community? There is a strain, a frustration that the black man has, that he can't get a job, the system won't hire him but they will hire his woman.

That's hard on any man, black or white. She's bringin' home the bacon and how can you show that you're a man? This breaks down every piece of manhood that you ever established, so it breaks down that the only way that you can show you're a man is through your penis. So you dukin' every girl you see and you get in trouble with your woman and shit get heated, babies comin' and you can't handle it and you're out . . . We want to talk about why is it like that. Not about love songs, because frankly how many babies can you attribute to Luther Vandross's singin'? You know?

BC: There was an article in the *New Republic* called, 'Rap, the Black Music that Isn't Either' by David Samuels. Basically what he says in there is that rap spectacularizes ghetto life, like the TV programme *Cops* does, makes gang lifestyles like a gladiator spectacle and makes white kids from the suburbs sort of the happy spectators of the downfall of the black community across America. Do you think that's true?

IC: Is this guy black, is he from the community?

BC: He's at Princeton. Between 20 and 30. I don't know, I just read it.

IC: He's at Princeton . . . you have a lot of people with different objectives, you have movies about the community like *New Jack City* which is basically on the action tip, and then you'll have a movie like *Boyz n the Hood*. Neither one of them being a comprehensive reflection of the black community. I mean, I give information to the people in Atlanta, that the people in Atlanta never even thought about. It's a form of unity, it does form a unity that we're startin' to put together. The kids in New York can have the kids in Texas dancing the same way, dressing the same way, talking the same way, then they haircuts the same, we starting to get more unified across the country. Whereas rap music . . . I can space out on the fact that a lot of the so-called whitey kids also know this information and that says something. But if I was to say that most black people get AIDS through IV drug use and not through sex – you can get it through sex, but most black people get it through IV – how can you tell me that the million people that buy my records can't learn from that? . . . Naw, I'm telling this guy, it's not only music, it's not only black, it's a source of information. I don't know how this guy can say it's not black and it's not music, I mean nobody can rap like black kids.

BC: That's true. However, in LA it seems that more and more communities seem to be getting involved, from Cypress [Hill] to the Boo Yaas to [Kid] Frost, I've heard of Irish rappers, Asian rappers. What do you think of that?

IC: It's cool. Where there's a cry from the black community there's a cry from the Latin community, there's a cry from the Asian community, you know what I mean? Why can't we hear all that?

BC: Do you subscribe to the idea that rap is the CNN that black people never had, like Chuck D said?

IC: Of course. He hit it right on the head. It's a formal source to get our ideas out to a wider group of peers.

BC: What extent do you believe in self-determination for black America? Are you talking about a nation within a nation or sort of more black capitalism?

IC: I believe black unity is the key, is the key to everything, the key to all our problems. But what happens is we were taught to love white and hate ourselves and we look to whites in awe and we're so forgiving. We want to fit into the white community but we don't really want to fit into the black community. In the fifties, you could only go shop at the black-owned market, but now you have a white market which you shop at because you can, you see, so we gotta break this down. There's the ancestors, the white ancestors who we got to hold accountable for their actions. We got to hold them accountable for what they done to us and we got to teach us to love ourselves.

BC: How do you and Jinx work?

IC: He's the music man, he gives me the music, I put the lyrics on it and we really compromise on what goes on top of that. Sometimes he'll be on a roll, he'll say, Cube, get lost for two hours and come back and everything will be hooked up. 'Cause he don't want to try that shit, right then and have me say no, so I leave and come back and say, okay I like this, I like that, take that out, move this around.

BC: Do you write every day?

IC: Every chance I get.

BC: Do you believe there's an LA sound?

IC: I think we just took rap out of its simplicity and we put in a lot more time and effort because we knew we had to come back that much flyer. You know, we knew New York had a grip on it, so we knew we had to work that much harder. So what we had to do was work, work, work, work and really get busy and put the shit out that much better. I think by doin' that, our music found its fullest, we used a lot more live instruments, our breaks – we put a lot more effort into them.

BC: Do you think that gangsta sound has been influenced by lowrider culture?

IC: I mean all of it's a part of it. Lowrider, airplay, the brothers, the gangs, the police, the prisons, all of it's influence for the music, for me I wouldn't even – Well if I was still with NWA . . . with gangsta rap, it's just that a lot of it is like a cartoon, a comic, a lot of shootin' but not a lot dead. With my raps I think you get a lot more than dis this, I killed this or this or that, I think I'm a lot more sincere to reality.

BC: I think *Death Certificate* proves that, but what is so scary is that the press are calling NWA this 'great party act' which I don't understand . . .

IC: What it is, they listened to my record, they're used to listening to our records and seeing our community. But what's happening is they're startin' to see themselves implicated, you know, they don't like that. They might be disappointed in who they are, when somebody else is telling you who you are, that don't . . .

BC: Do you read your press?

IC: Not really. I'm not a media fan to be honest, I don't really like doin' interviews, I think my records speak for itself, my records is final. If there is something they don't understand I'll clear it up, but some of them try to give me the take back, tryin' to set me up like, he don't like me any more, but it don't matter, 'cause I don't really respect the magazines that print those articles. People ask me about *Billboard*: I don't respect them, *Billboard* doesn't buy my records, *Billboard* doesn't sell my records, most of the people that read *Billboard* got my record free, so how could I respect them? They don't know me, they don't know my community. Criticism is cool but I look at them as they trying to take food out my mouth and when you look at somebody trying to take food out your mouth and out your friend's mouth, when you meet them you might not be as professional as they expect you to be. You might just want to run up and kick their ass, you might just do that. Criticism is cool but once you start fuckin' with people's livelihood and way of life, then, I'm serious: you write something about me in your magazine then you trying to take food out my mouth and it's on. Criticism of a record or song that's cool, but if you say don't buy it, then you messin' with my life, man.

BC: There's a lot of careers built on that – which brings me to the next question. What about Tim Dogg, man?

IC: Tim Dogg dissed me on his first record. I wouldn't talk to 'em. I'm like, you don't even know me, how you gonna do me like that? Just a second . . . you watchin' the music awards, I want Chuck to win it so bad but I know they gonna give it to Jazzy Jeff . . .

BC: Fuck that man.

IC: Jazzy Jeff and the Fresh Prince, goddamn it, I'll never go to this shit, all this shit is so muthafuckin' fucked, if you want to win the American Music Awards, don't do it like PE, do it like Hammer . . .

BC: Same as NAACP Awards.

IC: Until they change they name, they don't get no props.

BC: Rap music seems to be consistently down on homosexuality. Should it be taken the same way as the way a lot of the stuff that's said about women? Or – it seems to be more general in relation to the gay question.

IC: Most rappers as far as I know are straight men, and it not just a white thing, it's more of a society thing, even ladies are sick of it. We are part of the country and we fall under the same ills of it; you get ten straight males conversing about homosexuality and see where it gets you. It could be ignorance, it could be fear, it could be a whole lot of things. But most of the time to get a response, it is usually at another people's expense, everybody is straight that buys your record and you are straight. Nobody really cares about that person you cuffed on the back of the head, that's why I think we have the homosexual thing. I'm not saying it's right, to kids it's real new, it's real new, some of the kids that buy my records can't even understand fuckin' with women. We fall into society's hands and the influence of parents.

BC: Are rappers like Jazzy Jeff fiddlin' as Rome burns?

**Kiilu, JMD and Mattematicks work on tracks
at a rehearsal studio in north Hollywood,
1992.**

Mtulajazi kicks a beat at Heavyweight
session, Pharcyde Manor, south central Los
Angeles, 1992.

**Bird and engineer at Hollywood Sound,
Hollywood, 1993.**

**Getting open at the Heavyweight session,
Pharcyde Manor, south central Los
Angeles, 1992.**

Aztlan Underground at the Chicano Moratorium, east LA, 1991.

IC: That's rap music as entertainment. How can I fault that, how can I fault him 'cause he never meant there to be a message.

BC: Why do you think Islam has become so important?

IC: 'Cause Islam is the first black organization really that's become big, that is not getting funded by whites, that don't fear whites and speaks their minds. They not only teach you of religion, they not only teach your history, they teach you how to eat, how to survive, how to defend yourself, how to get respect from your mate, whether it's from the male or female. For the woman they show you how to take care of your black man, for the man they teach you how to respect your black woman. For the kids they need that, that's why it's become the influence.

BC: And that's why it's in rap?

IC: It's become an imprint on how things should be.

Part Two

BC: You start *Predator* with the admission procedure to the prison system . . . how come?

IC: I call it the first day of school; if you look through the history books most of our black leaders have been put into prison or put into jail. For some reason God has made 'em go through this trial to be put inside of a cage and I guess find theyself. That's where most of the prophets get they fire and raise the people when they get out of being in a place like that. I figured for all the leaders it's the first day of school whether they been put in there for a day or for ten years, it's some kind of trial, for some reason. Look at all the leaders . . .

BC: I understand using the Bomb Squad on *Amerikkka's Most Wanted*, but I'm not sure about why Das EFX [East Coast rap group renowned for their use of old school tenets] would have played such an important role on this record.

IC: They're only on one record.

BC: One song, but it seems they influence the whole record – the style, am I hearing that wrong?

IC: Yeah you hearing that wrong; no man, they just be on one record. I like how they rhyme, but I wouldn't dare try to copy, I did that just to let the new school and the old school, just let 'em know I could still keep up with the new brothers comin' out, but I never do my records like nobody, I just do my records like theyself. I prove on this record that I can flow, you know, more than I did on the other records. *AMW* is my first album and it was pretty much straight up, *Death Certificate* had a political agenda to it with certain topics and issues, and this record I just wanted to make a hiphop album. I don't like doing albums like the last one or using the same producers, but I was halfway through the album before I even heard of Das EFX.

BC: How come you decided to put out the album so quick?

IC: 'Cause I had a lot of material, I decided to put out the album quick. I'm real creative, I gotta release it or it'll back up if I don't keep releasing what I'm thinking at the time, I'll back up and have too much to think about and I get real crazy. I got to be, anything I have to say, I can't really get on the news and just say what I feel so I have to put out a record, not a record that's got to wait months to come out to hear what I have to say on certain issues. As long as I'm thinking about it I might as well keep makin'.

BC: Did you record change after 29th of April [LA Rebellion]?

IC: No, there's a lot of things in there I mention, but I had a lot of songs done before then. There's a few that speak upon the riots that I hadn't done. 'When Will They Shoot', and 'It Was a Good Day'; 'Dirty Mack' and all them was written before they happened. It was like the whole spectrum from the day *Death Certificate* dropped to the day *Predator* dropped. Those are the events I wanted to speak of, I wanted to do a little something different that people don't expect, 'It Was a Good Day', 'Gangsta's Fairy Tale 2' that people don't really expect.

BC: Did the 'Cop Killer' controversy affect the material on the record?

IC: I don't think – no, I didn't change nothing. It made me Say Hi to the Bad Guy, 'cause I believe in standing straight up on that type of thing.

BC: Do you think Ice T made a mistake [in withdrawing the 'Cop Killer' record]?

IC: Ice T is a force in hiphop, so any decision he made was the right decision, and I believe that because I don't know the situation. I'm not really equipped to comment on that man's business, I trust him to do the right thing for the music and for himself. Even if I had a problem I wouldn't tell the media, I would go straight to him, 'cause I feel that's the way we as black people need to deal with our problems. The media tends to twist and turn what I talk into the recorder, who knows it might go into they head and come out a little different.

BC: You think the LA 4 [four African American men charged with the beating of white truck driver Reginald Denny on the first night of the Rebellion; the beating was filmed and transmitted live across the country from a traffic helicopter overhead] should be released?

IC: Yeah, I think if you look at the situation, I don't think them brothers under any other circumstances would have pulled that man out the truck. When you look at anarchy, when you look at no law, no order, man, individuals are liable to do anything. I think that's what happened, if there was no verdict that day, and he was driving through the neighbourhood he wouldn't have been pulled from the car. They could plead temporary insanity on that thing. It's insane, if George Bush was in the middle of that thing he would have been looting. Come on man, free shit, anybody, anybody sitting there in the middle of free shit, you can do anything you want to do, police rolling past the area, no control, no law, no order, no nothing. I know a lot of people that would have been tempted; you gonna try to put them in the same position as the police officers? The police are in a controlled state and they deal with situations like that every day. That's bullshit, they were supposed to be professionals. They talk about a fuckin' Hyundai [Rodney King was driving a Hyundai when he was beaten by the police officers] going 90 miles an hour, those things go 75 tops. There was a lot of lying, a lot of bullshit and definite racism, whether it was the 'Gorillas in the Mist' comment about black families . . . These muthafuckers trained for years how to deal with this situation and they let the racism get to 'em and they just beat the shit out of this guy, so how you gonna take some kids in the middle of all this confusion, mad and everything is going on, you know . . .

BC: I totally know, but they're not gonna be released, it's the wrath of white America coming down on 'em now.

IC: And they gonna get them for attempted murder and you know give 'em life in prison. I know people that's done murdered muthafuckers, killed 'em, and they got four years, so the media event they gonna try to throw the book at these kids, it just shows the hypocrisy of the system that's never gonna work for us and we just gotta do for ourselves.

BC: T Bone was saying you recorded the whole trial.

IC: Yeah, I couldn't watch the whole thing; some of it was boring.

BC: Do you think the prosecution was fucked up?

IC: I think white people in that area generally see that there's good black people and there's bad black people. I think that's the way they see it, and if they done thought Rodney King as one of the good niggers they would have found them guilty, but I think they saw him as a bad nigger so he deserved what he got. That's how the jury saw that thing.

BC: At what point did you decide to put flow back into the album?

IC: It was my third album, I just wanted to make jams, man, I wanted to make songs, whatever I wanted. I didn't want to be tied down to a certain agenda, that's why there aren't a lot of tie-ins between the songs. *Death Certificate* was strategically put together and I didn't want to do that with this one, 'cause I had already done it. Let's do this record pretty bone dry, just jams, and it worked for me. Of course I got to drop my knowledge in there somewhere when I flow. I wasn't stuck to a certain agenda and it seems like reporters are mad at me 'cause I didn't . . .

BC: They're gonna be mad at you either way.

IC: I do all my albums different, I have all kinds of topics, some of 'em gonna be jams, some political, some be like dis, some be like dat. You never gonna be like this sounds like that record, never. It's just part of a chain, and I got many more in the future.

BC: You ever think about falling off?

IC: Yeah, that's what keeps me on. It keeps me studying why people fall off, it keeps me on my toes.

BC: You spent a lot of time on this album answering questions posed on the *Death Certificate* album; is that you talking back?

IC: Yeah, I was kind of pissed off 'cause they summed up my whole album in two or three songs. I spoke on all races, not just black or white, or Korean, I spoke on everybody that I deal with in my community . . . and they just chose two subjects and I'm like, okay fuck you and fuck you here's how I do my records and that's all, that's how I'm comin' out in '92 and '93. Okay I said it, so that's my philosophy, same muthafuckers that was callin' me all these names wanted to get my comments on the uprising. I ain't got nothin' to say, I already said what I had to say.

KING TEE

Since his first single 'Payback's a Mother' released on Greg Mack's Mackdaddy Records and distributed through Macola in 1988, King Tee has contributed hard humorous rhymes to the musical culture of LA. With long-time partner DJ Pooh, he has been one of Los Angeles' best-kept secrets, not enjoying the kind of record sales that some of his peers have. Tee had been responsible for introducing groups such as Madkap, Nefertiti and the Alkaholics. In late December 1992, I visited Tee in the executive suite at Capitol Records. He was suffering from an unmerciful hangover.

Brian Cross: When did you start rhymin'?

King Tee: Five or six years ago. Before I started rappin' I used to DJ. I never thought of rappin' until people heard me at parties and liked the way I sounded. I was DJing at 15 years old for a radio station in Houston, Texas, KYOK and KTSU, at 16 years old. It was amazing to everybody because I was so young and could rock the turntables. I moved down to Texas with my mother 'cause she had met some old nigga who wanted to move down to Texas. I was enrolled in school down there for two or three years, but I never went 'cause I was always down at the radio station trying to get somebody to listen to my mix tapes, that I had made at home using the pause button, you know . . . I knew about Greg Mack but I never met him down there though. When I was down there it was like when the Buffalo Girls came out and all that type of shit, shit was really just gettin' into the scratchin' and shit. But I knew about Uncle Jam's Army and all that . . .

BC: So the first stuff you did was with Unknown DJ right?

KT: Yeah, Pooh had hooked me up and we came up with some beats and shit, the first one was 'Payback's a Mother'. I was lucky 'cause when the record came out Pooh had been workin' in New York with Bobcat and all that. They were sending the records back and forth and Red Alert was hip to it. It was cool.

BC: Were you making tapes for people?

KT: I was making tapes, mixing not rappin', I used to make little four track tapes and sell them for about ten dollars a tape, 'cause I used to work at this Fila shop sellin' sweats.

BC: Whereabouts in LA did you grow up?

KT: Shit, I drank so much last night dude . . . I grew up down around 41st near Hooper, then I moved to Compton. I was around a lot, I done went to every school in LA, it was crazy.

BC: How do you remember the transition in LA from like the Wreckin Cru and the Dream Team to like 'Boyz n the Hood', deep bass, all that shit.

KT: I never listened to that shit, Egyptian Lover, all that fast shit, I was into slow-tempo slow hiphop shit. I was never into that fast breakin' shit. Yo, can I go to the rest room real quick, I feel like I'm going to . . .

BC: No problem . . . So you never listened to that fast shit?

KT: I was in love with 'She's Lookin' Like a Hobo' by Malcolm McLaren, that type of shit. And plus I used to get a lot of tapes from the radio in NY and I was really into that East Coast type of shit, I wasn't into the West Coast type of sound. [The NWA sound] tripped me out a little bit 'cause I knew about Dr Dre and what he was into, what his crew used to be about and all that type of shit, Wreckin Cru with lace and all that type of shit, lipstick and lip gloss and eyeliner, and then boom! It's like damn, these niggas is the ruffest gangsta rappers around and they used to sing like Prince and shit. But who am I to complain?

I didn't start writing songs until it was like time to write. I used to have freestyle rhymes in my head that I would just kick. When it was time to sit down and write real rhymes, it was time to go in the studio.

BC: You're given credit as the person who had styles in LA when everybody else was just doing old school slow gangsta style. Is that true? Was it the East Coast influence?

KT: Yeah, I was just trying to sound like I was from the East Coast, and that's how I developed the style I had, kinda different. It was all I listened to, shit that was comin' from New York. There wasn't nothing out here but the fast shit. That's why we didn't get no respect back then.

BC: When did you meet Pooh?

KT: I met Pooh in '85, '86, back in the day. I met Bobcat before I met Pooh. I was trying to DJ for Bobcat, he had this little crew called the California Cat Crew. I was auditioning. Right before that Bob had gone to NY to work with somebody, when Breeze was signed to Def Jam. I met Pooh and we started hangin' out, trippin' and shit, then we started makin' records.

BC: How does it all fit together?

KT: Basically me and Pooh was just on a different trip. We was listening to the East Coast, I don't know. People just started checkin' it out. I'm proud of where I'm from, and I always let that be known, it's just that I give props where it's due. What do we got here? We got

Hammer blowin' the fuck up, the West Coast like that shit, it's just an up-tempo kind of town here. It's just disco I guess, that's why me and Pooh try and be different.

BC: Do you want to talk about the development of your style?

KT: Umm, shit, my head is killing me.

BC: You ever make a love song?

KT: Ha, hell no. I'm not about – DJ Pooh did that Barry White shit – that's where I was talking about when a nigga start going around for some pussy and then he start dissin' a nigga that's been there for all his life. He meet a bitch last night and then he start sayin' this bitch before me, you know what I'm sayin' . . .

BC: What about your humour? Who do you listen to or get inspired by?

KT: DJ Pooh. I don't really think he'd be funny on stage. You just gotta videotape a whole day of him, let him be hisself. He's so fuckin' funny, especially when he's got the blunts going around, you just can't stop laughin', cause he's a funny muthafucker, that's the funniest muthafucker I know to this day. Back in the day I did listen to Dolemite, I watched all his movies too. My homeboy Jazzy Red back in Texas used to have me listen to Dolemite, and I used to like Eddie Murphy, he played out, though, to me. Blowfly and all that shit . . . Richard Pryor, but Pooh just takes the cake.

BC: Besides T you gotta be one of the few hardcore rappers workin' with a major right now, how do you feel about that?

KT: I feel lucky as a muthafucker. You talkin' about Ice T? He's the one that got me the deal here. I feel real fortunate, when I got signed here, it was just like Run DMC, the Def Jam shit was jumpin' off, there wasn't that many rappers signed to major labels. I been dealin' with censorship, it's a fucked up thing 'cause that's what rap is about, tellin' what it was about out there, and now you gotta take shit off. I didn't really have to deal with it until Ice T took the 'Cop Killer' record off the album. I never had to deal with censorship. I could say whatever, Capitol wasn't into that censorship shit. But after 'Cop Killer' every label started jumpin' on every curse word. He shouldn't have took the record off, 'cause that was really holding up freedom of speech. Everybody was behind him, his label was behind him. That's how it seemed to me, it just fucked everything up.

BC: What are you going to be doing when you're 50?

KT: Shit, layin' in a bed sick, like I am now.

I think in Japan you know we speak different languages, so to me the lyrics were hard to understand, you know, but I can feel the beat, the melody, the bass. I think that is how we feel it. Rap music, you know, the most important thing is lyrics, the message, what you are saying, 'cause I used to rap. It's different for me 'cause I live in LA three years so I know this kind of situation as far as gang situation and how you have to be taught to deal with it. In Japan it's pretty nice, you know, everybody respect each other, some people are fucked up but still it's easier, nobody carries gun. So they think gang situation is like idol type of thing, these are serious things, right? Violence is not idol, it's dangerous, that's their problems, they think violence is fashion. 'Cause they never had the fear; lyrics is the important part so they don't understand lyrics so they only see what rappers look like and think that's cool.

DJ Yutaka is a producer, DJ and hardcore B-boy immigrant from Japan.

SKATEMASTER TATE

Tate is LA's Cuban guru and jack of all trades. Cubano, surfer, skater, collector, DJ, producer. He is best known for Skate TV, and as band leader for Skatemaster Tate and the Concrete Crew and Acid Jazz outfit, the Stone Cold Boners. He finds rare samples and records for groups and movie productions and does A&R once in a while. Above all, Tate is one of those people who has turned the art of connoisseurship of popular culture into a living. His house is a treasure trove of American, Cubana and soul funk and jazz. He is a true curator in his own right. This interview took place in July 1992 at Tate's house. He supplied the smokables and I provided the drinkables – Guinness.

Skatemaster Tate: This is a group I was in in '86, Smash, Volume 4, Skaterock . . . *'and it's called the Skaterock rap and it goes like this, oh yeah'* . . . I'm like the (Gangstarr rapper) Guru right, five foot eight, hair ain't straight. *'My face is round and I don't wear no crown.'* Are you laughing? *'You know it but could I do it for you.'* Now I'm gonna do something funky. *'Oh yeah, that girl of mine, I love her so, but I can't let her see me rappin' all alone – that girl is high, you would not believe, the things she says she sees in me . . . Just like an egg in a frying pan, she walks like a woman and talks like a man . . . she's so high.'*
Brian Cross: Tell me how you got into this shit man.
ST: Well it's like this: 'I said a hiphop a hippety to the hip.' I heard 'Rapper's Delight' and wanted to be a DJ. Believe it or not I was a DJ in eighth grade 'cause the district I was in didn't have enough funds and I had to switch districts to a more academic kind of, a scholastic jock kind of fuckin' thing. And they had a radio station, KPPJ – I think it's still down there. And the summer between seventh and eighth grade, '72, '73 which is when all the dope shit came out, right, I was DJing on the station, and my brother was a rock and roll drummer for twelve years. So I knew all the dope shit, and we didn't have equipment for football so I got into the radio station. We rocked shit so hard that summer that people got

upset. So when we got back to school it was an education thing, with carts and reals and shit like that, we did PSAs [Public Service Announcements] and that's it.

After that I started collecting records. My brother collected Hendrix and Chuck Berry, Bo Diddley, I've still got the first 45s he gave me. I saw Hendrix in sixth grade with my mother and my brother and everybody but my dad. At the Palladium we saw him do three songs with Albert King, Buddy Miles on bass and Mitch Mitchell on drums. Me and my mom met my brother and sister right at the bottom of the stairs at the Palladium, and I seen this guy with a fuckin' big old afro and a big pink scarf, purple psychedelic. It was Hendrix. 'Cause my brother had brainwashed me, I used to draw him [Hendrix] in sixth grade. I go [to] George, 'Look, Jimi Hendrix!' And he says, 'Bullshit.' As soon as he heard one note, my brother just ran for the stage. Everybody did. Me and my mom went upstairs.

I was into early rhythm and blues, not what they do today (R&B), which is bullshit. So I got into music early. In high school I would DJ, but it was all a rock thing. I seen Zeppelin a bunch of times, Sabbath. We used to sneak into Long Beach Arena to see rock bands. Next time I hit the turntables was in college. I was a DJ at KVOC, Cypress, California, not to be confused with the hill. Right by the hill, though not as rowdy.

BC: You were doing skate for a while, was it hiphop . . .

ST: I was into punk at first, rock and punk, and then I was a punk in '79, '80, '81, then in '82, '83. I'll play you a dope punk song right now. I seen Stiff Little Fingers at the Whiskey, they were the dope dope. I just got the bug early, man, and it never left me. This is the musical shit, this is how diverse those muthafuckers were, from three chords to twenty. You know I got eighty crates of records here, and like twenty there [at his parents' house in Compton], sealed dope vinyl, collectables worth thousands of dollars, 78s. I got a 78 of James Brown. Check this out – dope cover, huh? James Brown's first record, I have like two hundred different singles of his.

BC: What were you doing when Egyptian Lover came out?

ST: I was a blunted muthafucker, collecting records, buying clothing and selling it to Flip, they made millions and I made thousands. I used to DJ at China Club, blues and psychedelia punk, I met the guy who discovered B.B. King. I'm a collector of Americana, rock and roll, blues. The minute I heard hiphop I loved it, it was infectious, but you couldn't get it all the ways out here, so I searched and searched and got what I could. That's all Sugarhill over there, on the left is Go-Go, on the right is early Profile, all the blue is all the Sugarhill shit.

BC: So when did you start putting out your own shit?

ST: '86 I put out the first record. '87, '88 we started playing, '88 we toured the States, '89 I went to France by myself. Caviar left me, man, 'cause he wanted to rap about smoking rock and drinking 40s. And I told him I don't do that in my band. I did this gig in France – 10,000 kids, skateboarders behind me skatin', and went to Japan last year when the album came out on Island, they like anything, man. They rock, they're a great audience. I'd go back there in a fuckin' heartbeat, fatman's heartbeat, a little bit quicker than a thin man's heartbeat. The [Stone Cold] Boners – you want to know about the Boners? They came about in '90. Acid Jazz had already came out, but the Boners came out as a result of me wanting to do something different, and um –

BC: So you still haven't explained how Tate became a beatbroker.

ST: I haven't explained about the Boners either. You're buzzed man. In the 1990s, you gotta learn to hold your Guinness.

BC: It's not the Guinness, it's that other shit.

ST: Hootymack. Me and OMD [guitarist] from Boo Yaa were chillin' in the pad, Eddie from Acid Jazz was there. I had a [sampled drum] loop up, he liked it, so he goes, 'Yo, give me something like that, mate.' I put a twenty-minute version on cassette. As he was leaving I handed it to him not rewound, he mastered the twenty-minute version on to CD and put a five-minute version on *Acid Jazz Volume 2*. And the kids danced to it. The first one I did by myself, Tate, no one else. He asked me for a name and I said I've got this Island deal so for all I care you can call it the Stone Cold Boners, so he did.

BC: So how did you hook up with Frost?

ST: Cypress [Hill] brought him by. I liked it, he heard that one track I did in '88 but hadn't met me. I always had the Latin vibe in me, and I always had the buddha vibe in me but I ain't gonna make records about it. I got a family and shit. But things change, and there's definitely gonna be a bit of the blunted in my next record, 'cause I don't care what anybody says, nobody can get as blunted as the Tate. I might have to bust out with one, the fuckin' buddha master.

Anyway the first time I ever put out a record was on Smash through *Thrasher*, the skate mag. I was into skate shit, I introduced them to TSOL, Screaming Sirens, Gangreen, got them on their compilation records. Then I went and up and said, 'Do you need anything else?' And they said, 'Yeah, why don't you do something?' And then when I did 'Five foot eight my name is Skatemaster Tate'. That's what I did in '86. I got a laugh out of that.

I'll always put out records. I'll put one out in '93 probably on my own label again. Demo tapes suck, they get recorded over, unless it's the dope shit, it's gonna get recorded over. So I put out vinyl. Me and Tupelo Joe. You just can't sleep, man. I like to sleep but I'm tired of people telling me what to do; you got to do your own shit. I worked many years, I cleaned toilets, worked at a gas station, I swept skateboard parks and finally ran one. So I've come a long way. As far as the work ethics in this country, they suck. There's one handful of people making all the money and there's two handfuls doing all the work. I got tired of being one of the two handful people. Buying and selling records, clothes, knick-knacks, bud, cars. I'm happy, I got two turntables, a speaker, and a ton of records, a nice car, my Cadillac convertible. You give me a dope 45 and I'm happy.

The last thing I did with Island, I put it together and pressed it and all that for like ten Gs and sold it to them for about eighty. Then I spent a little money on sampling and split it with the boys, but I still wound up pretty fat. I'm a businessman.

My dad played a little Cuban jazz. My brother played, my mother was a dancer a long time ago, my sister was a modern dancer. Tater no dance. Actually back in the day me and my homeboys used to do those jitterbugs with the chicks. Some of the first big rap groups in LA I saw were Cold Crush Brothers at Lingerie. I saw Ice T at Lingerie with about twenty people, me and Fishbone were the only heads in the house. When he had Sunset Boulevard, like LL had Farmer's Boulevard, he was busting the shit, he was bad, with fuckin' Lennie [from Body Count] come out of this trashcan with an Uzi. One of the dopest shows in LA ever was Trouble Funk at Myron's Ballroom, '87, when Go-Go was stomping the floors in LA. They thought they were in fuckin' DC, man, they showed up about 1 a.m. Did a stomp till about 3:30, I was dripping, watching the whole crowd MOVE, front to back side to side moving. I felt a sensation I had never felt before. Right, for three hours, and that was the first time I ever felt that unity thing in LA.

BC: What do you make of the Chicano vibe that's going down now?

ST: It's dope, you got the hardcore with Cypress Hill, the candy-ass with Gerardo, the halfway in between with Frost, Mellow Man too is both, hardcore and pop. Gerardo is straight up candy ass, pansy muthafucker, get a haircut. I like the diversity, the wide variety, Proper Dos, Lighter Shade of Brown.

BC: Why do you think it took until now to jump off? Considering the big contribution of Puerto Ricans in the old school.

ST: Took four hundred years for the black man, right? Well it took 410 for the Latin rapper. Right? When did 'Rapper's Delight' come out? '79? 413 years.

BC: What you been collecting lately?

ST: Been collecting a lot of Mongo Santamaria, a lot of Joe Cuba, Ray Barretto, Rico Salbrosso, Cachau. We sampled Tito [Puente] on the first record, 'Rancancan', and fucking 'Rancancan' was a twelve-inch dance single last year, so I don't want to give too many names away. Those guys have built-in audiences. They have been touring for forty years, they don't give a fuck about the pop tip, they're like the hardest-working people in showbusiness for real, the Latin musicians.

BC: Tell me about the oldies phenomenon amongst Chicanos.

ST: Back in the day when all that War shit came out, early Funkadelic, I'd watch my brother's baseball games in a lowered '67 Chevy with this chick with the biggest fuckin' bouffant, right, her name was Tina Bettini. She had a set that would wreck, she would just pump the oldies, and I would sit with my head on her sex 'cause I was such a cute little kid and listen to the oldies, learned a lot from her and my sister. It's a siesta thing, a mellow thing, a groove thing, a love thing. Plus half the people that put that stuff out were Latin, Suavecito, Malo, War. Even the brothers who put it out had the feel 'cause they were living in the *varrio*, the Chicanos were living in the ghetto. Back then it wasn't as segregated, the *varrios* and the ghettoes weren't all Latin and black as much as they are now. Barbecues and siestas are traditional, oldies and rhythm and blues are just Latin. Back in the day it was mariachi bands, you'd just fuckin' dig it, a good time, no attitude, no bullshit, no nothing. They took care of the children and shit.

I gotta drop a little bit of science here. There's leaders and followers in this world, and sometimes the leaders don't have the capital to put something out and the followers do and they get the credit, that's the way it is. I ain't no messiah, I know what I do and I hope they do too, but jazz never got its kick. Name me a jazz musician that made millions from his music; jazz don't play that. Miles Davis, in the *Guide to Jazz*, there's only about ten lines about him: 'A gifted musician but one who has entirely deviated from jazz to cool music.' See, even inside their own music, bebop, cool jazz was like punk rock, hiphop, right, not even accepted inside a book called *Guide to Jazz*. Right? Coltrane: he's not even in the book. Coleman, he might be in here. Bill Coleman, no Ornette, 'Scat: double talk, a succession of meaningless words done when the singers cannot remember their lyrics, or simply for the hell of it.' Tate used to do a lot of that!

BC: Who is writing history is the question, right?

ST: Mezz Mezzrow, he used to sell pot to Louis Armstrong. I have about five copies of the book he wrote about jazz, jazz lifestyle, and in the back is a glossary. He was so dope they named the Mezzroll after him, a fat joint with the ends rolled in. Me and Tupelo talked to Dizzie Gillespie in '86 and we asked him about Mezz Mezzrow, he said, 'Man, he had me so bad they named it after him, they called it Mezz.' And I bugged when I heard that, cause I read this book a million times, me and my friends used to talk like that, the four Fs, 'Yo man, did you weave the four Fs' – fool 'em, fight 'em, fuck 'em, freedom. And rubbers is to fuck in your car. We used to have it was like a bebop lifestyle, pseudo. We were fans. I love the whole jazz thing and I always will. All my jazz records don't have the bar codes on 'em. All mine are first pressings.

MATTHEW McDANIEL

Matthew McDaniel is a videomaker. He has been involved in hiphop in Los Angeles for many years. He used to work at the legendary KDAY. But for the last number of years he has through his own production company released two hiphop documentaries, *Rhythm Rock Live* 1&2. These hour-long videos feature rare candid interviews with rhymers from Scott La Rock to Ice T and Ice Cube during and after NWA. He has just completed an hour-long documentary entitled *Birth of a Nation 4-29-92* which tells the story of the recent 1992 LA rebellion from the perspective of the black community. He has carried the hiphop aesthetic into video.

Brian Cross: KDAY wasn't hiphop until Greg Mack got there, is that true?
Matthew McDaniel: Exactly, and what happened was it was AM, 1580 AM stereo; nobody had stereo, and in the Arbitron [system to measure listener ratings] to compete they had to be doing something different than the FM stations to get people to listen. Mack started the rap format before I was listening, 'cause I was in Pasadena to be quite honest.
BC: So how did you get started on the video/documentation thing?
MM: I lived in Pasadena in the projects, and when KDAY would have an artist in town, this goes back to when there weren't any albums, just singles. Shanté and UTFO would come out with a single, and they didn't put pictures on the cover. There was no rap magazines. Then one night I was talking with the Force MDs after a show and they started telling me their story. They were broke and hungry and they sung on the Ferry and they met this guy who managed the Juice Crew, Biz Markie, Shanté. I thought their story was interesting. I realized people wanted to know this. It was news in the Calendar section of the *LA Times* when the Dream Team got a deal with MCA. Rap was at the bottom of the music business, and Ice T shot this video at this DJ mixing competition in New York of Mixmaster Ice and Cash Money from Philly and Joe Cooley from LA. You know it was a DJ competition, and Ice T had a little camcorder back then. It was blurry out of focus, he was yellin' 'Fuck it up

Joe', you could hear him, and he brought it back and was selling them out of Greg Mack's store for 25 dollars a copy. So hearing the people in the projects say what they look like, hearing the story, and Ice T's tape . . . I don't have it but I saw it. So that's where I got the idea to do what I was doing. Then rap moved up.

BC: So were you involved in the music industry?

MM: Yeah, KDAY would send me out to little shows to say KDAY was in the house. I had been shooting stuff, the first interview I did was Ice T in '86 after KDAY had banned some of his records. He was living in Hollywood alone with his records. I interviewed Scott La Rock four months before he died. I got mad for a while. I'm glad what's happening with the censorship, the harder you come down on it the more it's going to jump off. Like when I was talking to Ice T. He says, when your mother says, 'Did you listen to your Ice T record today?' it's over, but if they say, 'You better not listen to that Ice T record'. . . this is funny cause this is years ago and millions of dollars later, boom. KDAY banned 'Killers' [an early Ice T single]. They didn't like him, he was about to put out a record dissin' KDAY and they talked him out of it. He did an interview with the Calendar section and he was calling Jack Patterson names and stuff. They were mad, and I would always try to keep my distance.

In '86 we would go to parks, Ice T had a big Cadillac Seville, he would have people walking along touching his car, a hundred people – it was amazing. He did a show at Manual Arts, wearing red, a bunch of Crips chased him down. He was always colourful. I learned a lot from him and I think a lot of rappers did. 'Six in the Morning' was a breakthrough. If you listen to NWA, 'Cruising down the street in my 64', that's how Eazy came out, T influenced a lot of people out here.

BC: What was responsible for the upturn in gang violence in '86, '87?

MM: We would do the show at skating rinks, but somebody was getting shot every week. That's pretty major to do a show and expect a life to be lost, so Greg stopped doing shows, period. I would go to New York to the New Music Seminar and that's when Hurby Luv Bug, Kid N Play blew up with 'Ola Ola Ay', [a single called 'Rollin' with Kid and Play']. He's like, when you gonna bring us out, why don't you do a show? I flew De La Soul out, had my commercials, did about three shows at World on Wheels. Big shootings started at my stuff in the parking lots. That was the end of that.

BC: Why was it '86?

MM: There's no real answer, things progress and move on with times. Why '92 for the riots? Nuff time had passed, Rodney King got beat down in '91. Also in music, things pass, people get tired of things. LL (Cool J) seemed so hard when he came, 'I put a muscle-down rapper face in the sand', and Kurtis Blow. But we didn't have anything to compare it to. It got harder, you got gangs killin' somebody, and you get your first representation of it on records. 'Diamond in the back, sunroof top, digging the scene with the gangster lean, ooohooooh', Zapp and all that. [Roger's song] was a national gangsta anthem, 'So ruff, so tuff, out here baby.' Something about that song, people would start throwing signs, and shit would happen.

Right now it's moving into a political thing away from the gangster thing, it's played out; that's why I'm calling the riot video *Birth of a Nation*. A lot of people started waking up on that day big time, Richard Pryor and rappers been talking about getting beat down for years. But you got video of Rodney King, the audio of cops laughing, everybody knows that they're guilty, and they get off. Your most conservative black people get a reality check, even the gangster thing has changed with the truce. It's not as bad as it was years ago, it was terrible; the gangster is turning more political. Zapp and Parliament, it's deeper than car music, it's heritage, it's a piece of culture. It's sampled a lot, it's very respected, it wasn't responsible for anything, and it brings out a feeling in people. It's good music. When it comes on you feel it, can relate to it. When that record used to come on, boy, whoo, stuff would just break out, Zapp, 'So Ruff So Tuff'. It's the shit though, perfect slow, gangsta throwing up signs. I can just see it on the dance floor, crazy.

I remember Kurtis Blow, when he was performing 'If I Ruled the World', his last, I don't know if you call it a hit, his last song. He had on a blue jacket and people were just getting riled up. All you saw was khakis and red shoes and beanies, I didn't really understand the seriousness of it. I'm alive, but shit did happen, the security though were no noke, no joke. One of 'em got shot, deep in the heart of Compton – nobody could do anything. I would see them fighting, big strong brothers. Bam! Drag 'em by the back of the collar, slinging 'em like a rag doll. And they would be strapped, come in the metal detector . . .

I got a story for you. I was gonna do a show of Jazzy Jeff and the Fresh Prince. My idea was to be with them the whole day on video – real original huh – and so they were going to the show at the San Morican Hall in Carson. I showed up and it was over. There was a fight or something. We went into the hall, talking to some girls, these cats in blue suits from Chicago called the Fresh Pack Four, they challenged the Fresh Prince to battle right in front of the place. Next thing I know, I look up and there's like fifty of the biggest Samoans I've ever seen, the Sons of Samoa. They had no guns, but then a 40 bottle came crashing down on the skull of the guy battling the Fresh Prince, then we break loose. I guess the Samoans were down with the Bloods or something. They cracked one guy through the plate glass window, I ran inside to this broom closet thing. They went to hide in the soda booth and there's ten bodies hiding there, we hear rubber burning outside. I'm like, 'Let's get the fuck out of here.' Fresh Prince is like, 'Fuck that, I'm not going.' He breaks off a chair leg. I'm like, 'You really don't know what time it is! Let's go!'

And you know part of who that was? The Boo Yaa Tribe. I was talking to 'em years later, they don't know for sure, they weren't even in the business then. I felt the wrath of the Boo Yaa Tribe, I was scared, it was terrifying. They're crazy. In a hand to hand you're comin' up short, I just ran for that broom closet, these big ass crazy Samoans, my heart was beating so fast, a guy crashing through the window. It was like something in a bad action movie.

I met a lot of people at the beginning of their careers. NWA popularized cussing on rap records so I started doing my stuff. My stuff was cool 'cause it was more uncensored and raw. I put my first video out thirty days before Public Enemy's first album. I sold four thousand, they sold eighty-five thousand. I didn't have the distribution and it was real raw; the trick is to show people the stuff they can't see anywhere else. The first one was cool 'cause it was about freestyling. I always banked on where I thought rap was going and I've been right. I should be a millionaire but that's not the way it works really.

Run DMC and leather and gold chains . . . is that what you mean? Run, leather, chains, beatbox, Uncle Jam's Army definitely . . . listened to KDAY, KDAY was it – you heard everything, you heard demos and everything else. The first rap show I went to, the first concert I ever went to when I was young, was New Edition and I think I was like eight. Other than that it was shows, I didn't really go to concerts. I was into rollerskating a lot, I rolled on wheels, and we used to do shows, oh yeah, I was with Young MC and he was the thing just coming out. I used to perform everywhere, all different shows, the stages were very small for open mikes, just like that mat over there, that's how big the stage was, and you just got up there and did what you had to do . . .

It's even harder. I think you know as far as the style, the style is just different, the lyrics are the same, but the flow is different, kind of. But I haven't found the title for my album yet, I was thinking of Split Personality but that's so common, though it deals with what we're trying to talk about, trying to figure out a way to where I can express myself. [The album was titled Black Pearl.*] I'm down with the women but sometimes they get me so mad I want to get down on them, this is why they call you a hoe, this is why . . . on this album I deal with a lot of freestyle, I didn't get too political, I think I have one political song and it's not hurting anyone's feelings. It's not talking about white, black or Korean. It just has to do with reality itself. My album is mean. It's supposed to be turned in tomorrow, mastered Friday, but doesn't look like we're gonna be through, but maybe end of March. I have two more songs to do, and I hate to work with a lot of people around, that's why I was kind of sad when you came in . . .*

YoYo is perhaps the West Coast's leading female MC. This interview was cut short by a tape recorder problem. I was subsequently unable to reschedule.

About six or seven months ago. We did 'Power of the P' at the Good Life and as soon as we got to 'and cherries, and cherries', the lady just said 'Oh no' and came and took that mike and was like, 'Oh no miss thangs we are not havin' that in here.' I mean there is no profanity in the song at all. She just caught on to what we were talkin' about, and everyone else was just screamin' like, 'Ah, that shit was dope.' Holding money in the air and snappin' their fingers and shit . . .

I brought you into this world. Our songs are about the black woman. This is how you love a black woman. 'Cause some men out there want to know, like damn, how do you . . . and then they'll be like ah, okay now I see maybe I shouldn't have done that girl like that. It makes you look at yourself and say 'Oh, okay'. It's funny 'cause it's all in the approach. You can come in through the back door and get the same point across, it doesn't matter how, just as long as you get your point across . . .

SIN are a duo of lyric kickin' females from south central Los Angeles. They are also members of The Heavyweights.

LENCH MOB

In 1992 Cube's company, Street Knowledge, put out four albums: YoYo, Kam's debut album, Cube's own *The Predator* and the debut from the Lench Mob. The Lench Mob bust out with voices that attempt to distil anger, frustration and fear into tonal articulacy. This interview was done in October 1992 at Street Knowledge's office two days before the group's first show supporting House of Pain. JD, Shorty and T-Bone were really excited about the show and eager to talk.

Brian Cross: The Lench Mob has been known for two years as the group at the back of Cube.

JD: Right. For two years known as Ice Cube's crutch, we been hearing all kinds of shit, but we had to back Cube up, 'cause Cube came from somewhere that was totally hectic. Even though they toured across the States he ran into a lot of behind-closed-door problems, so we learned how not to run into that from him as well as develop the skill.

T-Bone, by being there in the studio with Cube, boom, T-Bone get a drum, they start doing beats. So T-Bone call me, I called Shorty: 'Let's meet at T-Bone house.' We don't call Cube. T-Bone got three or four crates of records, so we get together, I might be brewed out, Shorty on a natural high, the brother don't drink, don't smoke, always come with some crazy stuff. For two years we just plotted and planned and we gotta hit 'em with something nobody came with. We gotta take the video thing to a different level, 'cause everybody know about a gangster in South Central, everybody know about the drug dealer, everybody know about the gangbangers, the hoochies, like Quik and AMG talk about, you know. Ain't nobody ever tripped on a south central group that's in full force. We come on a whole different level, we take the mindset that want to just kill innocent and kill for nothing and kill for the cause.

T-Bone: Me and Cube went to school together. We went to junior high, then high school and he was with the other group (NWA). He didn't really too much hang with them. They did the shows and stuff, then he would come back to the neighbourhood and we'd play basketball. But he'd take me to the studio. He got really interested in it, so when the other group broke up, he came back and said, 'I'm gonna start my own crew. I'm gonna get technical with it. I'm not going to just get somebody that can rap, I'm gonna get somebody that is down as far as all around situations, they can handle themselves on the road, in the streets, in the studio, outside the studio.' That's when Jerome came through with JD. JD had a security job, and Cube just like took us in on his wing. He was like, 'Yo, let's do this.' It was so weird because yo I'm working at my job twelve hours a day, and all of a sudden the next day I'm on a plane to New York, then in the studio hanging out with Chuck D, mentor, you know what I'm sayin'? Then all of a sudden we on the stage up front, rockin' crowds.

BC: What was your job?

TB: I was a printer. I was working at RR Dyne Printing Company, I was gonna make computer software manuals, *Sports Illustrated*, I was making twelve dollars an hour at that job. It was hard for me to break off with Cube, 'cause his group had just split up, and I was gettin' benefits. That's something that at 20 or 21 you don't want to give up. That was a career. But I figured, me and my girl sat down and talked about it, me and my pops talked about it, and if it came down to me, the love I have for rap, I'm gonna take that chance, 'cause I'm not gonna be one of those that sits down and goes damn, I shoulda did it, watching these brothers out there, printing up magazines which they are in now!

BC: But you guys are from out here, right?

TB: South central.

JD: I had like a block in my neighbourhood, a couple of brothers, Chevy Shank and Lennie Leonard these kids now, that's Charlie Jam, Chase and them. They used to come back from New York with records ain't nobody heard. That's when I started getting them fat laces and brass belt buckles with my name on them. I used to have a rap about that: 'Friday night, my fat shoe laces, Bruce Lee ties, bomber jacket on.'

TB: Very hiphop, B-boy.

BC: Did you go to Skateland and World on Wheels and shit?

JD: Yeah, that was a different era, it wasn't like at that time we was trying to rap, '83 when Run DMC came out with 'It's Like That'. That was the shit. We was at every Uncle Jam's dance party when they had the Playpen in Crenshaw back in the day, all the Sports Arena events, all the Fresh Fests, all of that shit, that was our beat you understand.

Shorty was going to school at the place called Westside Academy out here in Westchester, and we would meet up every morning. I'd catch the bus to town, we'd meet on Century and Prairie. We'd meet up every morning and have a sandwich or some old shit. Every Run DMC song we knew, we knew every muthafucking song. When '90 rolled around I was doing some crazy security shit, had a gun on my hip and all kind of shit. I was making some cool money, but that wasn't what I wanted to do. I had just had a little girl, she was two years old. I run into Cube at the Wherehouse Record Store on La Brea and Rodeo. Cube pulled up and he's like, 'Damn JD, what are you doing this shit for?' I gotta daughter, you know what I'm saying? I ain't out there selling no poison. I gotta support her. He came back and said, 'Do you still write?' And I said, 'Shit, I got a stack a rhymes.' So he gave me the number to his room at his mom's house. I called that nigger that night, and he hooked me up from that day on. He said, 'I be doing something, and I'm gonna tell you it ain't gonna be promising probably, but I want you to roll with it.' So my homeboy Randy, who T-Bone used to kick it with all the time, had told Cube, 'JD is kind of fresh, you should roll with him 'cause he know everything about the life and you could learn from it.' So I learned a lot about the music from Cube and he learned a lot of the war stories from me that you hear on the records.

We was kickin' it with Shorty and we takin' some pictures for the very first time – I think it was *Yo! Magazine* – I told Shorty roll with me out to Universal City, and we rolled and that day we kicked it. I introduced Shorty as my cousin, 'cause I don't usually bring anybody around with me, and that day just the chemistry clicked it with everybody. Shorty was in all the pictures with us. From that day on we just rolled, and Shorty can just tell you the rest.

Shorty: Yeah, that's basically how we came together. Me and JD we grew up together, did a lot of stuff together. JD was always serious, he took it real serious. I was just out there buckwild. As time went on I take a little fall, and I don't see JD for like two years. I see him and he tell me he's hooked up with Cube, and I don't believe him at first, I'm like yeah nigger right, you liar. He knew in order to prove to me he had to show hisself, so he and Cube – I didn't know T-Bone – he fly T-Bone and JD out to New York, and they come back from New York and JD show me a picture of him and Flavor Flav, and you know PE [Public Enemy] was hot at the time, and they was like my number one group. So JD says, 'Yeah, I got this tape that we did', and so we go and sit in the back of my car and listen to the tape. And I'm like, this is JD rappin' along with Cube. So I'm like, 'Yeah, man, introduce him to me one day.' The way my lifestyle was, JD was thinking I probably going to try and rob Ice Cube or something, so I'm like, 'Yo, I just want to know how the brother is.' I think we went over to his house, to Cube's mother's. Then one day we went to Priority Records, the same day we took those shots, and Cube asked me he said, 'Yo, we're going over to New Orleans to the BRE,' he says, 'Yo, you want to roll?' When we got together everything just clicked, the chemistry just . . .

JD: There weren't no big heads, no 'too bad', no 'fuck all y'all'. We all come out of the neighbourhoods. We didn't do nothing but play sports 'til the gang thing jumped off. Then it was like you either played sports or you gangbanged, so we each knew each side of the fence. So Cube and Jinx stayed with the music. T-Bone and my homeboy Randy, they were like playing ball, you know, and me and Shorty was the gangsters. We paired off like that, and you can just look at it all of us learning from each other and building off each other at the same time. You can't fuck with them.

BC: When did you start demoing this stuff?

TB: Probably like last October, November.

BC: So do you want to talk about the single 'Guerillas in the Mist'? Was it written after the Rodney King thing?

TB: That whole album was.

JD: It was during the trial 'cause we sampled one of the officer's voices and put it on the tape, I think it was officer Powell.

TB: It was Terry White, the prosecutor.

JD: When he says 'Gorillas in the mist', Cube had the trial on tape so we just took it up to the studio. Yeah, that was cold, the Rodney King trial was cold.

S: If our album would have dropped at the same time as the verdicts, they would have blamed all the rioting shit on us.

JD: You know how that shit go.

TB: When the riots was going on, I'm filming in the hood, like I say we just fresh out the studio. I got the tape playing in my car, not realizing that all the while the tape is going along narrating what I'm seeing. I couldn't believe that shit.

BC: I thought it was done after all that . . .

S: We started on that shit in '91.

TB: Naw, we were supposed to have the EP out in December. We started out in October, Cube was going to do his movie *Looters*. We could have had our album out, we just busy.

BC: What role does Cube play day to day?

JD: He's like the coach. He the quarterback, execute the plays and he be making shit happen.

TB: He the fullback, and me and him the receivers.

BC: You guys think anything's changed since the beginning of May?

JD: You mean since the riots?

S: Naw man. As far as the truce, that was cool. It opened doors in the community so people seen that when it comes down, we gonna need each other, regardless of I don't like you and shit. To get through what we got to get through, we gonna need everybody. In they life, nobody and they mama thought the Bloods and Crips could get together. It scared a lot of people too.

JD: The cops in Compton – I live in Compton – and they say the Crips and Bloods are still strong and the truce is still going strong.

BC: From what I hear the Chicanos are . . . .

JD: They still killing each other up over there. I heard a rumour in Compton they were having a picnic and a cookout so big that the police came put rags on they faces and seized dope dealer cars, all black, and shoot it up. We know at the party it ain't us, they knuckleheads we got to control, but we know it's the police. And now the Mexicans in Compton don't like the black people all standing together strong, so now the Mexicans and blacks are all shooting it out in Compton. There's been a few murders, they shot a little boy;

kind of bad, that's cold. Nobody want to see it really happen, they don't want to know what'll happen if we have all good rap, not the bad rap and the good rap, what do they call it, divide and conquer?

BC: Shorty, the Nation has obviously been a big influence on you, but did it influence the making of the album?

S: Just the truth, knowing the nature of a person, you can easily bring things to the light that other people in the darkness didn't know nothing about. Straight up. Wow, I mean I didn't know anything about Farrakhan, I seen brothers selling the products, the pies and things like that, but the knowledge and who you really are, I didn't know who I was. So when I first got introduced to it by this brother named Drew from Public Enemy, I mean it was shocking, 'cause I never heard nobody speak like this, tellin' us who we are and telling us to do for self. I kind of like glued my ears to it and I'm like, yeah. It took a while. I figured out what it really was about and finally I'm like every young man. Really everybody should want to live a righteous life. I been negative all this time. It's time to make that change, so I went over and made that 360 degree change and everything else negative is in the past. I stopped drinking, smoking, got married, stopped chasin' girls, it's the only way.

JD: Left me, he just left me. Now I'm sitting here, I gotta learn from him. I gotta be righteous, cause it's only right.

S: I'm sitting here, I gotta be an example 'cause I feel I could show a lot of people it's easy to change your life up. People think if they stop smokin' and drinking and partying ain't nobody gonna like me. They gonna think I'm a punk. But doin' that'll show you who's really your friend. They like you square, but that's just bein' who you are from the beginning.

BC: On the album, who is the devil?

JD: Who I portray the devil as is the police. We can't do no 'Cop Killer' – it won't sell – so I portray the devil as the police, their wicked ass system. Police are so cold man, 'cause if you could film them from thirty-five feet away beating down a man, if you look closer you can see the guy on the other side gettin' beaten, and you could get away with that, how can that not be divine evil? That wasn't right, weren't no way that was right. That's why we bucked the devil! Fuckin' cop with the flat top, standing over a nigger's face down on the black top, that shit has got to stop.

S: I can answer that and justify it, evil is the root word of devil. We portray the devil as anybody that is a wicked person. We got the fathers, they go to church, but the pops got the children to be just like him, so it all goes back to who's the father of wickedness and evil. You trace that back you got it plain as day. We talkin' facts, the truth, go back through history and check it out. They portray the devil as somebody in red tights under the ground with a pitchfork or something, go back through history. Just when you put it down, the devil is somebody that's evil. Goes both ways: you got our own people who is considered the devil.

CYPRESS HILL

Cypress Hill are a breakthrough group for the West Coast. Their combination of old school aesthetics with West Coast thematics and slang opened many people up to the possibilities of life outside straight gangsta rap. The group is comprised of Sen Dogg who is Cuban, B-Real who is Chicano and Muggs, an Italian-American. This interview was conducted at Image Recording Studios in late 1991.

Brian Cross: Is this an LA sound thing or is it not?

B Real: We made it for everybody, not just for people in New York or LA or of one race, everybody.

BC: So how did you guys get started?

Sen Dogg: We started back in the day when everybody started breakdancing and poplocking.

BC: You're all from Southgate?

SD: Yeah me and him are, [Muggs] is originally from Queens, New York.

BR: We figured we'd make it as long as we stuck together, you know, if we went off and did shit separate it's cool but it's always best to have a family thing.

BC: Is this a Latin thing?

SD: A lot of the groups out here are like pro one culture and shit, like Kid Frost – he caters just to the Latin, 'cause that's his thing. If you ask me – I'll tell you that [Frost] is a sucka and he can't represent my thing, that's where we step in. We feel you can all be down with your own, but not when it comes to the music; you all got to be together.

Muggs: We feel the niggas, the Mexicans, the Chinese, white kids, it don't matter.

BR: If you went to the show the other day you would have seen so many Asians you would have flipped, so for me it's not about colours. I think breakdancing helped us a lot, because for me rapping grew from my breakdancing experience. I got into the music more, more than to break to and shit. I was like, these muthafuckers are deep when I heard Melle Mel,

'Don't push me cause I'm close to the edge, I'm trying not to lose my edge', and all that. Raps like that, they had concept and shit right from the beginning, that kind of helped me get into it more.

BC: Did you guys always hang with Boo Yaa?

BR: Well, yeah we're real good friends, but we don't hang with them on a regular basis; it's like when we see 'em it's like real cool, like family, but we don't really hang with anybody but ourselves. When we hang with anybody they come and kick it with us on Cypress terms, you know, we don't like clickin' on to other people's shit. You can be down with us and we can be down with you but that's to meet halfway, fuck that, so we're mostly on the hill all the time.

BC: So where did the whole concept come from?

M: Just gettin' high and doin' beats, we was hangin' outside gettin' blunted and we got drum machines and started stayin' inside more. I started workin' on music and them writin' rhymes. We stopped hangin' on the streets doin' all that shit, brought it from the street corner into the studio, you know, and that's all it is.

BC: So were you always workin' with SP 1200s, man?

M: Yep.

BR: You shoulda seen what we did our first demos on, a little ghetto blaster, we gonna keep that piece of shit, it's like a little piece of history for us. Breakdancing days, man, you can tell it was a big, take your shit to the park and break-till-the-batteries-go-down-type blaster.

BC: So you guys just hung in Southgate the whole trip, didn't start hangin' in Hollywood or none of that shit . . .

BR: We came . . .

M: You heard of DJ Aladdin? We lived together for about two and a half years in Hollywood, 'cause I was comin' out here doing so much shit, every hour to do something.

BR: Man we went through hell to do our demos, man.

M: [B-Real] used to take the bus ride all the way from Gardena to my house just to do our demos.

BR: Almost every day. Praise God we made it, seriously.

M: I stayed out here for about two years, moved out when I was about 17, then moved back to east side. You're on the road so much you don't want to be goin' out to clubs. You want to be with your girl, do things. And I been going out since I was eleven years old to parties and clubs so I'm burnt on that shit. I've got too many things to do, too much fun to have, rather than standing around with four hundred other muthafuckers that don't know what they want to do for the night. Truthfully, if you had something better to do would you be at the club? I like dancing, don't get me wrong but, four nights a week?

BC: I don't understand it man, I mean I do it, but the people who do nothing else, fuck man.

M: I be chillin' in the house with a bottle of bubbly, my girl, fat joint, nice ass, the fish tank goin' on, candles.

**Self Jupiter gets open at the Soul Spot,
Hollywood, 1992.**

Ganjah K and Dr Suess at Hollywood
Sound, Hollywood, 1993.

Medussa gets open at Rudolfo's, Los Feliz, 1993.

Muggs, Jason Roberts, Everlast, Lethal and Danny Boy recording 'Jump Around' at Amerycan Studios, north Hollywood, 1992.

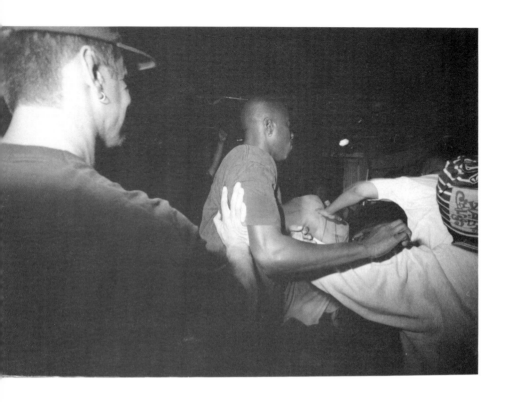

Slammin' at Guatelinda, Hollywood, 1992.

Fat Lip gets open at the Alley, Al's Bar,
downtown LA, 1993.

BR: I heard that, man.

BC: Did you think this record was gonna be this big?

M: Yeah, we knew it, but we figured the only thing that would stop us would be other things, you know. Management, record company, it happens too goddamn much, the record companies give up too quick. I mean Brand Nubian shoulda went gold/platinum no problem.

BR: We went in there and we told 'em like this is what we got, this is what we're doin, this is what we set out to be doin', and this is what we gonna do.

M: We directed most of the shit, like the imagery.

BR: We had most of the control.

M: We went halfway with them on some of the things but they did a lot of things right, you know, usually a record company drops a second single after three months, our first single has been out for eight months.

BR: They had patience.

M: They realized that they had made a mistake by not dropping 'Kill a Man' first which is what we wanted to do. 'Kill a Man' was blowin' up back east on the B-side. They dropped the video and it blew up.

BR: See you gotta give good groups some time, like us 'cause we were underground and we didn't have no radio play. The record company already knew we gotta shop them underground and it's gonna take a while, so let's just do this step by step, and they didn't get impatient.

M: Like 'Boyz n the Hood', Eazy E, it came out a year before you ever heard it on the radio. You heard it in the Swap Meets, in the cars, but a year later it came out on the radio, so [with] underground records you gotta let that shit sit and spread like a disease, it's gonna spread.

BR: And we probably wouldn't even be on the album charts like we are now, we're number 10 now, if they woulda fucked up.

M: It has a lot to do with timing and the record companies. It's like a basketball team, you can't win the championship with one star player. Got to have the whole company gotta be on the ball.

BC: Who wrote 'How I Could Just Kill a Man'? How did you sit down and figure it out?

BR: We did – how did we figure it out?

SD: It's just a freestyle song, man, it doesn't really mean nothing, [just] get together and write down lyrics.

M: You know what freestyle is about? Freestyle is about sentence to sentence, it's a whole story, sentence to sentence it's a whole story so if you pay attention you get the drift – it's abstract.

BR: 'Phunky Feel One' is a introduction freestylers, if you listen it's like 'The real one yes, the funky feel one freestyle has come'. Basic, just something to have fun to, man.

M: We just took the first part and repeated it like a hook. He wrote that shit a long time ago, man.

BC: What about the name Cypress Hill?

M: That's the block we live on in Southgate, Cypress Avenue.

BC: But they call it the hill.

M: Yeah, the hill. Gotta be there, be on the hill.

BR: There ain't no hill there, it's just a term. 'Cause in Southgate, I'll tell you what, there's muthafuckers that thought they were gonna be all that when they were older, there's muthafuckers that thought that we weren't and now it's the other way around.

M: You know it's like when you're 15 years old and you gotta BMW already and niggers like us we're walking around in old Levi's and patched sneakers not really giving a fuck, 17, 18, 19 you still like that and they all GQ'd and shit; my pockets was fat back then, I always had loot, but I just wasn't tryin' to be all flamboyant. They're workin' nine to fives now, still got that same BMW and same clothes they was wearing three years ago.

BR: From the muthafuckers that didn't have shit, but now we got shit, and I'm not talking material I'm talking the shit that means something to us. That just means we're on top of what we do. On the hill, life is like you climb fuckin' the hill, right, you strive to be the best of whatever and we did that. We're doin' that, and all of them muthafuckers they can kiss my ass while they try to walk that.

BC: Where do you think is the most important place for hiphop, the clubs, the streets?

M: Naw, it's the muthafuckers just poppin' the cassette in the box. You gonna be in your car, in your walkman, in your house, fuck a club, fuck a radio. I mean for sales I'd say it's the video. We get a lot of help from people who just wanna be down, they say, hey check this shit out man.

The old school shit's always been here, man, it never left, it's just been few, we're bringing it back. When you listen to Janet she's singing her choruses, man, Janet Jackson, I won't know one word on the whole album but I'll know every chorus 'cause that's how her album is. You gotta have concepts, but a lot of people have skills but they ain't rappin' about shit, they rappin' about money. Fifty muthafuckers already did that. They put out an album with three good songs, people don't be buyin' that shit any more. But that's the record company, their mechanism is to put out a record with three good songs, and whatever else is cool, three videos, three singles, three songs, sell a million singles.

BC: So that fact that all this legal shit is going down about sampling, did you think about that, 'cause you can't recognize . . .

M: No, if you listen you can, and I use them 'cause I don't give a fuck, but I try to stay original and fresh. A lot of these fucks got twenty-five beats out there, and every producer has twenty-five versions of each one.

BC: What about structure? Do you just keep listening and makin' it fatter and fatter?

M: Whatever I feel goes, I think is missing.

BC: A lot of that shit reminds me of jazz it's so fat, on the eleventh time you pick something up you ain't heard before.

M: Yeah. Well that's how I make it.

HOUSE OF PAIN

'See Dad, since you were a kid, they've invented a whole lot of ways for us to get in trouble.'

The Beaver to Ward Cleaver

In 1988, the Rhyme Syndicate put out a compilation called *Comin' Through*. It included a host of LA talents – WC, DJ Aladdin, Bronx Style Bob, Hen Gee, Evil E, Bilal and a young B-boy called Everlast. Now five years later after a solo album that wasn't, Everlast is comin' true. Teaming up with Danny Boy and DJ Lethal under the name House of Pain, they blew up in the late summer of '92 with the release of their debut single 'Jump Around' and followed that with huge sales of their album *Fine Malt Lyrics*. House of Pain have the distinction of being the first Irish-American hiphop group and like their brothers across the Atlantic, Scary Eire, they are freestyling on the experiences of an Irish upbringing. I interviewed them in February 1992 when Everlast and Danny were highly speculative about the possibility of their success. Danny and I had hung out all day in Woodland Hills with rapper Divine Styler. We consumed a number of 40s and drove back to Hollywood where at Danny's house we ran into Everlast and Leor (DJ Lethal). In this hugely jovial atmosphere I reluctantly conducted the following interview. Divine Styler contributed in the melee of abuse and mocking that ensued.

House of Pain's video was shot soon after on location at the St Patrick's Day parade in NYC. There they had an opportunity to meet T.J. English, the author of the book *The Westies*, the book that they had used to solidify their image of how Irish gangsters should behave. Since the interview House of Pain have become an American pop phenomenon – only time will tell if they can continue to collapse boundaries in the music and stay up.

Danny Boy: So ask some questions . . . The future is House of Pain, we are the future. To reach the nine still planets.

Everlast: I'm gonna put that out on film, that's the future of House of Pain, Borfix.

Brian Cross: What the fuck is that man?

E: A screenplay about nine still planets.

Divine Styler: Hey man, is this a House of Pain interview or is this a goddamn, no I'm just kidding, it's a collaboration.

E: It's gonna be the musical version of *Dune*.

DB: You want me to do the interview? When's the last time you been called a captain?

E: Me? The last time I was chillin' with your moms I think . . .

DS: Shiiiit.

E: You can just put our picture in the book with a blank page. Put *'a picture's worth a thousand words . . .'*

DS: So what do you all think of 3rd Bass as your rival hiphop group?

DB: As our rival hiphop group? Yeah, they're gonna put us up against 'em but you know it's really nothing because they're gone and . . .

E: FUCK 3RD BASS MAN!!!

DB: Sid Vicious rules.

E: Put it this way man, the Beastie Boys rule and the 3rd Bass gets the fuckin' pointed stools, G. It's like fuckin', I'll do 'em like an electric guitar . . .

BC: So is this a New York thing or is it an LA thing?

E: If you play it real it doesn't really matter, but we're from LA. If you think about it in the sense of influential years and where you spent 'em, my teenage years were spent here in LA. So really this is where I grew up.

BC: Did you hang with Irish people growing up?

E: Yeah, 'cause the whole neighbourhood was my family. Irish and Italian, that's all there was, and as a kid I didn't hang out with black people in New York, especially on the island.

DB: Bensonhurst G. I'm the only Irish in there. It's crazy. Fuckin' Bensonhurst.

BC: How did a bunch of beer-drinking, spliff-smoking Irish kids get into hiphop?

E: I really got into hiphop when Run DMC came out with that first record, cause out here in Cali where I was at the time, there wasn't no scene really for hiphop. But I got into it through that. When Divine Styler met me you couldn't tell what I was into. And then, after I met Divine, I started rhymin', 'cause I used to write bullshit little rhymes. We used to hang out with this Irish kid named Mick and he told us, 'Hey, you should start rhymin'.' And we talked about it, and when it came down to doing the demos the guy who was supposed to be my partner fronted for God knows what reason, and we sent out a tape, first to Ice T – Ice was starting this Syndicate thing – and I was young, this was like '87 when I really first joined with him. Then in '88 I put out a record on the Rhyme Syndicate compilation, they chose it for the single and the video, and from there I got an album. Did an album, they fucked me, I left.

Leor: So I've been DJing since I was 14 years old. I used to work with this one girl – I won't mention any names – but it didn't go through. Then she called me out of the blue and said that she knew someone that needed a DJ [Everlast] and I used to do beatboxing, I'll still fuck anybody up [starts beatboxing]. Ah, you can't print that, can you? Anyway, then we hooked up, started DJing for him, just recently got a hold of some equipment. I've always had beats running around in my mind, just had no way to express 'em, so I don't know, so I just been puttin' out some fat beats. That's it for me.

BC: So what are you guys gonna say when you're compared to Cypress Hill, man, 'cause I read that already.

E: I say anybody that compares us to Cypress Hill didn't really listen to the tape. I don't hear any similarities whatsoever.

BC: You gonna incorporate the Irish thing into the music too?

E: We haven't found the right way to do it justice you know, but as soon as we do, 'cause it's kind of a bugged out form of music you know? If you use it wrong, it'll just sound country, but if you use it right to make it sound Irish – [I] got a lot of Irish Rover records, a compilation of Irish boat music from Irish comin' over to America. Right now the Irish music is just in the lyrics. I'm American Irish, it's cultural history, Irish in the roots.

BC: Tell me about the Irish-American shit.

E: It's the House of Pain, money, that's what it is, some beer-drinkin' fighters, euphoric rangers . . . just a bunch of mystic sheep drinkin' electric tea, man.

BC: How did you guys get together?

E: After I did my first record, I was gettin' fed up with the promotion. No money was gettin' paid to me. And I came home (from a tour of Europe) and I went and moved back in with my mother, and got kicked out, and me and Danny Boy had been friends for a few years. I moved in with Danny Boy, he put me up and shit, and he wanted to do a group called House of Pain. It was gonna be a punk band.

DB: It was good on paper but that was about it.

E: The name just clicked in my head, it felt good to me. At first we started a band, it was all live, which it will probably come back around to sooner or later. 'Cause that's really what I want to do. We hooked up with Muggs, set 'em up, sent out some tapes and the muthafuckers went nuts. Tommy Boy signed it, and here's the House of Pain, word up. Danny Boy brought the Irish pride out in me.

DB: We're not trying to be like anyone else, like 3rd Bass and shit. Only good white group is the Beastie Boys. You put the 3rd Bass record on and you can't tell if they're black or white or what . . .

E: You can't tell their religion or culture cause they so busy bitin' off the black culture.

DB: The Beastie Boys gave us a lot of influence. Also old groups like Led Zeppelin, Jimi Hendrix. We just tryin' to show a different side people haven't seen, especially in hiphop culture, show that not everybody's tryin' to be black and not everybody's Afrocentric, and not everybody's trying to bite.

E: The Irish thing is just my culture, it's my family, there's a lot of cultures in my family, but dominated by Irish. Not everybody in the group is Irish, the DJ Leor is from Latvia. If you want to play on the Irish thing that's cool with me but so long as they don't play it out. That's not why we brung it up, to have it played out, sell it. A lot of muthafuckers be hittin' me up over the three dots in the logo.

DB: Why? That's *mi vida loca*, my crazy life.

E: In my lyrics, 'Put Your Head Out', it's from experience. If somebody like steps up to me or one of my boys, I'll put your head out, it's just automatic. It ain't really talkin' like I'm gonna be a gangster or just be tough guys wherever we go, 'cause I know when to keep my mouth shut. It ain't no front, this shit is real. I'm like Jimmy Cagney, I'm killin' shit.

BC: Yeah but Jimmy Cagney got killed . . .

E: That's alright, Jimmy Cagney only got killed once, but he killed many times, you know what I'm sayin'?

BLOOD OF ABRAHAM

Blood of Abraham is a new group in Los Angeles. They are firmly part of a new school sensibility rising from the ranks of LA's B-boys. Benyat and Mazik are Jewish, their DJ Lett Loose is African-American. Ben and Mazi attempt to negotiate the complex issues of their identity in their music. They are signed to Eazy E's Ruthless Records and will have their first album out in 1993. This interview was done after a long session at Paramount studios. Blood of Abraham are joined by producers Bilal Bashir and Brett (Epic) Mazur.

Brian Cross: Let's talk about the name, Blood of Abraham, what does it mean?
Benyat: Blood of Abraham, very simple. Father of many nations. We believe that Christianity, Judaism, Islam, all see Abraham as a prophet, from him stems Ishmael, which became Islam. Jesus traces lineage to Abraham. Abraham also being the first Jew so therefore everybody has got a little blood of Abraham in them unless they're atheist or somethin'. So Blood of Abraham is a universal name.
BC: When did you guys start rhymin'?
Benyat: It was first writing, writing the lyrics. More poetry or rhymes from the head, the beginning of my senior year in high school. From that it led on to rhymin'.
Mazik: Ya know, both of us have grown up our whole life with the hiphop culture. I mean our whole life the only way we could express ourselves is through hiphop, whether it was the breakdancin' or graffiti. It's like this is how we like to express ourselves, and people can see that it's true.
BC: You're from Vegas right?
Mazik: I'm from Vegas.
Benyat: I was born in Israel and raised in Nigeria and they brought me to the land of states around '83. I came here and that's when I got culture shock, so I got all those influences in me. My family never stayed in one spot. I never stayed in one school for more than a year

until tenth grade. That was the first time I went to school and knew somebody from the year before.

BC: You were pickin' up hiphop before you came here?

Benyat: Yeah, when I came here from Nigeria, for like three months on vacation out here, and in that little time, whatever I could grab I would because there wasn't much goin' on in Nigeria as far as anything really. I couldn't understand the languages on the radio, and the only thing we could pick up was *Soul Train* and *The Love Boat* in English, and uh – I'm talkin' the disco, afro *Soul Train* yeah, the real shit – so, *Soul Train* and *The Love Boat* and then on Saturday night like at 11:00pm there would be a western.

Epic: (laughing) That's America, huh? Westerns and afros . . . shoot outs and *Soul Train*.

Benyat: That's all we had. I got a distorted vision, I thought every American kid was rich, like they had a pool in the house, and had BMX bicycles.

Epic: Yeah, and then you found it was all true!

Benyat: Believe me dude, when I came here and found bananas in the supermarket that didn't have black blotches on it, nice clean bananas, that's a big thing. All the food there is natural. Anyway, the first thing I picked up was the breakdance movies, I remember, was it *Breakin'* or *Beat Street* that sold a cassette and a breakdance floor mat with it. It came like a whole set, so I'd bring that back with me and wear the fuck outta that until the next trip and, so I was influenced by a lot of shit. No one I knew was into what I was into. I found out entirely on my own me and my little brother Gil.

Mazik: When I was young, and I was in Vegas, breakin' was real big. I mean we had clubs every week that we could go to and like on Sundays at this one park at a junior high school, all the crews would go there. I've been breakin' since I was little. I remember all my friends were older than me, you know, DJs or what not and they used to get fresh records from the record pools in New York. They would get records in way before the shit came out. Like 'Have You Seen Davey' by Davy D and all the dope shit. There was only a few kids as young as me, and my mom used to be scared 'cause these big black guys would come to pick me up like 'Come on, David' and I'm like all little and in my long shorts.

Epic: This is definitely a group brought up in the new school, kids that were brought up with hiphop.

Mazik: I think in Vegas I missed out on a lot of dope shit. I didn't listen to music that much, 'cause I was too busy breakin' and into graffiti and all that stuff.

Epic: Back in the days [it was] the New York labels that were distributing hardcore hiphop like Select and Tommy Boy. When Tommy Boy was really an independent, they didn't care about distribution to Vegas. Originally I was from New York so I've been out here since I was two but I've been exposed to New York from going back and forth and I didn't get to appreciate it until I was like twelve, and I was stayin' with my uncle at the time. And I would come to LA with like Kangols and to them I looked like a freak. I mean, this little white kid with all this shit.

BC: When did you come out here Bilal?

Bilal: When was it? '84. I came to Santa Monica.

BC: Were you doin' beats back then?

Bilal: I was a DJ, that was my initial start. I been DJing since like '79.

Epic: Bilal was my inspiration, I remember back in high school, basically our crew was like, Everlast, Danny Boy, me Def Jef and Divine Styler and we would come over to Bilal's and it was just definitely a big schoolin' of hiphop to me, especially on the production tip.

Bilal: And Lett Loose, can't forget Lett Loose.

Epic: We all come from DJs, we all came from being DJs.

Lett Loose: I remember I used to go to Bilal's house and be like 'Yo Bilal, man get me some work', and he used to be like, 'Naw, man you're too young. I'd have to go through a lot of paper work and I'm not havin' it.'

Bilal: He was talkin' about goin' on tour and shit. That was then, this is now.

Benyat: I used to listen to all the shit like [I] read all the credits, you know when you only have two hiphop tapes in your possession as a kid you damn near know all the shout outs by heart, the whole inside cover, you know, Mark the 45 King . . .

Mazik: I don't consider us a concept group, 'cause everything is from the heart. We always knew that we wanted to be proud of who we are. The whole way we wanted to go was not to be imitating but create somethin' new and let the influences we grew up with affect that. It's like, I expect some friction on some things but that's cool. That's what makes the world go round, ya know, and it's like when you get your own album put your own opinions on it. Other groups like House of Pain or Cypress Hill, groups that are ethnically aware, they're not imitating another culture. They're respecting it and they're being influenced by it. And that's how I think we are, we're takin' an African-American art form and letting it influence us and with the love we have for it and I think you can't front on shit like that. If you actually love the music it's gonna come through on the record, if you're doin' it for the dollar signs that comes across on the first song. With us, if all this shit stopped right now, I think we'd be just as thankful and just as happy. It's been a dream come true for all of us were just real content with what we've done.

Benyat: We don't regret anythin' we've said.

Mazik: Nothin', nothin'. Everything has been dope.

Lett Loose: One thing I like about Blood of Abraham is they don't take other niggas' styles and wear 'em like a body suit. Most of the groups comin' out of LA right now, their influences are so high from other people you feel other people's souls, but with Blood of Abraham between them and Epic I can feel their soul.

Benyat: That's the truth. Every song we let the track move us, and whatever comes out comes out. The unity in the album is in the subject matter and the lyrics and that's it.

Mazik: At least if we went out, we went out knowin' we did what's true to our hearts . . . I wouldn't have one regret man.

BC: What are some of the songs about?

Benyat: 'Father of Many Nations', which is the tradition of Blood of Abraham almost. We got one about just people frontin' thinkin' they're all that.

Epic: It's the anthem of the superficial people in LA almost, ya know.

Benyat: Which livin' here in LA, you can't help but be affected by. I know other groups like Madkap talk about some stuff like that too. 'Stick to Your Own Kind' is on how society tells you and everybody else tells you what to do, and how we do whatever the fuck we want as far as what bitches I kick it with and who my boys are gonna be.

Mazik: Bitches? Girls, young ladies.

Benyat: I use the term 'bitches' very loosely.

Mazik: Yeah, *very* loosely. Stunts, hos, tramps, broads.

Benyat: (laughs) Yeah, bitches.

Epic: No, this is a very respectful group to everybody.

Mazik: We got 'Stand by the Steeple', which is basically not talkin' about Christians themselves, but the Christian system, the structure of the church.

Benyat: You could probably talk more on that topic than I could. But we took that topic which has been discussed before but applied it to us by bein' Jewish and bein' who we are and what it's done to us but more in a realistic way of 1993 of me goin' to the mall and being told I'm going to burn in hell because I don't accept Jesus as my personal saviour or wanting me to convert in front of May Company and shit, you know what I'm sayin'? Everything we deal with is something we've been touched with.

Mazik: I think it's abstract, but it's not abstract to the point where it loses you. You find yourself when you're writing hiphop. As you're writing you're like, damn, I've heard this before and we try and put a fresh twist on it. I think we have a lot to offer people, our culture and everything, we don't expect everybody to give a fuck.

BC: Aren't you guys dealing with the Simon Weisenthal Center, the same people who tried to block Cube's [*Death Certificate*] record?

Benyat: I think what they did about Cube was they blew that whole thing about Jerry Heller up, I don't think it was the Black–Korean thing as much as it was the part about telling a Jew to break up the crew or whatever that thing was, about put a bullet in his temple.

Epic: We were hoping we could school them.

Benyat: I know personally, they're trying to be the watchful eye for the Jewish community and they're . . . and they get bent outta shape as far as – they're extra cautious. It's like every little thing, you know, like havin' an Irish watch group or whatever to make sure nothing is being said bad about the Irish. It's cool and all but when it all breaks down . . . No matter what it is, music is a form of expression and it shouldn't be censored in any way. If an artist wants to say it let him say it, fuck it straight up!

BC: Are you going to Israel?

Benyat: Yeah, we're going to Israel as soon as we're done mixing the album in a month, to shoot the video; we just feel like there's some footage you can't get on Fairfax. You can't capture the Jewish essence [they all laugh]. There are all kinds of Jews, unlike America, there have been black Jews in Israel for years. There are Arabs and Jews whether they're living in peace or not, they're living together. I grew up around Arabs, like the store owners or other people in the city. That's the true melting pot if you wanna think about it. In Mecca, Malcolm X saw all kinds of people, and that's how it is. It's not about colour or religion, it's about people.

DJ QUIK

Quik for many typifies the worst of the Compton sound. He has been openly lampooned for his appearance on *Yo MTV Raps*. He was openly dissed by Tim Dogg, yet he still manages to make albums that go gold. His brand of less serious gangsta lean, woman-dissing lyrics and outrageous perm has made him as familiar a face in hiphop as many of his more progressive peers. He has extensively sampled the Watts Prophets and has recorded a track with them. Quik is 21 years old and owns a very profitable business. This interview took place at his manager's house in south central Los Angeles.

Quik: A long time ago man, my first hiphop song was 'Rapper's Delight'. It was like cool, you know, rap with some different shit, but when it started getting like serious and more youth oriented I was like eleven or twelve and I started getting into it. Me and KK from 2nd II None, we used to scratch together and share shit, and um, at the time the funkiest DJs were Joe Cooley and Bobcat. I was too young to go to Uncle Jam's, I just heard about it. I used to hear Joe Cooley's stuff . . . I never got to see a rap show until '89, '90. 3rd Bass came out with LL Cool J and rocked a show.

Brian Cross: What did you listen to then?

Q: Eric B and Rakim, Run DMC, way back in the day, Biz Markie, all of it as long as it was funky, except the underground New York groups like Ultramagnetics and shit. Only the big groups, Whodini, Salt 'n' Pepa when they were new. I could never hear Ultramags, Jungle Brothers. The west was real selective, at first, we got picky, we only like the funky shit, all the other shit got threw out.

BC: How do you see the shift from Egyptian Lover to Eazy?

Q: Egypt's shit was techno bass. Muthafuckers realized you can't play that dance shit all the time and impress bitches with your bass. So when we came out with the more lowrider based music, it redefined Los Angeles music much more than Ice T had done.

BC: So lowriding affected it?

Q: Definitely. We used to play 'Egyptian Lover' and shit, but it was mostly dance-floor based. How could you roll down the street with that Egypt shit at 130 beats per minute, 'da da duduEgyptshhhEgyptshhhh . . .' you don't look cool, when you could roll down the street with some 'boomchup boomshupchp . . . funky shit like your Cameo, all the Parliament shit, Sly, all the shit.

BC: It's a slower tempo and different timbre type thing. What is the difference now between the LA sound as compared to New York?

Q: I think there's a big difference. I think I take more time to really get into the music as opposed to like saying, that's a funky loop, let's loop it and lettin' it be like that. I would break that down mentally and then restructure. Me and my producer, he'll hear it, I'll hear it, we'll reconstruct it, add different drums. It's got to have an original feel, more original than if we just looped it. It's more open, it's broader, some loops are real compressed to get the most out of them, which brings in a lot of noise and a lot of static, which is okay with some folks, but me personally I don't like a lot of noise and static in my music.

BC: What about lyrically?

Q: All NWA shit. As a matter of fact, I really didn't get into them until 2nd II None got me into it. For me it was because they were from Compton, and they were really dope, as opposed to that guy who did that pop lock shit 'In the City, in the City of Compton' [Ronnie Hudson] . . . We had mouthpieces now, strong mouthpieces. Dr Dre went on to become the best rap producer in the industry at one point.

BC: Why Compton?

Q: It wasn't exactly the city. It was the aura the city gave people, the fear. I don't know what it is about my peers, some young people like people to fear them, me I earn my respect through my music. Fuck I know about this kind of shit, that's how I earn my respect. In St Louis they say damn it's tough out there and they say damn we need to be tough out here and crazy, they sick. In Denver they sick, St Louis they nuts. They kickin' more shit than we could ever dream of kickin'.

BC: But why not Watts or Carson?

Q: The city's closer to the boiling point. Gotta be crazy like that? I don't know. In a sense Watts is really rougher than Compton. I think it was the commerciality, it was a marketable concept as far as rap goes. And that NWA could portray this shit and make the music respectable.

BC: What made you decide to do so much live shit on *Way Too Fonky*, the second album?

Q: Who inspired me to do real funky shit on the album was the Brand New Heavies, who solidified the fact that you could bring the sound back in its entirety and have it be heavy.

BC: I heard you're doing something with the Watts Prophets?

Q: Yeah, I'm doing something with Amdee. I hooked up with him doing some sample clearances – we met and we hit it off real good. I'm gonna be working with 'em as soon as I get the time. I heard 'em when I was a kid, it was scary cause it was too radical for me. I was like five though, when I got into it. I think the real reason I remembered it and the reason I wanted to use it was because of how blatantly scary and formidable it was, it was thought-provoking and fearful . . . They were the first rappers in the truest sense, they been doing it since the sixties. If what you consider rap is philosophizing over rhythmic African type beats, they paved the way for this shit.

BC: Do you ever think of falling off?

Q: You mean becoming wack. I hope in all sincerity that I can maintain the funky style that I have. 'Cause what would crush me totally is if somebody were to say that I was wack, totally. Out of every song there was nothing likeable. It scares me, that's why I'm always doing new shit, reinvesting my money. This thing right here [goes to cupboard and takes out a battered Tascam four track], my first shit, 'Black Pussy', 'Tonite' was all done on this shit. First four track, then to eight track, then I started saving to put in this 24 track in my house [the mixing board had arrived just that day]. Now I'm ready.

Man, I was about to be in the film called Fly by Night, *I was doing the casting and shit, but I didn't get the part. I ain't no actor and shit I found out, but Tim Dogg was down there, and Black our manager look just like him, and I'm like, you look like muthafuckin' twins and shit. This dude had on locs and this dude had on some muthafuckin' ski glasses on and shit and I was like man, 'Fuck Compton, that shit didn't affect me and shit', and he was like, 'I know man, I don't know why niggers be trippin' and shit.' He was like bein' a man about the shit, came at it with a real man point of view. I was like I'm from LA and that song didn't even affect me, but I was like, 'Who do you think the best producer is in hiphop period?' 'Dr Dre, yeah I think Dr Dre gots 'em on, he's the best.' I understand what he talking about, just 'cause a muthafucker think he the best, you can hold yours too. That's what I got out of the whole thing . . . '*

Menace II Society are rappers from LA who recently changed their name to Nefarious.

Clear: We just did a party here and I threw on Cypress Hill, 'Hand on the Pump' and dudes were like, 'Take that shit off, man, throw on some oldies or Atomic Dog, right' . . . So I threw on some Sugarhill Gang hiphop, and they were like, 'Yeah' . . . something about the gangsta scene, majority of them are not really into rap, the newer ones are . . .

Shotgun: The diehard ones are not into it, though, only oldies.'

Clear: Yeah, 'get that black shit out of here' and shit like that. For a while we were kind of, not really scared but, our own people, it took a while for them to get used to it. We wanted to rap, and they were like, that's the black thing, so we had to go to a lot of black neighbourhoods and rock it there. They'd be like 'Hey, you guys are down,' so then we'd come back here and maybe they would listen . . .

Clear and Shotgun are from Brown Town, Chicano DJs and rappers from East Los Angeles.

AZTLAN UNDERGROUND

Interviewed by Raegan Kelly

I first saw Aztlan Underground (AUG) at the End Barrio Warfare *Rap por La Raza* event in July '91. I have seen Yoatl, Bulldog and DJ Bean perform on campuses, at MEChA (Movimiento Estudiantil Chicano de Aztlan/Chicano Student Movement of Aztlan) rallies, car shows and house parties all over California. This interview represents a combination of many afternoons and evenings spent in Bulldog's backyard talking about the group, hiphop, the Chicano movement, and their particular brand of inter/nationalist politics. AUG, formerly known as Brown & Proud, have been working with a distinctive combination of indigenous music, Latin rhythms, jazz, live instrumentation, and 'brown pride' since 1988. They released their first single 'Browns vs. Browns' and '1492: Fuck That' in the fall of 1992 and are presently working on their first album, to be released on their independent label, Xicano Records.

Raegan Kelly: Talk about AUG and hiphop . . .

Yoatl: The main track on our first single is about five hundred years of resistance and talks about how we as a people have suffered under foreign rule. By bringing it out and showing it we're showing a reverence, bringing out our culture and legitimizing it in the face of the white culture we were brought up under. That's the focus of it, seen as how this is the year of the so-called 'Quincentennial celebration' [1992].

Something we've always said is, we've already heard tons of stuff about us, that we're 'the Cesar Chavez group', but we don't have to play into that; we are down with everything that is positive, even Lighter Shade of Brown doing what they do. We want to be down, we are all barely emerging as Chicano, so we are definitely down for alliance with ourselves. I think the route AUG sees itself as taking as more along the lines of Maldita Vecindad & El General with their following in the Mexican/Chicano communities – or more in the light of Ice Cube, where we'll do anything but not if we have to change our message. We were dealing with certain A&R people in the industry and they were starting to hint, 'would be kinda nice for you to change this and that . . .'. We've been supported throughout Aztlan – Albuquerque, Arizona, Califas, Nevada – without ever recording, and it was kind of a lesson, a slap in our own faces to realize that we could exercise self-determination rather than believe in a major white-run label to carry out production for us. If we are talking about self-determination we have to exercise it in every possible way, and starting our own label is a way to do that.

DJ Bean: We're trying to reintroduce indigena music, rescuing mariachi music from the likes of PM Dawn, mixing it down with the Moody Blues, Carlos Santana.

Bulldog: And get our album out and turn around and help others.

Y: In reference to the whole gangsta rap thing, I feel that, on one level, if the person who's rapping can get the kids to identify with them, even if it is gangsta rap, if they are at the same time educating them it's alright, but most of the time it's like making money off the fact that your people are killing each other.

Luciano Cabanas: The rap tradition is developing in our community and infiltrating all over Aztlan – it is not new to us to communicate through the spoken word. An uprising is being felt everywhere, a consolidation of the base, like with Aztlan Underground. I know that the record industry is pretty conservative, so they define rap as a limited thing, occasionally white but mostly black only. But it's obvious as rap has grown and shown itself to be permanent, it relates to a Chicano experience as well as black. Just like the riots were at first described as being only a black–white thing, but they weren't at all.

RK: Could you define the terms Chicano and Aztlan for me?

Y: Aztlan represents the territories stolen through the Treaty of Guadalupe Hidalgo in 1848 by the US from Mexico . . . basically California, Texas, New Mexico, Utah, Nevada, Arizona, Colorado, parts of Wyoming – but really Aztlan extends to wherever Chicanos are born, live and die . . . The term Chicano, or Mechicano, was embraced because it was an underdog term. In Mexico they referred to the lowest classes as Mechicano, because the Spaniards used to call the Mechica peoples, the indigenous peoples, as *pinche chicano* and that was a really derogatory term, so in order to embrace the fact that we were underdogs and to embrace the struggle we took the term Chicano.

For us, someone who has suffered under colonization but who embraces our indigenous pride, who fights, we're warriors, you know, Chicanos are, when you call yourself that, you know your history, you know where you came from, you know where you need to go. If you recognize there's a struggle here in Aztlan as the blacks have in South Africa and in other occupied territories, then you're a Chicano as well. One of our mentors, Gabriela Hernandez, he points out that if we were in El Salvador we would be down with FSLN, we wouldn't be talking about Chicanismo, because it wouldn't be relevant. Whereas if a Salvadoreno comes to Aztlan, we're not saying for them to forget El Salvador, but you see anything we achieve here is going to benefit everyone. We end up being stronger if they take on the struggle. That's our legacy; we have the Treaty [of Guadalupe Hidalgo], that's our bargaining chip, so it could benefit them. The gringo is not going to say, 'Oh, he's

Salvadoreno and he's from Costa Rica, and he's from Peru.' No, we're all brown greasers to them. That's why we're nationalist in a sense but we're not excluding any other people of indigenous descent from down that way from our struggle, no way.

B: I'm half Irish, half Chicano . . . My mother asked me, 'How come you don't recognize my half?', and I said if I were in Ireland I would be fighting for the IRA. But I'm not, I'm in Aztlan, this is where I can do the best.

RK: Why the particular affiliation with Aztec icons in Chicano and lowriding culture?

Y: It's the most easily identifiable for now. First we need to educate the *gente* that they are indigenous. And the North American indigenous peoples and us – that's a relationship that we've been trying to cement since the late sixties early seventies. Ever since we had Chicanos up there at Wounded Knee shooting at the FBI – but at the same time we still have Indians saying, 'Oh, what are these beaners, Mexicans, doing here?', and Chicanos going, 'Oh man, punk ass Indian shit man, you know they racist against the *mestizaje*' [half Mexican half Indian]. There's two forms of colonization – difference is the English were exclusive, they didn't include the Indians in their religions, so on their reservations they were able to preserve some of their traditions, unlike the Chicanos who were included in the Spanish religion and lifestyle in that we were not equal but we could take on Catholicism. They were missionizing us, they made us confused, totally unconnected with our roots, whereas the North American Indians were still connected. That's the thing we have to get over. We go to pow-wows and you seem them sporting this American Flag, they do this flag thing and we're like, psssshhh – you shouldn't even be touching that.

DJB: Even today, to call someone out when you're ready for a fight you call someone a Indio – it's funny cause it'll be someone really dark who'll call someone lighter than him an Indian because it's an insult.

RK: Would you say there was a relationship between the nationalism of the 5 per cent Nation and Chicano nationalism?

Y: In a way it is separatist to the extent that these are all levels: the first level is to get the *gente* to realize that once you form a Treaty with a people, you are forming it with a nation, with a group of peoples who are identified by a certain thing that connects them all, and that's being indigenous. The Treaty of Guadalupe Hidalgo was the largest land mass treaty and water rights treaty in the United States and that treaty includes Chicanos, Hopi, Chumesh. It includes all indigenous peoples – that's like 15 million people. This is going to be used as a bargaining chip, because what we do in the Chicano Human Rights Council is record all violations of the treaty all the time and give our records to the International Council who gives it to our United Nations representative – what we're doing is laying foundation and justification for if ever we wanted to take over.

But what we're struggling for right now is getting the national Chicano movements together within Aztlan and letting them organize, like Chicano Moratorium, Chicano Human Rights council, and eventually form a National Congreso, which would be analogous to the PLO [Palestine Liberation Organization]. Then we would get together and talk about would we be separatist or would we just talk about self-government in a strategic sense under these conditions. So it's up in the air in that sense – we call ourselves a nation under the Treaty of Guadalupe Hidalgo, but we don't believe in the whole nation cultural mode of thinking.

RK: Could you talk about the concepts of *carnelismo* and *la familia*?

Y: It's been used a lot by the gangs, the whole concept of *carnale*, but chicanismo embodies *carnelismo*, the brotherhood, right? These guys right here are my brothers, I love them, they're my brothers – and the whole concept of uniting, that's like a big family – the Chicano people. Self-determination for the whole family. The family is real important growing up as a Chicano, the family values, really tied into chicanismo as a whole. Once again the ego is playing a role where we will divide our family and step on our brothers and sisters. Also in the indigenous people the family is important, so it's a part of our make-up. But at the same time different outside forces play into it so we forget sometimes.

RK: You speak on this division between Chicanos in 'Brown vs. Browns' . . .

Y: To us, the *vato locos* are in one sense all potential warriors. In the song we say:

> Imagine if you will all Raza gangs united
> Unified together and ready to fight against the real,
> The real enemy,
> All those people who don't want us to be free,
> Free in Aztlan.

That's all about anti-gang but we're talking about how they could all be potential warriors. Down for it. If we were really talking about revolution they would be the militia.

The gangs go around, 'I'm brown and I'm proud, Chicano.' But at the same time let's get beyond that. Maybe now we can, that's why it's important to us as a rap group, you know, take the medium to them. Rap is so powerful on a street level and Chicanos love it so we gotta take it to them with a message.

RK: So what about coalition-building?

Y: Coalition-building? We're down for it, of course we have solidarity with the African American movement and other movements, but at this point it's kind of premature for us to realistically think that we can try and come together at this point. In the Chicano community the consciousness is not together to be able to handle that. It's not that we don't want that; you see right away when we say that people think that we want to be so separatist that we're just down for our own, but it's not that at all. We see Woman Peoples of Color organizations and Peoples of Color organizations try and come together and we have Chicanas/Chicanos try and go with that but they're not even aware of where we're coming from. But we're down with it.

B: If you were to tell a cholo, 'Hey, I want you to be down with the blacks', he's gonna say, 'Fuck the blacks, man.'

Y: Perfect example: we had this party, we were trying to hold this AUG fundraiser for MEChA and other Chicano organizations, so we held this party at my house and all Sanfer [local San Fernando gang] came, you know this gang that I used to be affiliated with, when I was a Pee-Wee. In junior high I used to run with them, Frankie knows quite a few of them. Anyway they come and all the youngsters, they don't know who we are and the first thing they did was rush the door. The next thing they did is, uh, Claudio [former group member] was working the keg, we were trying to make some money, they took over the keg and kicked him out of it. Then DJ Chilly Bean was playing some dancehall, this big old *vato* came in, his name was Bouncer, hardcore tatooed up and down, and he said, 'Hey man, take that nigger music off', and he's scratching Jave's records and everything. And I walked in and said, 'What's up, man? This is my house – why you come in and try to mess everything up?' And he says, 'Tell that *vato* to take that fucking nigger shit off the fucking turntables, that's fucking nigger shit, man, play some fucking *raza* music man.' I go: 'Man, don't talk to me about being *raza* – I'm fucking fighting for your ass.'

J: And all they ever listen to is oldies . . . black music right?!

Y: I showed him my Aztec medallion, and he pulled it and threw it and said, 'Fuck this nigger shit', and I said, 'Man, that was an Aztec calendar', and he said, 'It was the niggers gave you that fucking idea.' I'm like fuck, you know, I shoulda told him what do you think oldies are, right? How can we begin to talk about coalitions when the average Chicano doesn't even understand about chicanismo or Aztlan.

B: We need to educate our own before a coalition can even work . . . Even back then [in the sixties] they thought they had coalitions, but they really weren't working. You didn't have the coalitions but the different groups respected each other. The Black Panthers knew about the Brown Berets and respected them, the Brown Berets knew about the Panthers and respected them, but they were taking care of their things in their places.

RK: Closing words?

LC: I say: 'It's better to die on your feet than to sing on your knees.' That's Zapata. Chicanos/ Mexicans go forward. If your thing is rapping, rap, art make art.

OFTB

(OPERATION FROM THE BOTTOM)

Coming from Nickerson Gardens, OFTB are concerned with providing a social realist view of their community to rival the exaggeration, stereotyping and untruths that exist in the mainstream of gangsta hiphop. This interview took place in August 1992 at Bustop's Watts home.

Bustop: I ain't no muthafucking gang member, I'm a gangbanger. We been together as a group going on about three or four long three years, whoo.

Fliptop: I had been incarcerated, and before people say, 'You crazy and you talk to yourself, you need something to get the frustration out', you know what I'm saying? I thought about a lot of the stuff that was comin' from me and I heard a lot of other rappers saying bullshit that you know that's animated, and I then start hearing that dope shit. I started rapping other muthafuckers' songs, so I said if I got the heart to rap that muthafucker's shit I can rap my own shit. I got the voice for this muthafuckin shit.

Brian Cross: You ever hear any of that old prison poetry?

FT: Yeah all that, the book called *The Life*.

BS: Deep down in the jungle where the tall grass grows,
           Lived the signifying monkey where the whole world should know,
           He was up in this tree sniffin' cocaine a bit,
           When he thought he come up with some of his shit,
           Now down on the ground in the great big green lived Leo the lion,
           Where he knew he was the muthafuckin' king,
           The monkey said to the lion one day

– what he say, uh some shit he said, '*big ole elephant your ass was sure to be kept the lion turned to him . . .*' some shit. I ain't muthafuckin', I used to know this shit by heart. Like I knew 'Mexicana Rose' by heart. I knew 'The Letter', 'Honky Tonk Bud' by heart. What he say, uh:

268

Dear miss adorable tight cunt bitch, while reading your letter I had an itch, I got the urge to take a shit, and finished your letter just as I quit – paper got scarce so I had to move fast, so I used your letter to wipe my ass.

Yeah, you talkin' about that shit was dope. I knew that whole book. I knew that shit where they say:

The hair on your cunt stand up like a steeple, and you can see the crabs walk around like miniature people, and you said you stole my old watch, some shit, the letter and the answer to the letter, my boy said I'm the fact finder, back binder, booty grinder, sweet pussy getter, back bone splitter, make many hos scream 'cause it wouldn't in fit her, cherry breaker, make money taker, sending punk ass broads to the undertaker.

I read every book Donald Goines has wrote. Iceberg Slim – that's where Rudy Ray Moore was gettin' a lot of his shit from man, and a lot of them brothers was right from jail, like Donald – was right in jail when he started to write his shit, 'cause he started that character Kenyatta.

BC: So how did you guys get together?

BS: We was always running together, we went to elementary school, junior high and correctional facility and all that other shit, projects, all around this neck, this whole neighbourhood.

Low MB: They was in jail, I was doing my little freestyle thing. They was doing their thing in jail, and we'd just call and [ask], 'What's up, nigga bam bam?' 'I got this stuff, what you got woowoowoo?' And then them niggas go out. All of a sudden we started gettin' serious, we started gettin' our shit, getting our songs down, get with our producers, went to the studio, layin' that shit, droppin' that shit, choppin' that shit, then that shit is out. TKO from Compton, Brian G from south central back this way, and OFTB. Things just started to fall in place, we all knew each other and shit but weren't really moving.

BS: I'd say the album is about 30 per cent new shit, 70 per cent old shit.

LMB: We write together, solo, we collaborate, we give or take a few – get you a dope hook, a dope beat and it's on. I don't really freestyle any more. Nowadays a muthafucker come up and try to rap on you, you walk up and try and bust on his ass, that's just the way it is. Me myself, I used to love to just come off the head, I could make up some dope shit right off the top, especially if I got dope beat and the shit'll be slammin'. I do it now, but now I be trying to write that shit down, everybody be layin' in bed and I'm still trying to write it all down, losing thought, and all kind of shit. For the public I don't fuck with it any more. It's for the posse fuckin' around exclusively, it ain't really doing nothing for you 'cause you just busting out on some muthafucker.

BC: You from around here?

LMB: I got a house somewhere else, it's a priority. I am from the hood, I always be from the hood, but for my family purposes certain things was going on that I had to get out of. So I moved the family elsewhere, my woman and my baby. Nigger gonna continue to be here. Don't get it twisted, my heart is here.

BC: Why you think that it's taken until now for Watts to get props?

BS: It's like this. We always felt it was the identity set trip. You have brothas knowing that everybody know in LA where the hardcore niggas at, right here, everybody know that. Gangbanging, killing, stealing, it's all here. Then these niggas come out from Compton and they never give those niggas here a shot, so we gotta start doing our own thing.

LMB: A closed mouth ain't goin' to get fed. We were like Watts is gonna get on the map, period. I feel like the record companies felt like they could deal with muthafuckers living in the house, middle class more than they could deal with a wild muthafucker livin' out here on the street. They don't even want to deal with the rappers, anyway. You gotta have a manager, where a muthafucker gonna meet someone to come down here and help set us straight. Ain't nobody gonna help me but me, like my boy said on his shit.

BC: You think the reality story will win in the end?

BS: We reality street rappers, man, niggas don't want to be considered as a gangster or a hustler, gangsters – that's the first person they be comin' for, the police, the mayor.

LMB: We gonna succeed in this shit, we done kick down the door, it's on, the bottom is here.

BS: Project kids, how many rappers in the game is really from the projects?

BC: Why you think it's not possible to be a rhymer and a banger?

BS: It's possible. The gang mentality ain't like every day, 'Let's go kill this nigger.' It's about respect, it's about watching your ass. We not gang-bangers but we gonna claim Nickerson Gardens.

LMB: You can't see us be doing no banging and then gonna go do a show, and think you gonna get away clean – muthafuckers gonna roll you up, I don't care if you as large as Michael Jackson. Muthafuckers gonna bang your ass if you be banging and disrespecting.

BC: So did anything change here since the riots?

LMB: What changed? Nothing changed. Oh yeah, something did change, they put Taco Bell back up. Peace treaty happened, in Watts it is still holding up. It's kind of a shaky but it's still holding.

BS: Frustration is back, muthafuckers looking forward to something for a while. Now they back to reality, but the man know that, it's set up to be that way. What they playing really is to get a racial thing started up down here, niggers better watch out, that is exactly what they up to. So they can go ahead to say, I told you, minority niggers and beans can't act.

LMB: Ain't no hard niggers, muthafuckers just gotta be theyself, that old I'm hard-and-I-fuck-anybody-up-and-I-kill-anybody shit. What goes around comes around.

BC: So what do you think it's gonna take to change some shit?

LMB: Oh, it's gonna take us to succeed and muthafuckers to see that and a lot of people to come down here and put a lot more money in this community and deal with our kids and not try to dis him and shit. See why he ain't got clothes, ain't in school, where his mother is, then they stop sayin' he was born to kill.

BS: You get the underground knowledge growing up in the pen, you grow up fast – I learned shit there – here so many talented niggas doing time. Can't nobody say they can't fuck up shit.

Coke: Make it like to appeal to Melrose, yeah. We definitely see that going on a lot, we think it's real foul too so we speak out on it a lot in our lyrics, keep a real undertone so . . . we try to keep the formats of each song different, even say the hook different, not just yellin' every time yeah yeah . . .

Motif: Then again you think, you can't really say they trying to direct it to a certain audience, singers just do what they do. Are you saying they really try to gear it towards crossover hiphop? . . . 'Cause it's like two or three years ago we were shopping a deal, so we know first hand, a thing was going on in the West Coast where it was like. If you didn't sound like NWA or Too Short or Hammer it was like you couldn't get no record deal out here. Now you got more of the real MCs comin' out, thanks to Ice Cube they tossin' it up a bit. That's why we think in '93 it's gonna come out, like Freestyle Fellowship has been out years; us we been out six years trying to get a deal. It's like you gotta a lot of people that been doing it a while comin' out, Cypress put a lot of work in, King Tee, muthafuckers like him in other places, it's cool.'

Motif and Joe are Madkap, a group from Pasadena. Their *Look Ma Duke No Hands* album was released in 1993.

THE PHARCYDE

The Pharcyde is a foursome of MCs who with their DJ Mark Luv have opened up the hiphop world to a post-gangsta LA sound. The Pharcyde represent LA hiphop of the new school, dedicated to eclectic samples, madcap humour and a love of the culture of hiphop. They also represent a vision of hiphop LA from pre-NWA days. Romye, Tre, Imani and Fat Lip were poppers and lockers back in the days of Venice Beach, Radiotron and Uncle Jam's Army. This culture is simultaneously preserved in the group through their dancing, but while their feet may be in the old school their heads are in the new. The Pharcyde have become phenomenally popular in 1993 on the strength of their album *Bizarre Ride II the Pharcyde*, a classic collision of swirling jazz, tight funk supplied by J- Swift, a comic approach to reality at best and a respect for styling, harmonizing and a vulnerability not often found amongst West Coast MCs. This interview took place as they finished the album at Hollywood Sound in late July 1992. J-Swift and Buckwheat (a featured rhymer and companion of the group) were also in the house.

Brian Cross: How did Pharcyde get together?
Fat Lip: I'm gonna make this short, make this sweet, make this short, make this sweet 'cause I gotta go rhyme to that funky-ass beat. Okay uh, I really don't give a fuck about nothing, and I'm about to go practise my rhyme, nice meetin' you B.
Imani: Word, alright Romye, what's up?
Romye: Okay, check it out. This is how it was, the group kind of originated in what we call the trendy scene, Egyptian Lover, Rodney O and Joe Cooley, it was a dance scene. I don't know what they called it on the East Coast but here it was called the trendy scene, everybody danced before they were rappers.
I: And we made tapes.
R: I'm from Pasadena, he's from Compton, everybody's from different parts of LA, stretched out, the Pharcyde tryin' to get to the far side.

Tre: Yo, ask me a question . . . we are the Beat Junkies.

R: Same as like the Flavor Unit or something.

T: Yeah, we are the Beat Junkies, a numskull state of mind.

BC: I heard somebody sayin' outside a club that you were gonna be the first new school group out of LA.

R: It's not really new school. It's really four individuals. I have my own thing going, he has his own thing going, Tre has his own thing, Fat Lip has his own thing. It's just individuals that we know. Since we're honest with each other we know what' going down, either it hurts or it don't . . .

T: It's all lies . . .

I: Check it out, we come from this place, open up your imagination, we see a plane, there's a highway and a sign that says, 'Ten minutes to the Pharcyde'. How do you get there? You get on the bizarre ride, the album, you just ride that bad bad baby for those ten miles, ten distances, ten quadraleaps for the 9 Tre, that's how we're comin' man.

T: Beats for the walkman.

I: Beats for the walkman, beats for the clubs, beats for the freeway, beats for the pubs, beats for the people, give me a sequel. This is part II you know I'm comin' in like this, I hope I don't get dissed. But I'm comin' for better or for worst with my grow, you know we smoke that's what we do, every day every day what I say. Hey hey hey not Fat Albert but we gonna be living phat for the 9 Tre, you know what I'm sayin'? Yeah, hopefully if people like us we'll be coming through but if they don't, I don't give a fo, sho no, fo sho no. I think it's just cool, I say it's music for life. Every place we went I kept thinking about that thing, 'Rule number four thousand and eighty. Record company people are shady', but [Delicious Vinyl owner] Mike is cool, [A&R person] Lamar is cool. When we sell our fifteen records and go lead, we can say, 'Yo, where's our money at? Yo, come up with the cash, we go double lead. We gonna be like don't be trying to vick [rob] me for my shit G.'

BC: Talk about the Brand New Heavies thing [Heavy Rhyme Experience].

R: Called no turning back, everything means nothing.

I: We always used to listen to the Brand New Heavies and it was like yo, it'd be cool to do something with the Brand New Heavies. Then Mike from Delicious called up and said, 'Yo, D got a brand new track, originally for De La Soul.' We was like, hey!

R: I don't think it was for De La Soul, dude.

I: Well for whatever reason, there was a track there for us so we said maybe somebody will listen 'cause everybody else was on there.

BC: How long did it take you to do?

R: We had two days . . . they gave us a tape.

BC: It sounds like you guys are the only group that actually worked with the Heavies.

R: Ah, ha. That's cool, that's dope.

J-Swift: We had no idea anyone was gonna like it. Romye listens to a lot of records, I listen to

**JMD at the Good Life, south central LA,
1992.**

(L-R) Aceyalone, Mikah Nine, Ganjah K,
Volume 10, Big Al in a cipher at Rudolfo's,
Los Feliz, 1992.

Marques Wyatt spins at Brass, Hollywood, 1991.

Vocal booth at Delicious Vinyl studios, Hollywood, 1992.

a lot of records, so we all work together on the production, it just comes together through me.

I: Yo, free Slick Rick man, fuck that.

R: I've always wanted to say that. The return of the B-boy.

BC: That's assuming he ever went away.

R: Yeah, but this year it's coming back in a big way. Kids been growing up with it, hiphop has been in them, comin' up. Graffiti artists doing t-shirts, getting involved again. I saw Crazy Legs up here, that's like part of history, [Grandmaster] Caz, last night the Jungle Brothers chillin' with Caz, and Whipper Whip and that's like goin' back to the days, here in LA, that's like deep.

JS: Whoever's responsible for KDAY goin' off the air, suck my dick. I used to listen to KDAY in the morning all the way to school.

R: But KDAY was like an easy thing, now people going out looking for it.

JS: But if you supposedly down with hiphop, you look for it.

T: A lot of the dope shit doesn't blow up 'cause it never gets heard. Brand Nubians never went gold – if KDAY was there it would have gone gold. Main Source should have gone gold. Gang Starr should have gone gold.

BC: The one before that as well.

Buckwheat: Straight from the Pharcyde, NWA is dope straight up, from the street. New York is cool but NWA is dope, Ice Cube is dope, Cypress Hill is dope, House of Pain is dope, even House of Pain is dope. The dopest white boys. I give NY my props, G, cause it's the mecca, but we're the mecca for them.

I: Let's not make this into an East Coast West Coast thing.

BC: Cool, it's done.

R: Walkman beats, G's only got jeeps, we can't afford jeeps, so walkman beats, the dopest walkman you can find.

FUNKDOOBIEST

FunkDoobiest is Son Doobie, Ralph M the Mexican (a veteran DJ of KDAY) and T-Bone (also know as Tomahawk Funk), the first act to be signed to Immortal Records. Immortal is a product of the success of Amanda and Happy at Buzztone, the ruthless management company of Cypress Hill and House of Pain. The following interview was conducted at Image Recording Studios in Hollywood during the summer and fall of 1992.

Son Doobie: I used to be a DJ and I turned to a rapper, and I hooked up with Ralph M and Muggs in high school like junior high. I also knew Leor 'Lethal' [DJ for House of Pain] and during high school I had written a couple of rhymes, bein' bored and what not, so I memorized them. I hooked up with Muggs and started comin' up with beats. At that time Cypress [Hill] was comin' along. I was in Cypress for about a eyeblink, but Muggs said I had a distinct style and he said I should go solo. I was solo at the time, then he knew Ralph so me and Ralph started hookin' up material. We would then turn it into Muggs and we would all work on it collectively. Then we hooked up with the third member of the group, T-Bone. He lives out there in Cypress where B-Real and Sen (Dogg) live, and he was rappin' too, and then the FunkDoobiest thing came together – the name came from a Cypress song – and ever since then it's just been us.

Brian Cross: You from out here?

SD: No, I'm from Brooklyn. But I came out here to finish my schoolin'. I been back and forth since '84. Pops and moms had one of them arrangements.

BC: So you were always down with hiphop?

SD: Oh, from the get go, just as far as I can remember, '80, '81. I was more into it then 'cause hiphop was makin' that initial voice in the industry. Grandmaster Flash, Cold Crush Bros, Fearsome Four, Fantastic Five, all that shit is dope. I still, I won't front, that's where I get my influences from, a lot of old school harmonizin', choruses, lingo I still use, it never dies, real hiphop. Ruby Dee, JDL and Grandmaster Caz, and even Whipper Whip had my moments too. I can't front, I thought they were the shit. Fuckin' Grandmaster Flash, DST, GrandWizard Theodore, those were my favourite DJs.

BC: Did you see a lot of them?

SD: Oh yeah, like Latin Quarter, Disco Fever, used to go up there damn, the Square Garden, when there was the first Fresh Fest, Fat Boys, Run [DMC], [LL] Cool J, that's what I meant by the initial mark they was makin'.

BC: Did you listen to KDAY and shit?

SD: Of course, it's sad that they didn't have no unity to find the funds to keep it going. Then you got some of these crossover stations playin' rap and they don't have a clue. But that's okay, I'm glad Muggs gave me the chance to come out and say what's on my mind. I'm not gonna disrespect no man 'cause they just tryin' to get theirs, just let me get mine.

I think I'm a fly MC. In my own mind I think I'm a superhero of funk. I've got this cape on and boots and the biggest VA across my chest, vocal avenger with my ears like extra large, the funk superhero. The hiphop crusader, protector of hiphop. I just combine all aspects of hiphop, 'cause like KRS said, wait till fifty years has past and then you can call it the old school. We just makin' our initial mark as far as people havin' a voice, like controversial songs talking to the people, or just tellin' them to be aware.

BC: What background did you come from?

SD: I was a latch-key kid. My parents were Puerto Ricans, nothin' but Puerto Ricans whether they was black or white a real Latino, strong pride type of background. I've always been a strong nationalist as far as hiphop, 'cause ain't no one has emphasized the contributions made to hiphop as far as Latinos are concerned. We was there from the fuckin' start, that was from the get go. They can talk all this we started this and blase blah, that's the bullshit, can't nobody say black nothin'. But as far as they were black Puerto Ricans, they were there from the get go, there was high yellow Puerto Ricans and they was Puerto Ricans that came as white as you. In hiphop there was no black or white thing, if you was dope, you was dope . . . writers, rappers, breakdancers, if you was white and you was dope you could get mad respect. People have also misinterpreted as far as the battling thing is concerned. There was a whole film made about who had the dopest style, and I think the style I'm a present for '93 is going to be the shit.

BC: Which movie you talking about, *Wild Style* or *Style Wars*?

SD: *Style Wars*. It's more about a documentary tip, who got the dopest style, and that's it. And it's funny you bring the two movies along 'cause the same word is in both pictures. I like that, battling, I'll battle for fun. Who got the dopest style, I believe one of them philosophies – the strong will survive.

BC: How do you define style?

SD: I think a style is the way you present your material as far as background, a piece of style. Where you come from as far as you may covet your surroundings, you understand what I'm sayin'? I think that goes with art, music and dance. Just lovin' an art and persistin' in it, to be the best, raw talent, no lights, no dances, no cameras, fuck nothin', just you and a mike and two turntables. That's it, do the best that you can. All the old school artists didn't have what they got now, all them sequined costumes, them beanie caps and baggie pants, that's corny. They was real. They may have had little hustler jackets on, pullin' on a Newport, chillin' with the Lee's or Levi's regardless. Havin' their kicks. They didn't wear their kicks to be seen, they wore their kicks 'cause that's all they could afford. But I don't even pay no mind to that, it's just raw, being real, that's all it's about, just be real. The style I have, the voice I have, I been doing that all along since the days with B-Real and the demos and all that. Then the superhero was born, after FunkDoobiest, then I started having that mentality like Caesar the Great or Alexander, all them people, 'cause that's how you get over, like a ruler.

I can't front. LA has had its contribution in hiphop, as far as the latter eighties and early nineties, got Cypress Hill, House of Pain, Ice Cube. I can't take nothin' away from that, they're dope. It's beautiful, and a lot of the old school rappers from New York have moved out here. A lot of the funk has started rubbin' off on freestylers in the clubs, they startin' to understand. That's not everybody, but then that's everywhere. There's wack MCs in New York just like there's wack MCs in LA. There's dope MCs out there as well as here; they might not be known, but they're out there, moving the people.

BC: So you guys are going to say some shit about the Native Americans?

SD: No we just addressing that we are Native American heritage, as far as T-Bone, me and Ralph who's comin from an Aztec Indian, T-Bone from a Sioux, and me an Arawak. We did it funky, not too serious or political. We think there's enough BDPs and PEs out there already pushin' the programme, but we present ourselves as down with the people on the reservations and shit. Some say this [hiphop] is a phase when you're young, but this is the longest fuckin' phase for me, longer than puberty.

Ralph M: From the age of six to twelve I used to just play baseball and shit. I used to just be into baseball. I got into hiphop when I was in the fourth grade, I started seeing breakin' and popping. There was a talent show and brothers be doing a number and shit with popping and locking and that shit was crazy creative. And from then on I always incorporated hiphop music into my lifestyle, it was always there and I accepted it and shit, I grasped it from the beginning on. Just grew up, didn't have turntables until I was like 13, in the seventh grade, I had one turntable, like Electrogrand or some shit. I used to try to save up and buy records, so I didn't really try to DJ until I was like 14. I practised an' stuff for like a year, and at 14 I started DJing at the clubs, high school flyer parts; like the underground thing now, they put your name on the flyer, so I used to go there and I would cut like 'Planet Rock'.

BC: Talk about trying out for the Mixmasters.

RM: Fuck man, I was in the tenth grade, that's what happened. At first I wasn't even gonna go, I thought I hadn't practised enough that day and I was like fuck that. Next thing you know I talked to my boy and he was DJing. A homeboy, he was older than me, he used to go to the parties and shit. He was like, yo man, we gonna go up there. It was at Skateland in Compton. They used to have all these parties up there, World on Wheels, and 321, all of those clubs. Before that they were doing that shit at the Civic Center.

So I walked in and in walked Tony G and brothers like chillin' and stuff. It was a crazy scene, all the Bloods and shit throwing up they shit in the corner and taking pictures and shit, 'cause they ran that shit. It was nothing but Bloods at Skateland USA. I was one of the last Mixmasters to try up; somebody was DJing, and I came in real quick with that doom dat doomdoom dat doomdoom dat doomdoom dat, that Davy DMX 'One for the Treble'. I had the bonus beats, I just came in and shit, then I did a little bit of mixing, then I went into the cutting and shit, I was doing this one song. Everybody was surprised, came around the turntables and shit, they thought it was cool. It was dope. When I got 12s, that's when I really really began to feel like I was a real DJ. Everybody, no not everybody, but I know a lot of niggas, a lot of the brothers had turntables and four-tracks and that shit. It was a way of life, that's how I look at it.

BC: You went on KDAY for a while after that, didn't you?

RM: Yeah, for about three-month period after that. I didn't know I was a Mixmaster and shit. I went one night to the Casa and shit and Tony G said, 'You a Mixmaster man, you got to get hooked up.' And I was like, word? I just wanted to get on the radio.

BC: So was there a lot of Mexican kids DJing or was it mainly black kids?

RM: Tony G, Julio G, not too many Mexican kids.

BC: So you and Muggs just used to hang out and do beats all the time and shit, right? When did you meet Muggs?

RM: About three years ago, '89, yup. After that we was just cool, I think through Son [Doobie] I met him, but really I had met him the night at the DJ competition that he had won. I was up there chillin' it. We cool for a while, just kept buildin' on stuff.

BC: Is there any music in your family?

RM: Yeah, my father, he was a musician or something. I seen some pictures. He listened to Creedence Clearwater [Revival], there's some bluesy shit in that. I use some of that, you know John Fogerty, but he's not down with sampling. I guess he has his own little stigma for this kind of music. Led Zeppelin didn't want to let a sample for that Kid Frost immigrant song, he didn't want to give it up. Ah Ah Ah haaa, that shit is dope, that shit works.

Reagan Kelly: Where did you grow up?

RM: In LA, on Olympic and Highland. I lived on Vermont too, but we moved when I was about five. I remember everything in my life, just trying to live day by day. When I was DJing, kids would shoot in the house, trippin'. What's up with that shit? It's just stupid shit when it comes down to it, just stupid shit. Like when I was in New York I felt a strong vibe, you better be on your p's and q's there. Out here it's real laid back, there you're like, tense. I still be on that vibe for a few days when I come back, on my shit, not really worried, not layin' back. When I was young I was DJing, dancing, taggin', I used to bust turtles and shit, fast man. I can still do that shit.

When you have respect and you give respect, there's a balance, you can get together with people and just talk. It's, I don't know, hiphop is just forever to me man, from the first time I heard a drum beat. Trying to stay up on the business end of things too. It's a different vibe out here, and I'm from here. When I was with [Kid] Frost I got to experience a lot of shit, went to France, Germany, Italy, Amsterdam. Oh no, they were on time with the shit in Amsterdam.

BC: Should be like that here.

RM: I could live there man, do my music, live there, go out there for periods of time and shit. Man they had so much green sensimilla, shit from Turkey, Africa, Thailand. This dude was rollin' shit in big funnels, yeah that's how we smoke here, something else for your mind, almost like heaven in a sense. You could go in with five dollars and come off. Italy, they were breakin' out there, they had Mellow Man Ace, they had Frost, they had records. I was tellin' kids, they had all the records from back home. Japan is jumpin' on the shit too.

RK: Japan lowrides and shit!

RM: For real? Wow.

FREESTYLE FELLOWSHIP

The Freestyle Fellowship have been one of the most influential groups in the new Los Angeles underground. They are five African-American men from south central, each with a long history in hiphop in this city. Not to say that their experiences are homogeneous, for Mikah Nine, Mtulazaji (Peace), Self Jupiter, Aceyalone, and DJ Kiilu each add an individual voice to their songs. Both structurally and thematically they grapple with the jazz analogy, swapping verses like horn players swap solos and lifting their rhymes to new levels of narrative complexity, while breaking boundaries in delivery. The Fellowship has recorded two albums. Their debut was an independent release entitled *To Whom It May Concern*. Their second album, released on Island Records, is entitled *Inner City Griots*. What follows is a discussion of the Heavyweights and other aspects of LA B-boyness with DJ Kiilu with interruptions and additions by Aceyalone, Self Jupiter, Mtulazaji (Peace) and Mikah Nine.

Kiilu: Basically I was working with a guy named Ebo, doin' beats every day, knocking out beats, and Matt was working on beats for all of them, individually. Mattematiks, who is my partner along with Ola and JMD, Matt was working on beats for KMC (Ganjah K), Aceyalone, and Ebo would take the beats that we would do and give them to Mike. I kept hearing about Mikah Nine. JMD had a band called Underground Railroad. He was coming down to the clubs I was spinnin' at, came down to Fat Beats, at Al's Bar, a free hiphop club last January.

    At that time, Acey and Mike were rappin' at the Good Life, Mike had been signed over on Arista, he did a song with Carmen Carter, did some shit with the Wailers, which they're just now playin' in the clubs. Everyone was just kind of established on the solo tip, but we had at the back of our minds to get together and play some shit. At that time the Freestyle Fellowship wasn't even a thought. The Freestyle Fellowship was like an umbrella, it was a loose term for everybody that was down with us. Which was KMC and Bombay (rest in peace), they had a group called the First Brigade. Bombay was killed not too long ago, in his home, execution style. The Underground Railroad was JMD's band. O'Roc used to rap in it with Acey and Mike. I came to a rehearsal and I got a ride home with KMC and Mike. Peace was a regular at the Good Life, but he wasn't totally tight with us yet, he was down. KMC and Mike started playin' some beats that were mine, and he tripped when he finds out that I had done those beats and, um, they came over to my house. We smoked a little ganja, I started spinnin' beats, everyone got hyped, and we made one of the best underground freestyle tapes. I mean there's about six singles right there, you could make an album out of that shit.

Ever since then me and Mike got really tight. We can talk about anything, politics. We admired each other's intellect. Through Mike I met everybody. I met Acey and Self Jup[iter] and it never really came to bein' a group for a while; everybody was tryin' to get a deal, working, making these songs, but going to the Good Life [Cafe] you know what I mean. They were just living the life of a B-boy in other words. We decided to make this tape [*To Whom It May Concern*]. Everyone was just puttin' in a song, the solo thing. A collaboration. That's when Jaysum B and Mello D of All and All were down. I was doin' some beats, Ola did some beats, Matt did some beats, and Jaysum B did some beats, it was all at Jaysum's house on a four-track. That became the springboard for all kinds of shit, shows, we sent the tapes out, we were sellin' 'em for five dollars. We were gonna start a record label but it got too hectic, we was too young and all that shit. There was just too many heads to try and start a business at that time. Island I guess came through with the best deal. Jaysum B started his own group, we took the name from the umbrella, and now the umbrella is the Heavyweights. Urban Prop, Menace II Society, JMD, KMC.

Brian Cross: So how did you start hangin' at the Good Life?

K: I never went at first, until I started hookin' up with Mike. I couldn't believe there was really some good rap in LA that I could respect, until I heard Mike and that's what brought me down there. Ola, and his roommate, R. Kain Blaze and Dynamic Flow started the Good Life. And the Freestyle Fellowship are the connoisseurs of the style that everybody's doin' down at the Good Life. Mike, Acey and Jup grew up together in 'the Jungle'. The way it is now it seems like destiny, like we known each other for ever. They met Peace through the Good Life. But it's not like we owe everything to the Good Life, it was bound to happen, somebody was bound to get signed.

But I think the common vector that brings us all together is that everybody's B-boy, everybody remembers the old school. A lot of kids today are [into] video, they seen the video, and that's where they learned how to dress, that's where they learned how to be a B-boy. And that's not really what it was about a long time ago. We always have to have something that shows we're B-boy, that we're not normal. And that's really what hiphop is about. I always like to show I'm down with hiphop in some way. That's important to all of us. Everybody remembers the old school and that's what keeps us together basically.

BC: Plus you guys were all breakers at one time, weren't you?

K: I didn't know them when I was breakin', but I was in a crew called the Shake City Rockers, which was really the first original Zulu chapter in LA. Ice T says now that the Syndicate was the original, but back in those days we hung out with the Rock Steady Crew and the New York City Breakers. We used to fly to New York and they used to fly out here. They gave us our beads, and put us down as the first Zulu chapter out here. The breakers used to be Al Ski and Cube G, myself, Tony Tone, ORKO and some others: Lenny Len, Suavy Smooth, Chevy Shenk, old school B-boys. When we stopped breaking', Cube G and Al Ski formed a group called the Almighty Homeboys, who are in the studio now; I used to DJ for them. They had the name Shake City Rockers, which they sold to the DJs. They produced Malcolm McLaren's last album. ORKO was the fuckin' best breaker, and he went out and hung out with Kuriaki and lived with him for three months in the Bronx, and took out all them breakers out there. Now I hear he's breakin' again.

BC: Muggs was saying the other day that there was really an electro sound out here, when he got here. It was probably because the whole B-boy culture was involved with breakin'. The breakers were better than the rhymers.

K: The electro thing really came from Uncle Jam's Army, which was mostly a south central thing. I was fortunate to have friends in New York, 'cause nowadays kids just get what's handed to them. Everyone can't be down with the underground scene. As soon as it gets trendy, it has to move, otherwise it loses its freshness. It was the first thing to really break the records out here that was hot in New York, they would break shit down in the coliseum. They would do New York half the night, the other half the night they would be playin' 'Planet Rock' beats with their rhymes over it. Whoever was listening to that on the radio or went to the coliseum some of them may have gotten into the NY shit, and others into the electronic shit, which we knew was gonna die soon – we were hopin' it was gonna die soon. All that shit was wack, the LA Dream Team.

BC: So the slate's wiped clean now. Is what you guys are doing totally outside of the whole Compton, south central thing?

K: I just think it's like brothers from the same city, but everybody can't do the same thing. Look at how many rappers are out in New York. Tim Dog says one thing, and you can tell it's straight hardcore Bronx-style lyrics, and you can look on this coast and look at NWA. It's kind of the same style, he wants to dis NWA but he's not really sayin' shit. He stoops to their level, and neither does NWA. We're not tryin' to do anything that's been done, that's why we don't sound like anybody. We all have hiphop backgrounds. Acey may have gone to different clubs, but we know guys like Ice Cube, we know gangsters, Crips, Bloods, dope dealers. We live in the ghetto, we didn't grow up in Beverly Hills, it's just that we heard something different.

BC: Did you guys listen to the Watts Prophets?

K: Yeah, the other guys could probably recite it back to you. You can probably hear the influence on the new album. And some of those guys might never have heard the Watts

Prophets. Music is like, it's a vibe, it comes from what you live in, where you are and where you're at, you don't have to listen to the same records to understand the same things, to understand what's going on.

BC: Define B-boy. My understanding of B-boy is total commitment to the culture, but most importantly not doing nine to five.

K: You think so? My thing is B-boy comes from breaker boy, I guess. The term is now so old that if you're a B-boy, you're living the life, 24-7. I used to have a job, but I was still B-boy. It's a state of mind. It's the hiphop, it's the culture. It's a total commitment. Committed to hiphop in one form or another, graffiti, DJ, promoter. I don't think you can be wack and be a B-boy, but I don't know. If Run makes a wack record can he still be a B-boy? I don't know, ask Fab 5 Freddy.

BC: So Acey, talk about when you guys started doing shit together, man . . .

Aceyalone: We was all together from high school I started rhymin', sixth grade, seventh grade. From junior high.

BC: Who did you start out imitating?

A: Well, I wouldn't say imitating, no I wouldn't imitate. I was doing old school, like Sugarhill Gang, Treacherous Three, stories, I started gettin' into some crazy shit. I remember all I ever heard about Microphone Mike is that he was wack, in the old days he was wack. That was because he was different. 'Cause I know he was kickin' the same style as now, but they wasn't ready for it. We was down with this other dude named T-Spoon, Jupiter and me. Actually it wound up being just me, Mike and Spoon. We was the MC Aces, all the way from '84 to about '86 or '87 and then we all split up.

BC: Most people that write about hiphop start with Kool Herc, but before that there was scattin' and shit.

A: Beatin' on drums. That's hundreds of thousands of years, beatin' on drums and chantin'. In Africa there was one person in the village that was the poet and he would come and the storyteller would come and tell different folktales as the music was playin'. It's still the same relation. I didn't even know my hiphop shit till late. I liked to make music and shit, like the Sugarhill Gang, makin' up our own words.

Jupiter: That's where the playin' with words started.

Kiilu: A lot of it started because there was a microphone attached to the turntable, kinda like crowd participation. Gettin' everybody to say 'Ho!' and clap their hands and stuff like that. Rap is different now, all these images. Yeah, they just came up with an image. Rap is at a point where you gotta have an image and stick with the image, like gangsta, or a stick-up kid, or a fuckin' peace guy, sixties, de la Dread, and the Freestyle Fellowship is a fellowship of brothers that freestyle, that's it – B-boys.

A: Not looking for the gimmick, or any of that, just freestyle.

K: That's why I can't stand all these video kids, you know, 'cause before you get into anything you have to research your roots, you can't just be watching six videos on *Yo MTV*

Raps and say, 'Yo, I'm a fuckin' B-boy and I'm gonna go put this scarf on my head and wear these shoes and go to the Good Life on Thursday night and yo, I'm in there.'

A: Yeah, but you gotta have sympathy a little bit, you know they want to get into it.

K: But they just look at the TV image of a B-boy and take the stoned face, say I can't talk to you 'cause I am a B-boy and they don't know shit, they only know new shit.

A: And I don't even want to talk about the clubs. Let me tell you from an MC perspective: you walk into a club and you a B-boy and you with your crew or whatever and you see all these flyers say hiphop, hiphop, hiphop and you cannot wear a hat. What B-boys don't wear hats? No tennis shoes, and they say hiphop, the promoters can wear it and their friends. They'll have people performing on stage, (A Tribe Called) Quest or whoever, with just their regular gear, with the same gear on. They wear their tennis shoes and their hats and their fans can't even get in. I don't know, man. And then, on the mike. Besides the club we did where the MC rocks, not hoggin' the mike but keepin' the party alive. Now it's like nobody talks on the mike, it's just all music, no crowd participation, if there's a wack song you just gotta sit through it.

K: That's the thing about LA, there's all these little bourgeois kids, got enough money to make a flyer. They throw hiphop on there, but it's like a clique, if they don't know you, you ain't rappin'.

A: Out here the hardknocks listen to hiphop, but they not really into the old school, just the gangster shit. In NY the little stick-up kids listen to the old school. Out here it's more bam bam bam. I work at a school with kids, they straight up B-boy, the hiphop lifestyle now.

SJ: I grew up listening to jazz, my granddaddy playing like jazz, one year old to 15 years old. Up-tempo jazz, Ornette Coleman – I was named after him – and grandfather played with the Duke Ellington band, he played the trumpet and the trombone, his name was Poppa Stubbs.

Peace: Before I got hooked up I was rhyming with a producer by the name of Jammin' James Carter, and who's now producing for Lighter Shade of Brown and some homies of mine, KMC. We was kickin' some flavour with them and everything was cool. I was settin' up for an album, bein' peeped by a couple companies, but nothing came through so one day I decided to go to the Good Life. So we decided to go up there and I dropped for the first time. A friend of mine had been telling me about Mike and Acey, especially Mike, and he was saying he's got a crazy style, man, he's fresh. The second time I went, sure enough there was Mike and he was blowing up. And after Mike heard me blow up, he was peepin' me, Eddie [Acey] was up there. Eddie bust, it was like, you know this cat got flavour – he said what's your name and I said 'Peace'. He said, 'Peace, all right, money, you fresh.' I kept going back for a while, and before you knew it I was hangin' out with the Fellowship. I was taken in by the First Brigade, KMC and Bombay (rest in peace), and they picked me up and they put me in the First Brigade.

BC: Who was you listening to when you started out?

P: When I came out here from Texas, I encountered Big Daddy Kane. I'm a new school rapper. I can't really recount the history, but I was listening to BDK, live from New York. I had heard Rakim, so I mixed up Rakim and Cool J and came together and came up with the style I got, used it 'til I came up with a stable base of my own. I just started flexin' and practising.

BC: When did you come here from Texas?

P: I came out here in '84. 1984, I was in junior high.

BC: So did you dance?

P: I got helluva rhythm. I can groove, poppin' was my thing. That's how I got to rhyme; if you can dance, you should be able to rhyme. But I wasn't heavy into breakin'. When I came here I hooked up with some guys from Jordan Downs, the M&M Crew, the Soda Pop Crew, everybody's crew would get on deck on Fridays at Watts Towers. That's when I used to take on MCs, strangling them with mad force. I used to sit up at the railroad racks writing rhymes for the next day.

Mikah: I was like writing my rhymes and they were writing their rhymes, but they had a crew and they rapped together. I rapped by myself. And I noticed they had little folders, they were coming with these little flimsy portfolio notebooks with their rhymes in 'em and I was like, okay they're into the music. And it was like a B-boy renaissance at the time. It was like Lee's with the permanent creases, belt buckles and BVDs. It was slightly after Run DMC's first album. We weren't the only MCs at that high school. Birmingham High was in the valley. I'm not sure where it was, I think in Van Nuys. It was B-boys on deck. I had a fat folder, a motherfuckin' fat portfolio. I was pretty bad, I used to tag all the time.

At school, I went in during the pep rally and I went up to the bench and started beatin' on the bench boom chat da boom boom chat, the 'Roxanne' [by UTFO] beat, the Intelligent Rapper part. At that time that was like the lick. Before I knew it some two hundred people were around the bench and before I knew it I heard Acey. I noticed him first, then I noticed T-Spoon and they were stylin', they weren't just rappin'. They weren't just styling they were tryin' to make the rhymes correlate to some kind of iambic pentameter, they were rappin' in meter, period. It impressed me and shit, at that time I wasn't thinking about meter. I was, damn this thing is fresh, and so I kicked my rhyme and it was a long-ass rhyme, and I rhymed all the way through lunch. And later on after school they asked me to be in their crew, and I said yeah.

BC: Where did you figure out how to style the way you do?

M: Um, I knew I had a knack when I was in junior high. It was me, this girl and this other dude, we had to do a project for algebra, and I elected to rap all these formulas. She did it like Sequence, he kicked it like Dolemite, and I came out with a rhyme that was fresh, and I knew I had a knack, 'cause they sounded like a commercial, 'Buy a new car for 14.99.' You know that shit? I hate that fuckin' white supremacist shit. That shit fucks me up. That's when I knew I could rap. I kept writing rhymes, tellin' my friends. It really came to fruition when I listened to solos, listening to the words, listening to the songs, I noticed that the ones that I liked, there was a certain degree of difficulty in the language used.

Muthafuckers said come join my crew, so I did, and ended up battling some of them and taking out this fool named Diamond D and we chilled. We got jerked, we paid our dues and shit, I think that what really brought it all together was our drive to really be singled out from all other MCs. Style was of the essence. I personally believe that good music well played will always win in the end. You can tell a person that's got a style when they project. When they project they don't necessarily have to articulate, but you can feel where they're coming from, if they look satisfied and things appear to correlate.

And that's when I got together with my own brothers and we decided we were going to start our own company independent of the white man. But then we wound up makin' a logical compromise under the situation, where we accepted whatever trade-offs occurred. But it is a temporary thing. We goin' to take our shit on the road and we gonna give out pamphlets and paper and shit that tells about stuff that we know what's happening to us on our side. Niggers have got their mouths busted and their nose busted behind rap, they have got slammed and pistols pulled on them behind some fuckin' hiphop and that's part of the reason why I have started to distinct myself with style. I am working to make that distinction, and that's the reason why we're a fellowship of freestylers because freestyles are the ultimate forms of expression.

If you want to do anything in life, that you want to consistently pursue, you make it your life. We really are down with this shit, every one of us, our different personalities, the way we relate. It's on such an enlightened level, it's all love. This shit is the best, I don't believe this is happening.

BC: So where did you start hanging out?

M9: Radiotron, World on Wheels. World on Wheels was where the Crips kicked it, and Skateland was where the Bloods kicked, but the women were just too fly, and you'd always see some Bloods and Crips under cover checkin' it out. Skating and playing video games. Another good place was at Rogers Park in Inglewood, and St Elmo's Village, a lot of people over there smoked out now. But I grew up there. There was a thing they used to do called LA Street Scene, we used to rap. Me and Eddie were the best at getting into clubs; we wore reversible clothing and used stealth and cunning 'cause we didn't want to pay but we wanted to push up on the honeys. We kicked it in the streets a lot.

I started rappin' in the sixth grade on a bus that was going to Wadsworth Elementary. I heard King Tim III on a tape, I heard Cold Crush Bros, I heard Sugarhill Gang, I heard Grandmaster Flash and Furious Five. That's what did it for me, I just kicked it in the back and I used to rap my bags. I used to roast anyone, 'cause the bus ride was long, used to beat on the widows and shit, always be rappin'. Always. When I say kickin' it in the streets I mean beatin' on cars, rappin', drinking 40s. The big thing was to rock houseparties, till homies started shootin' each other over some bitch or shit, to rock it, you know, everybody be there, and you get so much props. Schools of thought, logical progressions and shit. The bedroom was always a spot. I remember our best DJ was DJ Punish, and he was swift, he just finished like a little five calendar spin and shit, getting out in July, he's been in for six years come summer, and he was down with our crew to the fullest. Everybody was a hustler, I knew a lot of taggers, rappers, MCs, that's just doing a lot of shit that's going downhill. You a hustler till you can see what you doing.

NEFERTITI

Nefertiti is part of the new generation of female MCs on the West Coast. Her wisdom exceeds her age as do her skills on the mike. She is signed to Mercury Records and her album should drop in the autumn of 1993. This interview took place in October 1992 at the Burbank studio where DJ Pooh was laying tracks for her album.

Brian Cross: Is it worse being a woman rapper?

Nefertiti: Not for me, I would have to say. I was born into the Nation of Islam, so I always believed that when you respect yourself, you get respect, you know what I'm sayin', so I never had problems.

BC: Were you brought up Muslim?

N: Yeah I was born in the Nation of Islam. I'm from Chicago so I never really let that stop me. I figured I was just a rapper so, not women or men, I saw both come up so I never really took it to the sex thing. I just thought it was a rap thing.

BC: So you got involved with Bobcat when you were really young.

N: Yeah I was twelve. I met Bobcat, his brother went to Taft with me. My parents still live in Woodland Hills. I started out doin' shows, callin' and booking myself in the show. I started out doin' the shit for free, opening for shows, and people liked me. I was good or whatever, so I continued to get billed and then people would call me and ask me to do shows. My first big show was Public Enemy at the Palace, I got mad props from that and went on to do Rap Mania. During that time Bobcat was producing all my tracks. Rap Mania was the East Coast/ West Coast thing and that's where I got all my major, major props because I was, as far as write-ups were concerned, I was considered to be one of the best of the show. Actually I had the best audience, it was cool. Bobcat was working all of my show tapes, we were working off the SP in the garage spittin' the lyrics into the headphones and stuff like that. Bilal Bashir was doin' my stuff and then I hooked up with Griff and went off with Professor Griff for a while.

Then I came back to school, basically what I was doing was establishing a business, and I would just let people know who I was. That has always been in my blood. My father's an entrepreneur, and I had these record companies come after me and shit. That was real cool, it made me feel good 'cause I didn't have to go and solicit myself any more 'cause I had already done that. The way I approached the record company was like I'm bringing this to the table and you're bringing that and it was never a dependent type thing. But before I started really getting into the record companies I hooked up with Jim Brown and the Amer-I-Can programme, and I been teaching in that for three years. I taught in prisons and stuff. The reason I bring that up is, because it taught me my responsibility and stuff, and I keep a level head with everything. It keeps me humble.

BC: You're only 18.

N: Yeah, I got a good track record, only because of my parents and my upbringing and my beliefs. I believe like that in that Newton's Third Law, for every action there's an equal and opposite reaction. So if you do good only good things will happen to you.

BC: You were just doin' local shit.

N: Yeah. I did some stuff with Farrakhan the last time he spoke here. My first show was Monterey Jazz with Solomon Burke, and how many people go there? That was my first show and I had a live band, so I been doin' this for quite some time.

There are certain rules in rhymin', unspoken, to me. Whenever I see someone like Kool Herc or [Grandmaster] Caz I'm honoured to be in the same room with them. Music is music and whatever you feel like expressing is your expression, but if you're gonna get into the rap thing and start with that, have enough respect for the art to recognize certain things. It's like me gettin' up and trying to redo a John Coltrane song but I'm gonna turn around and say, 'Fuck jazz.' I wouldn't redo an Anita Baker song 'cause I don't sing, I wouldn't even disrespect her like that. When you see someone taking rhyming to a level it just ain't, it gets frustrating, as an artist maybe on the grassroots level.

BC: Talk about the influence of Islam on hiphop.

N: Like I said, for every action is an equal and opposite reaction. Islam has always been either right or wrong, like with every religion. Religions are man-made, and men aren't perfect, so you can just take it from that. I feel like Islam will always be a part of rhyme, because it has always been the most dominant religion as far as blacks are concerned. It is always looked on as the most militant, just as rap being considered militant, so how can you not have Islam with rap? You can't have one without the other. Plus Elijah Muhammad said this was gonna happen anyway. This isn't nothing new, it's been talked about before, it's 360 degrees. Things always go full circle.

It's a history lesson, a crate of records is like a history book. Since schools are producing fools, how can I use my education as a tool? They take that away and then what. Rap came from our conditions: we used to sing in the fuckin' cotton fields, any condition that you put black people in we manage to do something out of it. We're all really POWs here in

America, and we've managed to come up with jazz, to get out of the bondage so-called. So no matter what you do, we're gonna do something that's gonna make us swing anyway. Take away sampling, hey we're gonna play live now. We're poor people no matter how rich we are. We're really all prisoners, so it's like when you take away sampling and bring in chaos, record companies and all these people that didn't even start the thing, it's like a big con game. 'Hey kids, we see that this is something that you can make money off of, let me come and facilitate this shit.' They're pimpin' us. Eighty per cent of the money made in rap doesn't even go to the rappers. That's the whole pimp game right there. Why wouldn't they take sampling away from us? It's black on black crime, here we are rappers not getting along with James Brown. It's the division again of the black family.

Okay, the title of the album that I wanted to use is *L.I.F.E.: Living in Fear of Extinction*. Fear motivation is the first element of motivation, then you have incentive motivation, and then you have attitude change, those are the three forms of motivation. Fear is where we're at now, we're at the last plantation right now, and that's mental slavery, mental bondage. 'Cause physically we could kick ass if we wanted to. But right now it's the fear that keeps us from doing things, from attaining our goals, and that's what we talk about in the programme.

BC: Talk a little bit about the programme.

N: The programme teaches them responsibility for self-determination, we talk about drug abuse, family responsibility, right now Amer-I-Can is holding LA together. We're the ones who did the truce, we have somebody from every gang in LA in our programme. We call the shots. When I go to a city, I go to where it's really goin' on, the hood, the people who call the shots.

BC: You gonna stick with [Amer-I-Can programme head] Jim Brown?

N: Definitely, that's a lifetime thing. I always wanted to be a teacher and he's allowed me to do that. I've been facilitating and it's taught me how to basically get through life.

BC: Is that involved with Islam?

N: His programme doesn't deal with religion or race, just people changing themselves.

BC: I know there was people from the mosque . . .

N: There's a lot of Muslims involved with the programme. We work with Catholics and Jews and Koreans. Because we believe that problems of today are social. These are problems everybody has, so how could we limit it? If you deal with changing a person's mind and how they think, then you deal with changing the world. Rap is bigger than people understand, it's not gonna evolve into us making millions of dollars. It's gonna be action, people are not just gonna be dancing, they're gonna be moving, we're gonna be the next politicians. It's not gonna be Clinton that the people listen to, the new generation is raised on hiphop.

I'd be a fool to say everybody's gonna be positive. I listen to NWA too, but hiphop is gonna evolve, even . . . I don't know. It's a deeper level. The Panthers are gonna evolve through rap again. MOVE is gonna evolve through rap. You can't run from it, it's a sign of the times.

I experienced being in gangs, I've experienced putting gangs together, I got a lot of shit to talk about. I'm lucky to be here today, 'cause I have a friend MC Trouble who died at my home; that changed me for ever. That's what gave me my reality, from that day on I've been on a straight mission. I got people that keep me alive in the media, and me being seen on the grassroots level. I don't think the record company knows what they have on their hands. I'm not sayin' I'm gonna go platinum. I'm gonna wake some muthafuckers up, even just two or three . . .

BC: I have met people who say Farrakhan is a fascist, which brackets out all those people that chose him to be their leader, all the people in the prisons, on the street.

N: They control our thoughts. How can you have a world that isn't chaotic? I feel like as people we should tear the shit down, totally rebuild the whole system, rebuild it to a point where it's right and it's righteous. It's gonna be better, how could it not? Anything would be much better.

URBAN PROP

Urban Prop is T-Love and Suggah B (BJ), two women from south central, Los Angeles. They both emerged from the Good Life Cafe's Thursday-night freestyle sessions and were signed to Capitol Records, making them the first female MCs from the Good Life to be signed as well as the first act from the Good Life to sign a major label. They have been informed not only through the 'new school' aesthetics, but also through their relation to gangsta hiphop and lifestyles in their struggles as young women of colour. The interview took place in August 1992 at Hollywood Sound Studios where they were recording their album.

Brian Cross: When did you start rhymin'?
T-Love: Okay. I'll break it down like this. I been writing rhymes since fifth or six grade, but as far as trying to get a deal, I've been trying to get a deal since I was 18, and my first MC battle was Derrick from Pharcyde at a house party in the hood, and I was in seventh or eight grade. Which is funny that he would be in a group now.
BJ: I been rhymin' for four or five years. I started off as a dancer, went from there on to rhymin' but I've been writing since about the fifth grade, in which I would write for each class at graduation until I would graduate. And then I started turning them into songs, and then I figured I could get my groove on but I could probably flex even better so, you know.
T: She used to dance for MC Trouble.
BJ: Yeah my homegirl, rest in peace T, and Femme Fatale, and the whole little . . .
BC: So how did you guys meet?
BJ: Tara was my big sister back in Fairfax.
T: She was in tenth grade and I was in twelfth and she had a group called Femme Fatale, and my group of girls was called Ladies Chaos. My group consisted of five or six girls and her group consisted of five or six girls like Cali and all of them. But me and BJ, we had the same exact style, like wearing funky Pendeltons and monkey boots and having your hair all

fucked up and not permed, not giving a fuck. Because you know at Fairfax or in high school in general people have a tendency to like, 'Ooh girl, you have to look your best at school', and especially at Fairfax High. It was a fashion show being on Melrose and all. And everyone automatically linked us together 'cause we looked so much alike. So we just started lying and saying, oh yeah, that's my little sister, and it's funny 'cause like we kicked it at all the Ultrawave dances. Ultrawave was like trendy, like old school rave, five minutes of funk, and then Dream Team's In the House, and Lisa Lisa and the Cult Jam; it was like, that's where the Soul Brothers came out of, in fact that's where the Good Girls [Motown recording artists] came out of. What was they called?

BJ: The Dapper Girls.

T: And that's where the dance contests started up, and that's where hiphop in California started getting linked up to dancers. So we hung around at all these places. Everyone was still hanging in their turtlenecks, and their creepers and their plaid pants and all that. Me and BJ we came from Melrose and the Mod scene before these people even thought of Mod or Ska. We came from JB, John Burroughs, a junior high, she went to Bancroft and they had their scene too.

BJ: Yeah then I got kicked out and sent to Burroughs which is the story of my life . . .

T: So she was my homegirl. All the others were my friends but, we were like, 'Oh, you heard that Clash shit!' And none of the others were down with that, and then I didn't see her again until a gang of years.

BJ: Yeah, until one of Skatemaster Tate's little underground things.

T: Down on Ivar. And I saw her and I was like dang, and I spoke to my other friend Sophie and I was like, 'What is BJ doing, does she want to join a group with me?' I was going solo 'cause I had never found a girl who could flex or had a look like a real MC. Most girls, you ask 'em, 'Oh, you heard the Ultramags shit or did you bump the Ed OG and the Bulldogs shit?' And the girls be like, 'Huh?'

BJ: Or like, 'Uh, uh. But girl, I know I can look good!'

T: Or 'I'll fuck 'em.' So BJ's the only one who was down.

BJ: That's what they say.

T: So I asked her like last August ['91] and then we were together.

BJ: Actually it's cool that she asked when she did because I had had such a frustrating time trying to get my demo together on the solo tip because previously I had been in a group with my friend called Tammy and she had gone off to become a colleague at Howard University and I was on my way to move to London because I had just gotten back and everything was set up for me to live there. She asked me and I was like cool you know and I heard she could really get her flow on and Tasha [MC Trouble] had taken me to see her one night a while before so . . .

BC: So did you guys go through the Good Life?

T: The Good Life was something that I had stumbled upon. They had little circulation things that said, 'Come down to the Good Life for the food', with 'Hiphop and Blues and Jazz' at the bottom. But you know, I am always half hesitant when they say hiphop because you know they have cheesy MCs in there and all. But I heard they were Muslim and had Muslim food and I went down one night and I just kind of checked everyone out and the second night I went I flexed on the mic and basically I went up ever since when I could make it. It was cool that people could flex. She already knew Mikah Nine from the Freestyle [Fellowship]. I kinda knew him from a friend of his, Sophia, so I knew her, so I got to know him. I didn't know any of those guys from before.

BJ: I knew 'em from the hood.

T: That's how I met Unity [Committee] and Dino [Volume 10] and Darkleaf and all those guys. All the people that I know now, most of 'em I met from going down there. The MCs, the good ones anyway, I know from the Good Life. Me and BJ would just go there to chill, but we would rock the mic occasionally. It's right around the corner from me.

BC: Who did you guys listen to stylewise, who influenced you?

BJ: Kool Keith, Mikah Nine, he always came with funky styles, the whole freestyle amalgamation. Also on the female tip I might say [Queen] Latifah. She's the only female MC that will get on the mic, like, 'Well, I'm like female.'

T: Well I'm not trying to dis Salt, who's always, like En Vogue who come up in their little red dresses and say, 'Well, can we please have the mic?' But I've tried to be cute and show some cleavage and it never worked until I started elbowing my way past the muthafuckers. You have to con and connive, the shit that I have been through to get the mic, especially, at somebody's listening party. Like Tribe Called Quest, and you run over there, and they're all passing it over your head, and I'm not like, 'Honey, let me have that mic please.' I know some girls do that and I'm lettin' 'em know that shit don't work. 'Cause now me and BJ can approach the mic like ladies, 'cause we've earned our respect.

BJ: Now we don't have to fight for the mic. My favourite all-time MCs would be Apache, Kool G Rap and Rakim, as well as Treach.

BC: What about like Sha Rock [of the Funky Four Plus One], the old school?

BJ: Oh yeah, those are just like the ancient school. Busy Bee, I like the way he used to get the crowd hyped, Schooly D, back in his day, King Tee.

T: My favourite, the Sequence, that's what told me. I came from like a block of rappers, soon as like the 'hippety hop, good times'. Dang, I mean Sugarhill Gang; it was like a block of twenty children male and female of the same age playin' and as soon as it was dark and the lights were on it would be twenty of us sittin' on the street sayin' all the lyrics. It was the shit if you knew all the words to the song. When I heard the Sequence I was like, dang that means that I can do it, 'cause girls was doing it. I would always come out with this fresh rhyme that I wrote, it would still be in the same style that they had. But girls would be like dang, Tara, and now I'm like right, but all of us, all my play brothers and little sisters, we was like rappin' all the time. I'm just like the only one who stayed at it, me and this other Jamaican group.

My friend Mike used to bring Kool Keith. The hardest part of rhymin' is what you're going to write about, and when I heard Kool Keith he'd rhyme about anything. 'Oh, I stubbed my toe on the front porch. And now I'm about to roast you 'cause I'm about to scorch you.' I was just like oh, we could say anything. I thought King Tee was just dope, Pooh and King Tee were just dope and people underrate them so much, I think.

Egyptian Lover was there, Ice T was there, those were like my main influences. Not so much like I'm bitin' their style, but just that those were the people that gave us something to do. Uncle Jam's Army was the shit, different parks, Ice T out there with his Cerwin Vegas and his DJ and King Tee. This is what we used to do when I was fourteen, go to the parks at Memorial Day or whatever. We'd just hear on KDAY, listening to the mix shows, Dr Dre and Bobcat on Saturdays. I didn't know them but I had a friend that knew 'em, so when you hear that they're doing it you think maybe I can do it.

When Sugarhill came out we were like, that's cool but I could never do that, but when Ice T came out, we were like, 'Ice T, that's my homeboy. I go to his house every day.'

BJ: Or you just might see them at the liquor store, while you were standing around waiting for some bum to buy you a beer.

T: Chill Rob G was definitely underrated. And Latee was dope.

BC: There was no women involved on the West Coast at that time?

T: There still ain't no women if you ask me, shit.

BJ: There was out in New York. Roxanne Shanté and the Real Roxanne and Sparky D, Antoinette. Here we had Roxanne's Sister and Roxanne's Mother, the West Coast took Roxanne and ran with that shit. On the West Coast we had maybe two or three girls.

T: Girl groups none, JJ Fad and Sugar and Spice. Nothing after that but 357, YoYo and MC Trouble. The rest of the girls, either they made it, or one song shot, like JJ Fad. One girl who I thought was good, MC Smooth, and Soula. But there's no girls, I don't think, none approaching it like we do. We're not out to dis girls because we know how hard it is to get a deal and shit, 'cause these brothers out here be treatin' these girls kind of shoddy. They put out these little fake ass little records and you never see 'em again. They be getting shitted on.

Girls who are MCs need to stay true to the game as long as you flex and show you can flex, 'cause that's how these brothers get seen. They don't stay home and do their nails or sit with their bitches, they go to the clubs. Right now if you're 22 years old in LA you better get out and find yourself a club and hope that there's gonna be open mic. It's always good to start at the Good Life, there's always open mic there. A lot of MCs have flunked 'cause they never flex, and once they get the deal they don't go out, and no one knows who they are. That's where the buzz is, in the clubs. Underground is the way to come up now.

BJ: Females, you got to get into writin' your own rhymes, you definitely got to write your own rhymes. I'm not frontin' because if Treach came to me and said 'Yo, I'm gonna write you a rhyme', I would take it, don't get me wrong. But be able to write your own, so when these dudes bone out, you're not stuck. With rhymin' it's about how witty you are with the words, not like singin'. Like nobody would say Luther Vandross can't write for shit, 'cause he has a voice too. But with rhymin' it's on the spoken word. You have to look at writing like, some girls are like, 'Oh we're in the industry and we'll make money and we'll get to meet Jodeci and shit.' But it's not as glamorous as all that.

BC: How come there's not women DJs and producers?

BJ: There will be, give me a minute.

T: The Poetess has a female DJ and . . .

BJ: Jazzy Joyce.

T: Look to the Urban Prop's second album. I tried to, I don't know what the other girls been doing, but comin' from me, it was like I want to rhyme, so that's what I do first. When you're trying to make a living working nine to five you don't have time to write lyrics for yourself then do a demo and then learn how to work that equipment. Once guys get a respect for you as an MC, if you ask them about that button or how to truncate, they're a lot cooler. Someone who taught me a lot was E-Swift, King Tee's DJ. He did a lot of shit with me. Some girls are scared I think. When I talk to a girl, I see if she's serious. I would rather be on open mike than going down the street in a Porsche. Fuck a Porsche.

BJ: It's a charge, dude.

T: It's such a challenge. Being a girl makes it even better. Guys are always turnin' people's heads, but girls don't turn guys heads usually.

BJ: Only if they got a lot of titty. If you ain't big enough they won't even pay attention to you on the mike, but we can change that.

T: We style, we do concept. I think we are a very versatile duo cause we can get on a concept and talk about that and we can also style, flip it back and forth. Another MC who is responsible for T's second birth, the first birth was me from elementary to 18. But the person who was in charge of getting me to go damn, let me get my pen was Puba. When I heard 'Step to the Rear', that was like my favourite thing that I heard then. His voice is funky and his style is funky, so he was in charge of the rebirth, and BJ has a style already. What's cool about girls if they want to they can bite.

BJ: They can always bite a dude.

T: Thing is you have to be good to even bite. I hate when people kick it too much together, especially a guy and a girl, 'cause you can tell. 'Damn, you sound just like a lady Rakim.' Don't say I sound like nobody, say I sound like T-Love. There's no other girl group who can rip on us. They will not touch the mic. I grabbed the mic at the A Tribe Called Quest listening party and Nefertiti did too, she had no problems. She's like an aggressive female, this is the type of MC that we need.

We're on Capitol Records, we can't say nothing, we have a record-breaking deal. I've paid my dues. I've been like an immigrant for years, I have kissed people's butts, been treated like shit. Yes, I have a good deal, thank you, for the first time in six years I have finally built an ego. I am tired, you can see the rings around my eyes from years of struggle, so I'm glad the first struggle is over.

BC: There's a real division between the hiphop scene and the alternative scene. The other night when Trulio Disgracias played at the Music Machine, everybody left.

BJ: And that was fucked up. I was trying to push people back.

T: It's like an attitude though. There's an attitude in hiphop and alternative, 'cause in alternative people are like playing an instrument since I was five and I can't even get paid, doing sessions with El Debarge. Then you've got Tone Loc making like bank. Dope money. Hiphop is money right now. People at the Coconut Teaser are like, 'Oh, you rap'. Don't be like, 'Oh, you rap', 'cause we have to protect our voices and we been payin' our dues too.

BJ: Another reason why, is because back in the day a lot of these alternative bands were making the music funky but it didn't attract the black crowd. And the few that went were shunned so they're like, 'Well fuck you. I'll go see Rakim.' Now they want a little piece of the ghetto and the ghetto won't have 'em. They got their ghetto passes revoked like Ice Cube says. They didn't want us.

T: We want everybody to be able to listen to it, if you're white or Japanese or Mexican or Indian it doesn't matter, we want you to listen to it and say I felt it and take it home. But if it gets to that point . . . I have been called prejudiced because I have said, I want to make music that will appeal to my people.

I was making music for a while, rapping over alternative-type music, and I brought the tape down to the hood and none of my brothers really liked it. They said, 'T, why are you rappin' over that white boy music?' It's not white boy music, I know that. All this rock was black music anyway, but I'm not going to argue with them. They have their troubles in jail every other day so I'm not going to add to them and be like, 'You should listen to Jimi Hendrix.' So I took the tape back and asked if we could make it a little more funky, and they looked at me and said, 'Why?' And I said: 'Because none of my brothers liked it and it's really important for me to be able to bring a tape back to the people who are responsible for me rapping in the first place and have them like it.' And they said I was prejudiced.

It pisses me off. I said: 'Yeah, my friends are prejudiced. If you go to the hood they will not like you 'cause you are white, but I'm looking to them first. If in the interim, I can pick up white listeners et cetera.' It happens all the time. I feel like I scored, but my heart is to the black people; when you're MCing and talking about story and concept you're hoping that people will listen before they sell more drugs, before some girl goes and fucks some dude and gets AIDS, before she gets pregnant. I'm not trying to say white people don't have their problems, but at the same time, we came here with problems and have had problems since we've been here. We don't have a say in the White House. We don't even have enough juice to bring drugs into the country. I see my race, I try to give them something and those are my people and I love them to death, period. And I have been called prejudiced 'cause I want to sell to my people. You shouldn't be, music is not colour. Whatever, hiphop is a muthafucker. Where's the record company gonna put us? They're not gonna put us on Sunset with a big marquee, they're gonna put us in the hood. Why would I argue with that?

BJ: Since we're on the subject of the Mandingo thing, print this, okay? For all you little hiphop bambi beanie wearing, ain't never been to the hood, got to commute to come see your boyfriend on 65th and Slauson. Just let me interject, if I see you I'm jackin' you for your daddy's Benz, I just want you to know that. Because I'm not havin' it, I'm tired of it, you all know me too, BJ. Yep, that's me, I'm the one, me and Tara and Allison, the girl that used to have the red hair. Please print this: give it a rest, please give it a rest.

We have a song about that too. If you guys want to be down with the hiphop scene that's cool, but don't think that 'cause you are a caucasian woman with blond hair that you got it like that. You don't, you do not have it like that. And that goes for you brothers in the alternative scene that think, 'I just can't find any black women who understand me and my music', that's not true. Me and Tara and a few of my other friends, black sisters on the scene. This is a big problem, I will do the bug dance if you do not print this. We have this problem in the hophop scene, these blonde girls who put on a beanie and borrow somebody's khaki suit and think they got it like that and they do not. I'm not havin' it, for all the little pseudo-Tairrie Bs, I'm sick of it. I'm from the ghetto and this is how we wear our shit in the hood. For all you white boys and girls in the scene with your little shelltoes [old school Adidas sneakers], all down with hiphop, dude, step off. I mean don't step off, it's cool but it's like we're nothing but a fashion statement right now. I'm a B-girl 'til I die, when they bury me they're gonna bury me with some shelltoes on my feet and some gold around my neck because that is how I feel.

T: In the hood that's how the homies are buried. We went to a homie's funeral the other day and he had on locs [a particular type of sunglasses] and a baseball cap and a white khaki suit. Why put him in a double-breasted suit? I don't have a problem with a white boy or a black boy wearin' shelltoes, but there is an attitude that goes with it that pisses me off.

BC: It's about money.

T: Exactly, we like you if you are who you are, and if we don't like you we are going to tell you we don't like you 'cause you have a fucked-up personality. What BJ is talking about, one night I was at Brass and I was dancing with my friend Michael here, and there was this Caucasian girl who had on Zulu earrings, a cute little African medallion, a body suit with big jeans, and Nikes with a baseball hat, with her ponytail pulled through. I thought she looked cute. She had her little black man with her though, her little Mandingo, that didn't bother me either, whatever. But what did bother me though is I put my hand back to do a little funky fresh move, and bumped her by accident. I turned around, 'Girl you okay? I am so sorry.' She turned around, put her hand on her hip and did a litle turkey neck move. I don't care who you are, what you are, wearing a hiphop outfit and being with a black man does not give you the licence to turn around and do a chicken neck at me, especially if I'm apologizing to you. You don't do nothing like you're a sister who's from the hood who's had some abortions, and had their daddy beat 'em up and an uncle molest them. Bitch, don't you even try that. I have seen white guys go out there on the gangsta tip with their Pendeltons on. They got that from the blacks and Mexicans in the hood. They gonna try and 'What's up with you cuz?' I don't think so, had he lived in the hood, maybe. Leaves the club and gets into daddy's BMW and he's driving north, while we get into a BMW that my cousin had to get by selling drugs. Be yourself. Whatever is yourself from whatever your struggle is.

BJ: I'm tired of being treated like a fashion statement. Going to the clubs and the white boys are like, ohh a sister. If you think I'm fly then step to me, but not 'cause now the trend is black girls.

T: Black people are in like it's a sin.

BJ: What you gonna do next week, kick me to the carpet? The reason why people wore khakis and house shoes and beanies and Pendeltons in the hood was because the shit is inexpensive. And that's why we wore it, not to be cool. But naturally because we're so gifted at accessorizing and shit it was cool . . . just like on the slave ships they threw us chitlins, the worst part of the pig, and we managed to make that shit taste good. That's how gifted we are. The khakis and Pendeltons are about that, about chitlins. We couldn't afford to go to Vidal Sassoon's so we went to the Swap Meet and the shit that was durable, cool for gang-banging, you could get your roll on in 'em. Then you could pass it on to your brothers . . .

When I see you pseudo Tairrie Bs walking down my street I'm takin' you for your gold, I'm taking everything you got. And it's not out of character for me. We even got little white girls trying to fuck people with little nines (nine millimeter weapons) and shit; I will pimp slap you and take your strap from you, I'm serious. We are not marketable products, we are not on the slave ships. Go up to Brentwood and sit up and listen to what you want to listen to, leave us alone. Just like what Treach said if you ain't never been to the ghetto don't never come to the ghetto, 'cause you won't understand it.

T: I don't care so much, but what bothers me is the attitude. It took me three hundred and something years to get this attitude, I earned it. I'm not takin' it out on the white kid, I'm pissed the fuck off at his ancestors. The characteristics that are attributed to the black attitude – a man grabbing his penis like don't fuck with me, I'm hard, or twitching the neck – those are the characteristics white suburban kids are picking up from the television or whatever. Like, oh so that's how they do it. My mom always told me to play it neutral so that I could make money, so I cooled it on that shit, but you don't see any white girls trying to do everything T-Love does, 'cause she's too neutral.

BJ: To summarize the whole last section of this damn fucking interview, you didn't want to join us in the fields when we were picking cotton, so don't be down here doing all the things you think black people do, it's not cool. Just be what you are.

EPILOGUE

The Freestyle: T-Love

The album's completed. No more air-conditioned studios with plush leather couches. No more of those money-thieving, junk food machines which were the source of nocturnal nutrition. Gone are the corny engineers, the 'dope' producers, the ever-flashing photographers and nosey-ass interviewers and, most of all, gone are the lyric sheets for the songs that are going to be on the album. What's an MC to do at this point? Go down to the club tonight? Yeah – that sounds like the thing to do.

As you stroll casually to the front of the long line, the doorman spots you and immediately whisks you and your posse into the club. Putting away the now unnecessary cover charge, you make your way to the bar. Standing in a dark and remote corner wit ya peoples, while simultaneously spurning all others trying to make a play for your attention, you laugh, pass da pipe, sip ya brewski . . . damn, you feel triumphant!!! You think to yourself, 'Shit, this is why I wanted to rap'; to get da contract, get da duckets, get da freaks and to fuckin' chill.

Damn, there's a helluva crowd down here tonight. Thick wit all ya homies: DJs, MCs, dancers, producers, editors, A&R riff-raff, actors/actresses, singers, booking agents, band members, publicists, groupies, etc. 'No I don't need a new manager,' you say to yet another rudely aggressive person who has the gall to insist on conducting a one-way inaudible business conversation in a noisy-ass club. With a 'Uh-huh, yeah', you take his business card from his hairy hands and shove it in your back pocket with the twenty others.

Finally, you make your way to the over-capacity dance floor. Overhead, dim lights flash in red and blue, filtering through the never-ending upward bound cigarette and bud smoke. This is where the party's at – where the vibration from the bass of those chunky-ass phat beats that the DJ's spinning is best felt. Booommm!!! Right in the chest. Yeahhh . . . . . . groovin' with the freak o' da week, lampin', when – all of a sudden – 'Mike check, 1-2, mike check, 1-2!!!' The DJ is now flashing funky instrumentals and an MC is up in the booth, coaxing all the MCs in the house to come up to the mike and give up the freestyle. What's an MC to do? Profile or freestyle?

Freestyling is the ability to rhyme straight from the top of the head, as opposed to rappin' lyrics which have been previously written and memorized, or 'from page' as some MCs would word it. Done to a funky instrumental beat, or to human beatbox, even done a cappella, it is rapping in its freest form and where rap, as we know it today, has evolved from.

Freestyling is to an MC what a solo is to, say, a trumpet player in a quartet. In a solo, the trumpet can blow out an array of spontaneous musical notes as long as those notes played correspond with the key register and time signature which the composition as a whole is based upon. In a lyrical freestyle, the MC can rap about whatever he/she wants, in any style he/she chooses. The only confinements in the rap are: first, it should rhyme; second be comprehensible and third, be on beat, if done to music. In split seconds, spontaneous stories (fictional or non-fictional), dis's, toasts, boasts, etc. enter the brain of well-versed MCs and exit the mouth – all in a 'free' format that rhymes, is somewhat tangible, and makes overall sense.

Freestyling is important to the livelihood of true hiphop music because: 1. it helps keep the music form alive by encouraging creative competition among the artists, 2. it helps to define the line between an MC and just a rapper and 3. aids in the feat of never letting people forget where hiphop/rap came from.

Hiphop music, in just the years since its birth, has already gone through several phases and has proved to be a pliable and ever-changing music form. Partially responsible for its rapid evolution is its constant breeding of competition. Where there is competition, there is change. And in order for an MC to be considered a worthy competitor, he or she must practise and freestyling is just that: drills for skills. It opens the mind, and helps to keep fresh and new ideas flowing, which improves the competition amongst MCs, therefore upgrading the quality of true hiphop flavour in rap music. As long as there are MCs such as LL Cool J, Freestyle Fellowship, B-Real (Cypress Hill), Son Doobie (FunkDoobiest), Leaders of the New School, A Tribe Called Quest, the Guru (Gang Starr), striving to be the best as well as the most diverse and staying in tune with everyday changes, hiphop music will continue to evolve and breathe.

The main difference between an MC and a rapper is freestyling. Which brings me to the second way its presence in hiphop music is substantial. Rappers usually stay to memorized lyrics. In a studio and on wax they can be doper than dope but live, on an open mike (and that's only if they would even have the balls to get on the mike), they suck shit. It is scary to freestyle, to risk making a mistake in front of others; but MCs just go for it. By just showing the effort to try, it shows that you're committed to all facets of the music form, not just the ones that earn the duckets.

When I first started rhyming, I couldn't freestyle to save my life, so I always avoided it. Then one day, my homeboy was like, 'How can you call yourself an MC and you don't even freestyle?' It was that day that I began to try; first just freestyling on paper, just writing without stopping to think about it. Then I started doing it aloud when I was alone (in the shower or driving in my car) and then among close friends who wouldn't laugh at my fuck-ups, and finally in front of groups of MCs and at clubs. I'm not great at it, but whenever I'm challenged, I go for it. The secret is that mistakes are only mistakes when you let them be.

True hiphop will survive as long as past, present and future MCs keep their commitment to the trade. Rappers who tend to assist in the exploitation of the music, will come and go with the trend. True MCs will always stand the test of time. Ultimately, freestyling's presence in hiphop music is important because it doesn't let fans and wannabees forget where rapping came from and the skills it used to take to be considered dope-way before today's abundance of wax deals, recording studios and MTV. Freestyling is a way to teach (or remind) people about their roots and give them a dose of what it used to be like back in the old school. As long as today's MCs as well as those of yesterday earn and receive due respect, hiphop music as a whole will gain the respect it deserves.

In conclusion, freestyling in rap music is important because it raises the level of quality and creativity by way of competition, thereby helping to eliminate monotony, it forces MCs to prove their commitment to their trade and last, it teaches the history and culture of hiphop as well as the basics of what it takes to be an MC to the heart.

In seeking a major label deal, I realize that I will become a commodity that will need a 'marketing strategy' (and all that other record business bullshit) but while I'm making concessions, the label's execs will be making them too. It's either real hiphop or nothing at all. Back in the day, MCs would hype parties and clubs, urging crowds to participate and enjoy themselves, and they'd be freestyling it the whole nine.

Rap has come a long way since then but as long as people acknowledge the original elements (such as the necessity to freestyle), rap music, even when it by chance hits pop acclaim, will always be rap music, pure and true.

It's a sunny Saturday.

HOOO!!!!!

To me, as well as to the other kids that lived on my street, it meant a day without school. We slept in, did chores, then hung out on the block all day. Who needed to go to the park or the schoolgrounds when there was a huge posse of maybe twenty-five or more kids hangin' and playin' right in front of where you lived?

By the time the sun was at its hottest, every kid from every house or apartment was out and representing. To anyone walking or driving down this narrow residential street located in the heart of the west side, it looked as if youth had abducted the block. There wouldn't be a single adult in sight. Like Peanuts or the Little Rascals, parents were like transient traces of authority, supervision – heard but not really seen.

There were just kids, kids, and more kids. Some would be riding their bikes or skateboarding, rollerskating or climbing trees. Some of the girls would be playin' hop-scotch, some of the boys would be engaged in a couple of innings of stickball, older kids would be 'smackin' bones' (dominoes), playing spades, or backgammon. Oh, that's me by the way, the dark brown chunky one with the glasses, book in hand.

One thing I remember is the sound of Saturday. Always there was laughter, screaming some cry-babies crying, yelling, talking and – ah yes, music. There was always music . . . tunes in the form of Motor City oldies, Barry White, War, Teddy Pendergrass, James Brown, the Isley Brothers, Chaka Khan and the Commodores escaped some kid's family backyard barbecue in large decibels. Sounds of such jazz greats as George Benson, Herbie Hancock, Carmen McCrae, Richard 'Groove' Holmes, Roy Ayers, the Crusaders, Yellow Jackets, Weather Report, Miles Davis, Coltrane, Bird emanated from my crib. That was mom's doin'. An older kid, while labouring under the hood of his car, would have the car radio tuned in to the now defunct radio KDAY. The AM airwaves of the greatest black radio station of all time would be travelling in the patterns of GQ, Prince, Heatwave, Slave, Chic, Cameo, Rick James, New Edition, Teena Marie, Con Funk Shun, Brass Construction, Lakeshore. Songs like 'Double Dutch Bus', 'Square Biz', 'Super Freak', 'Tainted Love', 'Fascination (Keep Feeling)', 'Gigolette' – symbolized music that *we* would appreciate, that we could claim for our generation, not that there was anything wrong with Herbie Hancock, Teddy Pendergrass, Barry White or Miles Davis. It's just like, well . . . that was the stuff our parents were playing, ya know? These were the older folks that were corny and old and didn't understand the 'ways of the youth'. The folks that we strived to be different from. They listened to Al Green, we listened to Cameo; they wore flared green polyester pantsuits, we wore straight-leg Jordache and Sergio Valente jeans; they sported generic sneakers from Kinney, we sported K-Swiss, Nikes and Adidas. They would always stress the quality and price of that 'Puff the Magic Dragon' polo shirt they bought you from Sears. 'I wanted an Izod/Lacoste shirt – it's an alligator, not a dragon.' Their reply? 'It's almost exactly the same shirt, but it's half the price.'

How could *anyone* who listened to the Spinners know anything about what it was to be young, geared and filled with energy and angst (except when it came to homework)? The differences between the adults and kids on my street were like night and day; like the difference between *American Bandstand* and *Soul Train*. When were we going to get that, that umph – that piece of something that was ours, that we would could claim for our generation? For our older cousins and uncles, it was Isaac Hayes and disco, for our parents it was Chuck Berry and the Motown sound, for our grandparents it was bebop, jazz and blues.

Then, in 1979, it happened. Our generation's rebellious equivalent to the birth of rock 'n' roll had finally come. From the moment that Sugarhill Gang's 'Rapper's Delight' was played for the first time on KDAY, the hangin' out faithfully done on Saturdays by the kids on Carmona Avenue had become a dire necessity, an obsessional ritual. It's like, you had to be out there, hangin', representing; showing off that you knew all the 'Rapper's Delight' lyrics by heart. The 'hangin'-out' sessions had even expanded to Friday and Sunday. Homework assignments due on Monday would be done late Friday night. Kids were on their best behaviour in order to steer clear of punishments that would prevent them from hangin'. Gone was the dilly-dally attitude towards Saturday chores. The thing to do was to get up early and just knock the shit out, so there would be more time in the day to be out on the block; most of us had to go in the house when the street lights came on.

Rap, for the most part, was the common ground that was responsible for bringing us all together into one big posse. Earlier cliques separated girls from boys, the youngest from the oldest. We'd come together for the sake of rap. Whether young or old, male or female, if you could recite the lyrics to 'Rapper's Delight' in its entirety, you were the shit. Period.

Songs that came later, like Kurtis Blow's 'The Breaks' and Grandmaster Flash and the Furious Five's 'The Message', are what kept Carmona Avenue thriving. We'd go door to door, gathering all the kids together so we could form these huge teams to play stickball, kickball, football or hide 'n' seek. Then there would be a bagging session followed by the much anticipated reciting session.

I remember being the first kid on my street to take it one step further than simply mimicking someone else's rap. By the time I was ten, my diary, which had previously been filled with puppy-love poetry, was filled with 'paddy-wack'-type rhymes. Though each rap varied in topical content, each had one main thing in common: they were all written in the style and syllabic pattern of 'Rapper's Delight'. I'd just changed the words and substituted them for my own. I'd be sitting in class on a Wednesday morning, daydreaming about the upcoming weekend, where at our usual reciting session I'd be kicking my own shit instead. The kids, especially the girls, had been impressed.

The day KDAY played 'Funk You Up' (Ding Ding Dong), by the girl group, the Sequence, was the day I'd made a decision as to my future career. I wanted to be a rapper. My peers laughed and my mother tried her damnedest not to. I remember her asking, all the while trying to keep a straight face, 'So you gonna quit elemetary school?' Never discouraged – 'cause I'd made up my mind dammit! – I continued to write my rhymes and had even given myself the first of my three MC names: Sweet Tara Tee. By the time I'd turned twelve I'd advanced to writing one hundred per cent original rhymes. No more raps in the same pattern as 'Rapper's Delight', 'The Message' or 'The Breaks' for me. I was my own rapper now, mostly rhyming over-exaggerated, truths and braggadocio stuff.

Hiphop became the major focus of practically every boy on my street, from the Jamaican kids who lived up the street, to the gangsters who lived on the other side of Venice Boulevard. Most guys were rappin' a little here and there. And the girls? Well, they'd mostly buy the tapes and wax. Just about everybody was making tapes from KDAY. Hiphop had moved in for good as far as the kids on Carmona were concerned. Dr Dre, then still in the Wreckin Cru, would come to visit his girlfriend who had lived across the street from me. Everybody would go to hang in front of her house so they could chill with him and Lonzo and Yella. There'd always been fly rides with bumpin' systems – pumpin' our street with

DJ Kiilu's bedroom, south central Los Angeles, 1992.

O' Roc's bedroom, south central Los Angeles, 1992.

Link's bedroom, Long Beach, 1992.

Kingski's room, Los Angeles, 1992.

T Love's room, south central Los Angeles, 1992.

Muggs's room, Bell Gardens, 1992.

Alim's room, south central Los Angeles, 1992.

King Dizmost's room, south central Los Angeles, 1992.

Tomas's room, Miracle Mile, 1992.

Father Amdee's room, south central Los Angelos, 1992.

Mattematick's room, south central Los Angeles, 1992.

Aztlan Underground's room, San Fernando, 1992.

Danny Boy's room, Hollywood, 1992.

Skatemaster Tate's room, Hollywood, 1992.

Mike Nardone's room, west Los Angeles, 1992.

The Hut, Woodland Hills, 1992.

beats and the latest in West Coast and East Coast rap music. But when Dr Dre started hangin' out on our street, rap, for the first time, was directly hitting our block. Shit, he was the only rap celebrity that most of us had ever come in direct contact with.

With the start of KDAY's Mixmaster shows, every Friday and Saturday night, the introduction of LA's first real hiphop club, Radiotron, and movies like *Breaking* I and II, *Beat Street* and *Krush Groove*, LA youth had been completely taken captive by this music and culture, rumoured to have been started in the Bronx.

House parties equipped with dope DJs and open mikes became the norm by 1982. Egyptian Lover, Mix Master Spade, the Wreckin Cru, Toddy Tee, Ice T and DJ Bobcat were all the early West Coast mentors. Uncle Jam's Army was the place to go boogie and every year on Memorial Day at Cheviot Hills' Rancho Park, Ice T and DJ (Chris the Glove) Evil E would haul turntables, mixer, Cerwin Vega speakers and mikes and would perform – for free!!!

And every year, I'd pray that I could work up enough nerve to ask Ice T for the mike, and every year I'd chicken out. I never even thought about trying to push my way through the hordes of over-eager male MCs at Radiotron. I was still writing my rhymes every day. I'd branched out to writing stories, which to me was the hardest thing to write. Even to this day I avoid stories like the plague: they're not my forte.

No one I knew or hung with freestyled. We'd always kick memorized rhymes. In fact, freestyling wasn't even an issue or an 'in-order-to-be-a-dope-MC' requirement. It wasn't until I started hanging with this kid from NY that I discovered what freestyling was. 'Do you freestyle?' he had asked me. I was 15 then, and had been rappin' for a while. I was like, 'No, what really is freestyling?' He explained the term and I was hit with yet another aspect of rappin' to avoid like the plague. I'd try to freestyle two lines and would fuck up immediately. No, freestyling wasn't gonna be my cup of tea. I tried to put it out of my mind and continued kicking memorized text.

A year and a half later the same NY kid blatantly asked: 'How can you call yourself a rapper and you can't even freestyle? That's the first thing you're supposed to learn how to do. Anybody can write lines that rhyme. All my friends were freestylin' before they was even writin' 'em on paper.'

He was right. In staying true to hiphop and being a legit MC, it was important that I learn to freestyle. So in my room, late at night, I'd put on a Run DMC or Parliament instrumental and go for it. After months of thinking that I was improving, I'd get in front of the kids on my street and choke, not being able to get past four or six lines. 'Damn, I was just flowin' off the top of my head in my house earlier today!' They'd all look and be like: 'Yeah, right.' Immediately on the defensive, I'd tell them to try to freestyle their rhymes. Silence.

By 17, I was focusing on my other weak point: stories. I'd been checking the lil' stories in Doug E. Fresh and Slick Rick's 'Lottie-dottie' and 'The Show' and decided it was time to perfect it. Stories are usually the most difficult. While it's true that everyone who even rhymes a little can probably rap a story, the most difficult thing is to write a good one. The type of story that will compel people to actually listen and enjoy it. Two of the best were 'Mona Lisa' and 'Children's Story' by Slick Rick. Kool Moe Dee's 'Go See the Doctor' was cool, too.

The worst stories? I won't name names but I will say that many MCs have the tendency to get off the main storyline too often in their verses or include far too many insignificant details, dragging the story on and on and on . . . (yawn).

I did learn from Big Daddy Kane that whether you're rhyming stories or boasting lyrics, similes, metaphors are good ways to make your rhymes exciting. Remember, though, that repeatedly using 'like a' gets tired. The use of extraordinary rhyme pairs or couplets, opposed to the everyday expected ones (there she sat, lookin' all fat, now she gotta gat and a big top hat) makes for diverse rhymes as well. A good example of utilization of extraordinary rhyme-endings or couplets is Rakim's 'I Ain't No Joke': 'Write a rhyme in *graffiti an'* every show you *see me in* deep concentration 'cause I'm no *comedian* . . .' Or try adding some flavour to those ole everyday rhyme-endings, like when Rakim says, 'They think that I'm a new *jack*, but only if they knew *that*, they who think wrong are those who can't do *that* – style that I'm *doin'*, they might *ruin* patterns of paragraphs based on *you an'* . . . '.

By 18, I had learned what to do to make a rhyme turn out dope, be it story or otherwise. I knew how to experiment and create different styles. And I'd learned the three most important factors on which to this day I base all rhymes that I write: if it's not, one, what you say, then it's two, how you say it, then it's three, all the above.

Good examples of what you say are KRS One, Ice Cube and Chuck D (Public Enemy), who I feel kick somewhat straightforward styles because emphasis is on what message they are actually trying to convey. When dropping a substantial message or heavy story, simple styles are better vehicles with which to get it across to listeners.

Others emphasize the styles they kick as opposed to adhering to a story or a particular point of view. A good example is Black By Demand's 'All Rappers Give Up', where even I had to keep playing it over and over again until I was able to grasp what was being rhymed. Another is Grand Puba Maxwell's 'Step to the Rear' on the Brand Nubian debut album. Puba wasn't rhyming about one specific topic, he was just doing a boast type of the thing. He kept it exciting with a dope style:

> Step to the rear Grand Puba's on arrival
> Raised in the ghetto singin' songs called survival
> Standin' on the corner givin' all the girls Puba snacks
> Try to steal my style and ya likely to catch a heart attack
> Figured the way to get paid is to grab the mike–rehearse ya know
> Smooth as Jermaine – so honey don't take it personal
> There's no need in tryna dis the swinga
> Baby all you get is two sugs up and a finger.

Examples of conveying a significant message or story are Brand Nubian's Derek X's (Saddat X) first verse in 'Slow Down':

Hey baby – ya hips is getting big – now ya gettin thin
Ya don't care about your width
Now Woolie Willie gotta pair of my sneakers
Wonder where he got 'em from 'cause I hid behind the speaker

And C.L. Smooth's verse in 'Reminisce T.R.O.Y.':

I reminisce for a spell, or should I say think back
22 years ago to keep it on track
The birth of a child on 8th of October
A toast but my grandaddy came sober

In the past, LA MCs had always used more straightforward styles, not really focusing on stylin' or how a rhyme is worded. Having been in many rhyme sessions with LA MCs, I'd noted that there was never any emphasis on freestyling. So there was never any pressure to do it. Then I'd heard Ultra Magnetic MCs and rumour had it that the majority of their album was freestyled. Kool Keith's style was so wild that I challenged myself to be able make my rhymes wild too. I began practising my freestyling techniques.

I started my freestyling by doing a process I call 'free-writing'. I would go back and kick what I'd just written, trying to somehow make it go with the beat. The rhymes would basically be wild or wild-style, referring to a style that sounded similar to the ways that Kool Keith was kicking his lyrics. The difference between a wild rhyme and a well thought-out rhyme is like the difference between night and day:

Well thought-out:

I like to chill, I like to hang
I make a bill, when I do my thang

Wild-style:

I likes to chill, kickin' it with my peops, I creeps
up on my style while I get ill

This free-writing improved my styling skills which gave me an incentive to start practising my freestylin'. I'd be in the shower, in bed, driving in my car, walking to the store. For months all I did was drill, and after a little I was doing it at rhyme sessions with my homies, on open mikes, everywhere. From never being able to go more than four lines (two bars), I was doin' 32 lines (16 bars) and more. My styles improved so that in my written rhymes I'd reached a level as high as in freestyling styles – not just actual words and couplets.

I'd come full circle as an MC. I could write entertaining boast, stories, and message rhymes as well as kick flocks of styles and freestyle. It had taken a little more than a decade but I'd done it.

Whatever happened to all those kids on my street? Well, let's just say that LA hiphop has yet to hear more of the Carmona Avenue crew. One kid is signed to Mercury, I'm signed (at least for now) to Capitol and there's about two more groups working on their demo. The rest who ain't in college are just sippin' de Brewski, sellin' dub sacks and freestylin' to a gangsta beat. And in the end it ain't 'bout no salary.

APPENDIX

CAPA Report on Police Abuse in L.A.

1965 — 91

This outline was compiled from statistics gathered by the Coalition Against Police Abuse, a local independent umbrella organization offering structural and organizational support for local community groups, and documentation for legal use in fighting these kinds of abuse. This outline is in no way comprehensive. For example, the *Los Angeles Times* recorded 32 fatal shootings at the hands of the LAPD and Sheriff's Department in 1986, whereas below we list only eight for that year. The intent is to provide an idea of the situations in which shootings often occur, and potentially demonstrate a pattern of specific populations targeted. While a great many of these cases end up in court, officers rarely undergo criminal prosecution for their actions.

Date	Name	Age	Sex/race	How killed/where/by whom
5.5.65	Leonard Deadweiler	28	male/black	Shot by LAPD during traffic stop while rushing pregnant wife to hospital. Officer claimed accidental discharge.
11.6.69	Donald Lee Oughton	29	male/black	Deaf mute man stopped by LAPD while walking home. Shot point blank by LAPD when reaching into pocket for ID.
17.7.70	Guillardo and Guillermo Sanchez	21 22	male/ Chicano	Brothers shot during arbitrary raid on downtown tenement building. LAPD officers entered the site firing.

11.1.74	James Baldwin	30	male/black	Shot by LAPD on 70th and Avalon after being pulled over by LAPD. Officers charged with planting a gun on Baldwin's body after shooting.
2.2.76	Jimmy Blando	21	male/ Chicano	Blando, after summoning LAPD for protection, flees in terror, is pursued and shot 13 times by LAPD, finally falling at Pico and Hoover.
11.2.76	Barry Gene Evans	17	male/black	Two LAPD officers approach Van Nuys apartment building investigating a burglary, meet Evans on walkway, and after a brief verbal altercation, beat him down and shoot him three times in the back.
18.6.76	Anthony Brown	35	male/black	LAPD was called to handle a mentally disabled and irritated Vietnam veteran. SWAT converged on the Brown house, fired tear gas, Brown came out with a knife, was shot instantly.
19.1.77	Ruben Cortez	37	male/ Chicano	Car crashed after being chased by LAPD in east LA. Officers fired four or five rounds into car before arresting Cortez, who died of gunshot wounds to the head.
21.3.77	Travis McCoy	40	male/black	LAPD arrest McCoy for taking several cases of beer off a truck at 39th & Normandie, order him to lie prone, and shoot him in the back, claiming accidental discharge.

16.4.77	Edward Ramirez	16	male/ Chicano	Goes to the aid of a man struggling with three undercover LAPD officers dressed as 'bums'. LAPD shoot him in the head, claim he was wielding a walking stick. Witnesses differ.
20.4.77	Anthony Reeves	27	male/black	LAPD officer with loaded shotgun orders arguing men to exit their car. Reeves, whose door was jammed, exits through window and is shot in the face. His body was left to lie in the street for 45 minutes.
5.5.77	Armando Montes	19	male/ Chicano	Off-duty officer observes robbery at 11th and Main St. Suspecting unarmed Montes, he pursues, altercation ensues, and he shoots Montes point blank in the back.
19.5.77	Gregory Williams	20	male/black	Off-duty officer working motel security shoots victim in the face, possibly for intervening in an on-going beating of another man. Williams was unarmed and left to lie bleeding for 45 minutes.
4.8.77	Ron Berkholder	35	male/white	Berkholder, naked, unarmed and wounded, was approached by LAPD officer at 5 a.m. and shot six times while holding his hands up.
30.3.78	Dwayne R. Standard	19	male/black	Officers handcuff Standard at site of a burglary, throw him in the car, and shoot him while 'trying to subdue him'.

19.10.78	Janice Peck	20	female/black	An LAPD car chase ends in Peck, a burglary suspect, crashing. As she exits the car, officers fire 24 times, shooting her 12 times.
6.11.78	Kenneth Short	22	male/black	LAPD, responding to 'male mental case', grab Short, beat him about the head with a flashlight. He dies in holding cell 25 minutes later of fractured neck and spinal cord.
3.1.79	Eula Mae Love	39	female/black	Shot by LAPD in her front yard over a $22.06 gas bill. She had a money order for the bill in her purse when shot. There is a dispute over whether or not she was wielding a kitchen knife at the time.
18.1.79	James H. Richardson	19	male/black	Student walks towards two LAPD officers responding to call in south central. Believing Richardson to be subject of call, they stop him, he withdraws hand from pocket and officer empties one round into him. He dies holding a piece of foil.
2.2.79	Abel Gill	16	male/Chicano	Gill, fleeing the scene of an argument, is pulled over by Sheriff's Deputy and shot in his car point blank.
26.4.79	Carlos Washington	15	male/black	Shot in head by plain-clothes LAPD officers in backyard of Mafia murder case witness the officers were protecting.

19.5.79	Jerry E. Wright Jr	20	male/black	Responding to burglary call, LAPD officer grabs victim of call, kicks him and throws him on ground, where he dies of complications from beating and sickle cell condition.
1980	Jilardo Plasencia			Shot in Willowbrook.
1980	Philip H. Holt	27	male/black	Resident of Watts paralysed by shot delivered while trying to surrender to police in his automobile.
1980	Kenneth Randolph Ramirez	19	male/ Chicano	'Accidentally' shot to death by LAPD.
31.7.82	Donald Ray Wilson	36	male	Died of chokehold and teargas on Vermont and 66th at hands of police.
1.82	Delois Young	**	female/ black	Fetus shot and killed by deputies during illegal drugs raid.
1982	James T. Mincey			Death by chokehold.
1982	Alonzo C. Williams			Shot to death.
5.3.83	Patrick Andrew Mason	5	male/black	Shot dead in bedroom from three feet away by police officer who entered without bidding. Patrick was playing with a toy gun.
10.1.84	Hugh Thaddeus Clark	55	male	Officers beat Clark, breaking his collarbone, ribs and killing him on 50th St near Broadway after stopping him under suspicion of drunkenness.

18.4.84	Carlos U. Rodriguez		male/Chicano	Off-duty officer shoots and kills Panorana City resident during 'scuffle'.
21.5.84	Fernando Jimenez		male/Chicano	One-legged man shot by Sheriffs for 'attacking them with crutches'.
26.8.83	Unidentified male			Motorist killed by Sheriffs who think he has a weapon.
4.10.84	Michael McCoy Taylor	40	male	Off-duty RTD driver beaten about head with nightstick, while handcuffed in Pomona. Injuries are fatal.
10.84	Glenn Gorin	26	male/white	Shot with concussion grenade and submachine guns in Malibu home during 4 a.m. drug raid. A gun collection and 25 caffeine pills were found.
21.10.84	William Sisoyer	54	male	Beaten to death while being served a traffic warrant in Southgate home by Deputy.
24.10.84	Miguel Angel Herrera	30	male/Cuban	Witnesses watched him beaten to death with a flashlight and baton at Kenwood and 30th while standing with hands clasped behind his head.
2.1.85	Sylvester Henderson	28	male	Unarmed man shot and killed on Brooks Avenue in Venice after brief 'scuffle' and chase.
6.2.85	Battering ram unveiled		Pacoima	14 foot battering ram used to attack Pacoima 'rock house'. After breaking through five rooms, no drugs were found.

12.3.85	Santiago Calderon	58	male/ Cuban	During a pre-dawn raid looking for evidence in a murder trial, LA SWAT team burst into Calderon's house and shot him several times as he lay in bed.
20.3.85	Edwin Rugley Jr	20	male	Dies after being subdued with plastic 'pain compliance instrument' for joyriding on 97th Street.
11.4.85	Cornelius Garland Smith	35	male/black	High on PCP and breakdancing in the street, LAPD tasered him four times and he died.
26.4.85	Battering ram encore	Central Ave		Used on Central Avenue storefront to confiscate 3 grams ($100) rock cocaine.
10.6.85	Otis Robinson Sr	62	male/black	For reasons known only to themselves, deputies beat and handcuffed Robinson, and then broke his neck while he lay in bed.
28.7.85	Francisco Gutierrez	46	male/ Chicano	Unarmed immigrant standing with nephews in Culver City backyard. Not understanding 'Freeze' command of onlooking Deputy, turns and is shot point blank with a 12 gauge shotgun.
28.8.85	Unidentified male	35		Dies after being tasered by LAPD.
10.10.85	Danny Smith		male/black	Unarmed RTD driver shot six times in the back by LA and Culver City police officers.

21.10.85	William Roy Retana		male	Dies after 17 days of coma induced by being beaten by a nightstick by LAPD officers.
2.86	New and improved battering ram introduced by Sheriff's Department			
4.86	Yusuf Bilal	38	male/black	Muslim man shot three times in the back by south side CHP officer for running a red light. Officer's account differs radically from that of eye witnesses.
19.5.86	Robert Zapata			Shot fatally with taser gun.
23.5.86	Arthur Bruford			Shot by off-duty LAPD officer.
6.86	Unidentified male			Man dies from 'non-lethal' stun gun.
22.6.86	Michael Zinzun	36	male/black	CAPA founder loses left eye in beating by police after protesting about violent arrest of another man in Pasadena.
24.7.86	Alfredo Munoz	22	male/ Chicano	Beaten so badly for escaping Lennox station by deputies on 19 July that the officers were temporarily fired.
26.8.86	Jesus Martinez Vidales	17	male/ Chicano	Kicked, beaten and skull fractured in Panorama City by same officer that beat Sean Walker on 23.4.88.
20.2.87	Manuel Diaz	16	male/ Chicano	Locke High tenth grader shot on E 88th St by pursuing LAPD officer who 'tripped over a piece of wood'.

9.3.87	Pascual Solis		male/ Chicano	Responding to a domestic dispute call, deputy shot Solis six times, reloaded, and fired four more times. Same deputy shot Elzie Coleman 26.5.90.
12.3.87	Gregory Spain			Shot by south side Task Force who 'mistook reflection of a key ring for a gun'.
5.87	Virgil Lee Williams		male/black	Shot eight times without warning following a fight between Williams and a friend.
5.87			male/ Chicano	Off-duty Sheriff's deputy shoots youth point blank who is trying to climb a fence and holding a screwdriver.
11.5.87	Manuel Hernandez	27	male/ Chicano	Kicked and beaten by deputies, shot four times when he picked up a discarded push broom to deflect the blows.
19.5.87	Eliberto Saldana	20	male/ Chicano	Deputies tried to restrain Saldana using the taser. He picked up a pan in self-defence, they emptied their guns into him.
27.8.87	Eddie Ropati	41	male/ Chicano	Grabbed a deputy who was chasing his stepson through his house. He was then beaten and shot by several deputies.
11.10.87	Carlos Brummel			Transient shot by LAPD on Skid Row after he 'threatens them with 4 inch pipe'.

17.12.87	Acacio Ramirez			Dies of beating by LAPD.
14.2.88	Chester Briggs		male/black	'Valentine's Day Massacre'. Kicked, beaten, tasered twice, and shot five times by LA deputies.
9–10.4.88	Gang Sweeps			1453 people arrested over two days, corralled in the coliseum, concentrated on Pacoima and south central, only 66 felony charges made.
9–10.4.88		19	male/black	Unarmed 19-year-old shot during arrest during gang sweeps.
9.4.88	Roger Guydon	60	male/black	Beaten by LAPD officers during raid of home. House was destroyed, no drugs found.
23.4.88	Sean Walker	25	male/black	A security guard stopped by an unmarked LAPD car, beaten, verbally abused and arrested in Sepulveda.
1.8.88	Massive Drug Raids			Destruction of several project apartments.
20.8.88			male/black	Deaf youth shot by SWAT team.
22.9.88	James Earl Bailey	27	male/black	Beaten and shot to death in Compton by LA deputies. Died in his father's arms.
16.1.89	Melvin E. Thompson	32	male/black	Upset over the Miami shooting, the Don Jackson brutality case on Martin Luther King's birthday, and his wife's desire for a divorce, Thompson challenged deputies to shoot him. They shot him 25 times.

3.89	Richard Moss	37	male/black	Vietnam veteran arrested for outstanding traffic warrants. Died in jail after two days from 'seizures and a fractured hip'.
23.1.90	Oliver X. Beasley	27	male/black	Shot investigating a traffic stop with fellow Muslims in south central.
26.5.90	Elzie Coleman	27	male/black	Mistaken for a gang member, chased and shot (by same deputy that shot Pascual Solis) 23 times. Fell on mother's porch, deputy reloaded to fire again, witnesses pleaded with him to stop.
3.11.90	Tracy Mayberry	31	male/black	Hit over 60 times with a baton near Hollywood, died at the feet of four officers. Coroner called it a drug overdose.
1.1.91	Nicolas Contreras		male/ Chicano	Shot by LAPD for firing into the air on New Year's Day in south central. Tossing pistol away when shot.
1.1.91	Pedro Casteneda	28	male/ Mexican	Shot five times in El Monte for firing small calibre pistol into the air on New Year's Day.
12.2.91	Pouvi and Italia Tualaulelei	22, 34	male/ Samoan	Brothers living in Compton. Pouvi was shot 12 times, Italia 8 times by the same officer [Al Skiles], mainly in the back, while kneeling. Officer claimed self-defence.

3.3.91	Rodney Glen King		male/black	Beaten, tasered half to death for speeding away from pursuing Foothill Division LAPD.
23.3.91	Emiliano Camacho	40	male/ Mexican	Father of three shot by deputies after answering his door holding a 29-inch wooden stick. Left bleeding for four hours.
3.8.91	Arturo Jimenez	19	male/ Chicano	Shot by Sheriff's deputies outside Ramona Garden's housing project for objecting to Lynwood deputies beating his friend at a birthday party.
9.8.91	Freddy Santana	26	male/ Chicano	After being told to lay prone by LAPD, Santana reached to remove a paint can from his belt and was shot three times.
13.8.91	Keith Hamilton	33	male/black	Kicked, beaten, and tasered by deputies, then shot nine times as he lay on the ground. Hogtied and left to die.
28.8.91	David Angel Ortiz	15	male/ Chicano	Fled a stolen car and ran to a friend's house. Deputies shot him three times from behind.
2.9.91	Steve Clemons	28	male/black	On Labor Day Picnic with wife and four children. Shot as he ran from deputy and left to bleed to death.
2.9.91	Darryl A. Stephens	27	male/black	SWAT team burst into his West Covina apartment looking for evidence in a case in which he was not a suspect. Shot him 28 times in the back with assault rifles.

| 14.10.91 | Joseph Ornelas | 25 | male/
Chicano | Acting crazy, Ornelas stole a broom from a store and tried to hijack a truck. Beaten and choked to death by deputies. |
| 29.11.91 | Henry Peco III | 27 | male/black | Shot in Imperial Courts Housing Project by undercover LAPD dressed as gang members. Over 43 shots were fired. No weapon was found on him. |

DISCOGRAPHY

Afrika Bambaataa and the Soul Sonic Force, 'Planet Rock', Tommy Boy 1982
Aztlan Underground, '1492 Fuck That', Xicano 1992
Beastie Boys, 'Beastie Groove', Def Jam 1985
　Check Your Head, Capitol Records 1992
Blood of Abraham, 'Father of Many Nations'
　'Stabbed by the Steeple'
　'Stick to Your Own Kind', all from the album *Future Profits* Ruthless/Relativity 1993
Body Count, *Cop Killer*, Warner 1991
Boogie Down Productions, *Criminal Minded*, B-Boy Records 1987
　By Any Means Necessary, live 1988
Boo Yaa Tribe, 'New Funky Nation', 4th & Broadway 1990
Brand New Heavies, *Heavy Rhyme Experience*, Delicious Vinyl 1992
Brer Soul (Melvin Van Peebles), *Ain't Supposed to Die a Natural Death* A&M
　As Serious as a Heartattack, A&M
　Brer Soul, A&M
　Don't Play Us Cheap, Stax 1972
　What the . . . You Mean I Can't Sing, Atlantic 1974
Oscar Brown Jr, *Sin and Soul*, Columbia 1962
Captain Rapp, 'Bad Times I Can't Stand It', Saturn 1983
Don Cherry, *Multikulti*, A&M 1990
John Coltrane, 'Equinox', Atlantic 1960
Cypress Hill, 'Kill a Man', Ruffhouse/Columbia 1991
　'Phunky Feel One', Ruffhouse/Columbia 1991
　'Latin Lingo', Ruffhouse/Columbia 1991
Davy D(MX), 'Have You Seen Davy', Def Jam/Columbia 1987
　'One for the Treble', Tuff City 1984

Def Jef, *Soul Food*, Delicious Vinyl 1990
De La Soul, 'Plug Tunin'', Tommy Boy 1988
Dre, *The Chronic*, Death Row/Interscope 1992
Eazy E, 'Boyz n the Hood', Ruthless/Macola 1986/7
   'Dopeman', Ruthless/Macola 1987
Egyptian Lover, 'Egypt Egypt', Egyptian Empire 1983
Fatback, 'King Tim III' Spring 1979
Freestyle Fellowship, *Innercity Griots*, Island Records 1993
   To Whom It May Concern, Sun Music 1991
Slim Gaillard, 'Fried Chicken O' Routee', Hep (1947) 1990
Grandmaster Flash and the Furious Five, 'The Message', Sugarhill 1980
Lalo Guerrero, 'Chuco Suave', Real 1947
   'Marijuana Boogie', Real, 1946
Herbie Hancock, 'Rockit', Columbia 1983
Erskine Hawkins 'After Hours', RCA (1940) Bluebird 1989
Chuck Higgins, 'Pachuco Hop' (Combo 1952), Specialty 1990
House of Pain, *Fine Malt Lyrics*, Tommy Boy 1992
   'Jump Around', Tommy Boy 1992
   'Put Your Head Out', Tommy Boy 1992
Iceberg Slim, 'Reflections', ALA 1975
Ice Cube, *Amerikkka's Most Wanted*, Priority 1990
   'Dead on Arrival', Priority 1991
   'Dirty Mack', Priority 1992
   Death Certificate, Priority 1991
   'Gangsta Fairytale', Priority 1990
   'It's a Man's World', Priority 1990
   Predator, Priority, 1992
   Leathal Injection, Priority 1993
Ice T, 'Colors', Warner 1988
   'The Coldest Rap', Saturn 1983
   Home Invasion, Priority 1993
   Iceberg, Warner 1989
   OG, Warner 1990
   Power, Warner 1988
   Rhyme Pays, Warner 1987
   'Six in the Morning', Technohop 1986
Quincy Jones, *Mellow Madness*, Warner 1973
Jungle Brothers, 'Black is Black', Idlers/Warlock 1988
Kid Frost, 'La Raza', Virgin 1990

'Terminator', Electrobeat 1985
King Tee 'Payback's a Mother', Mackdaddy 1988
LA Dream Team, 'Dream Team's in the House', Dreamteam/Macola
   'Rockberry Jam', Deamteam/Macola 1985
Lench Mob, 'Guerrillas in tha Mist', East West 1992
Lightnin' Rod, *Hustler's Convention*, Restless (1972) 1991
   'Sport', Restless (1972) 1991
Thee Midnighters, 'Whittier Boulevard'
Charles Mingus, *Symposium on Jazz*, Bethlehem 1958
NWA, 'Dopeman', Ruthless/Macola 1987
   Efil 4 Zaggin, Ruthless/Priority 1991
   'Fuck tha Police', Ruthless/Priority 1988
   Straight Outta Compton Ruthless/Priority 1988
Paris, 'Bush Killa', Scarface 1992
Charlie Parker, 'Moose the Mooche', Dial 1946
Parliament, 'Chocolate City', Casablanca 1975
Pharcyde, *Bizarre Ride II the Pharcyde*, Delicous Vinyl 1992
Roy Porter Soundmachine, 'Funky Twitch', Rotine/Luv 'n' Haight, (1975) 1991
   'In the Groove', Rotine 1969
   'Jessica', Rotine 1974
   'Party Time' Rotine/Luv 'n' Haight (1975) 1991
Public Enemy, *It Takes a Nation of Millions*, Def Jam 1988
   'Rightstarter', Def Jam 1987
   'Show 'em Watcha Got', Def Jam 1988
   Yo Bumrush the Show, Def Jam 1987
Rammelzee vs. K-Rob, 'Beatbop', Profile 1983
Rhyme Syndicate, *Comin' Through*, Warner 1988
Run DMC, 'It's Like That', Profile 1984
   'Peter Piper', Profile 1986
Salt 'n' Pepa, 'Push It', Select 1988
Schooly D, 'PSK', Schooly D Records 1986
   'Saturday Night', Schooly D Records 1987
Sequence, 'Funk You Up', Sugarhill 1979
Archie Shepp, *Fire Music*, Impulse 1965
   'Semper Malcolm Semper', Impulse 1965
Spanish Fly, 'Spanglish', Enjoy 1982
Sugarhill Gang, 'Rapper's Delight', Sugarhill 1979
Toddy Tee, 'Batteram', Evejim 1986
   'Just Say No', Evejim 1988

Tone Loc, 'Wild Thing', Delicous Vinyl 1989
Tribe Called Quest, *Low End Theory*, Jive 1991
UTFO, 'Roxanne Roxanne', Select
William De Vaughn, 'Be Thankful for What You've Got', Roxbury Records 1974
War, 'Low Rider', United Artists 1975
Watts Prophets, *Rappin' Black in a White World*, ALA 1971
The World Class Wreckin Cru, 'Cabbage Patch', Macola 1987
   'Fly', Macola 1988
   'Turn Out the Lights', Macola
Malcolm X 'No Sell Out' (music by Keith LeBlanc), Tommy Boy 1983
Young MC, 'Bust a Move', Delicious Vinyl 1989
Zapp, 'More Bounce to the Ounce', Warner Brothers
   'So Ruff, So Tuff', Warner Brothers

and the following Compilations/Soundtracks

Black Voices on the Streets of Watts, ALA 1970
Greatest Hits of the Zulu Nation Volumes 1-4, Enjoy/Streetsounds 1988
Sweet, Sweetback's Badaaasss Song Sondtrack, Stax 1970
Wattstax Soundtrack, Stax 1972